The International Guide to Foreign Currency Management

Gary Shoup

Glenlake Publishing Company, Ltd.
Chicago • London • New Delhi

Fitzroy Dearborn Publishers
Chicago and London

ISBN: 1-888998-00-8

Li| 'earborn Publishers, Chicago and London
IS|

G

1261 West Glenlake
Chicago, Illinois 60660
glenlake@ix.netcom.com

Table of Contents

Acknowledgments

I wish to express my deep appreciation to Chalouy for her steadfast encouragement throughout this endeavor. I am especially grateful to Steven and Kimberly for their unwavering support. Thanks also to John Walsh; his suggestions and support were vital to the completion of this project.

About the Author

Gary Shoup, author, lecturer, and commodity trading advisor, is an authority on the subject of foreign exchange, and a pioneer in foreign currency management. As a former Merrill Lynch broker and futures specialist, Mr. Shoup established a clientele ranging from individuals to Fortune 100 corporations. He introduced hedging strategies to corporate managers at a time when the concept was virtually unknown outside the agricultural community. Working in conjunction with his firm's international bank, he was among the first to combine interbank and exchange features in currency hedging programs.

As this book demonstrates, Mr. Shoup skillfully imparts highly technical information in a breezy, often humorous, always easy-to-follow style. His sales experience comes to the foreground in the last chapter. Here he discusses techniques for presenting a risk management program to corporate decision makers. Unless the principals of currency hedging can be successfully communicated, they will not be implemented. For this reason, his sales concepts are crucial to the success of the risk management program.

Preface

The first edition of this book went into print two years ago. Since that time, profound changes have occurred, and are occurring, in the world of currency. Yet, as currencies change in value, name and even regime, we note the validity of that old saw, "the more things change, the more they stay the same."

Exposure of corporate cash flows to foreign exchange still plagues the bottom line, but now even more so. The strategies for managing this exposure are as valid as ever, and the need to employ them even more urgent. New types of risk management derivatives are engineered on a regular basis, yet the basic building blocks described herein remain unchanged. The concepts presented are like former class mates at a high school reunion. They may have aged, but Joe is still Joe, Sally is still Sally, and they are all still relevant.

Today, Asian and European currencies are front page news. Beginning in 1997 and extending well into 1998, shock waves emanating from the collapse of the Asian currency peg regime are generating headlines on a weekly, sometimes daily, basis. The degree of influence exerted by exchange rates on national politics, global economies, and on the social fabric itself, has caught much of the financial world by surprise. We can better understand the cause of this turmoil by recalling some of the intrinsic properties of currencies.

Currency is narrowly defined as a medium of exchange. Historically, currencies redeemable for precious metal fulfilled this role admirably. Currency was considered to be, well, precious. The non-redeemable fiat currencies of today's world, however, have value only because the issuing authorities declare them valuable by fiat, or legal tender acts. *How much* value a particular currency has is determined by the willingness of the issuer to curb supply (monetary policy) and maintain credit worthiness (fiscal policy), as measured by debtors and creditors who function in the currency. For this reason, fiat currency is more than a medium of exchange, it is a statement of national policy. The value of a fiat currency reflects the amount of credence ascribed to that policy.

This being the case, whenever a pegged currency, such as the Korean won or Indonesian Rupiah, makes a policy statement that is quite different than the statement of its underlying U.S. dollar peg, the fate of the relationship between the two is pre-ordained: it will change. Barring wage and price controls, change almost always occurs first between *internal* values. We perceive this as a growing disparity of current and future purchasing power between the currency pair, reflected in relative prices and interest rates. When the divergence is excessive, not even the strongest central bank can maintain for long the relationship between *external* values, which is the nominal rate of exchange that defines the peg. Exchange controls don't work. They simply promote parallel (black) market pricing. Hikes in the overnight interest rate don't work. They act simply as a poison pill used to depreciate the currency before short sellers can get to it. Intervention doesn't work, at least not for long. No central bank can corner a market the size of the interbank. Defending the value of a currency by any means other than a revision of monetary or fiscal policy is futile. The value will change. Whether it can be traded at its new value is another matter.

As the effects of the diverging policies between the pegged currencies and the U.S. dollar sweep through Asia, many currency watchers feel a sense of *deja vu.* A similar collapse of the Bretton Woods system, another pegged currency regime, occurred 26 years earlier. The eventual magnitude of that devaluation was perhaps even greater; the Bretton Woods peg rate initially was one ounce of gold to US$35. The Asian currency peg regime and Bretton Woods collapsed for the same reason—the statements of policy represented by the currencies lost their credibility. The major difference between the two events is the pace. Today, we are truly connected internationally. Everything happens more quickly to more people in more places.

Meanwhile, as one currency arrangement unravels, another is introduced, one that promises to be of even greater historical significance. This, of course, is the euro. Less than a year before its introduction, it was highly debatable whether the united European currency would ever be launched. Now, ready or not, it has been sprung upon us. According to the present schedule, for three years, between launch date January 1, 1999 and January 1, 2002 at the latest, the world will cope with a duel currency system. The euro and the currencies of the European member countries are each available for private transaction until the introduction of coins and bank notes in 2002 when the national currency ceases to exist as legal tender. During this time, the question regarding the "correct" rate of exchange between each member currency and the euro will be debated at length. Forward intervention by the European Central is the primary means available to keep the "correct" rates in line. (We know how well intervention works.)

Another important change for risk managers occurred outside the foreign exchange markets. From its headquarters in Norwalk, Connecticut, the Financial Accounting Standards Board (FASB) responded to several well-publicized incidents in which derivative losses exposed a company to actual or potential ruin. The board drafted a statement entitled, "Accounting for Derivative and Similar Financial Instruments and for Hedging Activities." The objective is to make corporate derivative trading for hedging purposes more transparent to investors. Two years later, the standard was approved.

Beginning with the fiscal year of June 15, 1999, many derivative instruments now carried off-balance sheet, such as options, forwards, futures and swaps, become balance sheet assets and liabilities measured at fair market value. In essence, profits and losses from derivative trading, be it for hedging or speculation, will be posted in real time for all to see.

FASB 52, the current standard for foreign currency exposure, allows hedging results for transaction exposures to be "deferred," along with value changes in the exposure itself. The proposed standard amends FASB 52 by providing hedge accounting for cash flow exposure, which was previously disallowed. This is a welcome and long-awaited development in the field of currency risk management. After all, transaction exposure and cash flow exposure are simply two sides of the same coin.

In the spirit of give and take, however, the method of hedge accounting itself will change. Value changes of derivatives used for hedges will be reported (not deferred) for each period, along with the offsetting values of the exposure. Hedge gains and losses not offset due to hedging inefficiencies go directly to earnings, which certainly will encourage the advent of more efficient hedging.

There are also important changes in the criteria necessary to allow hedge accounting, the most notable being the increased scrutiny given to the underlying hedge program. In other words, not only gains or losses, but the strategy that created them, will become more visible. The trend toward more transparency in the area of derivatives is unmistakable. The ability to *fashion, present* and *explain* the rationale of an effective currency risk management program has never been more essential.

When this book was first written, over one trillion dollars worth of currency was traded daily. Today, the figure is closer to $1.5 trillion and climbing. In terms of size, the currency market towers over stocks and bonds. In terms of volatility, foreign exchange is "red hot," and it looks as if it will remain so for a long time to come. One thing apparently has not changed: foreign exchange managers continue to walk a rough-and-tumble path, with every new trading day fraught with risk, opportunity and challenge. I hope the lessons derived from the following chapters help pave the way ahead.

Introduction

Life down on the farm has changed for good. Drive down any rural byway, and you'll spot almost as many roof-top satellite dishes as silos. With data links to Chicago and New York, real-time price moves for cotton, corn, and cattle blink across monitor screens nestled in homes among the hills and valleys. Farmers today keep one weather eye on the sky and another on digital data flow. They're able to react at once to the fluctuations of a world market place.

Embracing this new technology was not easy. Twenty years ago, it was rare to find a farmer marketing his products through Chicago from an office, for example, somewhere in Iowa. Agricultural products then were marketed the way they always had been. When the corn came in from the field, or when the fat cattle came out of feed lots, the farmer trucked his goods to the nearest elevator or auction barn to sell for whatever they would bring. Of course, all his neighbors were there. Together, they would finish selling the entire output from a year's worth of interest and labor in two or three weeks. With a buyer's market trying to absorb the harvest glut, the prices paid would often set new lows. Like clockwork, the producer traditionally sold every year at the bottom one-third of the price range. This pattern was so predictable that speculators consistently bought agricultural futures during harvest time to profit from the seasonal low of the cycle.

In the late 1970s, inflation and futures trading took off together, and I joined in as a commodity broker. I discovered that my natural bent was more toward educating than speculating, so I headed into the countryside to "teach those farmers a thing or two." With a copy of The *Wall Street Journal* and a set of basis charts, I began knocking on doors. If invited in, I would spread my wares on the kitchen table and, within a half hour, explain all about hedging with futures. Scribing in the air with my arms, I would illustrate with a flourish how my listener could greatly enhance *his* future. After all, I would add, hedging farm products is simply playing by the speculator's rules and they're the ones making the money.

The typical reaction was discouraging. After I told the farmer my story, he would tell me his. "Not a gambler," he would say, or "how about that fellow up the road who lost his farm hedging commodities?" I heard about the truck load of eggs dumped in some poor trader's front yard overnight because he overstayed a position. (Remember trading eggs?) I heard about the commodity broker who took "that one fellow" to the cleaners' and then ran off with his wife.

Perhaps as disheartening were the success stories I heard. It was never a personal experience; usually it was about a neighbor who locked in the very top dime of the market. "Won big," the prospect would whisper, casting a wary eye around the coffee shop. "Can you do that well?"

Although I "educated" many farmers, only a few opened hedge accounts. Fewer still actually traded them. I was convinced I would stir up more interest if I were making book on next year's crop instead of trying to hedge it. I was not alone. Most brokers I talked with at the time were experiencing the same thing. We were amazed at the resistance to a management tool of such obvious benefit.

We now know, looking back, that the reaction could not have been otherwise. The concept of risk management is not absorbed in thirty minutes over a kitchen table. Management advice coming from a stranger unaware of the farmer's personal operation was all too easy to dismiss. We learned that the educational process involves a two-way relationship. To be successful, brokers in the commercial end of the futures business need to know their clients' businesses inside out. They must become business advisors, not just brokers.

Today, risk management is much more sophisticated, and the educational process is keeping pace. More hedging tools are available for fine-tuning individual operations. Now, most large farm operators would not consider going into a planting season without a hedge program firmly in place. An increasing number of loan officers insist on it; however, even in this sector, risk management is not at all universal. A good deal of anecdotal evidence suggests that a lot of farmers who do not hedge would do so if they only understood it better. Still today, a great many farmers could teach a great many of us brokers a thing or two about risk management.

We have come a long way from our agricultural roots. Raw materials and commodities of all types can now be price managed through the tools available. It has reached a point where, for example, a refiner can buy crude oil, crack it into products, sell the heating oil and retain the gasoline, all with a keyboard, a monitor, and a modem. Producers and users of copper, nickel, aluminum, lumber, and gold can lock in cost and revenue the same way a farmer can lock in the price of wheat, cotton, diesel fuel, and hogs.

The most exciting growth is in the area of financial products. There is, of course, the image problem. With commodity brokers on the phone daily with their clients, passive investment strategies often turned into active speculating, some times hard to distinguish from outright gambling. Unwary users suffered heavy losses, especially during the 1980s when the raging bull market suddenly began its long descent.

The engineers of financial futures distanced themselves from such activities. The word *commodity* was dropped from the phrase *commodity futures*; after all, stocks, bonds, and currencies are really a breed apart. Even the word *futures* had a speculative ring to it, so the term, *derivatives,* was pushed to center stage. This term is now used to define exchange-traded futures, over-the-counter options, options on futures, interbank forwards, private party swaps, and more. Financial futures were formally introduced to the public in 1972 by the Chicago Mercantile Exchange (CME), in the form of a contract for 125,000 Swiss francs. Banks were dealing in forwards long before that, but few people knew of it. Currency and interest rate futures came of age about the time commodity futures peaked, virtually exploding in popularity during the 1980's. They are still growing. Outstanding bank balances in exchange-traded derivatives jumped from $583 billion in 1986 to $3.5 trillion by the end of 1991. The demand is not confined to exchange-traded instruments. Trading in over-the-counter derivatives grew even faster, from $500 billion in 1986 to $4.1 trillion by the middle of 1991.[1]

The different products now available permit us to manage the price risk in foreign currencies, equity portfolios, bond portfolios, and money markets both domestically and overseas. Selecting from the tools now at hand, a corporate treasurer can literally construct his own exchange rate and yield for any major country, either locking it in, swapping it, letting it float, or anything in between.

With the advent of financial futures, we brokers (now "risk management consultants") re-armed ourselves with charts, tables, printouts, and literature. Again we sallied forth—not into farm kitchens this time, but into conference rooms. Education began anew, but the response is no different. There is a familiar ring to it. "We make apparel, dies, frozen entrees, software, engine parts; we don't gamble in currencies."

The solution, of course, is the same as before. Would-be practitioners of foreign currency management must begin by educating themselves. They must understand their clients' businesses, and know how they relate to off-balance sheet hedging, FASB 52, counter-party credit risk, translation versus transactional exposure, visible versus hidden exposure, and all the rest. Finally, we must be able to help financial managers present the currency management program to whoever must give the final stamp of approval.

Currency risk management is where agricultural hedging was twenty years ago; however, there is a new wrinkle. American business cannot afford a ten- to fifteen-year learning curve. In many cases, company growth (in some cases, company solvency) depends on risk management becoming corporate policy tomorrow.

It is difficult to overstate the case. The stakes are enormous. Willingly or not, U.S. commerce is being carried out in a dynamic economy on a global stage. Increasingly, companies of all sizes are exporting, importing, or competing with someone who does. Corporations now routinely arrange financing in overseas capital markets. Portfolio managers, as a matter of course, today look overseas for new investment opportunities. The trend toward a global economy is unmistakable, accelerating, and probably irreversible.

International activity does not occur without currency exchange. Every contract or transaction that crosses currency borders results in exposure to foreign exchange risk. John F. Sandner, chairman of the Chicago Mercantile Exchange, addressed this subject during an interview with *Futures Industry*.[2] His remarks refer to price-risk management in general, and exchange-traded derivatives in particular, but, with the international currency markets now exchanging more than one trillion dollars a *day*, they are very appropriate here:

> "The biggest growth industry in this country, maybe the world, is managing risk. If you can't manage risk, there's going to be a tremendous cost to taking this risk which will be passed on to the consumer...Today, [risk management] is commonplace. If you're a corporate treasurer or have assumed some type of fiduciary responsibility, if you haven't considered futures and options for risk and asset management purposes, you had better be able to explain why not."

This study course is for corporate treasurers, financial managers, and operations managers who have been delegated the responsibility of looking at the "foreign currency problem." This course is also for bankers and brokers who are interested in increasing their business in this exciting area. Our purpose is to help you *develop* and *present* a foreign currency management program. The best-developed program in the world is wasted effort if it doesn't get the nod of senior management or members of the board. In my experience, senior managers (especially CEOs) seem singularly unimpressed with bells and whistles. They tend to be "bottom line" people, who favor well-tailored programs, based on solid, easy-to-understand concepts. This course is designed to help you develop and present just such a program.

CHAPTER 1

The Problem with Foreign Currency

We once lived in an isolated country; American business cut its teeth on domestic consumption. When we did go overseas, we often monopolized the field, be it in soybeans, computers, chemicals, or airplanes. We worried about only one currency: the U.S. dollar. To our advantage, this currency is still the world's leading reserve, the one most in demand as a store of value and as an invoice currency. Most world trade is still denominated in dollars; petrodollars in the middle east; Eurodollars the world over. Trading from this position of strength, corporate America was largely able to avoid exchange rate risk. Today, the tactic still most often employed in the United States for dealing with foreign currency risk is simply not to deal in foreign currency.

According to a recent study of 12,000 U.S. corporations filing with the SEC, less than 10% made any mention of foreign exchange in their reports.[1] Other studies confirm this non-involvement in foreign exchange. A survey by the Philadelphia Stock Exchange indicates that only about 30% of all U.S. managers hedge risk of *any kind*. In contrast, less than 40% of European managers do *not* hedge risk.[2] These figures illustrate the provincial nature of American commerce. Europeans, unlike Americans, have a long tradition of cross-border trading. They are aware of the dynamics of currency exchange rates and know how to deal with them, often to their advantage. In fact, it's quite common for French companies to set up in-house cost centers having all the earmarks of an international banking operation. Many commercial entities in France seem to thrive on currency exposure, and manage it with as much enthusiasm as they do other segments of the business.

They are not alone. Today, London is the world's leading financial center for foreign exchange, having taken that position from New York by default. Japanese traders traditionally look at foreign exchange exposure from a strategic point of view as inherent in the sale. They recognize the opportunity it affords. They often *assume* the currency risk, always *account* for it, and usually *manage* it to their advantage.

The dollar may still be king, but its crown is slipping. The fact that the attempt to avoid foreign exchange risk is exacting a heavy toll on U.S. commerce can no longer be seriously disputed. Today, U.S. dollar-denominated bids on overseas projects—the same projects for which European and Japanese competitors bid in local currency—are not nearly as successful as they once were. The global business environment has become much more competitive. Gaining market share today often means direct investment in assembly shops, inventory, advertising, and other expenses all requiring local currency. Today, overseas customers demand price sheets and catalogs denominated in *their* currency, not ours. Letters of credit invoiced in U.S. dollars, payable upon shipment in, say, 90 days, are becoming too risky to foreign buyers. The volatility of the currency markets is too great. More than ever before, when a U.S. company balks at addressing its overseas customers' concerns about U.S. dollar invoicing, there is a competitor in the wings who is eager to do so.

We are learning that ignoring currency exposure risk does not make it disappear; it merely transfers the risk to the customer (or when sourcing abroad, to the supplier). As far as long-term business relationships go, it really doesn't matter which party carries the exposure on the books. Left unmanaged, the eventual fallout affects buyer and seller alike.

This point was illustrated during a recent seminar sponsored by the U.S Department of Commerce to promote export business. One of the speakers was the export manager for a mid-sized industrial fastener manufacturer. He began by relating the ground rules by which his company approaches international marketing, one being that it transacts only in U.S. dollars. Midway through the presentation, he made the point that no company should get involved in exporting unless it's for the long haul. To support his argument, he told about the trials his company experienced during its attempt to market its product line in the United Kingdom. It took several years of effort at great expense and with numerous set-backs, but eventually they prevailed and established themselves as the number two supplier in the UK.

Not long after the company's market was established, the British pound started dropping in value against the dollar, which "was driving us crazy." Their major competitor, a European company, continually undercut them. When asked how they handled that, the speaker replied, "well, we just couldn't compete, so we had to back away from England." It turned out that the European firm could well afford to price them out of the market. Its own foreign operations were doing consistently well, with the company hedging its currency exposures whenever the opportunity arose.

This illustrates the amorphous nature of foreign currency exposure. It crops up in unexpected places. As this export manager discovered, the exposure risk was not confined to a specific asset or liability, but involved an entire market. In some cases, the entire business can be at risk while management remains blissfully unaware of any exposure at all. Examples abound. They crop up whenever a group of foreign exchange managers gather in corners to exchange war stories. As one strives to outdo the other, someone always comes up with the question, "have you heard about Laker Air?"[3]

Laker Air, a British air charter company, enjoyed a robust business in the 1970s. It captured a market niche by providing travel service to British vacationers flying to the United States. It was quite popular, then, to plan itineraries around overseas shopping trips to New York. With strong pounds in their pockets, compared to the dollar, British citizens could buy consumer goods in the United States at a hefty discount to what they would pay in London. The savings often paid for the air fare and, consequently, flights to New York and back were booked solidly weeks in advance.

Business was so good, in fact, that Laker Air placed orders for five additional DC-10s. Suddenly, things took a dramatic turn. The British pound topped out early in 1981. From $2.40, it dropped sharply to $1.90, continued downward for the next five years, and finally bottomed in 1985 around $1.10. From the perspective of the British traveler, however, the pound wasn't dropping as much as the dollar was soaring. Discounts in New York disappeared and Mediterranean vacations became more alluring. Laker Air started flying a lot of empty seats across the Atlantic.

The swift decline in revenues was not the only difficulty facing Laker Air. Its outstanding dollar-denominated loans for the new airplanes resulted in increasing pound liabilities at the same time its pound revenues were decreasing. The dollar balances remained the same, but it was taking ever more pounds to pay them. The result, of course, was bankruptcy.

It is increasingly difficult to sort out the exposures a business might face. As the global economy becomes more interwoven, it becomes more complex. It is not always easy to know which currency affects which product. A company does not have to buy or sell internationally to be exposed to foreign currency risk. This fact has been brought home to a number of U.S. corporations, none more so than to Chrysler Corporation.

Throughout most of the 1960s and 1970s, Chrysler was involved in extensive overseas operations. Beginning in 1977, however, it became mired in red ink and without sufficient reserves to maintain its international presence. A decision was made to retrench, and to concentrate in North America. To implement this strategy, the company sold off its investments in Latin America, Europe, and Australia.

After downsizing, Chrysler focused entirely on the domestic front. It sourced its parts from U.S. suppliers, assembled them in Michigan, and sold the finished products to America. It became the quintessential domestic manufacturer, almost totally submerged in a dollar-denominated economy; however, as it was reorganizing, Toyota and other Japanese car companies began to unload their exports on California docks. Approximately 60% of the cost of these cars was denominated in yen, at an exchange rate of 200 to the dollar and rising. With a cost of goods denominated in a relatively under-valued currency, manufacturing costs were much lower in dollar terms. The Japanese priced them in dollars accordingly.

Still reeling from skyrocketing oil price increases, American consumers welcomed the economies of these new imports, including their attractive sticker prices. The Japanese car makers poured their brand new dollar revenues into war chests to be used to capture an even greater share of the U.S. market. Chrysler, at a major cost disadvantage, could only stand aside and watch its market share disappear.

It is interesting to note that Chrysler had no foreign currency exposure on its books. Its assets and liabilities were denominated solely in dollars. Yet it was staggered by an outside currency exposure of such magnitude that its stock was being sold to skittish buyers for as little as six dollars per share. Chrysler certainly had suffered a currency mismatch. This exposure surfaced in two areas: Toyota, Honda, and others carried the mismatch on their books and reaped the profits from it. The second mismatch was in the market place, where yen-cost-based cars were winning the competition with dollar-cost-based cars, to Chrysler's dismay.

Nothing is forever. Beginning in 1989, the yen/dollar exposure started turning the losses of the 1980s into the profits of the 1990s. At less than 100 yen to the dollar, the yen was becoming quite precious in dollar terms. The upsurge in domestic automobile sales, compared to those of Japanese imports, is one result. The Japanese illustrate one method of managing a dollar/yen exposure: Toyotas and Hondas are now manufactured in the United States.

Another example occurred with the Mexican peso. The economic growth in Mexico throughout the early 1990s became a magnet for investment funds, underpinned by a currency pegged at approximately three to the U.S. dollar. With the exchange rate locked in place, trade flourished. The actual value of the peso didn't seem to matter, at least not until December 20th, 1994, when the financial authorities of Mexico decided to float the currency. Who was to know that the peso was 40% overvalued? Thirty-cent pesos became eighteen-cent pesos in a matter of weeks. The fallout was felt around the world as the investment-capital flow into many growing markets suddenly changed directions. Whenever the currency of a major trading partner plunges 40%, people seem to take notice.

Foreign Currency Management

The concept of foreign currency management is quite straight forward. The first step is to identify the areas of operation subject to foreign exchange exposure. After discovering and analyzing the exposures, the decision is made as to what, if anything, to do about it. Some exposures might offset others, thereby reducing or eliminating the overall risk to the financial statements. Certain exposures, such as operating exposure, may endure for years, which may limit the available range of management tools. Other exposures might be better left unmanaged because managing them would create a more unacceptable exposure somewhere else.

Exposure, in a general sense, means that some segment of business is sensitive to currency exchange-rate fluctuation. The risk depends upon the potential degree of fluctuation. Risk, therefore, increases proportionately with an increase in the volatility of foreign exchange rates. Market turmoil may affect a currency directly, when resulting from a change in the fundamentals of that particular currency, or indirectly, such as when a currency gets caught up in a general market panic. In recent years, volatility in all major currencies has increased dramatically. Its effect on the U.S. dollar can be seen in Figure 1-1 on page 13. Why has volatility increased in recent years? Some of the major causes are:

- Values of currencies of our major trading partners and of the U.S dollar are now governed by a floating rate regime. After the 1993 meltdown of the European Rate Mechanism (the official pricing matrix of various European currencies), virtually none of the major currencies remained officially fixed (or "pegged") in any meaningful way. Their rates of exchange are determined by ever-changing market forces which are political, economic, and psychological in nature.

- A massive volume of currency now exchanges hands on any given day. Currencies trade in the wake of efficient and instantaneous information flow. This flow does not readily differentiate among fact, rumor, and deception. Minor news items, even rumors, may quickly translate into major market moves before analysis can dampen the effect. The heavy volume, or *liquidity*, of the market may make exchange rate movements less violent than those of thinly traded markets, but it does not make a move any more predictable. Actually, greater liquidity may provide greater momentum once a trend gets under way, whether or not it is economically justified.
- Inherent in the growing volume of trading is the ability to almost instantly and effortlessly substitute one currency for another. Currencies flow rapidly and unimpeded in a single global market place. There is evidence that increasing the degree of substitutability in the international money supply may actually increase volatility beyond that which would otherwise occur.

This is today's world of foreign exchange. Its unpredictability creates risk for companies in every nation. Unpredictable rates of exchange can have an adverse effect on business or return on investment. This used to be the cost of "going offshore," but the distinction between global and domestic economies is fast disappearing. Today, a sudden change in the money markets of Tokyo can disrupt the economic well-being of retail shop owners throughout the United States, whether or not they ever venture out of town.

Prudent management dictates that business risk should be managed to whatever extent possible. "Managing risk" means finding a way to eliminate it or reduce it to acceptable levels. Foreign currency management techniques depend on how pervasive the risk is. It may be a one-time occurrence, for example, in an account payable or receivable, or it can be endemic to the operating structure of the organization. Let's look at an example of risk occurring as a single event, and see how it might be managed.

Figure 1-1: Effect of Volatility on U.S. Dollar From 1976 to 1995

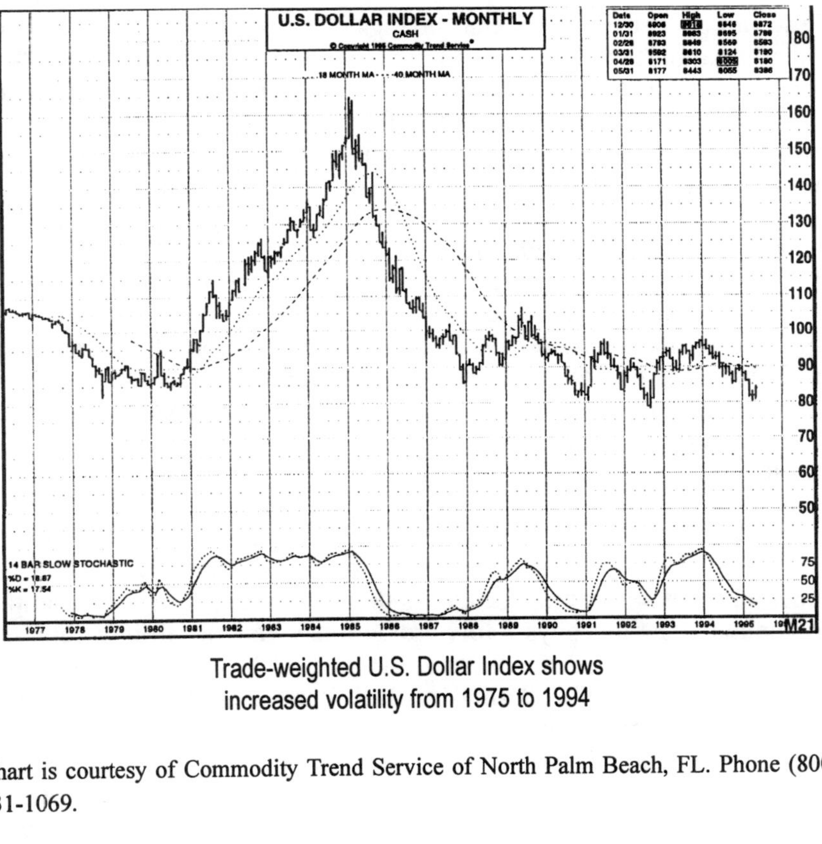

Trade-weighted U.S. Dollar Index shows increased volatility from 1975 to 1994

Chart is courtesy of Commodity Trend Service of North Palm Beach, FL. Phone (800) 331-1069.

Hedging a Dutch Guilder Exposure

A U.S. manufacturer of kitchenware signs a purchase order for plastic extrusion machinery from Amsterdam. The price of the machinery is 1,000,000 Dutch guilders. When the P.O. is signed, the rate of exchange is .50, or two guilders for one dollar. The price to the manufacturer, therefore, is $500,000.

The machinery will be shipped in 6 months, at which time payment is due. For these six months—from the time of sale to the time of payment—the manufacturer has an exposure in Dutch guilders. If the exchange rate stays the same, he pays $500,000 as anticipated. If there were a shift in rates and the guilder fell in value to $.45 by the time the payment came due, the manufacturer would benefit. He would pay the 1,000,000 guilders as contracted, but they would cost him only $450,000. He would pocket an unexpected savings of $50,000. The risk, of course, is that the guilder might increase in value instead. If it were worth $.55 when payment was due, the 1,000,000 guilders now would cost the manufacturer $550,000, for a loss of $50,000.

This exposure may be handled in any number of ways. The company may decide that its policy is to remain exposed; thus affording the opportunity to gain if the guilder decreased in value. The company may demand a clause written into the sales agreement indemnifying it against foreign exchange loss. Alternatively, it may decide to watch the market and take action only if the guilder began an upward trend in value; or it may "hedge" the transaction at the time the order is placed. A simple way to do this would be to exchange $500,000 for 1,000,000 guilders when the contract is signed, perhaps through the foreign exchange department of the manufacturer's bank. The guilders, then, are held in an account in the Netherlands and paid out when the shipment is made. The exposure is eliminated and the transaction is insulated from any potential changes in exchange rates, up or down. There is no unanticipated gain or loss.

Another way to achieve the same results is to buy a "derivative," or something that substitutes for the 1,000,000 guilders. For this example, say the manufacturer buys a forward currency contract from a commercial bank. It acquires the contract at the time of the purchase agreement. It has a value of 1,000,000 guilders at the current exchange rate. Only a small fraction of the derivative is charged initially, and a bank credit line is set up to handle this cost. The manufacturer picks up leverage because it doesn't pay anything out of pocket up front. Six months later, when the payment becomes due, it sells the derivative. At the same time, it pays 1,000,000 guilders for the shipment. If the guilders have increased in value and are now worth $.55, his cost is $550,000 instead of the anticipated $500,000, but the derivative also has increased in value. The manufacturer sells it for a gain of $50,000. There is no net loss.

On the other hand, if the price of guilders has fallen to $.45, the manufacturer pays out only $450,000; however, there is also a loss of $50,000 on the sale of the derivative; therefore, there is no net gain, either. The foreign currency exposure has been managed and the amount of the payment is as anticipated, no more, no less, whether measured in guilders or in dollars.

In reality, the gain or loss from a derivative transaction would probably not offset the gain or loss of the exchange rate change precisely. There may be tax implications, or, when dealing with two transactions in two different markets, the rate changes may occur at different rates of speed. Also, there are transaction costs to consider. Yet, if the hedge is properly constructed, these factors should be insignificant compared to the reduction in risk of exposure.

Is Hedging The Answer?

The above example illustrates a problem of much greater magnitude than the imprecision of offsetting gains and losses. This problem underlies all risk management programs. Simply put, should the hedge be entered in the first place? Does it benefit the manufacturer? Only hindsight reveals the answer. If the dollar made a major advance against the guilder while the hedge was in place, it would produce a loss of major proportions. The fact that it was offset by a savings somewhere else may not be enough justification, especially when the loss, or "hedge burden" as it is sometimes known, is being explained to a senior manager who has had no input in the risk management program. This may be the single biggest obstacle to foreign currency management. Unless there are clearly defined objectives, safeguards in place, and clear communications at every level of management, a hedging program may turn into a disaster.

The record is littered with casualties. In 1984, Lufthansa had placed a major purchase order for airliners from a U.S. firm. Its economists were forecasting a stronger dollar. Perhaps aware of Laker Air's experience, it locked up the Deutsche mark/dollar exchange rate with a forward contract. The economists guessed wrong. In one year, Lufthansa had lost somewhere around $150 million, and one or two financial managers reportedly lost their jobs. The chairman of Porsche found himself unemployed two years later. He had engineered the company into a dependence on the U.S. market for 61% of its revenue without hedging against a downturn in the dollar. Porsche suffered a major financial setback as a result. It was about that same time that Volkswagen began sorting through a loss of $259 million to a group of currency traders who had falsified documents in an illegal "bucket shop" operation. Meanwhile, in the United States, Zenith Electronics Corporation was explaining to its stockholders a $13 million loss on a forward contract. Jerry K. Pearlman, chairman and president, remarked that "it's the kind of mistake we will never make again."[4] It's a "damned if you do and damned if you don't" situation, and it's no wonder that U.S. corporate officers would rather just forget the whole thing.

Conclusion

It is evident that ignoring currency rates while engaging in international business is no longer a viable option. Simply staying out of foreign markets is no guarantee against foreign exchange risk, as discovered by Chrysler Corporation. Invoicing foreign customers solely in U.S dollars might well bring about an exposure even riskier than that incurred from transacting in foreign currencies. Such a policy simply turns very visible accounting exposure into less visible operating exposure, which may be harder to manage. No matter how exposure is viewed, foreign currency management indisputably will play an increasingly essential role in today's new business environment. In spite of the pitfalls and war stories, the list of companies who successfully hedge their exposures, large or small, is rapidly expanding.

Exposure to foreign currency risk is created by unpredictability in the foreign exchange markets. The larger the volume of currencies traded on a world-wide scale, the more exchange rates are subject to volatility and the more unpredictable they become. Different exposures can occur within an organization and affect different aspects of the business. Results may range from a windfall in operating income to insolvency. The outcome is rarely certain. Management techniques to reduce or eliminate exposure differ according to the perspective of the company. Short-term transactions can be hedged with financial instruments, but longer-term risks often require changes in operations.

The most important criterion of a foreign currency management program is that it fits within the overall policy of the company. In most instances, there is no policy to refer to and one must be developed. Hedging currencies should always be the implementation of a program reviewed, accepted, and understood by all levels of management. Senior management must be involved, if not in the tactical decisions, certainly in the strategic ones. Everyone involved must understand the possible consequences of all "what if" scenarios. Controls must be implemented and authority to make decisions in a timely fashion must be granted. Perhaps the most difficult part of foreign currency management is presentation of the concept. This is the reason it often takes a year or more from the time a program is first presented until it is implemented. A major objective of this manual is to enable financial managers to understand and explain the concepts, the objectives, and the possible results of a foreign currency management program.

CHAPTER 2

What is a Currency, Really?

Simply put, currency is money. Money serves many functions, however, and an in-depth discussion of currency is often an exploration of its various functions. According to John Stuart Mill, a currency:

> ". . . is a machine for doing quickly and commodiously, what would be done, though less quickly and commodiously, without it. . . ."[1]

In other words, the function of money is to serve as a medium of exchange. Qualities that are important to this function include serving as a standard of account and a store of value. Some currencies have other attributes. They may be "freely held," for example (not all are). They may be "investable," or invested for profit. They may be freely convertible into other currencies.

What is a Currency?

There are three types of currencies. The first is *specie*, which is money coined from precious metal (gold or silver). It most readily meets the requirements for a relatively stable store of value because it is naturally limited in supply. It is the most exchangeable and convertible of all currencies because the value of the precious metal from which it is struck is universally recognized and accepted.

The second is a commodity-backed, or redeemable, currency. This most often takes the form of paper notes backed by gold or silver. The

United States has had both silver and gold standards at various times in the past. To the degree that paper money is readily convertible at a ratio of one-to-one into the metal that backs it, a commodity-backed currency also has a relatively stable value. This type of currency is riskier to hold than specie because its convertibility depends on the issuer making good its promise to redeem the paper for the commodity that backs it.

The third type of currency is a fiat currency, which is an unbacked paper currency. It is considered to be currency only because the issuer mandates it to be "legal tender." In other words, creditors are compelled by law to accept it in payment of "all debts public and private." There are three properties common to fiat currency:

- The currency is intrinsically worthless. It is a piece of paper with a number on it.
- It is unbacked. It carries no promise of redemption for anything other than another piece of paper.
- It is virtually costless to produce, or at least whatever it is exchanged for is worth more than the production cost of the currency. Also, the cost to produce 10 units of fiat currency is the same as the cost to produce 100 units-the only difference is the number printed on it.

The movement of goods across borders is greatly facilitated by a common money, or medium of exchange, with which to swap one product or commodity for another. For most of human history, this medium was something of value, such as gold or silver. As governments began to look for new, less obvious ways to clip their currencies, paper monies came into being. Some were redeemable for specie; others were not. This was the beginning of fiat standards.

The qualities important for media of exchange are being compromised as currencies the world over have moved from specie to redeemability and then to fiat money (legal tender). For example, in a cash transaction, someone acquires something of value by exchanging units of currency for it. For a currency unit to be accepted in exchange, it must have value and the value has to be maintained while the currency is held, unless the government mandates that it be accepted as payment for debt, which it does through legal tender laws. The qualities of fiat currencies are fading as governments debase them. Fiat currencies cannot serve as standard units of account because they are continually inflated, losing value relative to other goods. They can no longer be considered stable stores of value because their values are entirely determined by what the issuing governments say and do. Otherwise, they are worthless. The only property left unchanged is its use as a medium of exchange—mandated by legal tender laws. In the long term, as the German hyper-inflation of the 1920s showed, even this function may be compromised—proving economist Ludwig von Mises' reported statement that "government is the only body which can take a valuable commodity such as paper, put some ink on it, and make it totally worthless."

Governments, being governments, tend to change the value of fiat currencies when they find it expedient to do so. The money is not stable in value, and when its value changes, the value of everything denominated by it also changes. Some fiat currencies are also restricted in their use due to exchange restrictions. Perhaps the single role for which a fiat currency is unconditionally qualified is that of legal tender.

Every industrialized country and most developing countries use fiat currency for domestic and international trading purposes. Because it has no intrinsic value, fiat currency is considered by some financial scholars to be "price indeterminate" (the value cannot be determined or predicted mathematically); thus, it is subject to constant price analysis. This is the major challenge of foreign currency management.

The Evolving U.S. Dollar[2]

The political and economic history of a country can be traced through its currency. In the United States, the politics of currency began with the pre-revolutionary colonies and independent states—with the profligate spending habits of the Massachusetts colonial government. These were financed in part by plundering nearby Quebec. When one such expedition failed in 1690, the Massachusetts government printed paper notes to pay the soldiers so they would not mutiny. Suspecting the fiat paper would be unacceptable to the public, the government promised to redeem it for specie in a few years (from tax revenues) and to never issue paper money again. Both promises were broken in short order.[3] This set the stage for other fiat currencies in the colonies, which soon ruined public credit throughout much of New England.

The experience of turning currency into waste paper was not lost on the founding fathers. The Constitution of the United States addressed the problem by giving Congress the "power to coin money and to regulate the value thereof." In effect, it adopted a specie standard. Following the Constitutional bidding, Congress authorized the minting of a dollar coin that contained 371.25 grains of fine silver or 24.75 grains of fine gold. In addition, *foreign coins* circulating in the United States were specified as legal tender. (This made sense because one ounce of gold is one ounce of gold whether minted into a Canadian Maple Leaf or a South African Krugerrand.) In 1800, roughly 80% of the specie in circulation in the United States was foreign.

The specifications for U.S. coins did two things: they established a bimetallic standard, and they set an official exchange rate between silver and gold. Also, aware of the dangers of allowing politicians access to a money machine, Congress denied the executive branch the power to issue paper money or fiat currency.

The role of a central bank is intended to safeguard the legal tender and control its supply and circulation. During the early nineteenth century, the First Bank of the United States (1791 to 1812) and its successor, the Second Bank of the United States (1816 to 1836), were chartered by Congress. By 1827, legal tender privileges for many foreign coins were progressively canceled. The millions of paper dollars issued by the First Bank of the United States created an inflationary price rise of 72 per cent in the first 5 years of its existence. The bank charters were not renewed by Congress in 1812, nor in 1836.

Between 1836 and the Civil War, state chartered banks issued a huge volume of fractional reserve paper bank notes. Had they been forced to meet their contractual obligation to repay their notes in specie, the system would have been more stable. Instead, the state governments stepped in repeatedly (starting as early as 1814) permitting banks to stop all redemption of notes and deposits in gold or silver, and yet to continue to operate! The government accepted the paper money for tax payments, giving it a quasi-legal tender status, which set the stage for today's use of fiat paper money, inflatable at the whim of the body politic.[4]

Circulating Bank Notes

A quasi-private banking system with state charters (many owned by the states) emerged as the country moved west. Each bank was free to issue its own notes, which were supposed to be receipts against gold and silver held in the bank's vault. It soon became a well-known practice for banks to establish themselves in distant towns, far removed from their central vault. Thus assured that their notes could not be readily redeemed, they began to overissue. Gold receipts took on the character of an unbacked currency, especially at a distance from the issuing bank in a day of slow communications and expensive travel. The value of the gold receipts reflected this. The notes became subject to discounting, the amount often in direct proportion to the distance from the bank's vault.

Greenbacks

The circulating bank note regime limped along until the Civil War. As the war dragged on, the treasury department issued large amounts of bonds to finance the mountainous cost. It obtained backing for the bonds by draining the gold reserves from major banks. When the government was unable to create more debt and the bonds appeared to be in jeopardy of default, Congress again abandoned the specie standard. Through the Legal Tender Act of 1862, it monetized the debt with printing runs of "greenbacks," an irredeemable fiat currency, setting a momentous precedent. Also, for the first time, the Act gave the executive branch control of the currency, marrying the federal government and banking. The greenback lasted until 1878, but by then the National Banking Act of 1863 had given the treasury department a permanent role in U.S. monetary policy. To this day, legal scholars argue over the constitutionality of the Legal Tender Acts.

National Bank Notes

The National Banking Act 1863 also provided for the chartering of the national banks and allowed them to issue bank notes. These notes were backed by U.S. Treasury Bonds. The supply of bonds, and therefore the supply of money, was determined in part by the Treasury Department through fractional reserve requirements (which could consist of greenbacks as well as specie). Additionally, there was a pyramiding effect caused by reserves of smaller banks being held at the larger banks. The small-bank reserves became deposits at the larger banks, which would then hold only a fractional reserve against the supposedly iron reserve of the smaller banks. The National Banking Act also allowed for the expansion and contraction of the federal debt. This system of controlling the money supply by bond issuance and retirement was extremely cumbersome and was only marginally effective. Consequently, banks began to issue notes on demand deposits, which did not require reserves.[5]

With this monetary system, there was no way to quickly respond to unpredictable demands for withdrawals. Moreover, the reserves of all banks in a particular region were interconnected. Many times, withdrawals at one bank turned into runs on all banks throughout the region. Bank panics, restricted credit, and suspended payments became commonplace. The country lurched from bank runs to economic collapse, culminating in a major financial panic in 1907.

Federal Reserve Note

The Panic of 1907 made the banks realize that they were in over their heads with fractional reserve banking, and they began to call for a central bank (to rescue themselves). Congress finally was convinced, and the Federal Reserve System was formed in 1913. A board of directors was seated and empowered to carry out the provisions of the charter. Its mission, according to Congress, was to establish a network of Federal Reserve Banks, and to furnish the country with an "elastic currency." The "Fed" fulfilled the objective by converting commercial bank deposits to currency, primarily through the lending powers of its discount window operations. Although, like its predecessor, this new Federal Reserve note was based on the bank's deposits, it was fully backed by gold. The United States ended convertibility to gold twenty years later, in 1933.

After World War II, the gold standard was resurrected on the foundation of the Bretton Woods system. Under this system, the major world currencies were pegged to the U.S. dollar, which was, in turn, pegged to gold at a fixed price of $35 per ounce. The system lasted until 1971, at which time the convertibility of dollars for gold was abandoned, and the U.S. dollar once again became a fiat currency.

Gold

Gold has been officially demonetized world wide. It no longer is used for coinage (specie) at least for exchange purposes. Coins are sometimes minted as an asset class for investment purposes, but no major currency today is backed by gold. Practically every country engaged in trade has turned to fiat currency.

Nevertheless, gold plays a major role in the global currency system. As of 1991, gold accounted for almost one-third of the world's entire monetary reserve.[6] Although no currency is officially pegged to it, nations with non-convertible currency still settle international payments from stores of gold. The best known example is the Soviet Union which, until its collapse, paid for grain imports primarily by selling gold on the international market. Gold and oil still serve world wide as proxy currencies for foreign goods.

In the developing world of Southeast Asia and elsewhere, substantial numbers of private citizens consider gold to be a form of currency, and it is often stored or worn as chains, rather than entrusted to a bank. A cottage gold exchange industry thrives in these regions. Shops that exchange gold for local currency are found on every street. The ubiquitous balance scale sits on the countertop, where 24 caret gold chains of one length are exchanged, along with the appropriate amount of cash, for those of another. Here, gold is priced strictly by weight without regard for artistry or workmanship.

The influence of gold on the monetary system is so extensive that, in its *Annual Currency Exchange Report*, the International Monetary Fund (IMF) publishes the restrictions and procedures for gold imports and exports for each country. Unlike official currency, gold moves confidentially much of the time. Figures of stocks are difficult to obtain. The gold stock of the former Soviet Union may be anywhere from 290 tons to 2,000 tons as of the end of 1989. Until recently, China has not disclosed its figures, declaring gold to be a strategic metal. As far as we can tell, total cumulative gold production at the end of 1991 was approximately 100,000 tons, of which central banks and other monetary authorities were holding perhaps a third.[7]

The gold market operates in three locations. Each one is the center of a unique function of the overall market. Zurich, Switzerland, for example, is the world's foremost depository of physical gold. The daily price is established in London, where five finance officials meet twice a day. After reviewing the latest gold transactions in the international financial markets, along with other market indicators, they announce the "fix" or the price standard for the morning, and again for the afternoon. Physical transactions in every country are based on the London AM and PM fixes. The third function of the market takes place in New York, or more precisely, at the New York Mercantile Exchange COMEX Division. Gold futures contracts traded in the pits provide a continuously updated pricing mechanism for storage and deferred deliveries of gold.

A cursory understanding of the gold market can benefit anyone involved in foreign currency management. The history of money is one of political maneuverings, and recent historical events surely cannot inspire confidence that fiat currencies will continue to function internationally as media of exchange. Specie currency, gold, or some other proxy currency may well be required for future international transactions—at least sometimes in at least some countries. This could simplify international trade because, as a currency, gold is one of the easiest to manage with currently available markets.

Eurocurrency

Global in scope and free from government oversight, the Eurocurrency market is comprised of a network of banks and other financial institutions. Its function is to borrow and lend "foreign currency." In other words, it makes loans denominated in a currency other than the home currency of the lender or borrower. The currency itself never leaves home; only foreign currency *deposits* are loaned, in the form of book entries or debits and credits. These deposits are not assignable, and they remain in the home country bank.

U.S. dollar deposits, which comprise 70% of the Eurocurrency market, are known as Eurodollars. These dollar deposits are loaned extensively abroad, mostly through international branches of American banks, but also through foreign banks. The predominance of Eurodollars in the Eurocurrency market is due, in part, to the dollar's stature as a lead reserve currency with its perceived low exchange risk. In addition, the Eurodollar deposit interest rate, known as the London Interbank Offered Rate or "LIBOR," is often somewhat higher than comparable-term rates in the U.S market due to U.S. banking laws requiring greater spreads between yields paid out for deposits and those charged for borrowing. The U.S. government restrictions give Eurodollar loans a competitive edge resulting in a large demand for Eurodollars not only from foreign borrowers, but from American companies as well.

As the name implies, the Eurocurrency market originated in Europe, primarily in London. Today, however, the term describes *any currency loaned or borrowed anywhere except in its home country*. The yields paid are called *Eurorates.* For example, Eurorates are quoted for Euromarks, Eurolira, Euroyen, Euroswiss francs and so forth. It is easy to understand why the traders of Eurorates are also in the foreign exchange market. Interest rates and exchange rates are interrelated; in fact, it is difficult to separate operations in one area from those in the other.

Currency as a Commodity

Currency is a medium of exchange, but currencies are not the only things that can qualify as such. Various commodities have been used at different times throughout history. Gold and silver were the most common, but others served as well, including barrels of oil, bushels of corn, beaver pelts, baskets of eggs, or whatever people valued. In fact, there are still some old timers who talk about grocery shopping as "having to go trading." Modern day trading, also known as barter, is just as straight-forward.

The only qualification is that the individuals involved both agree: each must believe that what he is receiving has greater value (subjective) than what he is giving.

In more recent history, there has been a gradual evolution from precious metals as media of exchange to today's currencies. In the United States, we moved from coined gold to deposit receipts for gold, to gold- and silver-backed notes, to notes convertible for gold (but only by foreign governments), to fiat currency notes. Regardless of this progression toward value-indeterminate money, currencies are still commodities in some respects. As long as they are perceived to have value, they can be bought, sold, and traded, just like gold, wheat, and pork bellies. Throughout this manual, currencies will be treated like commodities. Extending the concept of commodity barter to foreign exchange will help explain the principles of currency management.

Price, Rates and Value

The terms *currency price*, *exchange rate*, and *currency value* are often used interchangeably. This may lead to confusion because the meanings do differ. Specifically, *price* in very narrowly defined, *rate* is less so, and *value* has a much broader, more conceptual definition.

The *price* of a currency is relevant when it is treated as an asset. In other words, a currency can be bought or sold, just as other things of value can be, for a certain dollar amount. The price of a British pound unit may be $1.50, and a unit of Japanese yen might be priced at $0.01. Based on these prices, the *exchange rate*, or *rate of exchange* can be expressed in several ways. The Japanese yen, for example, has an exchange rate of 100. There are 100 units of yen to a dollar. It can also be expressed as .00100 because there are .001 units of dollars to a yen. Regardless of the difference between them, *price* and *rate* are used interchangeably in this manual unless otherwise noted.

The hardest thing to quantify is the *value* of a currency. The starting point must be the values and preferences of individual consumers. Value is *subjectively* determined by individuals, then aggregated in a market setting. Thus, for a currency priced freely at the market, its price is usually a function of its perceived value. An officially determined price may have no relationship to value. According to *The Wall Street Journal*, Iraq recently began the practice of lopping off the hand of anyone who confused the two terms by trading the Iraqi dinar at its dollar value (less than a cent) rather than at its official price ($3.22).[8]

We often hear of "hard," "soft," and "exotic" (very soft?) currencies. Hard currencies have certain properties, such as convertibility, accessibility and tradability. These include the U.S. dollar, the Canadian dollar, the major European currencies and the Japanese yen. They all "float" somewhat independently, meaning that they are priced by a free market, hopefully close to their true values. Their rates of exchange are accepted almost without question because they are under constant market scrutiny. Long lines of buyers and sellers line up on either side of the price, hoping for it to move one direction or the other. The rate at any moment is both visible and well supported.

It is often more difficult to forecast future *hard* currency exchange rates than future *soft* currency exchange rates. The rates of soft currencies are "stickier." In fact, rates may be officially cemented in place. In contrast, hard currency prices are definitely not fixed. Prices of hard currencies are continuously "discovered" by an ever-changing market. There are exceptions. The Swiss franc and Dutch guilder are hard currencies that, through official policy, remain closely tied to the price of the Deutsche mark. Also, an increasing number of soft currencies now float independently, although retaining some exchange restrictions. As a general rule, however, the rates for hard currencies are determined by the market and are subject to daily change; the exchange rates for soft currencies are often officially established and remain relatively constant.

Hyperinflation

Hyperinflation occurs when a government inflates the currency (necessarily a fiat currency) as a matter of expediency to meet some political objective. The objective is usually one requiring massive deficit spending. It is a futile exercise to try calculating values for currencies in hyperinflationary environments—they may change from moment to moment. The question for currency managers becomes, "How much longer will this untenable situation be allowed to continue?"

Perhaps the Reichsmark of Germany is the most widely known example of hyperinflation in currency. After World War I, a conference of European nations drew up terms for Germany's war reparations. Compliance by Germany with such stringent terms was impossible. Using the crushing depression that followed as an excuse to print more fiat paper money, the currency printing presses in Germany never stopped running. Currency depreciated *hourly*. Restaurant patrons began to pay in advance because menu prices rose faster than they could eat. As the story goes, one wage-earner trudged home with his wheelbarrow filled with heavy wads of Reichsmarks—his daily pay. He stopped at a meat market and, parking the wheelbarrow outside, went in to check the price of sausage. Leaving the store, he found he had been robbed. The thief had dumped the money on the sidewalk and made off with the wheelbarrow.

The story has a ring of truth about it, considering that in the final spasm between December, 1922, and November, 1923, wholesale prices increased almost 100 million percent![9]

There are more recent occurrences of hyperinflation, which increase in times of turmoil. Russia and eastern Europe are prime examples. So is Brazil. In 1993, the economy of Brazil grew at 4.5%, a respectable figure on the surface; but it was based on a currency system out of control. Since 1960, prices had multiplied 22 *billion* times. The *cruzeiro real* was replaced four times, simply by lopping off three zeros each time. The rate of inflation exceeded 211% every year of the last decade, and was 2,567% in 1993. The system worked, to some extent, because a large portion of wages was indexed to inflation (although only a privileged minority of the population earned these indexed wages). As an index component, the currency served as a unit of account within a type of barter system. It was worthless as a store of value, and virtually non-investable. The government indexed tax revenue to inflation by collecting a proxy currency, called the *ufir*, which was constantly adjusted in value. The fact that the majority of the population received non-indexed wages, and therefore was spiraling into insolvency, made the system unstable. No determination of either current or future exchange rates could be considered meaningful. Things have changed. The current Brazilian *real,* pegged to the U.S. dollar, is the result of a serious effort to put meaning back into the currency.

Currency Pegs

Exchange rates for some currencies are "pegged," or based, on another currency. Usually, a soft currency is pegged to a hard currency, which forces the government of the soft currency to restrain its policies so they are no more inflationary than those of the hard-currency country. Sometimes the peg is not a currency at all, but a mathematical indicator, such as an index or basket of currencies. Price discovery of a pegged currency is straight-forward. The price is a constant percentage of the price of the currency it is pegged to. Of course, it does little good to know that today there are 50 Congo francs to the French franc and tomorrow there will be 50 Congo francs to the French Franc if we don't know what the French franc will be worth tomorrow.

Along with the price uncertainty of the hard-currency peg is the uncertainty of whether the pegged rate makes economic sense. It depends a lot on government policy. Remember that fiat currencies are priced by the market or by edict. An officially priced fiat currency is whatever the issuing authorities say it is. The only thing backing it up is that the people have grown accustomed to it. If there is little faith in the value of the fiat money, the government may simply refuse to permit convertibility of the currency, or it may put into effect heavy exchange restrictions to impede convertibility. Such restraints prevent capital flight from the country, a phenomenon that often occurs when the official price is unrealistic in light of underlying economic factors. When the official price overvalues the currency, the market-determined exchange rate may change rapidly due to rising inflation. "Parallel markets," a euphemism for black markets, spring up to convert the currency at more realistic prices, if people can get away with it. Conversely, the price of the currency may be kept artificially low to obtain a competitive advantage in international trade. In either case, a careful distinction must be made between the pegged exchange rate and real value.

Exchange Rates

The rate of exchange between two currencies tells how many units of one currency can be exchanged for one unit of another currency. This is expressed as a ratio. American tourists who travel abroad are familiar with the concept. Crossing the border to Canada, one of their first stops is at the government currency exchange booth, where they hand over, for example, $500 dollars in travelers checks in return for, say, 675 Canadian dollars in cash.

Two generic currencies can be used to discuss the concept of foreign exchange. One will be "foreign currency," designated "FC." The other will be "home currency," or "HC."

Now, if it takes one unit of HC to purchase two units of FC, the exchange rate for these currencies can be expressed either as 0.50 or 2.00, depending upon our perspective. For the rate of 2.00, the ratio fully written out is as follows:

$$\frac{FC}{HC} = \frac{2.00}{1.00} \quad \text{or,} \quad FC/HC = 2.00$$

This represents the number of FC units required to buy (or to exchange for) one unit of HC. The same rate of exchange can be expressed another way:

$$\frac{HC}{FC} = \frac{.50}{1.00} \quad \text{or,} \quad HC/FC = .50$$

This refers to the number of HC units required to buy one unit of FC. The ratio used depends upon the method of quoting exchange rates. Different methods are used in different markets. When "HC" represents the U.S. dollar, the first ratio is called the *indirect quote* and the second ratio is the *direct quote*.

Reciprocity

Direct and indirect quotes are reciprocals of one another. Dividing either into 1.00 produces the other. Standard practice is to express both ratios to four decimal places; for example, assume the following exchange rates between the U.S. dollar and the Deutsche mark:

$$\frac{\$}{DM} = .5708$$ *direct* quote, one Deutsche mark equals $.5708

$$\frac{DM}{\$} = 1.7520$$ indirect quote, one dollar equals DM 1.7520

$$\frac{FC}{\$} \times \frac{\$}{FC} = 1$$ Example: .5708 x 1.7520 = 1.00 (rounded)

Notice, then the reciprocals:

$$\frac{1}{.5708} = 1.7520; \qquad \frac{1}{1.7520} = .5708 \text{ (rounded)}$$

Reciprocal exchange rate symbols such as "HC/FC" and "FC/HC" are written as ratios, therefore it is important not to confuse the value on the right side of the equation with the solution to a division problem. In other words, $FC / HC = 2.00$ does *not* mean that HC goes into FC twice. Rather, the expression signifies that x units of FC are to *one* unit of HC as two is to one (2.00/1.00). An easy way to avoid confusion is to remember that the denominator on both sides of the equation is always 1.00.

Exchange Rates and the U.S. Dollar

Unless otherwise noted, "exchange rate" is understood by the industry to mean the rate of exchange between the U.S. dollar and some other currency. This convention grew out of the Bretton Woods system, where the dollar was the international currency peg. Actually, exchange rates can be applied to any two currencies, and the combinations are almost endless. By convention, an exchange rate that does *not* include the U.S. dollar is called a *cross rate*. Cross rates are calculated directly or, more commonly, by determining the rate of each currency against the U.S. dollar, then factoring the dollar component out of the calculation by cross division (hence the name). (See Figure 2-1.)

Nominal vs. Real

Consider the following relationships occurring over a period of time:

Start of period	*End of period*
100 HC = 100 FC	100 HC = 110 FC

This is all the information required to recognize a change in nominal rates. When referring to exchange rate changes without any elaboration, it is the nominal exchange rate being discussed; the number of units of one currency required to purchase one unit of another. In addition to nominal rates, there are real rates of exchange. A real rate of exchange refers to the comparative values of two currencies; specifically, how much purchasing power is available when using each currency. To illustrate the distinction, let's look at a few examples of changing rates. For these

Figure 2-1: The Canadian Dollar / Mexican Peso Cross Rate

Assume that the Canadian dollar exchange rate is approx. 73 cents, or .72870 to be precise. The Mexican peso is .29802. These rates can be expressed as:

$$\frac{.29802}{1} \quad \text{and} \quad \frac{.72870}{1}$$

To find the cross rate we "cross divide" the two ratios by inverting the last term and multiplying:

$$\frac{.29802}{1} \quad \text{X} \quad \frac{1}{.72870}$$

The dollar component "1" is factored out, leaving $\frac{.29802}{.72870}$ or .40897.

This is the exchange rate of the Canadian dollar and Mexican peso. One peso equals .40897 Canadian dollars. The reciprocal (1/0.40897) expresses the number of pesos that equal one Canadian dollar which, in this case, is 2.4451.

examples, a "basket of goods" will symbolize purchasing power. The basket will be designated "BG."

7/1/94	**7/1/95**
100 HC = 100 FC	100 HC = 110 FC
100 HC = 1.00 BG	100 HC = 1.00 BG
100 FC = 1.00 BG	110 FC = 1.00 BG
Base rate	Change in Nominal Rate No Change in Real Rate

In the example above, 100 units of HC buys one BG on July 1, 1994. FC has the same value because it can buy the same amount. Having identical purchasing power, HC and FC are "at purchasing power parity" on that date. After one year, the exchange rate between the two currencies has changed. Due to inflation, FC is now worth less, at least in terms of HC. The same amount of HC buys more FC (110 instead of 100). It also cost more FC to buy the same 1.00 BG; therefore, the *relative* levels of purchasing power remained the same. The new exchange rate still provides for exchanging one currency for the other without a loss or gain in purchasing power. Since HC and FC are still at purchasing power parity, only the nominal exchange rate has changed.

The shifts in relative inflation rates appear to actually cause a *compensating* shift in exchange rates. In fact, the theory of Purchasing Power Parity (PPP) predicts that this shift will occur. This theory argues that the price of a currency in one country relative to that of another seeks a level that "equalizes" the costs of goods in both countries. According to the theory, if equalization does not occur—if parity is lost—goods will flow out of one country into the other until purchasing power parity is re-established.

Any change in the exchange rate is, by definition, a change in the nominal rate. When the move compensates *precisely* for the difference in purchasing power, *only* the nominal rate changes. Let's compare the above example with the following:

7/1/94	**7/1/95**
100 HC = 100 FC 100 HC = 1.00 BG 100 FC = 1.00 BG	100 HC = 110 FC 100 HC = 1.00 BG 100 FC = 1.00 BG
Base Rate	Change in Nominal and Real Rates

Here, there is a change in nominal rates: 100 HC's relative value increases from 100 FC to 110 FC; however, there is no compensating adjustment in purchasing power between the two currencies. A unit of each currency still purchases 1.00 BG as it did the year before; therefore, on July 1, 1995, one unit of HC still equals one unit of FC in terms of *purchasing power*, but they are no longer equal in terms of *price*. Any portion of a nominal rate change that does not represent an identical change in purchasing power represents a change in *real* exchange rates; thus, in this example, both nominal and real rates have changed.

What about the automatic shift predicted by PPP? Actually, what PPP theory predicts often does not occur in the near term. This is because of differences in demand, supply, transportation, government trade restrictions, or foreign exchange restrictions. Any of these constraints may prevent two currencies from achieving parity in purchasing power. Still, over the long run, freely traded currencies tend toward parity. A good example of this is the changing buying patterns of U.S. and Canadian citizens living near the border. Throughout most of the 1950s, American motorists would drive on fumes into Canada to fill up with "low cost" gasoline. By the time the 1990s rolled around, Canadian grocery shoppers with bare cupboards at home would cross into nearby American cities for similar savings.

Under different conditions, a change in the real rate can occur while the nominal rate remains constant. This is shown below:

7/1/94	**7/1/95**
100 HC = 100 FC 100 HC = 1.00 BG 100 FC = 1.00 BG	100 HC = 100 FC 100 HC = 1.00 BG 110 FC = 1.00 BG
Base Rate	No Change in Nominal Rate Change in Real Rate

Here, there is a change in the relative levels of inflation. On July 1, 1995, 100 HC still can purchase 1.00 BG, the same as a year earlier, but during the year, FC depreciated. It now takes 110 FC to buy the same goods. There is no compensating change in nominal exchange rates (100 HC still equals 100 FC). The net result is approximately a 10% change in real exchange rates. This commonly occurs when the currency price is "stuck," perhaps at an official rate. The economics surrounding the currency may change, but the rate remains the same. To maintain this nominal rate, stringent exchange controls sometimes are put into effect, preventing the currency from trading at a more realistic price.

The following example below shows another common occurrence:

7/1/89	**7/1/91**	**7/1/95**
100 HC = 100 FC 100 HC = 1.00 BG 100 FC = 1.00 BG	100 HC = 120 FC 100 HC = 1.00 BG 110 FC = 1.00 BG	100 HC = 115 FC 100 HC = 1.00 BG 115 FC = 1.00 BG
Base Rate	Change in Nominal and Real Rates	Change in Nominal Rate Only

The FC economy experienced 10% inflation between 1989 and 1991. In 1991, it took 110 FC to purchase 1.00 BG, which cost 100 FC in 1989. Between 1989 and 1991, the HC economy's inflation rate was 0%, and there was a nominal rate change of 20%. The difference between the nominal rate change and the relative inflation rates constitutes a real exchange rate change. Purchasing power parity does not exist.

Over a longer period of time (five to ten years), real rate changes tend to balance each other out and PPP is regained. In this example, the real rate variance disappears by 1995, when PPP is restored. Recent history shows that, in the near term, volatility of both real and nominal rates of exchange is usually a daily occurrence.

CHAPTER 3

Currency Arrangements

The major currencies, like those of most trade-oriented countries, trade freely. They float, either independently or in a group of sorts, in relation to the rest of the world, but none of these currencies float independently of governmental interference. Rather, they are "watched over" or managed to some degree by the central banks. Many so-called "floating" currencies are pegged in one fashion or another thròugh bilateral or multilateral agreements.

Countries will often peg their local currency to a major currency to "protect" its value. The process of "pegging" constitutes a pledge that the government will do what is necessary to keep the value of its currency at a specific rate, or within specific rate boundaries of the stronger currency. Effectively, this constitutes a promise that it will debase its currency no faster than the one to which it is pegged is being debased, on average. A "soft" fiat currency may be more readily accepted internationally if it is perceived as tied to a "hard" fiat currency. Other countries, for the same reason, will peg their currencies to a composite, or currency basket. Pegging one currency to another also facilitates trade between the countries by reducing the foreign exchange risk.

Convertibility

Oftentimes, a central bank will attempt to support the price of its currency by restricting its convertibility in some fashion. Such exchange restrictions are especially tempting if the official rate of the currency can not be justified by the economics of the country. Rates might be controlled for a number of specific purposes. A central bank may want to keep its currency highly valued at home, but valued lower abroad for competitive reasons, or it may want to maintain a higher currency rate for international borrowings, to promote foreign capital investment, or to defend its international reserves. In any event, if a currency cannot be easily converted, it cannot be freely traded, so its rate is not subject to the whims of the market place.

Of the 26 countries which reportedly allowed their currencies to independently float as of 1991, only five did so with no exchange restrictions.[1] Exchange restrictions affect the availability of a currency and, consequently, its value. A currency may be officially priced by making it unavailable at a lower rate of exchange that more truly reflects its value. As a result, parallel markets often exist when there are exchange restrictions. These markets, though limited in scope due to risk of government prosecution, exchange currencies at rates more closely related to economic conditions.

There are many forms of exchange restrictions; for example, payments of current transactions for consumer imports may be unduly delayed. There may be multiple exchange rates, with some transactions taking place at market rates and others at higher "official" rates. There may be cost-related import surcharges (as opposed to product-related tariffs). Some countries require advance import deposits or repatriation fees; or the rate of exchange is allowed to float freely against some currencies and not others. A selective float of the currency can be effected by bilateral payment arrangements between two countries that are not available to others. Sometimes foreign exchange or convertibility of the currency is forbidden at any price. The IMF has identified four examples of the multiple currency practices in common use today[2] (see Figure 3-1).

Figure 3-1: Examples of Multiple Currency Practices

Dual or Multiple Market System—Multiple markets often consist of an official market in which the supply and demand for foreign exchange associated with certain specified transactions are controlled, and a free market that handles all other transactions. The free rate is almost always lower than the official rate. Less selective in their impact than the imposition of individual rates for given transactions, multiple markets typically penalize broad categories of suppliers of foreign exchange to the official market—usually exporters—and subsidize groups of purchasers—such as the government or special interest groups.

Figure 3-1: Examples of Multiple Currency Practices, *con't.*

Fixed Exchange Rate on Given Transactions—Specific foreign exchange transactions can be either subsidized or penalized by the authorities, forcing the purchase or sale of exchange at an over- or undervalued exchange rate. Fixing the rate on certain transactions is often practiced to hold down official expenditures on the servicing of government-guaranteed debt, to encourage migrant labor, to repatriate foreign earnings, or to penalize profit remittances abroad by foreign companies or travel abroad by residents.

Taxes or Subsidies on the Value of Transactions—Similar in impact to fixing the exchange rate for given transactions, and equally selective, these practices typically target current account transactions. Examples include export bonuses or subsidies, mandatory advance import deposits (which pay no interest or less-than-market rates of interest), taxes on remittances abroad, and taxes on foreign exchange sales by commercial banks.

Excessive Spreads—Multiple currency practices result when the central bank prescribes buying and selling rates for spot foreign exchange transactions with a spread of more than 2% from their midpoint rate.

Source - Developments in International Exchange and Payments Systems, IMF

The list of exchange rates in Figure 3-2 includes a variety of terms that identify restrictions in convertibility, price, or both.

Figure 3-2: Various Terms used to Identify Convertibility and/or Price

Free market central bank rate
Floating rate
Commercial rate
Free market rate
Controlled rate
Financial rate
Preferential rate
Nonessential import rate
Floating tourist rate
Public transaction rate
Agricultural product rate
Priority rate
Market rate
Essential import rate
Export rate

Source: *The Wall Street Journal*

Exchange Rate Regimes

Like the governments that invoke them, exchange systems rise, hold, sway for a while, and then disappear. They are distinguished primarily by the degree of flexibility, or inflexibility, in the determination of currency value. The International Monetary Fund (IMF) has defined seven broad classifications, or regimes, in which exchange rates are determined.[3] These are listed in Figure 3-3 from the least to the most flexible, using 1992 data.

Figure 3-3: Exchange Rate Regimes

- *Single Currency Peg*—The central bank pegs to a major currency with infrequent adjustment of the parity. (About one third of all developing countries have single currency pegs.) Major currencies used are the U.S. dollar, the French Franc, the Indian Rupee, and the South African rand.
- *Composite Currency Peg*—The central bank pegs to a basket of currencies of major trading partners to make the pegged currency more stable than if a single currency peg were used. The weights assigned to the currencies in the basket may reflect the geographical distribution of trade, services, or capital flows. They may also be standardized, such as SDRs and ECUs.
- *Limited Flexibility vis à vis a Single Currency*—The value of the currency is maintained within a certain range of the peg (for example, Saudi Arabia's riyal peg to the U.S. dollar). There is also a core Deutsche mark block within the European Monetary System (EMS) which has more restrictive boundaries. This arrangement consists of the Deutsche mark, Swiss franc, Dutch guilder, and Belgian franc. The guilder and Belgian franc generally maintain a higher degree of correlation with the Deutsche mark. The Swiss franc, being an actively traded currency in its own right, correlates with the Deutsche Mark to a lesser extent.
- *Limited Flexibility through Cooperative Arrangements*—This applies to countries in the Exchange Rate Mechanism of the EMS and is a cross between a peg of individual EMS currencies to each other and a float of all these currencies jointly vis à vis non-EMS currencies.

Figure 3-3: Exchange Rate Regimes, *con't.*

- *Greater Flexibility through Adjustment to an Indicator*—The currency is adjusted more or less automatically to changes in selected indicators. A common indicator is the true effective exchange rate, which reflects inflation-adjusted changes in the currency vis à vis major trading partners.
- *Greater Flexibility through a Managed Float*—The central bank sets the rate but varies it frequently. Indicators for adjusting the rate include, for example, the balance of payments position, reserves, and the parallel market developments. Adjustments are not automatic.
- *Full Flexibility through an Independent Float*—Rates are determined by market forces. Some industrial countries, as mentioned above, float their currencies within this regime. The number of developing countries in this category has been increasing in recent years.

Source: IMF Survey, October 26, 1992

Bretton Woods

Perhaps the most widely recognized exchange rate system developed in the last fifty or so years was the Bretton Woods arrangement. In July, 1944, a group of international financial leaders gathered in Bretton Woods, New Hampshire. Their goal was to rebuild a war-torn world economy through a resurgence of international trade. The International Monetary Fund emerged from the talks, along with a new world bank. There also emerged a new world currency system. In essence, the decision was made to confine the world's major currencies to a single-currency peg regime.

This system was deemed by international financial leaders to be a satisfactory substitute for their long sought-after goal of a universal currency. Based upon the agreement, the major currencies (consisting of the U.S. dollar, the Canadian dollar, the industrialized European currencies, and the Japanese yen) were aligned with each other by establishing a permanent exchange rate for each currency to a single standard, and thus to each other. Except for periodic realignments, no currency was permitted to drift more than 2% up or down from its pegged rate. If a currency broke through this limit, it was driven back into place by central bank *intervention.*

Intervention is a procedure used by central banks, individually or in concert, to manipulate currency supply and/or demand, and thereby price. For example, assume the market demand for a particular currency rises because of rumors of an impending realignment; the trading activity drives its exchange rate more than 2½% higher, beyond its permitted limit. One or more central banks begin to sell that currency by exchanging it for other currencies held in reserve. Supply of the currency increases until the price falls to the pegged rate. By the same token, central banks would intervene to buy a currency if it fell below its permitted range.

The standard chosen for establishing official rates of exchange was the U.S. dollar; therefore, the Federal Reserve had a unique function within the system. It was obligated to value the dollar by converting it, upon demand of any member central bank, for 1/35 ounce of gold. In effect, the currencies of the industrialized world were gold backed, and the U.S. gold reserve was the collateral. This role gave the U.S. dollar increased stature as the lead international reserve currency, the one most often chosen by a country to keep as foreign reserves or as a conduit for international trade.

The Bretton Woods system of 1944 was not fully implemented until 1958, when the private sector was permitted full exchange privileges for all participating currencies. Full conversion brought down the last major obstacle to foreign trade, but by this time, cracks were already appearing in the system. As the 1960s rolled around, member nations began having serious doubts about the U.S. commitment to the gold standard.

The problem became apparent when the U.S. current account began running deficits. The large cash outflows required by the post-war Marshall plan, along with the cost of the Korean war, were beginning to show up in the inflation figures. Dollar reserves grew in other countries as dollars were spent abroad. Reacting to the expanding supply, foreign currency values began to rise, *vis à vis* the dollar. Central banks, following the provisions of the accord, responded by selling their currencies for dollars, in effect trying to inflate their currencies to match the U.S. inflation, and thus pushing the U.S. deficit higher still. Additional debt was piling up from the Vietnam War and rising oil prices. As uncertainty mounted over the convertibility of the dollar to gold, foreign holders began to demand gold for their dollar deposits. It began to look like an old fashioned bank run.

The U.S. authorities tried vainly to stem the tide. They issued "Roosa" bonds, denominated in foreign currency, to foreign authorities.[4] The currencies taken in from the sale of these bonds were then used to buy in dollars. They swapped dollars for foreign currency, used the currency to buy dollars, then closed out the swaps by paying back additional foreign currency for additional dollars. They borrowed against their IMF credit line to repurchase dollars. They attempted to flood the gold market to drive down demand and stem its rising price. Their efforts came to nought, and in August, 1971, President Nixon put an end to it by abolishing gold convertibility for the U.S. dollar. When the final tallies were in, it was noted that one-half of the total U.S. gold supply, about ten billion dollars worth, was gone. The currency system struggled on for another two years, with a few attempts to re-establish the gold standard, but by 1973, the Bretton Woods accord was no longer operational (see Figure 3-4).

Figure 3-4: The Bretton Woods Period: U.S. Gold Stock

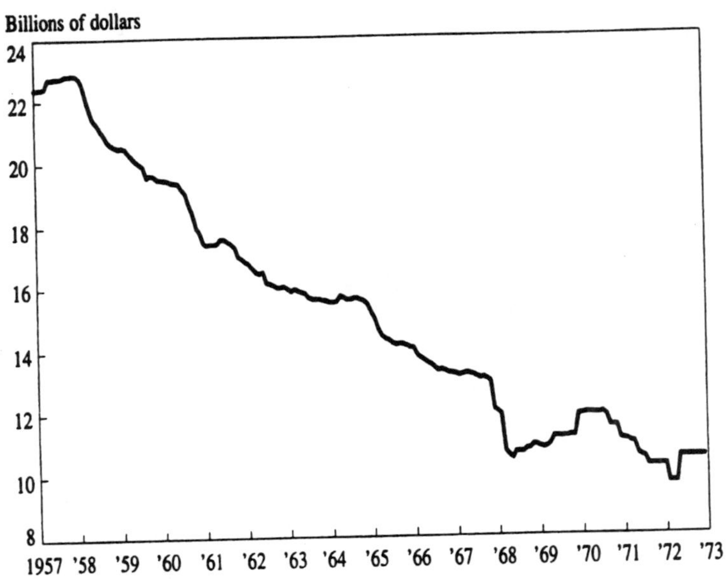

Source: Data Resources

The Snake in the Tunnel

As one pegged-rate system drew to a close, another had already been designed to take its place. In 1971, the Werner Plan introduced an exchange-rate system for the currencies of the European Economic Community (see Figure 3-5). The plan was to gradually restrict the movement of exchange rates until the currencies moved up and down in lock step, in essence as a single currency. Originally, six countries were in the plan (France, Italy, West Germany, Belgium, Luxembourg, and the Netherlands). The currencies were pegged in a more restrictive fashion than that of Bretton Woods. Whereas permissible movement in the former system was 4½% (2¼% up or down), it was now 2¼% from top to bottom. This group of currencies comprised a composite that could move in a broader range of 4½% against the U.S. dollar, which was still used as the "intervention currency." In this manner, the currencies in the Werner Plan were allowed to fluctuate, but together, like a banner serpentining between the broader boundaries. Hence, the mechanism became known as "the snake in a tunnel."

Figure 3-5: The Werner Plan

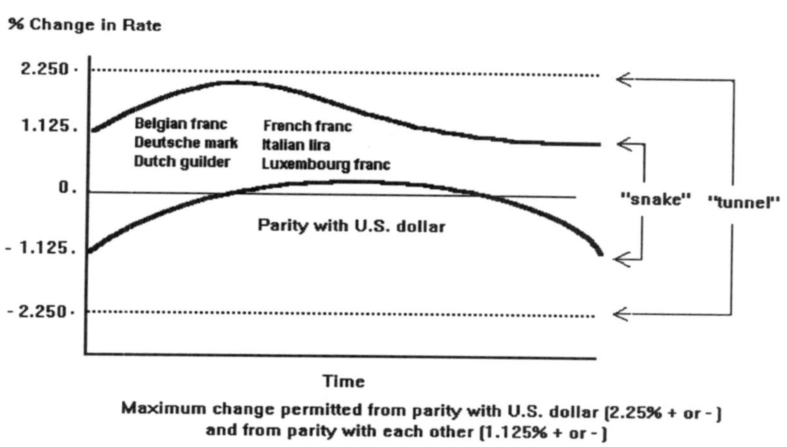

European Rate Mechanism

The most obvious difference between the Bretton Woods system and the Werner Plan was the lack of an underlying unit of intrinsic value (gold). As a very restrictive basket pegged to a single currency, the system was untenable. It was superseded in March, 1979, by the *European Monetary System (EMS)*, a system championed by West Germany and France. The original six member-nations of the Werner Plan now made up the EMS. They were joined by the UK, Ireland, Denmark, and later by Greece, Spain, and Portugal.

The EMS aligned its currencies using a formula known as the *European Rate Mechanism (ERM)*. The ERM was structured along the lines of the Werner Plan, but without the restrictive band of the "snake." The tunnel remains, albeit without the U.S. dollar as a peg. The dollar was replaced by a currency composite called the European Currency Unit, or ECU, which is the forerunner to an even grander plan. The European Community leaders set a goal in 1991 during a summit in the Dutch town of Maastricht: a single European currency under one central bank before the twenty-first century.

The tunnel, now defined by the ECU, still constrained most of the currencies to a range of 4½%. (It was less confining to the Spanish Peseta and the Portuguese Escudo, which were allowed 6% leeway.) Enforcement of the system was through intervention, the same method employed by the Bretton Woods system. The central banks of the Common Market, individually or collectively, would enter the market, buying one currency and selling another, whenever a particular currency drifted too far from its established rate. Eventually, diverging economic policies in the European Community made the imposed constriction unsustainable, and the range was increased to 30% overall.

Currency Composites and Baskets

We usually think of a fiat currency as a type of bank note, printed and issued by a single governmental agency; however, several currencies can be bundled together and packaged as a separate currency in its own right. These are commonly referred to as currency baskets, or composites.

The International Monetary Fund (IMF) refers to "composites" and "baskets" almost interchangeably. A basket is simply a grouping of two or more currencies. Usually there is a daily summation of the prices of the various currencies in the basket. A number (or "numeraire") is derived from the sum of the prices, which becomes the "basket price." This figure may simply be an average based on the number of units of each currency in the basket. More often, it is a *weighted* average, based on the number of units, price, and *importance* of each currency to the basket. The basket price (sometimes called the *index*), is similar to a stock index, comprised of the price and number of shares outstanding of a group of stocks such as the Dow Jones Industrial Average.

The importance of any currency to the basket depends largely on the value of foreign exchange transactions involving it, relative to the others. Currency baskets are often used as pegs. When a country pegs its currency to a basket or a composite, it strives to maintain the price of its currency at a predetermined exchange rate to the basket unit. It accomplishes this by buying or selling its currency for a hard foreign currency until the desired rate is established or reestablished. The foreign currency used for this purpose is called the *intervention currency*, and it is almost always part of the basket.

The currency of Thailand can be used as an example of what determines a currency basket and how it is applied for pegging a currency on a day-to-day basis.[5] The Thai currency, the "baht," has been closely pegged to the U.S. dollar since the end of World War II. The exchange rate varies little, from 24 to 25 baht to the dollar. This stability was beneficial to both countries during the arms build-up of the cold war. As a SEATO ally and host to American armed forces during the Vietnam war, Thailand purchased most of its military hardware from the United States. Yet, before the cold war ended, other exchange rates had a growing impact on the Thai economy. Strong economic growth was fueled primarily by capital investment from Japan. By the late 1980s, almost every car on the crowded streets of Bangkok was a Japanese import. A thriving tourist industry serving European vacationers, including a significant number from Germany, adds to the myriad visitors and immigrants from both the eastern and western hemispheres. In addition, Thailand is a major exporter of rice and maize to neighboring countries, and a sizable Thai labor force has been established in the middle east.

In response to these influences, Thailand adopted a basket of currencies as an "official" peg for the baht. The basket contains Brunei dollars, Deutsche marks, Hong Kong dollars, Indonesian rupiahs, Japanese yen, Malaysian ringgits, Philippine pesos, British pounds, Singapore dollars and, of course, the predominant U.S. dollar. A government agency, known as the Exchange Equalization Fund, determines the value of the baht on a daily basis by considering the baht's price relationship to the weighted basket. It then announces the official daily buying and selling rates for the U.S. dollar, which is the intervention currency. It also announces daily minimum and maximum rates at which commercial banks can deal with the public for U.S. dollars and other currencies in the basket.

The advantage of pegging to a composite, rather than to a single currency, is the resultant dampening effect if one of the currencies undergoes rapid revaluation or devaluation. The other currencies in the basket are probably not rapidly changing in absolute value, so they appear to be moving in the opposite direction relative to the one currency. The basket price does not fluctuate to the same degree as any individual currency within it; therefore, a large measure of stability can be maintained regardless of what happens to one or more of its individual components. As a case in point, the ECU, the composite currency of the ERM, continues trading rather actively after the ERM itself effectively ceased functioning in late 1993.

Special Drawing Rights

During the 1960s, growing international trade created an opportunity for the IMF to begin its own fiat composite currency called the "special drawing right (SDR)," adding to the inflationary potential of member nations (see Figure 3-6). Unlike regular currencies, SDR units are not distributed as paper money. They are allotted as account balances, and are electronically transferred from one account to another within the SDR Department of the IMF. First issued in 1970 at a value of one U.S. dollar per unit of SDR, the intent was to distribute one billion SDR units a year for five years. As the IMF became more active in third world development, these amounts have been increased. As of April 30, 1993, a total of SDR 21.4 billion was allotted.

Several countries peg their currency to the SDR. For example, Libya recently officially priced its currency, the dinar, at 0.396 dinars to one SDR. (If there were .70 SDRs to the dollar, the dinar/dollar rate would be approximately .27 dinars to the dollar.) The SDR does more than serve as a peg. IMF members nations draw upon their SDR "reserves" to settle balances of payment among themselves. Transfers of SDRs among nations can be made in a variety of ways, such as swaps, loans, forward operations, and in trade for other currencies. The number of official holders of SDRs has expanded beyond the IMF members. As of April 30, 1993, fifteen organizations hold SDR assets, including the African Development Bank, the Arab Monetary Fund, the Asian Development Bank, and the Bank for International Settlements.

Although SDRs serve as a medium of exchange for international and regional organizations, it may also be used to denominate private financial instruments. So far, there has not been much activity at the private level. Should this activity increase, there may be potential for use of SDRs in the management of foreign currency exposure risk.

Figure 3-6: The SDR Basket

The SDR is a basket comprised of five currencies: the U.S. dollar, the Japanese yen, the British pound, the French franc and the Deutsche mark. The amount of each currency in one unit is based on the currency's *percentage weight*, calculated from its price and relative importance in international trade and foreign reserve holdings. Determination of these percentage weights is reviewed every five years; the last review was December 31, 1995. The percentage weights in use are: 40% for the U.S. dollar, 21% for the Deutsche mark, 17% for the Japanese yen, and 11% each for the British pound and French franc. Because these weights are a function of price, as well as trade, they change continuously to some degree.

The value of the SDR is determined daily from the exchange rates of its components, and is expressed in U.S. dollars. The example below shows the calculations:

Currency	**(1) Currency amount per SDR unit**	**(2) Exchange rate**	**(3) U.S. dollar Equivalent**
Deutsche mark	0.4530	1.60120	0.282913
French franc	0.8000	5.61850	0.142387
Japanese yen	31.8000	106.10000	0.299717
British pound	0.0812	1.53670	0.124780
U.S. dollar	0.5720	1.00000	0.572000
		Total	**1.421797**

Column (1) The whole or fractional amount of each currency unit that comprises the "basket" of one SDR unit, based on the currency's exchange rate.

Column (2) The exchange rate in number of currency units per U.S. dollar. For the British pound, it is conventionally expressed as U.S. dollars per pound.

Column (3) The U.S. dollar translation of each currency, based on the unit amount and the exchange rate. This is found by dividing column (1) by column (2).

The total is the value of one SDR. As shown, one SDR is equal to $1.421797. The reciprocal of this number gives the SDR units in one U.S. dollar. (1 divided by 1.421797 = 0.703335. Therefore, $1 = SDR 0.703335). It can be seen that the U.S. dollar is still roughly at its assigned 40% of the basket (57¢ is a approximately 40% of $1.42).

European Currency Unit

The European Currency Unit, or ECU, is the composite of the *European Rate Mechanism* (ERM), an exchange rate system. It is also considered the currency of the *European Monetary System* (EMS) which serves as the framework of the ERM. The ECU was established September 17, 1984 to serve as the currency basket and unit of account for the European Economic Community (EEC). The EEC expresses its budget and denominates its bond issues in ECUs. The ECU began as a currency basket of the ten European currencies that made up the EMS at that time. By 1990, there were currencies from twelve countries in the basket. Similar to the SDR calculations, the composition takes into account the relative importance of the currency in the overall trading activity of the EEC. Table 3-1 shows the composition of the ECU, along with the representative component weights. Although the composition remains constant, the percentages vary slightly with the daily currency prices.

Table 3-1: Relative Currency Weights of the ECU

Currency	Weight
Deutsche mark	30.52%
Belgian franc	7.84%
Luxembourg franc	0.31%
Dutch guilder	9.54%
Italian lira	9.86%
Greek drachma	0.66%
Spanish peseta	5.35%
British pound	12.42%
Irish punt	1.11%
Danish krone	2.50%
French franc	19.12%
Portuguese escudo	0.77%

Source: *Futures*, April 1991

The ECU is denominated in U.S. dollars. The price is monitored three times daily and fixed once daily by the Commission of the EEC. This official price is used to settle ECU balances of payment among central banks. The official rate does not always apply to private transactions, in which the rate may be negotiated or discovered by "marking to the market." In some ways, the ECU is more like a real currency than the SDR.

For example, a cash market, as well as forward and futures markets, exist for trading it. A central clearing center, comprised of a small group of banks, is in place to settle ECU accounts. For U.S. holders of ECUs, deposit accounts are set up and handled through their banks' European branches just like any other foreign currency account, for minimum deposits of ECU 10,000.

The ECU was considered by many industry experts and government officials to be the future common currency of Europe. Due to aggressive promotion of the ECU by the European banking industry, it became familiar to both private investors and corporate treasurers; however, the radical readjustment of the ERM in 1993 clouded the future of the ECU. Its exchange rate, *vis à vis* currencies both inside and outside the basket, has become much more difficult to predict.

U.S. Dollar Index

The Federal Reserve maintains an index of the value of the U.S. dollar against a basket of ten major currencies. The index is referred to as the *trade weighted exchange rate* (TWEX). It is trade-weighted in the same sense as the ECU and SDR: the currencies in the basket are represented by percentages that reflect their relative price in U.S. dollars as well as their relative importance in international trade. The component currencies and their trade weights are shown in Table 3-2.

Table 3-2: Components of the U.S. Dollar Index

Deutsche mark	20.8%
Japanese yen	13.6%
French franc	13.1%
British pound	11.9%
Canadian dollar	9.1%
Italian lira	9.0%
Dutch guilder	8.3%
Belgian franc	6.4%
Swedish krona	4.2%
Swiss franc	3.6%

The index offers a real vantage point when trying to determine the direction of the U.S. dollar, relative to other major currencies. When a particular exchange rate becomes unusually volatile, it is often difficult to determine if one currency has strengthened or the other has weakened. It is a matter of perspective, similar to the sky diver whose parachute has not opened: he notices that all his team mates are shooting *upward*. When *ten* currencies are going up or down against the dollar, it definitely says something about the dollar.

FINEX, the financial futures division of the New York Cotton Exchange, has constructed a futures contract from the dollar index, called the USDX. This contract has a potential for use as a hedging vehicle. Consumer product companies that receive ongoing streams of revenue from a number of countries whose currencies are part of the index might consider it; however, like any other currency, composite, or index, liquidity, convertibility, and tradability are paramount considerations for risk management purposes.

Trends in Exchange Rate Systems

There currently appear to be two trends. The major trend is toward greater convertibility. Developing countries, in particular, are moving from single-peg regimes toward those offering greater flexibility. There are two primary reasons for this:

1. High inflation rates racked the economies of many developing countries during the 1980s. To remain competitive in world markets, these countries made steep devaluations to reverse changes in real exchange rates. One way of doing this is to abandon the single peg to a hard currency in favor of a more economically justifiable peg to an inflation index or indicator.
2. The second reason is the increased volatility of the major currencies. Major moves up and down in currency pegs have greatly impacted the economies of developing countries using them. The recent financial situation in Southeast Asia is a case in point. Many countries in the region have pegged their currencies to the U.S. dollar. They have also availed themselves of large sums of yen-denominated debt, courtesy of the favorable-rate loans proffered by Japan to build a presence in the area. During 1993 and 1994, as the dollar (and the Asian currencies) tumbled against the yen, the repayment schedules of the debt became quite burdensome. When similar conditions existed elsewhere, some of the countries effected by volatile and shifting currency markets changed from single-currency pegs to composite-currency-basket pegs.

In Africa, inflation and volatility resulted in a devaluation that severely shook the political, social, and economic climate in fourteen countries. The *Communaute Fainanciere Aficaine* (CFA) is comprised of former French colonies or nations under French influence.[6] This block of nations use the CFA franc as a common currency. The CFA franc had been pegged to the French franc at a 50 to 1 ratio since 1945, making it the world's longest-lasting fixed-rate currency. As the French franc began to lose value to the dollar in the mid 1980s, and as the commodities of cocoa, coffee, lumber, and minerals exported by these countries suffered steep price declines, the CFA franc became very overvalued. As a result, the CFA zone's exports were soon uncompetitive with the rest of the world. It took 15 years of economic decline before the value of the CFA franc was finally cut in half, to 0.01 French francs, early in 1994. According to some experts, the long delay in rate adjustment was due to the fact that many members of the elite classes of these countries enjoyed the riches that the overvalued CFA franc brought in the way of Mercedes-Benz cars, French champagne, and other imports.[7] It should be noted, however, that the overvalued currency also provided for such imported necessities as medicines and basic foodstuffs.

The trend toward greater convertibility is often evidenced by a reduction in exchange restrictions. Multiple exchange rates are being shelved. Bilateral payment schedules are being replaced with multilateral agreements and liberalized capital movements across borders. More than ever before, developing countries, especially in Latin America and Eastern Europe, are allowing market forces to price their currencies.

China is one example. Convertibility of its currency, the yuan, had been restricted through use of a dual track rate system. The official value in late 1993 was about 5.8 to the dollar, with the daily rate established by the central bank through a managed float arrangement; however, 80% of currency transactions were conducted through "trading centers," which exchanged yuan at a market rate of approximately 8.7 to the dollar. In addition, a thriving parallel market offered "free market" rates of a sort which facilitated payments by foreign multinationals. Beginning January 1, 1994, the rates were unified under the trading center exchange regime. The resulting devaluation from the official rate is part of the price of China's entry into the global economy.

A countertrend is taking place, mostly in the industrialized countries. Currencies once pegged within the Bretton Woods system were set free to float when the system virtually collapsed in 1971. Because of the increased volatility experienced after its demise, several of the previous members have made repeated attempts to return to a peg system of some sort. Recently, beginning in 1987-1988, these have been taking the form of tripolar arrangements between Europe, Japan, and the United States. Currently, voices favoring a return to the gold standard are being heard with increasing frequency. So far, all attempts to increase exchange rate restrictions have met with little success. Table 3-3 shows the number of currencies in specified regimes in 1981 and 1991.

Table 3-3: Comparison of the Number of Currencies in Specified Regimes in 1981 and 1991

Regime	1981	1991
Single-currency peg		
U.S. Dollar	40	27
French Franc	14	14
Other	4	6
Total	58	47
Composite-currency peg		
SDR	15	6
Other	22	33
Total	37	39
Cooperative arrangement	8	9
Adjustment to Indicator	4	5
Other	33	51

Source: IMF

Movement over a ten-year period shows a large decrease in the U.S. dollar-pegged and SDR-pegged systems, and the greatest increase toward the "other" regimes, mainly the floating regimes.

The Great Debate

A subject that continues to be hotly contested among politicians is the desirability of a gold standard. Fifty years have now passed since the demise of the Bretton Woods Agreement, and its passing is still mourned by some. They argue that the only way to conduct international trade with some semblance of predictability is by having stable currencies. They point to a number of facts supporting their stance, not the least of which is the volatility constantly roiling the currency markets. The chaos currently taking place in foreign exchange is unsurpassed in modern times.

Malcomb Forbes, founder of *Forbes Magazine*, describes the currency situation as a house under construction in which every workman uses a ruler with different measurements.[8] Free-floating currencies that change value hourly raise havoc in a world that attempts to depend on them as a standard unit of account. In other words, the world must *price* currency, and "price" should mean the same thing from one day to the next. The only way for this to occur is to use a standard that politicians cannot meddle with. This standard, from time immemorial, has been gold. Another problem involves the "managed float." Freely floating currencies are never entirely freely floating. They are constantly being steered in one direction or another (meddled with). Too often, political expediency is at the tiller. The world really doesn't know whether the dollar devaluation of 1994 is an economic adjustment or a political maneuver because there is nothing of set value standing behind the dollar. For these reasons alone, many top monetary authorities feel that the time has come for a change.

Some suggest a new gold-peg system on the order of Bretton Woods. The problem, according critics of this proposal, is that pegged systems generally don't work because politicians do not restrain themselves. For example, the United States, entrusted to keep the dollar pegged to gold at $35 an ounce, simply inflated itself out of the arrangement. President Nixon did not shut the door on Bretton Woods when he closed the gold window. The door had slammed shut long before, when the United States ran through a large portion of its gold reserves to cover outstanding dollar obligations. The obligations represented every paper dollar sent abroad. By the time President Nixon acted, the run on the bank was already well under way.

According to others, the United States is already on a *de facto* gold standard. Gold trades freely. Dollars trade freely. Both are commodities. The world barters in commodities and, theoretically, there is nothing to prevent the use of one over the other when trading internationally or domestically (except legal tender laws). Then there is the matter of exactly how to peg the dollar to gold. What price should we use? What if we had returned to the gold standard in 1980, when gold was $850 an ounce? Today, a night out in Kalamazoo would be probably be the same as a night out in Tokyo, with its mind-boggling prices, dollar for dollar.

Some economists recommend removing politicians from the money business altogether. By removing the government money monopoly, allowing people a free choice in money, people will naturally prefer the good money over the bad money. Thus, in a system of private mints, operated as for-profit businesses without government interference, any mint clipping its coins or printing more money than it had backing for would soon be out of business.

The debate is heated. No argument has yet prevailed. About the only thing that can be predicted with any degree of certainly is that the debate will continue for a long time.

Conclusion

No one contests the fact that a flourishing international trade depends upon a stable medium of exchange. From the bronze age forward, only gold and silver have qualified for this role with any degree of consistency. Specie currency, coins actually minted from the metals, have a recognized intrinsic value world wide. One the other end of the spectrum is fiat currency, for which value is proclaimed, but the claim is accepted entirely as a matter of faith.

Fiat currencies play dual roles. They're used as legal tender, exchanged for things of real value, and invested, but they also serve as a statement of policy. The German Deutsche mark of the 1990s and the Reichs mark of the 1920s both have played the role in Germany of a medium of exchange, but are vastly different statements of policy. Accepting currency in payment of debts is an act of legality required by legal tender laws. Accepting a *particular amount* of currency as payment is an act of confidence, both in the central bank and in the politicians of the country.

This being the case, it is not surprising that fiat currencies of different sovereign states are difficult to peg to one another. They change with the politics that create them. No matter how noble the intentions, politicians eventually follow their own self interests, and they take their currencies with them. Perhaps that's why precious metals are still the only "predictable currencies." Only they are immutable.

It is far easier to manage currency at a commercial level than at a political level. With the demise of the ERM, commercial management of currencies, especially of European currencies, is more essential than ever. This is true because the only reliable statement that can be made about a fiat currency is that its value will change as the politics behind it change.

CHAPTER 4

Price Determinants

There is something fascinating about a suspended mobile, circling slowly below the ceiling. The position of each weighted string is dependent on all the rest. Move one and the others move to compensate for the change. It is much the same way with the economic variables that determine the price of a currency. Whether it is consumer spending patterns, changes in bank reserves, international investment decisions, or inflationary government policies, change the values of one measurement and the rest respond. The ever shifting balance is the exchange rate. One important variable is *anticipation.* Today's exchange rate represents the expectation for tomorrow's exchange rate.

Purchasing Power

The fundamental process for determining the exchange rate of a freely traded currency is still not well understood—which is no surprise. The value of any freely traded commodity is purely subjective. Theories for valuation abound, but the oldest theory is still the most widely used. This is the theory of Purchasing Power Parity (PPP). It had its beginnings in sixteenth century Spain, and has been used in one form or another to this day. We used PPP to explain the difference in real and nominal exchange rates (Chapter Two). To review, the theory states that the price of one currency, as defined in units of another, is determined by the level of prices in the one country as compared with the level of prices in the other.

Specifically, the PPP theory predicts that, everything being equal,, a basket of goods that moves freely across borders must eventually cost the same wherever it is sold. The driving force is competition. If a disparity in prices between two countries begins to grow, competitive pressures will soon cause the disparity to disappear. Goods and money flow in opposite directions across the currency border until price equilibrium is again achieved.

Imagine, now, that in an HC country, a basket of goods costs 500 HC units. In an FC country the same basket costs 1000 FC units. If the two currencies are at parity in purchasing power, we can deduce that the exchange rate, *hc/fc*, is 0.50 (500 HC equals 1000 FC). If this were *not* the exchange rate, according to the theory, *arbitrageurs* (traders who look for and take advantage of such disparities) would see that there was an automatic profit to be made by exchanging goods across the border until either the prices or the exchange rate fell into line. In reality, of course, the basket is a proxy for *all* the goods and services in one country compared to *all* the goods and services in the other.

The theory is expressed by the following equation:

$$hc/fc = P\ hc\ /P\ fc$$

where *hc/fc* is the exchange rate, *P hc* is the price of goods in home currency and *P fc* is the price of goods in foreign currency. Using this equation, *hc/fc = 500/1000 = .50*, where 500 and 1000 equal the prices of the respective baskets.

Purchasing power parity can be diagrammed as a function of exchange rates and relative price levels. Figure 4-1 shows PPP as a 45° line measuring two variables: exchange rate and basket price. At every point on the line, the equation *hc/fc = P hc /P fc* holds true, as relative price levels and the exchange rate move in direct proportion to one another. If, for example, our basket goes from 500 HC to 1000 HC, while remaining unchanged at 1000 FC, the change in relative prices would cause the exchange rate to adjust from .50 to 1.00.

As popular as it is, the theory of PPP has a major problem. Namely, it does not accurately predict variations in exchange rates. In fact, over the years, there have been large and persistent departures from the expected relative price levels and exchange rate levels, both long-term and short-term. The theory can hardly be relied on for making major currency decisions. It certainly cannot be used as a stand-alone forecasting indicator. Purchasing power parity theory can only *suggest* relationships. There are several reasons for this imprecision. One is the restrictions placed on exchange rates. Another is the restrictions placed on the free flow of goods, such restrictions as tariffs and transportation costs. Also, it is difficult to construct a basket of goods that actually has the same perceived value, and therefore the same supply and demand characteristics, from one country to another. Lastly, mathematical models can never precisely match the aggregate of all the *subjective valuations* taking place in the market. For example, our diagram predicts that price-exchange rate parity will fall somewhere on the PPP line, saying nothing about *where* on the line, or *when* parity will occur. Parity may be achieved by changes in the exchange rate, changes in the relative price level, or both—if in fact it is achieved at all.

Figure 4-1: Diagram of PPP

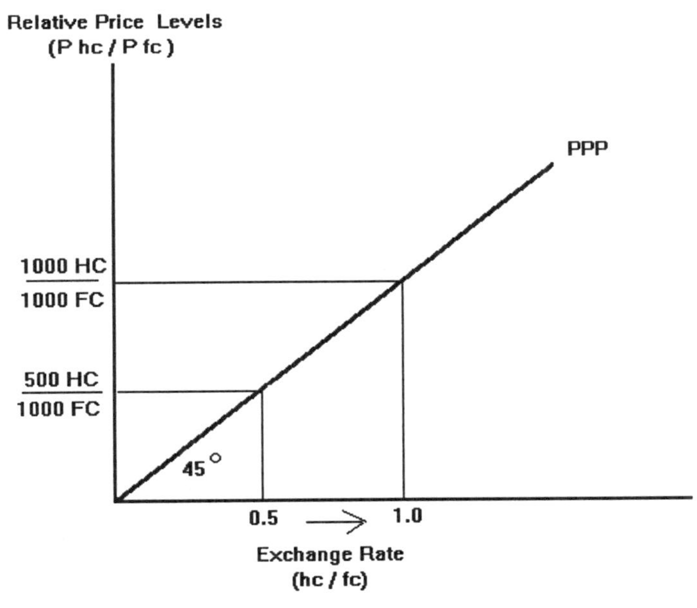

Source: *Purchasing Power Parity*, Merrill Lynch, 1990

One of the problems is the base line. The starting point of the PPP index is unknown, so there is no way to assess how much disparity there is at any given moment. Some analysts have used 1973 as a base year, which is the year that major currencies were set free to float. Others have used 1980, the last year in which the U.S. current account was in balance. The validity of these or any other base lines, however, remains debatable.

There is also a significant problem concerning the basket of goods. This goes to the core of a related hypothesis: "The Law of One Price." This theory says that identical goods must trade at the same price across all countries when valued in the terms of a single currency. Prices for certain goods follow this theory quite well. Gold is one. Crude oil is another. If gold is $400 an ounce and crude oil $15 a barrel in Chicago, gold is also $400 an ounce and crude is also $15 a barrel in Tokyo (or close to it, ignoring transportation and storage costs). What is the distinguishing characteristic of these two commodities? Universal supply and demand factors, primarily. Similar goods, or baskets of goods, are more difficult to find. A number of indices have been offered in lieu of baskets: consumer price indices, producer price indices, and various commodity-based indices to name a few. The problem is that each country has different preferences, different perceived values, different tastes, and different priorities. Each country has obstacles to completely free trade, such as exchange restrictions or tariffs. Also, manufacturers rarely respond instantly to exchange rate changes by raising or lowering prices. All of these factors permit price disparity to exist among countries or economic regions.

Nevertheless, the search continues for a basket of goods that meet all requirements of the PPP theory. In 1986, *The Economist* magazine, came forth with a novel entry: McDonald's Big Mac hamburger. It was proposed as an index somewhat tongue-in-cheek. After the jokes, analysts began to take a closer look at it. The Big Mac does fulfill at least some of the requirements. It is ubiquitous. It doesn't change when crossing borders. And although Big Macs don't trade on world markets, boneless beef, albeit with some trade restrictions, does. The levels of demand, popularity, and taste are somewhat consistent wherever hamburgers are sold, and the Big Mac is responsive to changes in national price levels. All told, the Big Mac may be a workable "basket" of goods.

Table 4-1 shows relative local currency prices of Big Macs in several countries as of April, 13, 1993, and compares them to the price in U.S. dollars ($2.28). The price implies which currencies are undervalued or overvalued relative to the U.S. dollar. A Big Mac in Hong Kong, for example, costs nine Hong Kong dollars which translates to $1.16. Therefore, the Hong Kong dollar is shown as being undervalued compared to the dollar. It should have an exchange rate of only 3.95, rather than 7.73, so the translation would come to $2.28, the same as the U.S. price. According to the survey, the Japanese yen and major European currencies are overvalued. The Danish Krona is the most overvalued (86%). In fact, subsequent to the publication of this index, the dollar index rose from 92.50 to 96.50, largely against European currencies. Perhaps not coincidentally, the Danish Krona later suffered the heaviest devaluation during the ERM collapse in the fall of 1993.

Table 4-1: The Big Mac Basket

Country	Price in LC		Price in $	FX as of 4/13/95	Implied PPP of the U.S. $	%
United States	2.28	$		2.28		
Argentina	3.6	Peso	3.60	1.00	1.58	58
Australia	2.44	A$	1.76	1.39	1.07	–23
Belgium	109	BFr	3.36	32.45	47.81	47
Brazil	77,000	Cr	2.80	27,521	33,772	23
Britain	1.79	BP	2.79	*1.56	*1.27	23
Canada	2.76	C$	2.19	1.26	1.21	–4
China	8.5	Yuan	1.50	5.68	3.73	–34
Denmark	25.75	DKr	4.25	6.06	11.29	86
France	18.5	FFr	3.46	5.34	8.11	52
Germany	4.6	DM	2.91	1.58	2.02	28
Holland	5.45	Fl	3.07	1.77	2.39	35
Hong Kong	9	HK$	1.16	7.73	3.95	–49
Hungary	157	Forint	1.78	88.18	68.86	–22
Ireland	1.48	Punt	2.29	*1.54	*1.54	0
Italy	4,500	Lire	2.95	1523	1974	30
Japan	391	Yen	3.45	113	171	51
Malaysia	3.35	Ringgit	1.30	2.58	1.47	–43
Mexico	7.09	Peso	2.29	3.10	3.11	0
Russia	780	Rouble	1.14	686	342	–50
S. Korea	2,300	Won	2.89	796	1,009	27
Spain	325	Ptas	2.85	114	143	25
Sweden	25.5	SKr	3.43	7.43	11.18	50
Switzerland	5.7	SF	3.94	1.45	2.5	72
Thailand	48	Baht	1.91	25.16	21.05	–16

% pertains to the percent of over (under) valuation of LC to US dollar
*FX quoted indirectly except as noted

Source: *The Economist*, April 17, 1995

Figure 4-2: PPP and Arbitrage

The tendency of currencies to gravitate toward Purchasing Power Parity through arbitrage can be shown by visualizing goods and currencies as units of value. Assume that the currency "HC" can purchase 100% of a basket of goods "BG," and that "HC" is equal to "FC." Assume also that "FC" can purchase 110% of the same basket. This sets up a "three-point arbitrage situation," so called because it involves three separate transactions. Place all three units arbitrarily in a circle, and connect them with a directional arrow of transaction. If the arrow can be made to generate a profit in one direction (with a loss in the other), automatic profits can occur from arbitrage.

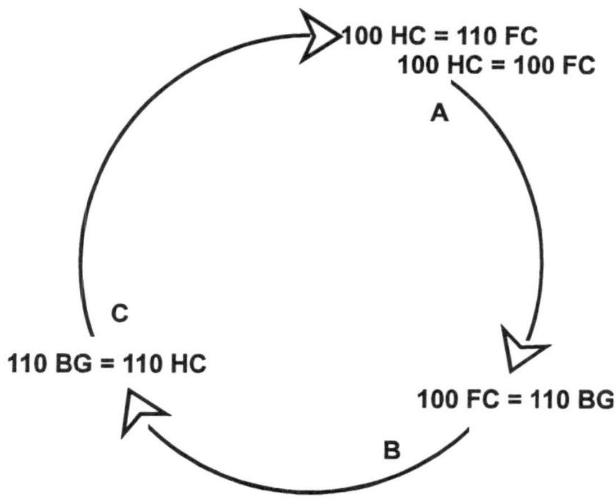

In this case, a trader swaps 100 HC for 100 FC (A), then buys 110 BG (B) which she sells for 110 HC (C). The circle continues to spin profitably as 110 HC is swapped for 110 FC, 110 FC is swapped for 121 BG, etc. Arbitrage activity sows the seeds of its own destruction through the laws of supply and demand. The continuous demand for FC purchases with HC will raise the price of FC relative to the price of HC until the trading profits disappear.

If "BG" were another currency rather than a basket of physical goods, the transactions could take place immediately at insignificant cost. This is why market arbitrage occurs instantly and parity is achieved within minutes. Our example, however, involves the costs of trading goods, including transportation, distribution, and so forth. These costs must be made economical before arbitrage can take place. For this reason, Purchasing Power Parity is usually achieved, if ever, only in a very long time frame.

Supply and Demand

All economic goods, including money, are subject to the Laws of Supply and Demand. Simply put:

1. If demand increases and supply remains constant, price tends to rise.
2. If demand decreases and supply remains constant, price tends to decline.
3. If supply increases and demand remains constant, price tends to decline.
4. If supply decreases and demand remains constant, price tends to rise.

With money, evidence of the Laws of Supply and Demand is discussed using different terminology. A "price decline" in money resulting from an increased supply is called *inflation.* Inflation means that each unit of money is worth *less*, relative to the goods being purchased; thus it takes more units of money to buy the same amount—the price tag has gotten bigger—hence the term *inflation*. Many people in the United States watch monetary indicators such as M1 and M2 to try to keep tabs on the money supply and the "inflation rate."

Dollar Supply (Supply of Money)

The money supply designated "M1" consists of cash in the pockets of the non-bank public plus money held in demand deposits, checking accounts, and travelers checks. M2 includes M1 plus overnight repos (repurchase agreements) and Eurodollars, savings accounts, money market fund shares, and small time deposits. There are other categories of supply tracked by the Federal Reserve (the Fed). One is the *adjusted monetary base*, representing *currency in circulation*, which is the currency held by the public and in all the vaults of depository institutions (which includes M1 and M2). Federal Reserve credits are the major source of this monetary base, which is adjusted for reserve requirement ratio changes. There is also a category known as *adjusted reserves*, which is simply the adjusted monetary base without the currency component of M1.

The growth or shrinkage of the money supply indicates how much money is available in the system. The more money available, the less value it has relative to other goods. An over-supply of currency, then, results in inflation. The Federal Reserve traditionally has turned to the money supply figures to try to determine whether the economy is expanding or contracting.

Pulsating the money supply can cause false expansion or painful contraction in the economy, but cannot produce real economic growth. In addition, money supply figures have correlated poorly with expansion and contraction of the economy, particularly recently. For example, prior to the recessions of the early 1980s, M2 growth did not slow appreciably. According to conventional economic analysis, a slowing of M2 growth would be likely to bring on a recession, but there had been no slowing growth. What went wrong? Perhaps the prolonged meddling of the Fed with the money supply has caused an expectation for, even a requirement for, *accelerating* growth rates for M2 in order to stimulate the economy. Like the heroine addict, an ever larger fix is required to get the same "high"; a *stable* M2 growth rate allowed the economy to lapse into recession. Thus, growth of M1 and M2 have little predictive value for the state of the economy. It now appears that the Fed is paying more attention to price indices such as the consumer price index, the producer price index, and various commodity price indices.[1]

Dollar Demand (Demand for Money)

As the money supply is inflated, the price level of consumables rises, creating a greater demand for money. Simultaneously, inflation creates upward pressure on interest rates which may stimulate new bank deposits and loans. Through fractional banking, there is a multiplier effect which creates new money. Thus, the prices of goods and services are determinants of the price of the currency. Supply and demand work together, affecting a currency's purchasing power.

One way to discover changes in the supply and demand for a currency within a country is to watch trends in the domestic availability and consumption of goods and services. This is usually done by watching price indices, changes in which are carefully monitored by most currency traders. A comparison of Gross Domestic Product (GDP) figures may help determine whether production is rising or falling, and therefore whether demand for money is expanding or contracting.[2]

Changes in inflation have a major impact on currency prices, yet it is difficult to measure inflation reliably. The Federal Reserve attempts to measure it using a "GDP Deflator" index to find the "real GDP." Other economists use the Consumer Price Index (CPI) to measure the rate at which changes in consumer prices are taking place. While both the GDP deflator and changes in CPI are inflation indicators, they sometimes diverge. Which one represents the true inflation rate? Valuing currencies by economic indicators leaves a lot of room for judgment calls and varying interpretations. Unemployment figures, securities market indices, commodity price indices, and other leading, lagging, and current economic indicators are all studied for anomalies and trends, to try to predict whether the price of the dollar is heading up or down.

Balance of Payments

A currency's exchange rate is also influenced by the relative price indices, inflation rates, and exchange rates between countries. In turn, these are influenced by the level and direction of cross-border transactions between them and other trading partners. The net totals of all international transactions, commercial and financial, that are conducted by the residents of one country are called the *balance of payments*. The balance of payments is comprised principally of exports and imports of goods and services. These trade flows depend on a number of variables that determine the country's competitive position. Over the long haul, competition is based on the assets of the country including its infrastructure, its level of technology and education, its natural resources, its labor base, its tax laws, its tariff laws, and its willingness to enforce contracts. Many of these factors only change quite slowly.

In the short term, a country's competitive position is directly related to its cost structure, income levels, and exchange rate. Countries with weak currencies (inflating faster than other countries) have products that appear cheap to foreign consumers; thus, exports usually increase. Conversely, foreign products appear expensive to domestic consumers; thus, imports usually decrease. Sometimes, the overall price increase of imports during a weakening currency leads to an initial increase in the trade deficit. As contracts take time to fill and buying patterns take time to change, this lag is known as a j-curve.

Currency Flows

Exporting and importing can also be expressed in terms of currency flows among countries. Paralleling the movement of goods and services, we export dollars and import foreign currencies. Usually this is done with bank debits and credits, not physically. The currency almost never leaves the country. Residents of the United States export U.S. dollars to Japan for computer chips and cars, to France for wine, to Mexico for labor, to Brazil for concentrated orange juice, to Hong Kong for capital investment, to Germany for sensing devices, and so forth. In return, from each of these countries U.S. residents import yen, francs, pesos, reals, Hong Kong dollars, and Deutsche marks which are payment for U.S. goods, services, and assets sold overseas. To complete the cycle, the currencies are returned to their respective countries in the form of payments for goods and services, investment in assets, debentures, and money market instruments, and through "foreign exchange," (buying and selling currencies in the currency markets). After all, what good are yen deposits in Chicago, or U.S. dollar deposits in Berlin?

Currency flow is similar to arbitrage, in that a weak currency automatically plants the seeds of its future strength. For example, the yen was very weak during the 1970s and early 1980s, producing a continuous flood of cost-competitive goods to the United States. Payments in dollars exported to Japan far exceeded receipts of yen. Simply put, imports from Japan far exceeded exports to Japan.

As a consequence of this "trade deficit," Japan built up large reserves of U.S. dollars, which it wanted to convert back into yen. It could only do so by returning the dollars to their source. Japan did this by trading them for U.S. goods and services, swapping them for U.S. debt and equity, or simply selling them in the currency markets. No matter which method was used, Japan, in essence, sold dollars and bought yen. The result was an increased supply of dollars in the world market, and a decreased supply of yen. This brought about the subsequent 1993-1994 price decline of the dollar to below 100 yen.

The Net Flow

The net flow of currency in and out of countries results from supply and demand changes caused by differences in real exchange rates and trade restrictions. This is often called a "trade imbalance," and can be measured by noting the quarter-to-quarter changes in the current account (see Figure 4-3).

The *current account balance* is the value of exports of goods, services, and income plus unilateral transfers less imports on goods, services, and income. This balance gives an approximate value for the current movement of foreign currencies *vis à vis* the U.S. dollar. When the balance is negative, it is called a *trade deficit*. According to Horace W. Brock, the trade deficit equals the net foreign capital inflow.[3] When the current account balance is positive, it is called a *trade surplus*. With a trade surplus, the surplus would equal the *net dollar outflow*. This equality stems from the fact that, after U.S. residents swap their dollars for foreign goods, and after foreign residents swap them back for American goods, there are dollars remaining abroad. These remaining dollars represent the balance on the current account, or trade deficit. Because these dollars must also be returned by some means or another, they arrive in the capital markets as foreign capital inflow. There are capital outflows as well, but the balance after all settlements are made represents the *net* foreign capital inflow.

Figure 4-3: Items included in the Current Account

- Exports of goods, services, and income, which is the sum of merchandise exports, service exports, and income receipts from U.S. assets abroad.
- Imports of goods, services, and income, which is the sum of merchandise imports, service imports, and income payments on foreign assets in the United States.
- Unilateral transfers (defined as foreign private and government transfers to U.S. citizens and government) less private transfers (representing gifts and similar payments by U.S. citizens, government payments associated with foreign assistance programs, and unilateral military transfers—usually a negative number).

Merchandise exports and imports are measured as the value of physical goods, excluding military equipment. *Service exports and imports* include receipts and payments associated with foreign travel and transportation, royalties and licensing fees, and purchases and sales of military equipment and fuel. *Income payments and receipts* refer to payments, receipts, and reinvestment of earnings on U.S. investments abroad, and foreign investments in the U.S., including interest, dividends, and branch earnings.

Source: *International Economic Conditions, Federal Reserve Bank of St. Louis, Aug. 1993*

The trade deficit must equal the net foreign capital inflow. This inflow represents the return of the country's currency in exchange for the country's capital assets. For any given trade deficit, a strong currency with higher purchasing power is exchanged for more capital assets than a weak currency with lower purchasing power.

It has long been recognized that changes in the capital account are indications of long-term trends in the economic environments of trading partners, and in their relative competitive positions. (See Figure 4-4 for a listing of items included in the capital account.) Brock contends, however, that net foreign capital inflow is directly related to the price of the dollar, and furthermore has an inverse relationship with interest rates, which also influence currency prices. For this reason, today there is much attention being paid to capital flows as a determinant of dollar-price direction. There should be. These capital outflows are a result of lack of confidence in the dollar and a growing regulatory burden in the United States. The ensuing declining rates of return on investment in regulated industries, relative to freer foreign markets, are a primary reason for this flight of capital. Beyond a doubt, capital flows impact currency prices, and vice versa.

Figure 4-4: Items included in the Capital Account

U.S. Assets Abroad

- Official Reserve Assets—defined as the net transactions by the Fed of sales and purchases of monetary gold, IMF allocations of SDRs to the United States, acquisitions of outstanding SDRs, sales of U.S.-owned SDRs for foreign currencies, changes in IMF holdings of dollars from transactions between IMF and member countries, exchange market interventions by the Fed, acquisitions of foreign currencies from the IMF or foreign governments, and net earnings on U.S. official reserve assets.
- Other U.S. Government Assets—includes U.S. government credits extended to foreign residents, capital subscriptions in or contributions to international financial institutions, repayments of credits by foreign residents, and net changes in other U.S. government assets.
- Private Assets—consists of: 1) direct investment, including equity capital flows, reinvested earnings, and inter-company debt flows of U.S. direct investors to their foreign affiliates; 2) foreign securities, comprised of net U.S. purchases of foreign stocks and bonds; and 3) U.S. claims on foreign residents by U.S. banks and their clients.

Figure 4-4: Items included in the Capital Account, *con't.*

Foreign Assets in the U.S.

- Foreign Official Reserves—net claims of foreign official agencies on U.S. federal, state, and local governments, and on other U.S. residents, including banks, financial institutions, and other organizations. This also includes U.S. government liabilities to foreign official agencies through military and other contracts.
- Other Foreign Assets—foreign direct investment, foreign purchases of U.S. securities, U.S. liabilities reported by foreign banks, and U.S. financial and commercial liabilities on unaffiliated foreigners reported by U.S. nonbanking concerns.
- Allocations of SDRs by IMF, used primarily for transactions among central banks.

Quarterly reports of the capital account reflect changes in U.S. assets abroad and foreign assets in the United States. Changes in values may indicate long-term trends in the economic environments of trading partners and their relative competitive positions. They are seen to have a growing impact on exchange rates.

Source: International Economic Conditions, Federal Reserve Bank of St. Louis, Aug. 1993

Government Actions

The ways governments create and manage currencies—a stalwart Deutsche mark, a politically driven Canadian Dollar, a run-away ruble—are governmental policy statements. In the main, political attitudes safeguard (or trash) a currency, while long-range fiscal policies determine the long-term value of a currency. Decisions made at "official" levels determine whether the British pound is worth about $1.50, rather than $3.50 or 27¢. Currency managers are less concerned with the broad brush stroke of long-term policy pronouncements, and more interested in whether the pound will be $1.52 or $1.47 *tomorrow*. To the extent that governments influence exchange rates, such near-to-intermediate potential price changes are almost solely in the hands of the central banks.

Figure 4-5: Trade Deficit (A less B) equals Net Capital Inflow (C)

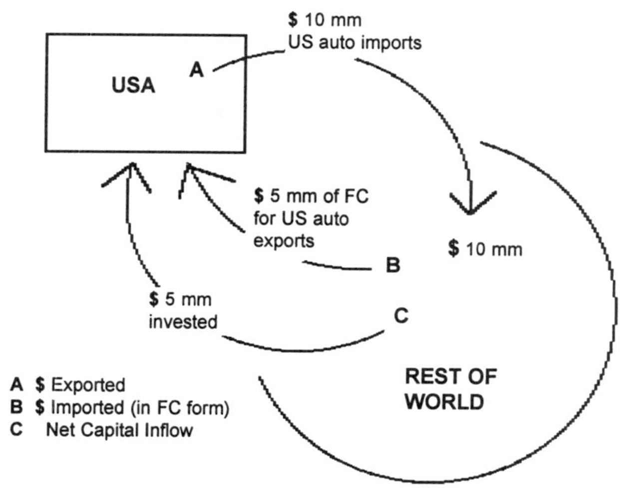

The net capital inflow is equal to the trade deficit, which is defined as a negative balance on the current account. In this diagram, "cars" symbolize all items entered on the current account, including goods, services, and income.

International trade can be viewed in two ways: 1) a flow of goods among countries, and 2) a flow of currencies among countries in exchange for the goods. Arrow A shows dollars paid out to the rest of the world in exchange for imported goods. Arrow B depicts the opposite flow of foreign currency for U.S. exports. When A exceeds B, resulting in a greater amount of dollars going out than foreign currency coming in, it is called a trade deficit. Arrow C, demonstrates that foreign currency must eventually return to its country of origin through the capital markets. This is called a net capital inflow.

A favorite pastime of fundamental analysts is "Fed watching." Scrutinizing the Federal Reserve is done on a minute scale. When the chairman of the Federal Reserve is prepared to speak before Congress or at a luncheon, anything he might possibly say is explored. After the speech, every word, every nuance, every raised eyebrow is analyzed—the Fed has that much influence over the foreign exchange markets. Because of the leverage in these markets, a move of 1/10th of one percent in exchange rates can mean an immediate transfer of hundreds of millions of dollars. A typical central bank has the ability to change the price of its nation's currency by many times that amount overnight by a change in policy. Fortunately, capricious actions by major central banks have been rare events. Much more common are currency movements resulting from manipulations of interest rates and foreign exchange, commonly called "intervention."

Managing the Float

After the Bretton Woods System collapse, the currencies of most industrialized countries were cast adrift to find their own levels, either independently, as in the case of the U.S. dollar, or as part of a group, such as the ERM. A true floating system is at the mercy of the market. Most governments are not completely happy with that state of affairs, so they "manage the float."

The term, *managed float* describes the concerted efforts to influence exchange rates by the central banks of first G-5 and then G-7 countries.[4] The initial stated objective of the United States, as a participating manager, was to "counter disorderly markets." (Of course, the markets were not really disorderly; they just didn't behave the way the central bank wanted them to.) The objectives were subsequently broadened to include "keeping exchange rates in line with underlying economic fundamentals." They then were expanded again, as stated in the Louvre Accord of February, 1987, to "foster stability of exchange rates around current levels."[5] As with all pegged-rate systems, *intervention* is the primary tool used to manage floating rate systems. This is the same tactic that was employed by the Fed to keep the dollar at parity with gold during the Bretton Woods era, when "parity" still meant $35 per ounce. When the currency price is higher than desired, the bank sells it in massive amounts for other currencies, building up foreign reserves in the process. It buys when the currency price is lower than desired, by selling foreign reserves.

The Problem with Managing the Float

International cartels, whether formed to protect the price of coffee, cocoa, oil, or currencies, eventually all encounter the same reality. Namely, there is no practical way to enforce the rules. Enforcement of the rules is the key to the cartel's success because whatever is in the collective best interest may not be in the best interest of an individual member. The G-7 nations operate something like a cartel, and they inevitably experience this conflict. For international trade, it is apparently to a country's short-term economic advantage to have an undervalued currency, as long as it is not debased to the point of causing rapid inflation. With a relatively weak currency, imports become less competitive with domestic products. In addition, of course, the country's exports become more competitive abroad. More is exported, less is imported, and the balance of trade figures look rosier. While this may make the statisticians and politicians happy, consumers prefer a stable "strong" currency. Thus, one major function of the EMS, for example, is to police against the practice of countries devaluing their currency for competitive trade advantage. Of course, if the central banks of several countries compete for a trade advantage, their currencies would be debased (inflated) at accelerating rates until they were totally worthless. While central banks may find other reasons for devaluing their currencies at varying rates, the long-term effects are the same.

For central banks to have any semblance of credibility in their attempts to manage the float, national interest must be subordinated; thus, when one nation's currency declines in value rapidly, creating so-called "disorderly market conditions," the country may be required to intervene, buying its currency in an attempt to strengthen it. It may also be required to raise interest rates. Intervention has the greatest effect when done in concert, all member countries buying or selling simultaneously. A central bank, pressured by the G-7 countries to honor the provisions of an international accord, may be under greater political pressure at home to ignore them. Market participants have observed so-called concerted intervention carried out with less than robust enthusiasm in all quarters.

Another problem with managing the float is that intervention does not permanently change anything; i.e., it doesn't work in the medium to long term. In fact, when central banks like the Federal Reserve "sterilize" their intervention efforts, they don't even change things temporarily. *Sterilized intervention* means that if the Federal Reserve buys its currency on the international market, it counteracts this action domestically to keep the money supply the same as when intervention started. For example, when the foreign desk of the Federal Reserve Bank of New York intervenes to buy dollars, thereby draining them from the international markets, the total supply of dollars decreases, but the domestic desk immediately counteracts the move by buying U.S. treasury securities (monetizing the debt), putting the same amount of dollars back in the system. The actual supply of currency hasn't changed. The inflation evidenced by the weakening currency in the international markets has been imported to the domestic market.

The rationale behind sterilized intervention is that *something* is being removed from (or added to) the system. In the above example, what are drained are treasury securities, by some considered to be dollar substitutes. Lower treasury security supply results in higher foreign currency prices for these instruments which, in effect, increases the value of the dollar, or so the argument goes. In fact, one school of thought goes so far as to assert that the desired benefits can be achieved without intervention ever taking place. The mere threat of intervention can change exchange rates (in the very short term). One need only notice the sharp jumps in volatility in the currency markets whenever the chairman of the Federal Reserve prepares to make a public statement.

Like the Fed's attempts to stimulate the economy, the threat of intervention and intervention itself is having less and less effect. Perhaps traders have concluded that intervention is little more than a hollow gesture. Also, currency traders as a group now have the wherewithal to match the central bank, and increase the stakes as well. More investment banks, commercial banks, pension fund managers, and global mutual fund managers from all corners of the globe are entering the markets, and the markets themselves have changed. There is trading twenty-four hours a day in every major financial center throughout the world. Over one trillion dollars worth of currencies change hands daily, and the amount is growing. America's six largest banks derived more than 40% of their profits from currency trading in the second quarter of 1993. Participants in this market trade for large sums, and attempts by central banks to control prices without ruining the domestic economy have not met with much success. It appears that central banks are beginning to realize the folly of it all and are becoming reluctant to intervene, except in minor amounts for posturing purposes.

Adjusting the Interest Rates

Floating rates can also be "managed" by adjusting interest rates. The relative values among currencies are dependent, in part, on the interest rates that are paid on each of them. The higher the interest rate a currency earns, the more valuable it is to a holder. Because a freely convertible currency paying lower rates can be easily substituted for one paying higher rates, the shifting demand may influence the price of the currency.

U.S. overnight interest rates are established by the Federal Reserve. All others are determined by market discovery. The discount rate is the overnight rate that applies when banks borrow from the Federal Reserve. It is the bench mark for short-term rates, and can be readjusted whenever the Federal Reserve decides it should be. That is not often. More often, the Fed will affect the interest rate market by open market actions causing shifts in the federal funds rates (the overnight rate used by Federal Reserve member banks to borrow from each other). In this way, the Fed adds to and drains reserves from the banking system.

The Fed may change interest rates such as the discount rate or federal funds rate to try to control inflation, or to strengthen or weaken the currency. It may, from time to time, enter into international currency agreements that demand an increase in interest rates regardless of other factors in the economy. The purpose of such an agreement may be to maintain the exchange rate within an agreed-upon range. For whatever reason interest rates change, exchange rates usually respond, but *how* the exchange rates change depends on *why* the interest rates changed.

The devaluation of a currency is often considered to be self-serving. Shoring it up, on the other hand, traditionally has been viewed as a sacrifice for "the good of the global economy." These points of view are jaded because the economic health of consumers in one country increasingly affects the producers in others. Also, domestic economies are damaged by the inflationary policies thought to promote export trade. In addition, sacrifice is difficult, no matter who benefits. The resulting political fallout makes most central banks unlikely to tamper with interest rates to honor international agreements; thus, actions by the Fed usually relate to real or anticipated changes in inflation levels, and are not usually intended to cause change in exchange rates. Nevertheless, currencies do react to Fed interest rate changes. They just don't move in any predictable way.

The Official Philosophy

Another important variable is the official philosophy about currency. Besides national defense and internal security, maintaining an honest currency should be at the core of the government's responsibility to its citizens. Although we speak of "managed float" versus "independent float" in an attempt to differentiate exchange systems, all fiat currencies are managed, if by no other means than limiting the printing presses, so the term, *managed float* is used appropriately. U.S. politicians argue constantly about how diligently the exchange rate should be managed.

The IMF Articles of Agreement among members stipulate that each country should intervene to counter "disorderly currency markets," or "when otherwise deemed appropriate." U.S. authorities interpreted this article quite narrowly between 1973 and 1977.[6] The volume of intervention remained small; however, in the late 1970s, the declining dollar created concern. The U.S. interpretation of "disorderly markets" was broadened to include prices that "had gone beyond what could be justified by underlying economic conditions." Intervention with large dollar purchases followed. Then, between 1981 and 1984, the pendulum swung again in the other direction. A "hands off" approach came back into favor. That ended with the Plaza and Louvre Agreements of the IMF members (G-7 and G-10) between 1985 and 1987. Both of these meetings concluded that concerted intervention was required for economic reasons. As Milton Friedman relates, "The Plaza conference was held because the dollar was deemed to have appreciated too much....(when) the Louvre Summit was held, the dollar had lost more the three-quarters of its earlier appreciation. The powers-that-be decided that was enough. The rate was *just* right."[7] Apparently, governments believe that they know what a currency's value should be and that they should have a major role in exchange rate determination, regardless of whether or not their management techniques work as intended.

For Want of a Franc

The showdown between the European central banks and the "speculators" (everyone else) took place in the last weeks of July, 1993. Strains in the European Monetary System began causing problems a year earlier, when the UK and Italy were forced to withdraw. The problem, according to much of Europe, was Germany. The Deutsche mark was a strong international reserve currency in its own right. It has become a leading reserve currency partly because it is backed by the Bundesbank, a very independent central bank, mandated by its charter to safeguard the value of the currency above all else.

Germany was being subjected to major inflationary pressures due to the massive amount of funding required to assimilate the former Eastern Germany. To counteract this, the Bundesbank maintained very high interest rates unflinchingly, even in the face of a severe economic slump and rising unemployment at home and throughout the European community.

Meanwhile, the Banque de France was called on to alleviate the French recession. The two central banks could hardly have been more opposite in character. The Bundesbank is furiously independent and, overtly at least, answers to no other body. Its mission is to protect the currency, even at the expense of the German economy (and certainly at the expense of the European economy) if necessary. The Banque de France, on the other hand, does not have the independent status accorded a strong central bank. In fact, such status is prohibited by the French Constitution. While many central banks are considered by politicians to be part of society's problem, being the independent, tight-fisted entities they often are, the Banque de France is called upon to be part of society's solution. The problem for France in 1993 was widespread unemployment and economic recession. The time-honored solution was to lower interest rates which, by extension, would devalue the currency. This would stimulate the economy at home and allow France, with the rest of Europe, to be more competitive overseas.

As a member of the ERM, France could not lower interest rates alone. Such a move would have to be coordinated with the rest of the members. Furthermore, Germany, holding the strongest currency, would have to lead the way. France, with other European nations in the same straits, urgently called upon Germany to lower its bank (discount) rate, then hovering around 7%. The Bundesbank, characteristically, refused.

A year earlier, the United Kingdom and Italy, faced with the same situation and faced with the same German response, had left the ERM to reduce interest rates unilaterally. The values of the British pound and the Lira fell sharply in the process. France, however, was a major advocate of ERM. The fixed-rate requirements of the system, along with Bundesbank leadership, had produced the *Franc Fort*, the cornerstone of France's long-term economic policy. Also, France was firmly committed to the Maastricht Treaty. This agreement called for a single European trading block, a common currency, and a single central bank. All these were very much in France's best interest. In contrast, the Bundesbank had consistently opposed the formation of a European currency to replace the Deutsche mark. With such a disparity of interests, it seems somewhat ironic that the co-founders of the EMS were former West German Chancellor Helmut Schmidt and former French President Valery Gisgard d'Estaing, two leaders who stood together on the side lines and watched their nations act as adversaries, playing out their hands.

When Germany refused to lower interest rates to any significant degree, it appeared to the rest of the world that France was facing an imminent unilateral devaluation. Currency speculators, flush with profits from recent attacks on the Spanish Peseta and Italian Lira, began to take interest. France, vowing to "break the backs of the speculators," prepared for massive intervention in defense of the Franc and the ERM.

Attacks on the Franc and the allied weak currencies increased dramatically in the last weeks of July, 1993. It was a replay of the final curtain drawing down on the Bretton Woods System, telescoped into one week of financial chaos. It was over by August 3, 1993: France had poured 300 billion Francs into the currency markets—over $50 billion dollars worth—virtually wiping out its foreign reserves. Denmark, fighting on a second front, threw in 50 billion Crowns (over $7 billion). After it was over, Denmark was forced to sell new bonds abroad to replenish its coffers. These bonds were denominated in British pounds. The ERM was in a shambles, its 4½% band expanded to a meaningless 30%. It was a week like no other, and the *Franc Fort* was no more.

Conclusion

Determination of exchange rates was once fairly simple. During the years of the Bretton Woods System, there were long periods of exchange rate stability. Despite the inherent problems, pegged systems lend a degree of confidence to currency price predictions—the Deutsche mark or Canadian dollar very likely would be the same tomorrow as it was yesterday and today. For almost thirty years, the Swiss franc moved less than 1¢ from its official price peg (1941 through 1970). There were major readjustments to the system if a currency got too far out of line with economics, but there were few surprises because adjustments could be anticipated well in advance.

This is no longer the case. Now, the Swiss franc moves more than 1¢ on an average *day* with no news. Economic factors such as purchasing power disparities and changing balances of trade appear totally disconnected from today's often-volatile currency markets. Why? Because the freedom of movement allowed by converting to an independent float and today's instant transmission of information through a global telecommunication network allow changes in supply and demand and other factors affecting currency prices to be reflected in the markets almost instantaneously.

A third reason is the sheer amount of money trading in the foreign exchange markets, which have been transformed from a billion dollar market to a trillion dollar market. A trader with several million dollars of his bank's money at risk covers his position at once when he hears that the chairman of the Federal Reserve has called a news conference. He doesn't wait to hear the results.

In today's swiftly moving markets, speculators often react to news, rumors, or tidbits of rumors without much analysis. They are poised to get in, get out, or get covered. They'll figure out what it all means later. They are not necessarily athletes or even analysts, but they have good reflexes.

Currencies that have followed a major trend for months can reverse it in seconds, turning trading profits into losses. The market often becomes proactive, anticipating changing economics, rather than reacting to them. Exchange rates can still be determined and predicted. Currencies can still be managed, but the rules have changed.

CHAPTER 5

Exchange Rates and Interest Rates

There is no doubt that interest rates and exchange rates have a profound effect upon one another. There are many theories regarding the relationship. One popular perception is called the “hot money” theory. It is accepted by many that a huge source of funds overhangs the currency markets worldwide. Whenever interest rates rise in one country, especially a major industrial country with an unrestricted currency, the theory purports that these funds rush in to take advantage of the increased yield. They remain parked in that currency only until the rate of interest moves back down, or interest rates of other currencies move higher, at which time they again flow to the currency paying the highest yield. Proponents of the “hot money” theory contend that the sudden shifts in demand have a dramatic effect on exchange rates, with the highest yielding currency rising quickly in price as buyers pour in.

With the very deep pockets of numerous large investors, including commercial and investment banks, and with today’s instant telecommunication and transfer capabilities, the “hot money” theory seems quite plausible; however, it is a false perception. There is no tremendous flow of funds chasing interest rates. Some money does, but not much; thus, “hot money” does not move exchange rates. The reason is that the automatic gains implied by this reasoning simply do not exist and trying to achieve such gains involves a great deal of risk due to market forces called *interest rate parity*.

Interest Rate Parity

The concept of interest rate parity and forward pricing are intertwined. Currency values (prices) exist not only in the present, but out into the future. The prices change from minute to minute, from day to day.

Today's price is called the *spot*, or *cash* price. All values in the future, beyond spot, are called *forward* prices. *The Wall Street Journal* reports spot prices and three forward rates, as shown in the example in Table 5-1 of Canadian dollar rates. The top figure in each column is the spot price.

Table 5-1: Spot Prices and Forward Rates: Canadian Dollar

Country	U.S. $ Equivalent.	
	Mon.	Fri.
Canada (Dollar)	.7443	.7481
30-day forward	.7439	.7458
90-day forward	.7428	.7448
180-day forward	.7403	.7426

Source: *The Wall Street Journal*, September 12, 1995
(prices as of September 11, 1995)

Although only three forward rates are reported in the *Journal*, there could be any number reported: a 4-day forward, a 31-day forward, a 47-day forward, a 268-day forward, and so on. Constraints on space dictate that just a few representative forwards are listed, as shown.

A major characteristic of this string of prices for a given currency is that they maintain a relatively constant relationship with each other. If one price moves up (or down), all prices for that currency tend to move up (or down). As can be seen above, although the quotes change from day to day, the relationships among them remain fairly constant. This is because, relative to spot, the difference in values between two currencies over a specific period of time roughly equals the difference in interest rates earned on those two currencies over the same period. Forward rates and interest rate differentials are functions of one another. If one moves, the other usually compensates. As with any attempt to quantify human behavior, there is some "slippage" between the theory and reality!

Example: assume a spot rate of *hc/fc* = .50 (or 2FC = 1 HC). Both of these currencies have an annual interest rate yield of 5%. Because there is no difference in interest rates, there are no value differences in the forward rates. Every forward rate along the entire forward listing equals .50, as shown on line (1) in Figure 5-1. If the interest rate yield for HC is suddenly increased to 6%, how would this affect the exchange rate?

First, the *spot* rate is subject to immediate adjustment to "factor in" the change in interest rates. The spot rate may adjust upward, downward, or remain unchanged, depending on the reasons for the change, and the market's assessment of the long-term prospects for the currencies. For this example, assume the HC/FC spot rate is adjusted downward (line 2). Next, the forward rates realign with the new spot rate to compensate for the interest rate change (line 3). These changes occur so quickly, they are virtually simultaneous.

Figure 5-1: Impact of Interest Rate Changes on Exchange Rate HC/FC

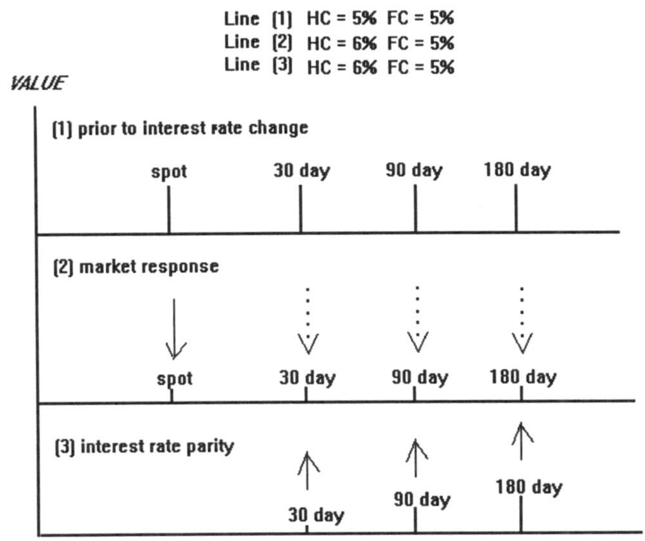

Unlike the adjustment of spot, which is indeterminate, the realignment of forward prices is determined by the change in interest rates. It expresses the difference in interest rates between the two currencies, and

is approximated by the formula for interest rate parity. Many analysts believe that the motivating force behind the price moves is arbitrage, the same dynamic that drives PPP. Unlike PPP however, interest rate arbitrage is certain and immediate. It happens as quickly as the *arbitrageur* can pick up the phone to make a transaction. If interest rates and exchange rates move away from parity even slightly, the "excessive" value is sold and the "deficient" value is bought for an assured profit with little risk. This is the popular explanation of why interest rate parity is re-established in seconds or minutes, rather than hours or days.

Because forward price differentials relate to interest rate differentials, and because arbitrage occurs, there is no advantage to moving out of one currency into another to garner higher yields. As long as the currency is hedged to prevent exchange risk, higher yields are factored out by the forward prices.

This can be easily illustrated. Let's say that a U.S. construction company purchases new road-building equipment from a manufacturer located in an FC country. The cost of the equipment is 1,000,000 FC, with payment due one year from the date of purchase. The corporate treasurer now has an FC payable on the books and is concerned about the exposure. He decides to hedge this liability, and looks at two options (assume FC futures trade on an exchange and the current $/FC spot rate is 1.00):

1. The treasurer can immediately exchange $1,000,000 for 1,000,000 FC and invest the foreign currency. (To eliminate extraneous risk factors, let's say he considers a money market instrument comparable to a U.S. treasury bill.) The FC payment is due when the instrument matures.
2. He can purchase FC one-year futures contracts, take delivery of the FC when the contracts mature, and make the payment. Note that a third alternative, borrowing FC and investing it for one year, doesn't work in this instance because it merely substitutes one FC liability for another.

The treasurer looks for the most economical option and discovers that both are virtually equal in cost, as shown by the following:

Value Date of FC	Exchange Rate ($/FC)	Interest Rate (one-year)
spot	1.00 ($1.00 = 1.00 FC)	$ = 10%
one-year forward	1.05 ($1.05 = 1.00 FC)	FC = 5%

With the first option, the treasurer foregoes the interest for one year on dollars (10%), and earns one year of interest on FC (5%). This represents a net opportunity cost equal to 5% of $1,000,000. With the second option, he earns 10% on $1,000,000 for the year because he doesn't trade it for FC; however, he pays a premium for the one-year futures, which costs 5% in dollar terms. Again, the net cost is 5% of $1,000,000.

This "one is the same as the other" result applies in every case. This correlation is known as *interest rate parity*. The correlation works in both directions. If the interest rate were 10% for FC, and 5% for dollars, the futures would be discounted from the spot, rather than priced at a premium. Let's look at this scenario:

Value Date of FC	Exchange Rate ($/FC)	Interest Rate (one year)
spot	1.00 ($1.00 = 1.00 FC)	$ = 5%
one-year forward	.95 ($0.95 = 1.00 FC)	FC = 10%

Now, the cost has a negative value (it is a gain), but again, the amount is the same, regardless of which option is chosen. With the first option, the treasurer can gain 5% by converting dollars to FC and investing it at 10% for a year, foregoing a 5% earning on dollars, or he can make the same 5% by purchasing futures at a discount.

Does the company actually realize a gain by hedging in discount currencies? Probably not. Remember that the treasurer starts out with an FC liability. He is seeking to eliminate the exchange risk it represents by acquiring an FC asset in one form or another. The discounted purchasing price of the futures (the asset) more than likely will be offset by the higher interest cost factored into the payable. By the same token, the 5% "cost" in the first example is offset by the lower interest rate charged for the FC liability.

The terms *premium currency* (futures priced at a premium to spot) and *discount currency* (futures priced at a discount to spot) are used to identify which currency has the higher or lower yield. By knowing either the futures price or the interest rate, the other can be approximated out to about a year distant. The calculations are less exact as the time frame exceeds one year because other risks come into play. Even so, forward contracts out as far as twenty years are not unknown.

An underlying assumption of the Interest Rate Parity theory is that the foreign currency interest rate is 0%. Obviously, this is never the case in a world of fiat currencies; however, the theory is still widely discussed. For those with a mathematical bent, calculation of Interest Rate Parity is shown in Figure 5-2.

Figure 5-2: Calculation of Interest Rate Parity

$$\frac{F}{S} = \frac{1 + R\,hc}{1 + R\,fc}$$

where *F* is the direct exchange rate of the one-year futures or forward; *S* is the direct exchange rate for spot; *R hc* is the one-year interest rate of the home currency (U.S. $, in this case), and *R fc* is the one-year interest rate of the foreign currency.

Assume S = 100, R hc = .10 , and R fc = .05.
What is the approximate one-year futures or forward rate (F)?

$$\frac{F}{1.00} = \frac{1 + .10}{1 + .05} = 1.0477619$$

Rounded, F = 1.0478

Simply stated, the difference between the spot and futures or forward rates is approximately equivalent to the difference between the interest rates. For both sides to be precisely equal, both denominators would have to equal 1.00, which would only occur if the foreign currency interest rate were 0%—which never happens. The higher the foreign currency interest rate, the greater the error factor.

The Anatomy of Interest Rate Parity

Conventional wisdom has it that forward rates are determined by interest rate parity because of arbitrage. In other words, interest rate differentials translate into forward pricing, so any mis-price between the cash and forward markets is instantly traded away. Interest rate parity works, according to this line of reasoning, because arbitrage makes it work. But does it really? It is just as easy to argue that arbitrage is simply an effect of interest rate parity, rather than the cause. Perhaps *arbitrageurs* act quickly when noticing a price disparity only because they realize that parity will occur *regardless* of what they do. It can be shown that this is what actually happens, and that interest rate parity is much more fundamental than the results produced by arbitrage.

Imagine the following scenario: you are approached by a benefactor who proposes to enhance your well-being. He offers you $1,000 with no strings attached. You are given two choices. Either you can receive the cash immediately, or you can receive the cash after an interval of one year. Which option would you choose?

There is a high probability that you would take the cash immediately. Why? For the following reasons:

1. The delay of one year represents 365 days of lost opportunity. You can purchase a lot of things with $1,000 during a year's time (this is the time value of money).
2. The money will be less valuable in one year because of the effects of inflation.
3. The future is uncertain. The benefactor may change his mind or lose the money during the year.

In short, there are three factors which affect the value of money to be received in the future: the time value of money, the inflation rate, and the borrower's (or benefactor's) credit risk.

Although we cannot determine in advance the present value of the future sum, we can measure precisely the *expected* present value. It is equal in value to the inducement that must be paid to turn *money in hand* into *money promised*. In other words, the present value of a future sum of money is reflected by the rate of interest that it earns. For example, assume the inflation rate is 3% and that this rate has been steady. This means the lender requires 3% in addition to the principal to maintain purchasing power for one year. The lender also wants to be paid for the opportunity cost (loss of use), which is probably about an additional 2%.

Thus a lender might choose to defer spending the money for one year, but only if he were compensated for the anticipated loss of value and use. In this example, the dollars would have to yield an additional 5% (disregarding credit risk), the minimum amount required to induce someone to save the money for future use. This 5%, of course, is the rate of interest. Since it includes the inflation rate, it is the *nominal* rate of interest. The nominal rate includes the real rate, which is the time value of money, 2% in this example. The real rate of interest may be either positive or negative. If it is negative, it acts as a disincentive to saving.

Thus, the minimum rate of interest earned by any currency must be the expected value by which that currency "depreciates" over time. The term *minimum* is used to restrict the situation to "secured" dollars. Dollars are secured if:

1. principal and interest are guaranteed,
2. the savings are liquid (may be redeemed for cash at any time), and
3. the time involved is short enough to preclude substantial market risk; i.e., one year or less. Restricting the situation in this way, the following statement can be made:

The anticipated depreciation of a currency equals the nominal interest rate for short-term money market instruments, such as treasury bills and Eurodollar deposits, denominated in that currency. The nominal rate includes the real rate, which may be positive or negative.

Figure 5-3 shows the current value of FC as 50% of HC; therefore, the spot exchange rate (HC/FC) is .50. Both FC and HC are anticipated to depreciate 5% annually, as reflected in the nominal short-term interest rate for each currency. Thus, the expected relative values of FC and HC will not vary from spot to one-year forward. This is confirmed in the forward exchange rates. Each forward rate, 30-day, 90-day, 180-day, etc. is identical, that is HC/FC = .50.

In Figure 5-4, both the rate of inflation and the nominal interest rate of FC have been increased by 5%; however, the real interest rate remains the same. The interest rate change is reflected in the new comparative values of HC and FC. Forward rates have gone to a discount to spot, because FC now is anticipated to depreciate faster than HC. The one-year forward rate, previously .50 (same as spot), is now 5% less, or .477.

Figure 5-3: Anticipated Depreciation of HC and FC with nominal interest rates of 5% per annum and real interest rates of 2% per annum

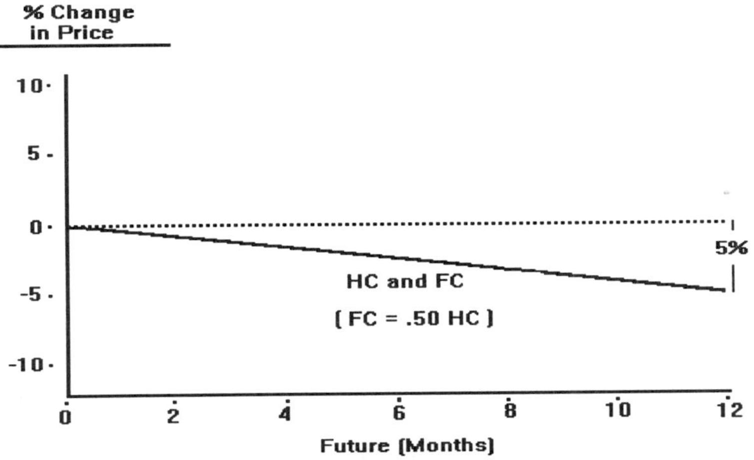

Figure 5-4: Anticipated Depreciation of HC and FC with nominal interest rates of 5% and 10% per annum and real interest rates of 2% per annum

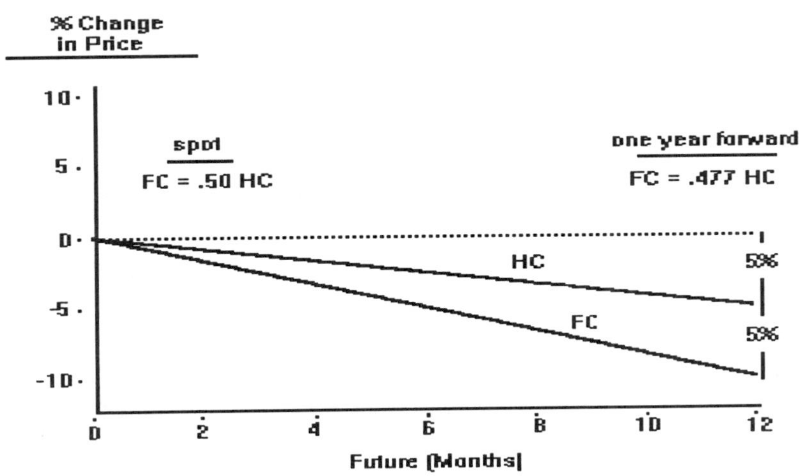

This can be confirmed using the formula for interest rate parity (page 82):

$$\frac{F}{S} \cong \frac{1 + R\,hc}{1 + R\,fc}$$

where S = .50, R hc = .05, R fc = .10

$$\frac{F}{.50} \cong \frac{1 + .05}{1 + .10}$$

Therefore, F= .4772727

This rate assumes that spot does not change. As long as there is no change in real interest rates and everything else stays the same, there is no *quantifiable* reason to expect a change in spot rates. Of course, that does *not* mean that spot *will not* change in reaction to the interest rate increase. It just means that a change in the spot rate cannot be predicted.

The above example illustrates a fundamental difference between spot and forward exchange rates, and between the spot exchange rate and interest rates: the spot rate is based on *known historical* and *current events*. On the other hand, forward rates and interest rates are based upon *anticipated events*. In effect, forward rates and interest rates are the same thing, expressed differently. They are the interest rate differential between the two currencies.

Chasing Higher Yields

Often, financial managers consider switching into high yielding currencies for investment purposes. Remember the "hot money" game? It is certainly possible to profit from higher yields on a short-term basis; however, chasing higher yields involves currency speculation.

As you recall, in the example of the corporate treasurer considering buying foreign currency immediately or buying a forward, his intention in either case was to hedge exposure by acquiring a foreign currency asset of some kind to offset a liability. It is hedging, in which foreign currency rates are fixed on both sides of a transaction, that establishes parity. In fact, interest rate parity comes into play only when there is no exposure to exchange rate movement. For this reason, it is often referred to as *covered interest rate parity*.

The concept of covered interest rate parity precludes profiting from higher interest rates. If the treasurer had decided to move from HC to FC to capture the additional interest, but did not wish to speculate in FC, he would need to purchase FC spot and simultaneously sell FC forward (say, one-year forward). As the treasurer discovers, the gain on interest is offset by the loss in translation on covered transactions.

Still, currency managers often make hedging decisions that result in gains from higher yields, but if the *objective* is to *profit* from the yield difference, then forward positions cannot be taken because that simply gives back the difference. The solution, of course, is not to lock in a forward position; but the manager must realize that, to the degree that the future price is not secured, he is speculating in currencies.

Figures 5-3 and 5-4 show how interest rate parity is achieved, and show that changes in anticipation of currency depreciation result in changes in interest rates which, in turn, cause changes in exchange rates (expectations, and actions taken on them, can create a self-fulfilling prophecy). Also, regarding spot rates and one-year forward rates, spot is impacted *first* by a sudden interest rate change. But are spot rates impacted *more* than forward rates? The answer depends on why the rate of interest changed.

Return for a moment to Figure 5-3, in which both HC and FC have a nominal interest rate of 5% and a real interest rate of 2%. This is re-drawn in Figure 5-5 as line A. What happens when the nominal interest rate for FC increases to 10% while the nominal interest rate for HC remains unchanged? Lines B, C, and D show three possibilities. Let's review the facts following such a rate hike:

- The anticipated depreciation of FC has increased from 5% to 10% annually.
- The spot rate reacted first to the change, if it reacted at all, and the forwards then realigned. (This sequence is theoretical. In reality, the changes are simultaneous.)
- FC becomes a discount currency relative to HC, and HC becomes a premium currency relative to FC.

- The discount and premium difference between HC and FC is expressed by the difference in interest rates, and is a precise amount.
- The new spot rate is indeterminate.

Figure 5-5: Possible FC Price Moves In Response to Nominal Interest Rate Shift from 5% to 10%

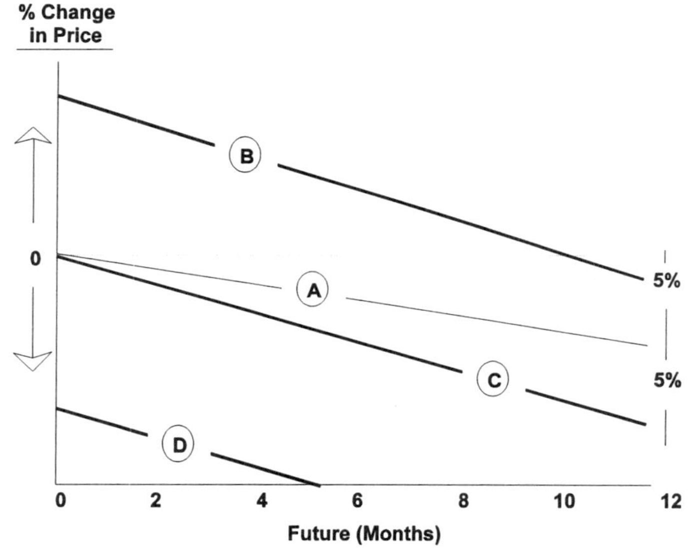

Because of the difference in how nominal and real interest rates affect exchange rates, one cannot determine whether the spot value of FC increased (B), stayed the same (C), or decreased (D). Only *nominal* interest rate differentials are reflected in forward rate changes, but both nominal *and* real interest rate changes impact the spot rate. In general, when the real interest rate of FC increases along with the nominal rate, the impact produces higher spot values, but what if the interest rate rose in reaction to a runaway inflation rate? Let's say that FC inflation jumped from 3% to 9%. Even with a 5% increase in nominal rates, the real rate would actually *decrease.* This might easily translate into lower spot values, compared to HC. Although this example holds HC constant, in the real world, all currencies undergo continual fluctuations in real interest and inflation rates. Also, economists do not all measure inflation the same way, regardless of the currency being analyzed.

Even if inflation and real interest rates could be adequately measured and future changes accurately predicted, imminent changes in spot prices still could not be determined. Remember interest rates are just one of many price determinants. In addition to those already addressed, there are expected inflation rates, future interest rate changes, future government policy changes, and future depreciation. When it comes to determining the effect of interest rate changes on spot, the following soliloquy of a currency trader describes the situation:

"The FC Bank raised its key interest rate again, so I better buy FC before it goes up . . . except the Bank had to act because of the government's new budget-busting spending program. Prices in FC-land are going out of sight. I don't think the bank did enough, maybe I better sell FC instead. Yet, if I sell and I'm right, and FC falls, then the bank will see that their hike had no effect-an adverse effect, actually. So, they might increase again. They did that before, and caught the shorts in a bear squeeze. I have to watch that. I wonder if the HC Bank is going to ride this out, raise rates, or lower rates to help out. HC-land has CPI figures coming out tomorrow. I think they'll be a little inflationary, too . . . maybe they'll have to follow suit. Maybe I should buy both FC and HC, or maybe I should sell both FC and HC and buy gold. Maybe I'll just go home!"

The prices of fiat currencies are "indeterminate" because traders have to try to second-guess the political motivations of bureaucrats.

Premiums, Discounts, and Costs of Carry

So far, the examples have shown foreign currencies with yields greater than home currencies. The higher the rate of interest, the steeper the negative slope of the line. It also works in the opposite direction. A currency paying lower interest than the U.S. dollar would be represented by a line with less negative slope than that of the U.S. dollar.

Consider the following group of currencies. Each currency has the anticipated depreciation value listed.

currency	depreciation
gold coin	3.00%
FCA	4.00%
U.S. $	6.00%
FCB	8.00%

Figure 5-6 shows the value changes in these currencies during one year. Notice the description of the vertical axis. The changes being plotted are changes in spot, or current dollar value (real dollars). To standardize the currencies, a "dollar's worth" of each one is depreciated by assuming positive real interest rates. Notice that currencies with interest rates less than that of the U.S. dollar depreciate less, whereas currencies with higher rates depreciate more.

Figure 5-6: Anticipated Depreciation of Various Currencies

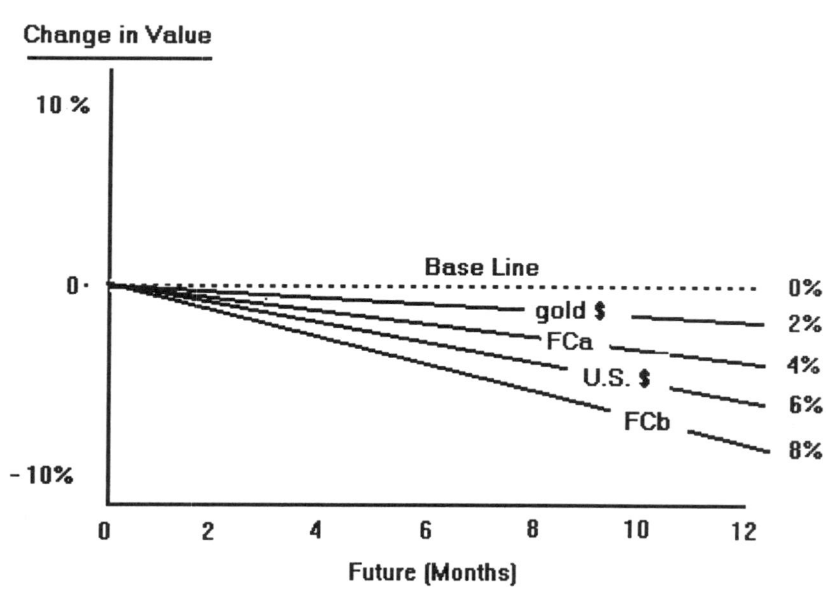

Let's change the chart slightly, as shown in Figure 5-7 on page 92, so now the vertical axis represents *nominal* dollar price changes. "Nominal" means that, at the end of twelve months, one dollar is still one dollar. Here, the dollar is used as a standard unit of account rather than as a store of value. This is required to compute exchange rates—one of the two currencies is used as a unit of account while the other varies against it. In this case, the dollar is the unit of account and FC is quoted indirectly (FC / $). Figure 5-7, therefore, shows each currency expressed relative to the U.S. dollar as an exchange rate. The price relationships are unaffected; the chart is simply tilted until the dollar line is the baseline. Note that Gold Coin and FCA are at a premium to the dollar, while FCB is at a discount. By using the dollar as the standard, all currencies with lower interest rates are rendered premium currencies, and all currencies with higher interest rates become discount currencies. Because the originary rate (time value of money) is small and constant, usually around 2%–3%, and credit risk of governments is rarely called into question, the primary factor affecting interest rate levels is inflation. Thus, we would expect Gold Coin and FCA to have lower inflation rates than the dollar, and FCB to have a higher inflation rate.

Figure 5-7 shows the differentials between spot and forward exchange rates when real foreign currency values are measured against the nominal dollar value. Those who trade futures may recognize the forward price differential as the *cost of carry*. This cost usually consists of interest, insurance, and storage. Because currency holdings do not require payment of insurance or storage fees, the cost of carry is simply the difference between the rates of interest.

With a world of fiat currencies being valued relative to the dollar, we can say that the nominal value of the dollar remains constant over time, while the real value may decline through inflation. In fact, this has been the case; thus, premium currencies are losing purchasing power more slowly than the dollar, while discount currencies are losing purchasing power more quickly than the dollar. The whole world is on a sliding scale.

Eurorates

The true value of an independently floating currency is under constant surveillance and revision in the global market place. No government regulation or restriction affects its convertibility or its value. If spot trades freely, the forward rates must be equally free of governmental constraints. This also applies to any rate of interest used in determining forward rates.

Figure 5-7: Anticipated Depreciation of Various Currencies In U.S. Dollar Terms

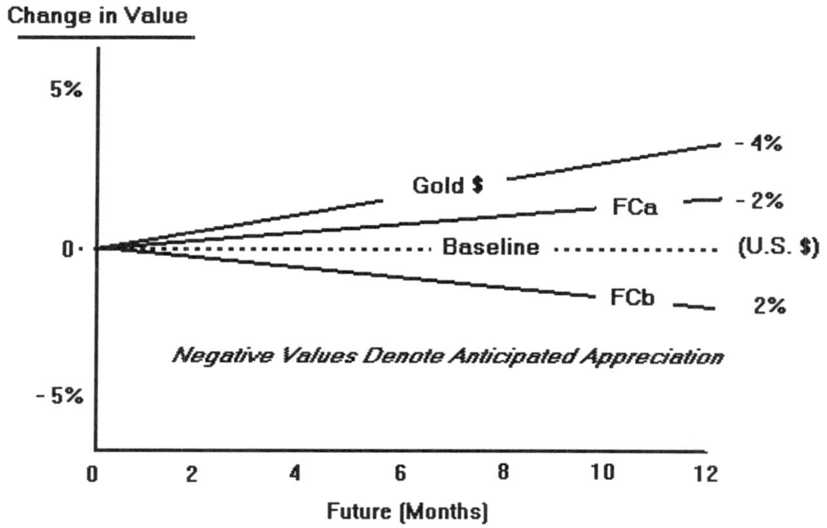

As previously determined, the minimum short-term interest rate earned by any currency is a money market rate for which principal and interest is secured. U.S. treasury bills fit the criteria, but are government issues, and therefore under government control. It is difficult to find instruments denominated in other currencies with the same characteristics as a U.S. treasury bill. A one-year government debt instrument in one country may have a very different yield from that of a one-year government debt instrument in another country for reasons having nothing to do with currencies. Government regulations, yield limitations from banking laws, liquidity risk, and a host of other political considerations affect short-term yields in a variety of ways. Unless we can use comparable interest rates, there is no way to compare forward prices accurately. There is one place where short-term interest rates are comparable across numerous currencies, and this is the Eurocurrency market.

Eurorates and exchange rates are so interrelated that, for all practical purposes, they are simply two separate ways of looking at the same thing. It is only natural, therefore, to speak of forward prices in terms of differences in Eurorates. To summarize:

> *Differences between spot and forward exchange rates for any two currencies are the Eurorate yield differences between the same two currencies.*

Forward Value Dates

Just like 30-day and 60-day treasury bills, forwards can be designated 30-, 60-, 90-, 180-day, and so on. To calculate forward prices, all months are considered to be 30-day months within a 360-day year. For example, 60-day forward is the same as two months, 120 days are four months, etc. Exact time periods are known as "even" dates, such as exactly one week, one month, two months, fifteen weeks, and so forth. There are also "odd" dates, for example 10-day, 29-day, 45-day, 50-day, etc. Even date references are used to simplify price comparisons for a general picture; however, once a specific transaction takes place, the forward contract is recorded and referred to by its *value date*.

The term *value date* refers to the date on which a forward rate becomes the spot rate. A contract for a one-year forward purchased on September 30, 1995, has a value date of September 29, 1996. On this date, the forward becomes the spot. The term *spot* also requires further definition. So far *spot* has been used to refer to *today's* price. In practice, the value date of spot is today plus two business days. A spot trade then is a trade that settles two business days from now. This grace period allows participants time to transfer the funds. The term, *spot*, is also commonly used for trades for which the value date is "in a few days." To avoid confusion, two-day spot is sometimes called *ordinary spot*. Most accurately, today's price is referred to as the *cash price*, for immediate exchange purposes; for example, vacationers traveling abroad stop at the border to exchange currency at cash prices.

As discussed above, a specific forward rate can be for *any* number of days in the future, one week, seven weeks, 113 days, four years and four months, etc. While the examples have generally referred to the one-year forward price, the nearer-term forwards are used to a much greater extent. One-year forwards are relatively illiquid in many currencies, and thinly traded. One-month, two-month, three-month, and six-month forwards are most heavily traded, and have become standardized. Most trading is confined to a six-month range because this time frame conforms to many scheduled shipping and payment due dates.

Finding Forward Rates

Approximate forward rate of a currency can be found when we know the difference in interest rates. Conversely, the interest rate differential can be found from the difference in forward prices. They are really the converse of the same ratio. The following formula may be used to derive the percentage of premium or discount of the forward rate over spot. You may notice this formula is very similar to the interest rate parity formula. In fact, this formula calculates interest for a specific period based on the annual interest rate difference.

$$\frac{F - S \times 360 \times 100}{S \times \text{Number of Days}}$$

Where: F = Forward rate, S = spot rate, 360 = the number of days in the year, Number of Days = the length of time in days between the forward and spot value dates

For example:

Eurorate HC	5.75%
Eurorate FC	15.00%
Spot	1.6860 (HC/FC)
Six-month forward	1.6080

Using the formula:

$$\frac{1.6080 - 1.6860 \times 360 \times 100}{1.6860 \times 180} = 9.25\%$$

= 9.25% discount of forward to spot, which is equal to the difference in interest rates

The formula is reversed to find the forward rate:

Eurorate HC	6.00%
Eurorate LC	15.00%
Spot	1.6860
Six-Month Forward	?

Transpose to the algebraically equivalent formula:

$$\frac{\text{S x (\% premium or discount) x (number of days)}}{\text{360 x 100}}$$

Because the months are assumed to be equal (30 day) months, months can be substituted for days. The equation can be rewritten as follows:

$$\frac{\text{S x (\% premium or discount) x (number of months)}}{\text{12 x 100}}$$

Solving this is straight-forward because the percentage of premium or discount is the same as the difference in interest rates; in this case, 9.00%. The number of months from spot to the forward value date is 6. The forward rate is calculated by finding the number of points (called "pips") to add or subtract from spot.

$$\frac{1.6860 \text{ x } 9.00 \text{ x } 6}{12 \text{ x } 100} \quad \text{or} \quad \frac{91.044}{1200} \text{ or .07587 pips}$$

Do we add or subtract these from spot? If FC has a *lower* yield than HC, it is a premium currency; therefore, forward is at premium to spot, and the pips would be added. In this case, FC has a *higher* yield; therefore, it is a discount currency, so the forward is discounted to spot. The pips, which represent the discount, are subtracted from spot.

1.6860 – .07587 = 1.610, which is approximately the six-month forward rate.

Compare this price with the first sample. By increasing the yield slightly, the slope of the FC line steepens, which *increases* the difference in FC value between spot and future prices (greater depreciation); however, the FC slope line moved closer to the much steeper HC slope line. This *decreases* the difference between spot and forward exchange rates.

Using an annual rate of interest does not introduce sizeable errors when working with forwards of less than one year. If there is a different rate for 30 days or six months (and there usually is), using them instead of the annual rate gives a more accurate reading of the forward nearer to those dates. This is true as long as the same rate period is used for both currencies. For example, a 30-day Eurorate for HC should be compared with a 30-day Eurorate for FC. The Eurorate must be for a time span that is no less than the forward date. A 30-day rate is not accurate for a six-month forward; however, the six month Eurorate can be used for a 30-day forward and be reasonably accurate. As with interest rate parity, the percentage difference in interest rates and exchange rates is very close, but not precise.

Value Changes

Let's adapt the model to more accurately reflect real world currencies. Values differences between currencies are often much greater than interest rate differences; for example, the Deutsche mark may be worth around 57% of a dollar with an interest rate differential between them of perhaps 2%. It is rather awkward to plot both the differences in values and interest rates by a standard measurement of value change.

Rather than comparing one dollar with one Deutsche mark, then, compare the dollar value over time with one dollar's worth of Deutsche marks over the same period of time. In other words, plot the exchange rates. Consider the following prices, reported as of September 14, 1995:

U.S. Dollar / Deutsche mark exchange rate:

Spot	.6725
6 mo.	.6781

Annual interest rate:

Eurodollar	5.88%
Euromark	4.44%

First, find the reciprocal of the Deutsche mark quote of .6725. This value (1.4870) is the indirect quote telling how many Deutsche marks there are in one dollar, and is found by dividing 1 by .6725 (1/.6725 = 1.4870). This gives equal beginning value to the dollar and the Deutsche mark line on the graph.

Figure 5-8 shows the value changes over one year. From a comparison of interest rates over a one year time span, note that the anticipated depreciation of the Deutsche mark is 1.44% less than that of the U.S. dollar. In six months, the difference should be almost half of that, or 0.72%, ignoring the short-term yield curve. Can this assumption be supported?

If we multiply the six-month exchange rate (.6781) by the beginning line value of 1.4870, the result should be the percentage by which the

Deutsche mark is anticipated to appreciate or depreciate in value against the dollar over a six-month period. Remember, if the Deutsche mark pays a lesser rate of interest than the dollar, the Deutsche mark will appreciate. At this time, the Deutsche mark was valued at approximately 100.83% of the dollar, for an appreciation value of .83% (.6781 x 1.4870 = 1.0083). This is close to our projected 0.72%. (1.00 + .0072 = 1.0072). Six-month Eurorates would give greater accuracy; however, no mathematical model is ever precise—trying to quantify the subjective actions of human beings is always risky business!

Figure 5-8: Anticipated Appreciation of Deutsche Mark against the U.S. Dollar

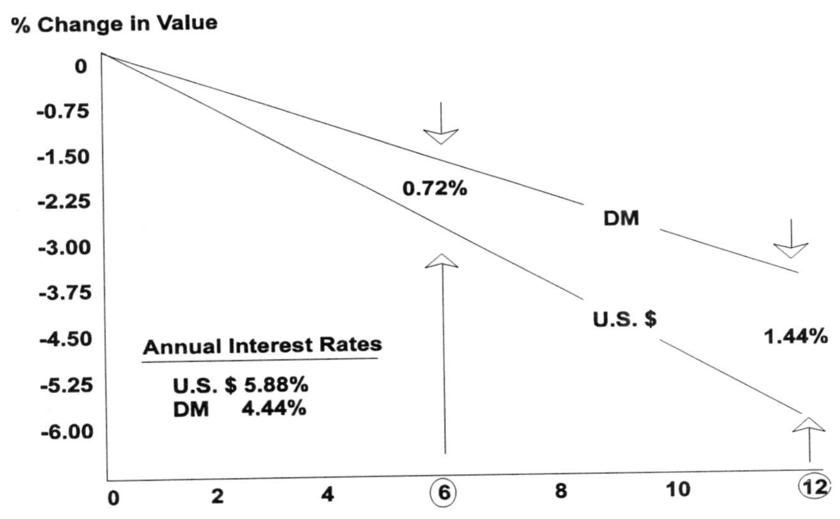

A few simple rules for constructing a chart comparing any two currencies can be found Figure 5-9. Any visual model is only a graphic depiction of the formulas covered earlier, but it may be a useful tool for visualizing the relationships between exchange rates and interest rates, and how each might respond to various external economic factors.

Figure 5-9: Constructing a Relative Depreciation Chart
(See Figure 5-10)

- Beginning from "0 value change," draw line AB to show the anticipated depreciation of the U.S. dollar from spot to one-year forward. Point B equals the annual Eurodollar rate (LIBOR) expressed as a negative number.
- In the same manner, draw line CD to show the anticipated depreciation of another currency. Point D equals the annual Eurorate of the currency (Euromark, Euroyen, etc.) expressed as a negative number.
- Find the constant value which equalizes lines AB and CD at spot by determining the indirect spot exchange rate quote (FC/$).
- To find a percentage difference in value at any time, multiply the constant by the directly quoted exchange rate in effect at that time. In the above example with the Deutsche mark, the constant is 1.4870. The direct quote for spot is .6725. The product of these two numbers is 1.00, which means that the spot rate represents 100% of FC value compared to dollar value, at this time. In six months, the direct quote is .6781. This is multiplied by the same constant of 1.4870, for a product of 1.0083, showing that FC is now 100.83% percent of the dollar in value (it has appreciated).
- If both interest rates can be found, we can find very approximate forward rates using the formula above. If the forward rate is available, one can work backward to find the approximate Eurorate. Remember, any differences between the lines on any specific date will equal the premium or discount of FC to the dollar for that date. In the above example, the difference in interest rates between the dollar and the Deutsche mark 1.44% for twelve months, so presumably one-half that for six months, or 0.72%. This is a premium because it is an appreciating value. Add the premium to 1.00 to arrive at 1.0072, which is the change in value from the spot rate of .6725; therefore, the forward rate should be 100.72% of .6725, or .6773. If the currency were depreciating against the dollar, the difference would be a discount subtracted from 1.00, rather than a premium to be added. Of course, the forward is actually .6781, not .6773, we can see the effects of yield differences between annual and six-month Eurorates, and the inaccuracy of mathematical models.

Figure 5-10: Relative Depreciation Chart

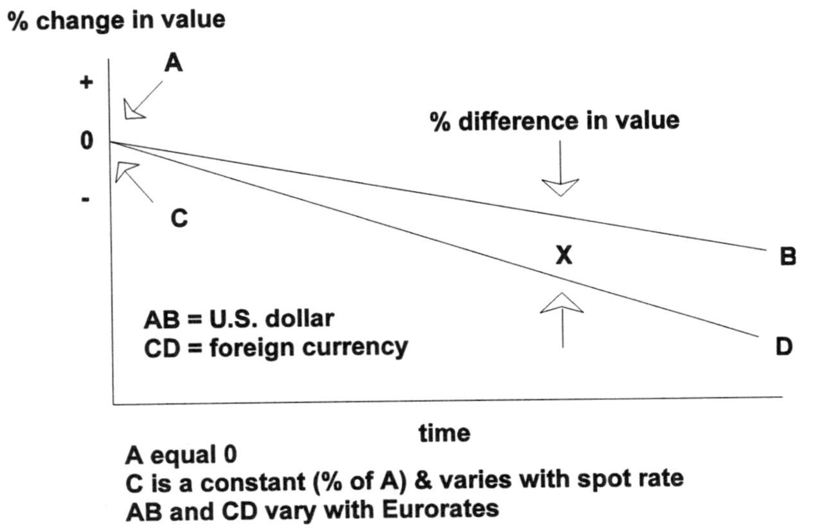

CHAPTER 6

The Markets

The currency market is, in fact, not one, but many currency markets. These markets share price information, and are interconnected. Foreign exchange transactions occur continuously among markets, as well as within markets. Some currency markets have physical locations, such as an exchange floor. Others are simply communication networks—markets without walls, so to speak.

When considering the currency markets, the interbank may be visualized as a cake, and the other markets as thin layers of frosting. In 1992, more than one trillion dollars worth of foreign currency transactions took place daily.[1] The interbank accounted for 96% of this total, the majority of which were exchanges in spot. Within the United States, 51% of all interbank transactions involved spot transactions, with an additional 32% identified as swap transactions. Of the remainder, 8% consisted of options on interbank transactions, and the balance were forward contracts (the "plain vanilla" corporate hedge vehicle). While this is only 5% of the market, which has a total daily notional volume equivalent to 960 billion dollars, there are almost $50 billion dollars worth of forward contracts traded *every day*.

The Interbank

The largest market is the interbank. It is sometimes referred to as "FOREX," although that acronym more accurately designates an association of interbank participants. Some simply refer to it as the "foreign exchange market." The interbank is comprised of a global network of commercial, investment, and merchant banks, along with a number of multinational corporations and other financial institutions. There is no central location, but simply a communication network. There are no floors, no currency pits, there is no open outcry. Currencies are exchanged by phone and computer. Because the interbank is a free-floating global market, it is unregulated by any government. Short of barring international currency trading, government regulators have no practical way to control it. (This does not mean they've stopped looking for one.)

Not all commercial banks are members of this network. It is primarily the domain of large international, national, and regional financial firms. Although its transactional services are sometimes extended to local branches to provide foreign exchange access to retail customers, the actual trading usually remains centralized at a dealing desk in the financial firm's main office.

Singapore, Hong Kong, Zurich, Frankfort, London, New York, and other major financial centers are on stream. The interbank never closes; the off hours are the non-business hours, the nights, and the holidays that roll slowly in and out of certain areas of the web. The trading volume is overwhelming. It easily absorbs transactions of such "customers" as the Federal Reserve Board and other central banks. After a few brief days of battle in August, 1993, France, its foreign reserves exhausted, went down in glorious defeat defending the *franc fort*. It was interbank trading that did it in.

The Foreign Exchange Broker

One participant in the interbank market is the foreign exchange broker. This person acts in the same capacity as any securities or futures broker. He is the intermediary between principals in a transaction. He brings the buyer and seller together, facilitating the transaction. For his efforts, he receives a commission paid by the principals. He doesn't realize a profit or loss on the transaction and has no economic interest in which way the market goes. Firms and individuals act as brokers on the interbank for a clientele of banks. Through their efforts, bank dealers find counterparts for transactions or acquire current information about the market.

The interbank system contains "resting orders," similar to those on an exchange. These are open orders as yet unfilled, awaiting a specific price. They are posted as bids ("buys") and offers ("sells"). The broker's role is to keep track of the current bids and offers, which are continuously updated and displayed on a computer monitor in a "quote stream." In response to an inquiry as to where the market is, he will report the highest bid and lowest offer currently displayed. To maintain confidentiality, he does not divulge the names of the banks making the bids or offers until a trade actually occurs. In very lightly traded markets, the broker often performs the additional service of phoning various banks trying to find a buyer or seller to fill a client order. Brokers need volume to sustain their business, and normally restrict their efforts to the key currencies.

The Foreign Exchange Dealer

Most participating banks in the interbank market act as dealers. The term *dealer* refers to both the bank and to the individual trader. Most foreign exchange dealers are employed by banks or by other financial institutions such as large brokerage houses. Some work for smaller, private firms or are self-employed. The primary difference between a broker and a dealer is method of compensation. Whereas the broker receives commissions, a dealer receives a "cut" on the deal. Because the dealer is a principal or trades on behalf of a principal, he places his firm's money at risk. Dealers may deal directly with other dealers or banks, or through a broker. A "deal" may take place for one of several reasons. The dealer, who we'll assume works for a bank:

1. is a market maker and responds to an inquiry for a quote from another dealer;
2. is an in-house or proprietary trader and takes a position seeking to profit from price changes in the market;
3. generates transactions for revenue by capturing spreads between bids and offers while offsetting market risk in his portfolio through other dealers;
4. initiates a transaction to obtain currency required for his bank's international operations;
5. responds to a client order to buy or sell a currency;
6. initiates a transaction to cover or offset a previous transaction for a client or with another dealer or broker.

The Market Maker

The dealer network runs on reciprocity. A major bank dealer is expected to make a market in the currencies he trades. As a market maker, he gives two quotes in response to an inquiry from another dealer. These represent the price at which he'll buy (bid) and the (somewhat higher) price at which he'll sell (offer). It's easy to see the importance of reciprocity. If a dealer is less than forthright in naming both prices, he'll soon receive very few inquiries. Moreover, he will find it more difficult to obtain fair prices when he makes his own inquiries to other dealers. Some U.S. branches of foreign banks act as market makers for their home currencies. This is especially important for small countries with infrequently traded currencies. The market maker is entrusted to stand behind the currency as the dealer of last resort, always available to either buy or sell upon request.

Interbank Transactions

Spot and forward currencies are both traded in the form of *contracts* governing exchange of one currency for another at an agreed upon price. Because foreign exchange is such a rapid-fire business, the contracts necessarily are very simple and straight forward. There are standard terms which are rarely changed, plus particular terms that "fill in the blanks" for each contract. The standard terms include the following:

- The contract is binding on both parties. It is oral rather than written; therefore, phone conversations between dealers are almost always taped in case of dispute.
- The contract is irrevocable and non-assignable.
- Both currencies are delivered on the same value date. This can be any date that constitutes a banking day in the countries of the currencies involved. (The banks must be open in both countries to make and accept delivery.) The value date for *spot* transactions is two business days after the transaction, except for Canadian dollar contracts transacted in North America, which are one business day. Contracting for a value date later than the spot date results in a forward contract.
- Delivery must take place in the home country of each of the currencies in the transaction. Spanish pesetas are delivered (transferred) between accounts in banks in Spain. Canadian dollars are delivered (transferred) from one bank account to another in Canada, U.S. dollars are transferred between accounts in the United States, etc.
- Delivery is based on wire transfer instructions given by the recipient. Each party gives delivery instructions to the other regarding name of bank, account number, and so forth.

- Delivery may be waived by either party through the process of *offset*, which consists of "buying in" or "selling back" an existing contract. Offset is central to foreign currency risk management.

Non-standardized provisions include the amount of currency exchanged, the value date or date of delivery, and the rate of exchange. Although any amount can be contracted, industry practice is to deal in increments of $1,000,000 (or $1,000,000 worth of currency). This compares to the 100 share "round lot" traded on stock exchanges. Trades for less than $1,000,000 are analogous to "odd lot" trading, and are much costlier to transact, per unit.

Price Quotes

The U.S. dollar is always one of the two currencies in any rate of exchange. Currency prices are quoted either *directly* or *indirectly*. Direct quotes express the number of U.S. dollars that equal one unit of foreign currency. For the most part, direct quotes are used in the examples in this manual. Indirect quotes express the number of foreign currency units that are in one U.S. dollar. The interbank uses indirect quotes for all but a few currencies. Traditionally, certain currencies, such as the British pound and Irish punt, are quoted directly.

The Spread

Banks are notoriously unwilling risk takers. Although bank dealers may be very agile in the fast-paced world of foreign exchange, the risk of loss from a major move in exchange rates is quite often unacceptable. The quantities of currency traded in a single day by one individual can easily amount to hundreds of millions of dollars. In these amounts, even a moderate adverse move could substantially affect the quarterly earnings of a mid-sized bank. Rather than trying to profit from changes in exchange rates, most banks generate revenues from the *spread* between the offer and the bid. Buying currency for resale (or selling currency for repurchase) is conceptually no different from borrowing money at one price and lending it at another; however, there is no assurance that currency can be resold or repurchased at a profit if it's held for more than a few seconds. Banks rarely buy and hold for any length of time. When they sell $10,000,000 worth of currency for one value date, they often resell it for another value date as quickly as possible. Much of the time, both transactions are done simultaneously. The spread between the bid and offer is measured in "pips," the same term used to designate the discount or premium points between spot and forward contracts. Consider the following:

Deutsche mark

Spot	1.4870	Bid	1.4865	Offer	1.4875
30-day forward	1.4847	Bid	1.4841	Offer	1.4853

A dealer might quote *spot* at a bid of 1.4865 and an offer of 1.4875, or "65–75," indicating a spread of 10 pips. Notice that the spot price above is the "mid-price." It is precisely midway between the bid and the offer. An interbank quote refers to a bid and offer of *U.S. dollars*. In this case, the dealer is quoting the prices at which he will buy or sell dollars for Deutsche marks, not Deutsche marks for dollars.

If asked to bid on 30-days forward, the dealer may respond, "41-53," for a 12-pip spread, showing a bid 6 pips lower and an offer 6 pips higher than the mid-price of 1.4847. Quotes for forwards of one year or longer have wider spreads up to as much as 200 pips, to account for the higher risk and lower trading volume of distant value dates. Consequently, most activity centers around spot exchanges and forwards out to 90 days.

Interbank Dealing

Let's assume that a U.S. bank—call it *Ourtown Bank*—discovers that it must make a deposit with its correspondent bank in Milan, Italy, and maintain that deposit for thirty days. It requires 8 billion Italian lira for this deposit.

To accomplish this, the dealer for *Ourtown Bank* calls the dealer who trades for *Crosstown Bank* and asks for a two-way quote on lira. The quote is agreeable, and the two dealers enter into a spot contract to exchange 8 billion lira for $4,959,702, based on the spot *dollar bid* of 1613. Two days later, when the trade clears, *Crosstown* transfers 8 billion lira from its account in Rome to *Ourtown's* account in Milan. In turn, *Ourtown* transfers $4,959,702 from its domestic (foreign exchange) account to *Crosstown's* (foreign exchange) account.

If *Ourtown* wanted to keep the lira to satisfy a payable, for example, this would be the end of the transaction; however, *Ourtown* needs the lira for only thirty days, at which time it wants to re-exchange them for U.S. dollars. For this reason, before the two dealers enter into the spot transaction, they also reach an agreement on the second transaction. The dealer of *Ourtown* asks for, and receives, a *dollar offer* for lira 30 days forward. The quote is 1627, reflecting a forward discount. This transaction, in which *Ourtown* resells the lira to *Crosstown* for $4,917,025, and the spot transaction are entered simultaneously.

Thirty days later, both banks reverse the direction of currency flows. *Ourtown* delivers 8 billion lira to *Crosstown's* account in Rome, and *Crosstown* delivers $4,917,025 to *Ourtown's* domestic (foreign exchange) account. The two-stage transaction leaves *Crosstown* with a credit of $42,677, which approximately offsets the higher lira interest foregone by Crosstown in the deal, plus the spread. (See Figure 6-1, 6-2, and 6-3 for a summary.)

Figure 6-1: Foreign Exchange Swap of Italian Lira

Sept 05	Ourtown sells $ for	8 billion lira	Spot	$4,959,702 bid by Crosstown
Sept 05	Ourtown buys $ for	8 billion lira	30 day	$4,917,025 offered by Crosstown
Sept 07	Ourtown transfers	$4,959,702	to Crosstown	
Sept 07	Crosstown transfers	8 billion lira	to Ourtown	
Oct 05	Ourtown transfers	8 billion lira	to Crosstown	
Oct 05	Crosstown transfers	$4,917,025	to Ourtown	

Spot bid Rate: 1613; 30 Day Offer Rate: 1627
Difference in dollars reflects both bid - offer spread and 30 day discount
Dealers bid and offer dollars for foreign currency, not foreign currency for dollars.

This double transaction is known as a *foreign exchange swap*,* It is by far the most common type of foreign exchange operation engaged in by commercial banks. You might recognize this operation for what it really is: a currency hedge by both banks. Assuming that both *Ourtown* and *Crosstown* start out with balanced lira accounts, the spot trade, by itself, creates a lira exposure for both. Ourtown contracts a lira asset, and Crosstown picks up a lira liability (because it has to get the currency for delivery from somewhere). The forward trade simply hedges the spot

* A *foreign exchange swap* should not be confused with a *currency swap*, which is a more complex transaction between private parties.

trade by locking in the return price; therefore, no intermediate change in exchange rates will affect the ending balance already locked in.

Foreign exchange swaps vary, depending on the needs of the participating banks. A *tomorrow/next* swap, or *roll over*, exchanges currency of the next business day and reverses the trade the following day. A bank expecting to meet a foreign currency liability within the next two weeks or so, but uncertain of the exact date, may do a spot transaction for the currency and simply "roll over" the contract from one day to the next, thereby remaining hedged until the payment date arrives. Other swaps are *spot/forward*, as in our example above, or *forward/forward*, in which a forward contract is initiated, then reversed at a later date.

Figure 6-2: Forward Contracts and Swaps

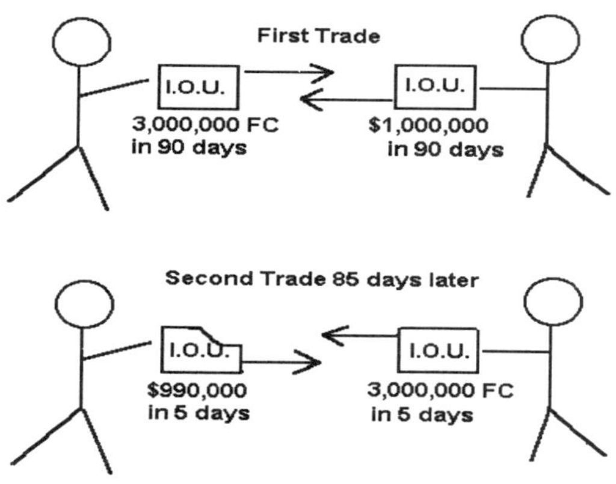

A forward contract between two dealers may be viewed as an exchange of I.O.U.s. The amounts are based on the forward rate in effect on the day of the exchange. In this case, the 90-day forward rate of FC/$ is 3.00. Delivery does not take place if either dealer decides to "swap back" the I.O.U. before the delivery date. The second trade is initiated at the then-current forward rate for the same delivery date, which very likely differs from the original forward rate. Here, the rate has changed to 3.03. The difference is settled in dollars.

Figure 6-3: Ourtown Bank and Crosstown Bank Offset Transaction

Date	Bought/Sold	Value Date	Price*
Jan. 26	B 1.7 bil lira	Feb. 2	1704
Jan. 27	B 2.4 bil	Feb. 2	1703
Feb. 1	S 1.7 bil	Feb. 2	1706
Feb. 2	2.4 bil lira received at		1703

*Indirect quote

Ourtown Bank buys 4.1 billion lira February 2 forwards from *Crosstown Bank*, and five days later sells 1.7 billion lira February 2 forwards to *Crosstown.* It would be cumbersome for *Ourtown* to deliver 1.7 billion lira to *Crosstown* in exchange for U.S. dollars, and in return receive 4.1 billion lira from *Crosstown* in exchange for U.S. dollars. To avoid this, the transactions that offset each other are canceled out. On February 2nd, *Crosstown* delivers 2.4 billion lira to *Ourtown,* and receives approximately $1.49 million dollars in exchange, which equals the contracted rate of 1613 lira per dollar. In a separate accounting, *Ourtown* simply credits $1304 to *Crosstown's* U.S. account, representing the loss on the purchase and sale of 1.7 billion lira.

Central Bank Transactions

When one or more central banks decide to intervene, they conduct their operations in the interbank market. Whether buying or selling a currency to influence the price, the trades are done as described above. Specifically, the central bank calls upon one or more bank dealers or private dealers, usually selected from a stable of those with whom it has dealt with in the past and has developed good working relationships.

Central banks may intervene overtly or covertly, depending on whether or not it wants to publicize its activities. If it intervenes overtly, it deals directly with various banks and is forthright about the reasons for the trades. It can operate covertly by going through non-bank intermediaries (perhaps brokers or private dealers), or apportioning the trades among a number of banks throughout the world.

The Futures Exchange

There are significant differences between the interbank and the futures exchanges. While the interbank is a network of participating dealers, futures exchanges are housed in central locations similar to stock exchanges. Four U.S. futures exchanges trade currencies. Two are also commodity exchanges which traded goods such as pork bellies and cattle long before they developed currency futures. These are the Chicago Mercantile Exchange (CME) and the MidAmerica Commodity Exchange (MidAm), both in Chicago, and the Financial Exchange, or FINEX, which is a division of the New York Cotton Exchange.

The third exchange, the Philadelphia Board of Trade, lists currency futures; however, at the present time, their currency contracts are rarely traded and not a factor in the overall market. (The related Philadelphia Stock Exchange with its listed currency *options* is another matter, and very much a presence in the market.) Besides U.S. futures exchanges, there are futures exchanges in other financial centers around the world. Their trading facilities are available through many U.S.-based brokerage firms and foreign brokers with U.S. branches. Some exchanges, for example, the CME and the Singapore International Monetary Exchange (SIMEX) are electronically linked to permit trades entered into on one exchange to be closed out on the other.

The primary problem with the futures market is the limited selection of currencies traded; however, new contracts are being added. Appendix II includes a listing of international futures exchanges and the currencies traded on them.

Trading Futures

Currency futures on the CME and MidAm trade like commodities, which they are. They are bought and sold by open outcry in the same manner as corn, cotton, and lumber. A separate ring (or "pit") dedicated to each currency is located in one area of the exchange floor. The CME has a glassed-in viewing area for visitors located high above the floor. From that vantage point, the pits appear to contain crowds of people bunched together, standing around quietly or engaged in activity that at times falls just short of physical combat. Information on which contract, how many contracts, whether they are being bought or sold, and at what price, is conveyed orally (shouting) and with hand signals (flailing of limbs). This is known as trading by *open outcry*.

The currency futures market is the beneficiary of a long and established heritage. Compared to the futures markets, the interbank is brand new. Futures have traded in Chicago since the 1800s, and the CME currency pits today are an outgrowth of a lot of trial and error. The MidAm is a smaller version of the CME which trades off the CME quote stream. It also offers contracts of half the size, an important feature when trying to manage smaller exposures.

Unlike the interbank, futures exchanges are subject to federal government restrictions. They are regulated by the Commodity Futures Trading Commission (CFTC), a federal agency akin to the SEC. While this may create some inefficiencies due to red tape, the overall market efficiencies are so great that trading volumes are large and growing.

Although nothing is more frenetic than the currency pits at the CME during the close of trading, customer loss due to mis-communication is extremely rare, and loss due to credit risk is virtually nonexistent because no credit is extended. It is strictly a cash business. The clearinghouse stands behind every contract traded, and futures brokerage firms financially substantial enough to be clearing members stand behind the clearinghouse. Every day, the books are squared to match up trades from the session's trading. Until the books balance, the market does not re-open.

The Futures Broker

The term *futures broker* is somewhat ambiguous. There is both a legal and a popular definition. Legally, a broker is an entity such as a financial institution that is registered to trade futures for the public; for example, the securities firm Prudential Securities is also classified as a futures broker. This means it is legally registered as a futures broker, or *Futures Commission Merchant* (FCM). This registration allows the firm to provide futures brokerage services to the public and to take custody of client funds. Another type of brokerage firm is an *Introducing Broker* (IB). Introducing brokers provide brokerage services in the same manner as an FCM, but are not authorized to accept client funds; therefore, they are not required to meet the strict financial requirements of an FCM. Introducing brokers, then, pass client funds through to the FCM with which they are associated for safekeeping.

The public often uses the term *futures broker* to identify any individual who is a member of the profession. Individuals who open and service client accounts and effect transactions while in the employ of an FCM or IB are legally referred to as "Associated Persons," yet are often referred to as *brokers*.

Futures brokers operate the same way interbank foreign exchange brokers do; they are compensated by commission. They have no economic interest in the profit or loss on a transaction, which is referred to as a "trade." The interbank market *deals.* The futures market *trades.* Clients may be speculators, pools of speculators, corporate hedgers, or mutual fund managers. Individual futures brokers operate from every financial center in the world. Very few trade on the floor of the exchange itself. Those who do are referred to as *floor brokers*, or *pit brokers*. The others phone or wire clients' orders in to them and they, in turn, trade with each other and the *floor traders* in the pit.

The Floor Trader

The role of the dealer in the interbank is paralleled by the floor trader on the futures exchange. Floor traders are members of an exchange who have direct access to the trading floor. Like dealers, traders trade for their own accounts or for the accounts of their firms. One difference between floor traders and interbank dealers has to do with the element of risk. There is no doubt that many interbank dealers can and do accept risk trying to profit from exchange rate volatility. The *Banque de France* discovered how willingly interbank dealers speculate with huge sums at stake. Also, many individual currency speculators trade exclusively through the interbank; however, as we pointed out, most dealers—at least most bank dealers—are far more heavily engaged in swapping currency than in naked speculation. Their objective is to derive revenue from the spread. Risk is often limited to the lag time permitted before completing the offsetting transaction of the swap.

Not so with the floor trader. Most traders in the currency pits maintain continuous exposures to exchange rates. They may be buying and selling currencies the same day, but usually not at the same time. By and large, the business of a floor trader is risk-taking, not risk avoidance.

The Speculator

Floor traders are speculators (everyone who trades currency futures is either a speculator or a hedger). Speculation is a serious occupation, and books are written about how to go about it. The major objective is to cut losses short and let profits accumulate. To keep losses small, traders must get out of losing positions quickly—ahead of the crowd. Floor traders do this by working in the pits for six hours, making bids and offers, opening and closing positions quickly. Unlike the interbank etiquette, there is no reciprocity here. Traders do not inform each other what they are *willing* to offer or bid. They just offer, bid, or say nothing.

This constant activity is responsible for a different "sense of time" common to many participants of the futures market. It is sometimes difficult for a corporate treasurer to relay to a broker that "long term" in currency hedges does not mean until next Tuesday. There's no sense even trying to communicate with floor traders. To them, any position held longer than a month belongs in a retirement account.

While it is important to be aware of the difference between speculators and hedgers, it is also important to realize that speculators play a crucial role in providing market liquidity, allowing hedgers to enter and exit the markets at will. There is no futures market without speculators or traders. Currency management (hedging) depends on speculators willing to make a market. The *raison d'être* for currency futures is to provide a conveyance for transferring exposure risk (hedging). As currency managers, the objective is to transfer the risk of potentially adverse exchange rate changes to someone else. If another hedger does not take the position, someone else must be willing and able to accept the risk; someone whose incentive is the potential profit from price moves. This is the speculator. Speculation gives the markets the liquidity and depth required to ensure ease of entry and exit, and is a necessary counterpart of risk management.

The Commodity Trading Adviser

Commodity trading advisers (CTAs) fulfill another role in the futures market. These people are similar to brokers in the sense that they trade with clients' money and have a fiduciary responsibility to them. Unlike brokers, they are compensated by management and performance fees, rather than by commissions; thus, they have a direct economic interest in the profitability of every trade. CTAs are similar to investment advisers in the securities industry. They manage individual futures accounts, limited partnerships, and public funds for speculators in the same way investment advisers manage mutual stock and bond funds. Some CTAs publish their advice rather than managing accounts. They do this through newsletters or by phone via a daily "hot line."

Although many CTAs trade the full range of commodity and financial futures, others specialize, for example, in grains, metals, or currencies. Most limit their efforts to speculation because speculators want to profit from trading opportunities. CTAs are compensated by how well they meet this objective. Risk management, being more long term and less opportunistic, gets little attention from an industry dependent on trading profits for its livelihood.

Tomorrow's Futures Market

Open outcry has a rich heritage. Unfortunately, the system is antiquated, almost quaint, and bound to change. Modern day communications and computer power will sweep away the sight of traders standing together in a single location to fix the exchange rates of the world. In fact, it is already happening.

The CME and its counterpart in Paris, the *Marché a Terme International de France* (MATIF), have taken a step toward computerization with the Globex system, a computerized communication network with a host computer that automatically matches buy and sell orders. Globex products include CME currency futures contracts and MATIF financial contracts. Terminals for accessing the host computer are located in New York, Chicago, Tokyo, London, and Paris. Exchange members who have undergone training in the use of the system are the principal traders. This network is an extension of the futures exchange, not a substitute. It allows almost 24-hour trading, with off times prior to and immediately following hours of exchange trading to permit updating. A number of other exchanges are also on line with automated systems. A trend is emerging in which open auction trading is being replaced or supplemented by computerized trading. Besides Globex, exchanges trading currencies and/or interest rates are fully or partially automated in the financial centers of Belgium, France, Germany, Spain, U.K., Japan, and elsewhere.

Currency Futures Contracts

The interbank network and the currency pits of the futures exchanges can be considered to perform twin functions in one overall market. There is so much interplay between them that prices in both markets rise and fall in parallel almost tick for tick. When a currency trades up 30 "pips' in the interbank market, it almost instantly trades up a comparable number of "tics" on the futures exchanges. The prices correlate well for the same reason other parities remain in line: arbitrageurs seize the moment if they don't. Just as the MidAm follows the CME, traders at the CME continuously watch the interbank.

Unlike interbank forward contracts, futures contracts are completely standardized. The only thing not fixed is the price. A contract for a particular currency contains a specific number of units to be delivered in a specific manner at a specific time.

Figure 6-4: The Trail of a Futures Trade

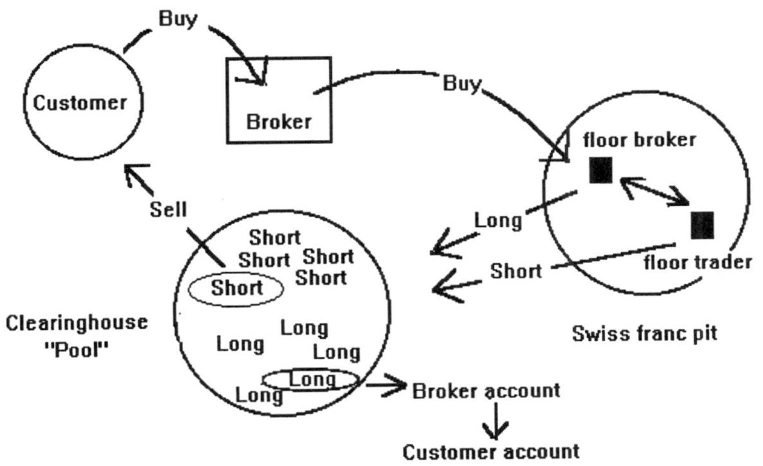

The path followed by a customer's order for a futures contract is complex. Here, a customer wishes to purchase a contract for Swiss francs. He phones his order to a broker who, in turn, phones the order to a floor broker on the exchange. The floor broker fills the order by trading with a floor trader who sells him the same contract. At this point, the floor broker has a long position, and the floor trader a short position. At the end of the trading session, both positions are entered in the clearinghouse account.

The clearinghouse holds all positions in an unmatched condition. They are assigned to the various customers' accounts, and marked to the market daily. When an offsetting position is assigned to the same account, the two are matched up, closing the position. Both positions disappear from the customer's account, resulting in a realized gain or loss.

The size of a futures contract is much smaller than an interbank contract, as little as a 1/10th the size of the standard interbank increment of $1,000,000. Another major difference involves value dates. For futures, there are only four standard value dates, and they are not even called value dates, but rather "last trading days." They correspond to calendar year quarters, falling on the third Mondays of March, June, September, and December (except Canadian Dollars which fall on the third Tuesdays). Other last trading days are listed, but are usually inactive. There are also "rolling spot" contracts, each lasting one week. When one expires, another begins trading. These are similar in concept to interbank spot transactions, and are available in Deutsche marks and British pounds on the Chicago Mercantile Exchange.

The interbank is well set up to facilitate delivery. Although forward contracts can be offset, they are usually delivered on. The futures market, on the other hand, is most efficient when offset is used to terminate contracts—which is more than 95% of the time.

The most confusing difference between the interbank and the futures markets is the different method of quoting price. The interbank quotes indirectly, with bids and offers made for U.S. dollars. The futures market quotes directly for the most part, with bids and offers referring to foreign currency. This language difference stems from the fact that currencies are considered commodities of sorts, and are traded as such.

Table 6-1 shows the contract specifications for currency futures listed on the CME.

Table 6-1: Contract Specifications

Currency	Symbol	Size of Contract	Form of Quote
Australian dollar	AD	A$100,000	direct
Brazilian real	BR	BR100,000	direct
British Pound	BP	£62,500	direct
Canadian dollar	CD	C$100,000	direct
Deutsche mark	DM	DM125,000	direct
French franc	FR	FF500,00	direct
Japanese yen	JY	J¥12,500,000	direct
Mexican peso	MP	MP500,000	direct
Swiss franc	SF	SF125,000	direct
Cross Rates			
DM/JY	DJ	DM125,000 x DM/JY rate	JY per DM
Rolling Spot			
British pound	RP	£250,000	direct
Deutsche mark	RD	US$250,000	indirect

The Options Market

Spot, forward, and futures contracts all represent agreements to exchange currency. Terms, such as the rate of exchange, are left open until the agreement is finalized in the form of a trade. Currency options, on the other hand, represent future spot, forward, and futures contracts and are bought and sold as a type of security. They are similar to any other type of option, including real estate options, stock options, etc. Options convey the right to the option purchaser to buy or sell something sometime in the future at a predetermined rate or price. For example, the option may convey the right to buy a particular residence for $200,000. In a similar fashion, a currency option may convey the right to buy or sell 1,200,000 Canadian dollars for 1,000,000 U.S. dollars. The buyer pays the seller for the right to buy or sell at a fixed price at a future time. He can choose either to exercise his right or to allow it to expire. The buyer can walk away from the deal at any time; however, the seller is obligated to fulfill his part of the bargain whenever he is called upon to do so by the buyer.

There are two types of options: *calls* and *puts*. Foreign exchange calls and puts can be defined at follows:

- A *call* is an option to buy a foreign currency (or foreign currency futures contract) for U.S. dollars at a specific rate of exchange.
- A *put* is an option to sell a foreign currency (or foreign currency futures contract) for U.S. dollars at a specific exchange rate.

Currency options, like other foreign exchange products, do not involve transfers of physical certificates or agreements. They are contracted orally and exist in the form of accounting entries. Also like other currency agreements, they are marked to market daily.

Exchange-Traded Currency Options

Currency options are specific types of contracts conveying rights to buy or sell spot contracts. These are listed on the Philadelphia Stock Exchange (PHLX) and several international exchanges. Like futures contracts, currency options are standardized in size. They are offered at specific exchange rates for specific value dates. Like other exchange-traded products, these options are available through security or futures brokerage firms. They trade the same way futures contracts trade. They also clear the same way, with the clearinghouse taking the role of buyer for every seller and seller for every buyer. If an option results in a currency exchange, the clearinghouse acts as the intermediary, effecting the exchange between buyer and seller.

To facilitate the combining of futures and currency options in trading positions, currency options on the PHLX are exactly one-half the size of futures contracts. The listed options on the PHLX and the contract sizes are shown in Table 6-2.

Table 6-2: PHLX Currency Options

Currency	Units
British pounds	31,250
Australian dollars	50,000
Canadian dollars	50,000
Deutsche marks	62,500
Swiss francs	62,500
ECU	62,500
French francs	250,000
Japanese yen	6,250,000
Cross rates	
Deutsche Mark/Japanese Yen	62,500 DM
British Pound/Deutsche Mark	31,250 BP
British Pound/Japanese Yen	31,250BP

Over-the-Counter Options

Over-the-counter options are bought and sold by banks and other financial institutions for themselves and for their clients. These are similar to exchange-traded options, but are not standardized. The size of the contract, the value date, the forward rate, and the price are all determined between the buyer and seller on an option-by-option basis. Pricing models are available to estimate a fair market value for options under practically any market condition. As with other interbank transactions, no clearinghouse is involved. This introduces a credit risk not encountered with exchange-traded products because the obligated seller may default. The advantage in dealing with over-the-counter options is the fact that they can be customized for the buyers' and sellers' particular situations. This benefit is somewhat offset by the lack of a well-established secondary market (although one is emerging). The buyer or seller may have a difficult time liquidating a position tailored for a unique financial condition.

Options on Currency Futures

An option on a currency futures contract is an exchange-traded contract giving the buyer the right to buy or sell a currency futures contract sometime in the future at a predetermined price. The CME lists options for each currency futures contract it trades. Futures and options on futures are traded with positions entered in the same brokerage account. One option exercises into one futures contract of the same currency and expiration.

An example will illustrate the purpose and outcome of trading currency futures options. Assume that Phil Smith is the treasurer of a U.S. firm called Baker Company. The company submits a bid valued at approximately $1,000,000 for used construction machinery being sold by a British firm. The bid is in British pounds, so a foreign exchange loss will occur if the bid is accepted and the British pound then increases in value.

Responding to this potential exposure, Phil buys 10 CME call options on March British Pound futures. These provide him with the right to go long March British pound futures at the (currently traded) price of 1.50. The 10 contracts are equivalent to 620,000 British pounds, with a value of $930,000. Baker Company's bid is accepted, and the British pound increases in value to $1.65; therefore, Phil exercises the options. The next day, the option position in his account is replaced by a long position of 10 British pound futures contracts priced at 1.50. Because the account is marked to the market daily, there is also a profit of $0.15 per pound, or $93,000.

Phil can either sell the futures and take the profit, or allow the position to be converted to British pounds during the delivery period, then deliver the currency to purchase the machinery. Either way, he has effectively hedged the exposure. When Phil exercised the calls and received the long futures positions in his account, a seller of the same options chosen by the clearinghouse was notified that his brokerage account now holds a short futures position of British pounds in place of his option position. This futures position shows a $93,000 loss, corresponding to the gain in the Baker account.

The Currency Swap Market

Recall that a foreign exchange swap is two interbank spot or forward contracts paired together, one offsetting the other. The effect is the same as borrowing and repaying funds denominated in a particular currency with the exchange rate locked in. A *currency swap* does the same thing. The primary difference concerns the participants, who are two private parties, rather than dealers; the length of time, which is often measured in years rather than weeks or months; and the repayment, which takes place incrementally rather than in a single transaction.

A relatively new development in foreign exchange is the advent of the currency swap market. This market is similar to the interbank. There is no central location; it consists solely of a telecommunication web, international in scope, and available to a growing number of swap dealers. Swaps in currencies and interest rates comprise a two trillion dollar a day business, rivaling the interbank in size. (The interbank does one trillion dollars a day in currency alone.) The "market makers" are members of the International Swap Dealers Association (ISDA) an organization that includes merchant, investment, and commercial banks, and other financial institutions. One purpose of the Association is to educate risk managers and governmental regulatory agencies to the benefits of the currency swap market. Another is to standardize agreement forms, legal obligations, and terminology. Like over-the-counter options, currency swaps are non-standardized. In fact, the definition is still evolving. New concepts and terms of agreement are constantly being developed and negotiated by potential market participants.

Reading *The Wall Street Journal*

One of the primary tools of currency management is a daily financial publication covering the foreign exchange markets. *The Wall Street Journal* is a good example. The *Journal* often prints information regarding currencies from a geopolitical standpoint in the "International" pages of the first section. The world credit markets and foreign exchange rates are covered in the section entitled "Money and Investing."

Cross Rates

The *Key Currency Cross Rates* in Figure 6-5 show the currencies of the major U.S. trading partners as they might appear in *The Wall Street Journal*. It provides an overview of the interbank market. The quotes are from "Late New York Trading Oct. 9, 1995," which is approximately 3:00 P.M. Eastern time, after the Chicago currency futures markets are closed. Notice that the U.S. dollar exchange rate is quoted indirectly in the columns and directly in the rows. For example, the first column shows that there are 1.1465 Swiss francs (*Switzerland*) in one U.S. dollar. The bottom row, under "SFranc" shows that there are .87222 dollars in one Swiss franc. The product of these two numbers equals one (actually slightly more due to rounding).

While "exchange rate" means the conversion value of two currencies, one of which is the U.S. dollar, a "cross rate" is the rate of exchange of two currencies, neither of which is the U.S. dollar. You may recall that cross rates are calculated by factoring the dollar out of the equation. For example, you can multiply the indirect quote for the Swiss franc (1.1465) by the direct quote for the British pound (1.5740). The product is 1.8046, which is shown as the SF/£ cross rate, or the number of Swiss francs in one British pound.

Figure 6-5: Key Currency Cross Rates Late New York Trading Oct 19, 1995

	Dollar	Pound	SFranc	Guilder	Peso	Yen	Lira	D-Mark	FFranc	CdnDlr
Canada.......	1.3407	2.1103	1.1694	.85167	.20100	.01336	.00084	.95390	.27096	
France.......	4.9480	7.7882	4.3157	3.1432	.74183	.04931	.00310	3.5205		3.6906
Germany......		1.4055	2.2123	1.2259	.89283	.21072	.01401	.00088		.28405
Italy........	1598.0	2515.3	1393.8	1015.1	239.58	15.924		1137.0	322.96	1191.9
Japan........	100.35	157.95	87.527	63.747	15.045		.06280	71.398	20.281	74.849
Mexico.......	6.6700	10.499	5.8177	4.2371		.06647	.00417	4.7456	1.3480	4.9750
Netherlands..	1.5742	2.4778	1.3730		.23601	.01569	.00099	1.1200	.31815	1.1742
Switzerland..	1.1465	1.8046		.72831	.17189	.01143	.00072	.81572	.23171	.85515
U.K.	.63532		.55414	.40359	.09525	.00633	.00040	.45203	.12840	.47387
U.S.		1.5740	.87222	.63524	.14993	.00997	.00063	.71149	.20210	.74588

Source: Dow Jones Telerate Inc., from *The Wall Street Journal* Oct. 20, 1995

Exchange Rates

Usually on the same page in *The Wall Street Journal* as the Key Currency Cross Rates is the table entitled, *Exchange Rates* (See Figure 6-6 on page 123). The heading describes these quotes as "Interbank selling rates by Bankers Trust Company." Recall that, with indirect quotes, interbank dealers offer dollars for foreign currency. Retail transactions, such as those between corporations and banks, are conducted at lower offers (fewer dollars per foreign currency unit) with *bids* providing fewer foreign currency units per dollar. Thus, "selling rates" refers to offers quoted directly, not indirectly. The table shows both forms of quotation.

There is a communication problem concerning foreign exchange. We often read or hear about a particular currency rate "going up" or "dropping." What does this mean? Did the exchange rate for the British pound go up or down between Monday and Tuesday? If the British pound weakened against the dollar, the British pound exchange rate went up *and* down, depending on how it's quoted. Care must be taken to refer to currencies, not exchange rates, when discussing market movement. Descriptions like "going up" and "going down" need to be carefully defined.

The *Exchange Rates* table below is similar to that found in *The Wall Street Journal*. All quotations are for spot transactions unless otherwise specified. Forward prices are also listed for many of the currencies traded in the futures market. Forward rates are shown for the British pound and Canadian dollar. Notice that both are discount currencies, so their Eurorate yields are higher than corresponding LIBOR (Eurodollar) rates.

Although forwards can be transacted for any "good" date, the 30-day, 90-day, and 180-day forwards have become standardized as market rate indicators. Dealers, arbitrageurs, and speculators normally initiate trades with *even-dated* forwards (exactly one week, one month, three months, etc.) Hedgers try to contract specifically dated forwards that correspond to their exposures. These may be even dates or odd dates. In either case, once transacted, a value date is fixed. Value dates for later offsetting trades must conform to the date fixed by the original trade.

Philadelphia Options

Currency options quotes for trading taking place on the Philadelphia Stock Exchange (PHLX) are usually printed on the same page as exchange rates. Below is sample price information for the British pound. The PHLX facilitates trades in regular options for March, June, September, and December, and two nearby months. Options expire on the Saturday before the third Wednesday of the month. Options contracts are exactly one-half the size of CME futures contracts to allow cross trading between the markets. Options expire five days earlier than the expirations of futures to allow coordination between exercise, delivery, and future contract value dates. End-of-Month (EOM) options are also traded on the PHLX, and the statistics for those expiring in the three nearest months are published in *The Wall Street Journal*. EOM options expire on the Saturday following the last Friday of the month, which is about a week later than regular options. *Long-term* options, with durations of 18 to 36 months, are not covered by the *Journal.*

Figure 6-6: Exchange Rates

Tuesday, February 15, 1994

The New York foreign exchange selling rates below apply to trading among banks in amounts of $1 million and more, as quoted at 3 p.m. Eastern time by Bankers Trust Co., Telerate and other sources. Retail transactions provide fewer units of foreign currency per dollar.

	U.S. $ equiv.		*Currency per U.S. $*	
Country	**Tues.**	**Mon.**	**Tues.**	**Mon.**
Argentina (peso)	1.01	1.01	.99	.99
Australia (Dollar)	.7080	.7093	1.4124	1.4098
Austria (Schilling)	.08250	.08243	12.12	12.13
Bahrain (Dinar)	2.6518	2.6518	.3771	.3771
Belgium (Franc)	.02814	.02809	35.54	35.60
Brazil (Cruzeiro real)	.0018517	.0018510	540.05	540.25
Britain (Pound)	1.4775	1.4855	.6768	.6732
30-day Forward	1.4754	1.4835	.6778	.6741
90-day Forward	1.4718	1.4797	.6794	.6758
180-day Forward	1.4673	1.4753	.6815	.6778
Canada (Dollar)	.7388	.7391	1.3536	.1353
30-day Forward	.7386	.7389	1.3539	1.3533
90-day Forward	.7382	.7386	1.3547	1.3539
180-day Forward	.7375	.7379	.1356	1.3552

Figure 6-7: Philadelphia Options

Tuesday, February 15, 1994

		Calls		Puts	
		vol.	last	vol.	last
BPound					147.74
31,250 British Pound EOM—European					
150	Feb	25	0.25	x	x
British Pound					147.74
31,250 British Pound EOM-cents per unit					
147 ½	Feb	20	0.97	x	x
150	Feb	20	0.25	x	x
150	Mar	4	1.02	x	x
31,250 British Pounds-European units					
142 ½	Apr	x	x	100	0.75
31,250 British Pounds-cents per unit					
142 ½	Apr	5	5.2	120	0.8
145	Mar	9	2.96	13	0.55
145	Apr	x	x	30	1.53
145	Jun	5	4.5	384	2.51
147 ½	Mar	285	1.67	114	1.6
147 ½	Apr	x	5.2	4	2.27
150	Mar	103	0.7	x	x
150	Apr	400	1.41	x	x
150	Jun	10	2.27	x	x

Figure 6-7 contains columns for calls and puts. Each column gives the *volume* (number of options traded that day) and *last* (the premium at the close of trading for the day.) The current mid-quote exchange rate (147.74) appears in bold print. This rate should be less than the selling rate shown in the *Exchange Rate* table.

The first row shows the *European end-of-month option* with a strike price of 150. It expires on the Saturday before the last Friday of February, the expiration month. Premiums are quoted in cents per unit of currency. For the British pound, each cent of premium is worth \$312.50. This option is worth only ¼ of a cent, or \$78. This small amount reflects the slim chance that the British pound will rise to 150 in 5 days. The strike of 150 is the price that the buyer would pay for the currency if he exercised his option. So the British pound would have to actually exceed 150 before the option has any intrinsic value.

The last category is regular *American options*, identified by "cents per unit." American options can be exercised any time until expiration, whereas European options can only be exercised on the last day. Compare the deep-in-the-money 142½ April call with the near-the-money April 147½ call and put. The premium for the 142½ call consists totally of intrinsic value. In fact, it is valued under current spot. Time value, as opposed to intrinsic value, increases the closer the strike price is to spot. Premiums for out-of-the-money options, such as the 150 call or the 145 put, have only time value. Options with strikes close to spot are the most active. This table and others in this section use x to designate options that are inactive or not traded that day.

Currency Futures

The Wall Street Journal publishes the daily futures prices in the Commodities section, but only the most active futures months in each commodity are listed. Currently, the *Journal* reports some months for most currency futures traded on the CME. It also lists currencies traded on other exchanges. The most active contracts are listed together under the heading *Currency*. Less-actively traded contracts, such as the CME French Franc and the FINEX currencies, may be listed in abbreviated form under the heading *Other Futures*. The *Journal* also prints quotes for Eurorate contracts such as Eurodollar, LIBOR, Euromark, Euroswiss, and Canadian Banker's Acceptances. Listings are added and deleted as trading volume warrants.

Figure 6-8 is a listing of the British pound and Canadian dollar futures similar to that in the February 16, 1994 issue of *The Wall Street Journal*.

Figure 6-8 lists the Canadian dollar contract size as 100,000 Canadian dollars. All futures prices are directly quoted as U.S. dollars per unit of foreign currency; for example, the first number in the table, .7390, indicates that \$.7390 is equal to one Canadian dollar. The market opened trading in the nearby March contract at this price. The trading range of the day was 17 ticks, from .7393 to .7376. The market closed about in the middle, at .7383, seven ticks lower than the previous trading day. The lifetime high and low defines the range of the March '94 contract from the first day it started trading. One tick in a Canadian dollar futures contract is worth $10; a one cent move (.7383 to .7483) is worth $1,000. Compare this with the British pound contract, for which each tick is worth $6.25, and a one cent more is worth $625.

Figure 6-8: Futures Prices (Currency)

Tuesday, February 15, 1994

	open	high	low	settle	change	lifetime high	lifetime low	open interest
Canadian Dollar (CME)—100,000 dlrs.; $ per Can $								
Mar	.7390	.7393	.7376	.7383	-.0007	7860	7394	35896
June	.7375	.7387	.7373	.7377	-.0008	7805	7365	2518
Sept	.7388	.7388	.7372	.7374	-.0009	7740	7330	662
Dec	.7382	.7383	.7366	.7372	-.0010	7670	7290	520
Mar'95	x	x	x	.7372	-.0011	7605	7376	368
Est vol 4,470; vol Mon 10,156; open int 39,975, +2,893								
British Pound (CME)—62,500 pds.; $ per pound								
Mar	1.4820	1.4830	1.4690	1.4730	-.0112	1.5550	1.3950	40772.0
June	1.4690	1.4730	1.4660	1.4680	-.0112	1.5300	1.4350	2310.0
Sept		x	x	x	1.4640	-.0110	1.4950	1.4570
429.0								
Est vol 18,106; vol Mon 24,8766; open int 43,523, -156								

In general, eleven contract months are available, including:

- Calendar quarters (January, April, July, and October) and fiscal quarters (March, June, September, and December).
- The current (spot) month, if it is not a calendar or fiscal quarter.
- The next two or three contracts beyond the farthest one above to bring the total number to eleven.

The currency contracts available to be traded as of February 15th, for example, are:

February (current year)	(spot)	October	(calendar)
March	(fiscal)	December	(fiscal)
April	(calendar)	January (next year)	(calendar)
June	(fiscal)	March	(fiscal)
July	(calendar)	April	(calendar)
September	(fiscal)		

In practice, only the fiscal months are traded, with interest concentrated in the nearest three; however, if trades occur in one of the inactive months, they will be published in *The Wall Street Journal*, space permitting. This is why five contracts of the Canadian dollar are shown in the above table, compared with three for the British pound.

Open Interest

The bottom line of the table lists the estimated volume (total number of contracts traded) on Tuesday and a verified volume figure for the previous day. Monday's total *open interest* figure is also reported. "Open interest" is the number of contracts transacted that have not yet been offset.

Open interest is calculated in the clearing operations. Every day, the clearing house maintains records of three types of transactions:

1. New buy orders and the corresponding sell orders initiated that day.
2. Previous buy orders and corresponding sell orders that have not yet been closed out.
3. Buy orders and sell orders that offset either new or pre-existing trades.

The clearinghouse "decouples" each trade, separating the buy side and the sell side. These form a pool of long (buy) positions and short (sell) positions. They are equal in number, since one long position and one short position make up every trade (see Figure 6-4).

These positions remain in the pool until they can be matched by account number with an offset. If the same account number appears on both a long position and a short position, it is assumed that account intended to offset one position with the other, so these two positions are matched up. Any position that can be considered a "type three" order automatically exits the pool and is closed out on the individual account, to leave a realized gain or loss. Positions remaining in the pool constitute open interest.

The size of the open interest pool for each contract month is shown in the right-hand column. The overall pool size and its daily change are listed in the bottom row along with volume. Note that the open interest figure is arrived at by counting either the open longs *or* the open shorts. So the total open interest shown for British pounds consists of 43,523 longs and 43,523 shorts still in the market.

Futures Options

The table of futures options prices is usually positioned near the currency futures table. Information on futures options is quite similar to that given for PHLX options. Calls and puts are not necessarily bought and sold in equal amounts, and volume and open interest figures are listed for both. The premiums for futures options are priced the same way as the underlying futures contracts; for example, the Canadian dollar March 7350 call has a premium of .57 cents (see Figure 6-9). Since one cent equals $1,000, the premium is $570. The premium for the British pound April 1475 put is $1,675 (2.68¢ at $625 per penny.) Futures options are all American style and can be exercised any time until they expire.

As previously stated, the major distinction between futures options and currency options is what the option exercises into when it is exercised. The currency (PHLX) options exercise into spot contracts with an immediate delivery of currency. A futures option exercises into a futures contract. The table does not specify *which* contract the option exercises into. Futures contracts are listed for every calendar month in the upcoming twelve months. Only four months are actually traded. If a currency speculator exercises an April 1475 put in British pounds, which futures contract appears in his account the next day? The option exercises into the futures contract for the next fiscal quarter month. Thus, April, May, and June options exercise into a June futures contract. July, August, and September options exercise into a September futures contract, and so forth. After exercising the 1475 April put, a short position in June futures, priced at 14750, appears in the speculator's account. Remember that a put conveys the right to buy dollars for British pounds and is thus a short position in pounds and a long position in dollars. Most of the time, there is no conversion. Options usually are simply offset before they expire.

Figure 6-9: Futures Options Prices

Canadian Dollar (CME)
100,000 Can $—cents per Can $

Strike	Calls - Settle			Puts - Settle		
Price	Mar	Apr	May	Mar	Apr	May
7350	0.57	x	x	0.24	0.52	x
7400	0.31	0.55	x	0.47	0.78	x
7450	0.16	0.36	x	0.83	1.09	x
Est vol 600			Mon 245 calls 331 puts			
Op int Mon			5,442 calls 5,026 puts			

British Pound (CME)
62,500 pounds; cents per pound

Strike	Calls - Settle			Puts - Settle		
Price	Mar	Apr	May	Mar	Apr	May
1475	1.30	2.00	x	1.46	2.68	3.22
1500	0.46	1.12	1.60	3.12	4.28	x
1525	0.16	0.56	0.94	5.32	6.20	6.58
Est vol 3,184			Mon 2,671 calls 3,665 puts			
Op int Mon			18,261 calls 18,802 puts			

CHAPTER 7

Price Forecasting

Forecasters use two methods to predict future currency prices: *fundamental analysis* and *technical analysis*. The first method analyzes variables outside the currency markets that seem to drive currency prices. The second method studies the past price movements of the currency market to try to predict future movements. Researchers schooled in one method often purposefully ignore conclusions reached by the other.

Fundamental Analysis

Fundamental analysis studies factors outside the currency markets that may drive future exchange rates. Since knowing everything that affects exchange rates is impossible, most fundamental analysts limit their study to a few selected factors, including economic indicators.

Predictive Value of Economic Indicators

Do economic indicators have predictive value? If so, how much? How often? Over what time span? These questions provoke elusive answers. Economists and market analysts spend entire careers trying to prove or disprove relationships between fundamental events and price movement. Changes in interest rates, gross domestic product, money supply, and inflation seem to precipitate changes in the value of currency, but can they predict future exchange rates with any degree of certainty?

In one study by Eric Sharp, editor of *Financial Data*, a comparison of changes in economic indicators and exchange rates between October 1989 and October 1990 indicated a paucity of *reliable* short-term correlations.[1] For example, the study found little evidence of positive correlations between changes in nominal exchange *spot* rates and interest rates. In fact, it suggested *inverse* correlations between real long-term bond yields and the price of some currencies. In other words, some currencies decline in price when real interest rates increase.

According to Sharp, no measurable relationship exists between changes in GDP and exchange rates. He also found no significant correlations between the consumer price index and moves in currency prices. This finding makes sense, since nominal and real exchange rates take years to converge. A correlation was found, however, between *real* growth in money supply and a decrease in currency values, and between changes in the current account balance and exchange rates.

Sharpe also examined the relationship between currency values and anticipated inflation. According to the monetarist theory of inflation, *anticipated inflation* is a function of the growth in money supply, less the growth in the GDP. Theoretically, any new money (new supply) not absorbed by new goods and services (new demand for money) becomes excess dollars. To correct the resulting imbalance in supply and demand, prices are bid higher, resulting in inflation. Thus, a correlation between currency values and anticipated inflation seems likely, and, according to the study by Sharp, a pronounced correlation actually does exist.

A major exception in Sharpe's study, however, is the British pound. This currency actually appreciated during a period when the money supply was expanding, the current account balance was decreasing, and anticipated inflation was high. This deviation might be written off as sampling error, but a more likely explanation involves *market expectation*. During the time span under review, the market anticipated a closer union between the Deutsche mark and British pound as the United Kingdom began moving toward greater participation in the European Monetary System (EMS). This move required higher interest rates for the British pound, for reasons involving international politics. In fact, the pound was made part of the EMS, and its yield did increase. Sacrificing the economy at home for foreign affairs had its price. The resulting economic upheaval in the United Kingdom prompted the country to abandon the EMS two years later.

So do economic events predict future currency prices? The answer is a modest "it depends." If everything else in an economy remains unchanged, certain economic variables do indicate where currencies must go in value to be "priced right;" however, in a dynamic economy, factors influencing the analysis always change. For example, perhaps the most important economic indicator for predicting exchange rates is the interest rate. Is there a connection between changes in *spot* exchange rates and interest rates? The answer is a qualified yes. It depends on why interest rates have changed. Central banks can certainly influence exchange rates, and they sometimes shift short-term rates for that purpose; however, these pre-planned moves in short-term rates may have unpredictable results in the currency market.

On the other hand, though short-term rates are *established*, long-term rates are *discovered.* Bond rates, or any rates over a year in duration, are almost completely market-driven. Since they reflect the anticipated depreciation of the currency in the future, bond yields are a useful indicator of future inflation. Therefore, any move in long-term rates is often accompanied by an inverse move in the rate of exchange for that currency.

Mixed Signals from Too Much Information

Economists have had little success predicting the future over the last two decades. With all the research available and with the overwhelming technology that allows immediate, global dissemination of changes in every conceivable economic variable, why is it so difficult to forecast price changes? Also, why don't currency prices act like they're suppose to, by following the fundamental rules of economics that govern supply and demand, value and purchasing power, and so forth?

One answer to both of these questions is the massive flood of economic data that washes over the analyst daily, giving mixed signals. Many professional currency speculators studiously avoid looking at yesterday's news concerning the markets they trade, for good reason. Financial dailies, such as *The Wall Street Journal*, publish yesterday's price moves in all financial markets. Their readers demand reasons for these price moves, so market commentary is published along with the closing prices. No matter which direction the market goes, some information can be interpreted to support that move.

Admittedly, some markets do move in a major way for reasons publicized in advance. For example, a company announces a technological break-through, and the world buys its undervalued stock until it is no longer undervalued. Stock prices go up and down because of *something concrete* most of the time. If they go up, all investors can profit.

Not so in the zero-sum game of speculative currency trading. Here, nothing of intrinsic value is being acquired. Rather, non-intrinsically valued things are being exchanged because of an anticipated price change. In a contract market, every buyer requires a seller. If both hold on to the contract, only one will profit at the end of the day. The other will lose. Therefore, fully one half of all traders are on the wrong side of the market. How can this be, if every trader has virtually unlimited access to virtually unlimited information? Why is one out of two traders consistently wrong? The reason explains why so many traders refuse to read the market news. The commentators always have an answer for what happened simply because the information flow can be interpreted to support either position. It is always bullish, and it is always bearish. Market reports are similar to weather reports. A person may explain why today's weather conditions exist, but still will not be able to predict the weather at a specific time in a specific place tomorrow.

In interpreting the continuous barrage of data, traders only agree that the current price is wrong. Half of them think it is too low, and so they are the buyers. The other half think it is too high, and they are the sellers.

Efficient Market Hypothesis

Another reason economic news and currency prices seem to have so little bearing on each other has to do with the efficiency of the market. The market does not wait for the analysis. It is like a foot race: the news breaks, the whistle blows, and the market participants are off, each trying to be the first one to fill the order. But in this race, the runners can start whenever they want. Many trade on news still in the process of breaking, or even on appearances that news might break, with no time for verification or analysis. The result is a market off and running on every whisper, whipsawing back and forth without any apparent justification.

Observers of this behavior fashioned the "efficient market hypothesis," which postulates that free markets instantly discount all available information. Thus, the current market price accounts for every tidbit of news the instant the market becomes aware of it. The implications of the efficient market hypothesis are staggering to practitioners of financial analysis. It means that the conclusions drawn from new occurrences or changing variables, whether economic, political, geographical, or otherwise, are useless for predicting market prices. The current price has already taken the probable conclusions into account before the analysis is even completed. No matter what the news brings forth, the market is already there. Remember the efficient market hypothesis the next time your broker calls and breathlessly whispers that he has a hot tip concerning an imminent move in the currency markets.

So if news analysis, and even news itself, lags the market, what *does* cause it to move? Nothing, according to advocates of this school of thought. It moves without direction. Only current price can be determined. Future price moves are completely indeterminate. In the words of the economist, the market is a "random walk."

Market Expectations

If the efficient market hypothesis is essentially correct, every change in variables outside the market, current or past, is meaningless to future price forecasting. However, most traders do not toss coins to decide whether to buy or sell currencies. Then what goes into their decision-making processes? Traders act on their *expectations.* Whereas the current price discounts current news, market expectation discounts future news. Therefore, today's expectation, not today's news, has a direct bearing on tomorrow's rate of exchange.

Few objective measurements exist for divining the future. Students of market expectation are immersed in a study of capricious, irrational behavior. A better name for this field would be "mob psychology." The market is often personified. Traders talk of a 'nervous' market, or a 'panicky' market, or what the market expected and what surprised it, as if the market were a conscious being.

Some justification may exist for the personification of the market. Sigmund Freud spoke of the impulsive behavior of the masses as if the mob were an entity onto itself. Carl Jung refers to patterns of instinctual behavior in defining his concept of the collective unconscious. The market does seem to have its own mind, albeit a rather irrational one. Markets plummet and soar on virtually no news. Reasons for this behavior are best described through the analysis of market expectation.

Trend and Sentiment

Many market analysts believe that markets are fueled primarily by the emotions of greed and fear. According to Dr. William Schmidt,[2] who has done substantial work in this field, fear is much more a factor than greed. In other words, price trends are driven more by aversion to risk than by potential of gain.

Consider a market that first moves up a bit, perhaps to discount economic news, or perhaps just randomly. The holder of a long position now has a profit, and the holder of a short position has a loss. Because fear overrides greed, traders with losses are more motivated than traders with profits. The trader with the loss feels relatively higher levels of emotional energy (fear). The trader holding a gain, on the other hand, experiences a sense of fulfillment from achieving a profit. He sits back and relaxes. Naturally, fear is a less secure position than a state of relaxation. Therefore, the "loser" is much more apt to act quickly. He fears greater loss, maybe major loss. Each additional tick upward looks like the start of a skyrocketing ascent, with no end in sight. The losing trader is ready to jump out of the market by buying back his short position at the slightest provocation.

On the other hand, after each additional tick upward, the trader sitting on a profit becomes more complacent. Even when the market sets back a little, he stands pat, feeling he has "hit it right." The growing relaxation becomes a bit stupefying. The winner begins to lose objectivity. He becomes overly optimistic, reluctant to let this pleasurable state end. Striving to maintain this stability, he considers a market reversal to be simply a correction affording new buying opportunities and not an end to the trend. So the winning "longs" readily buy on down moves. They are driven by greed and by the ease of financing new positions from the growing equity in the existing ones. The losing "shorts" are reluctant to sell to the longs, resulting in more demand than supply. The market compensates by moving even higher. Moreover, the move up is augmented by the shorts who, quick to jump ship, also become buyers by closing out their positions on every new high.

As this "band wagon" effect grows, new buyers, fearful of being left behind, enter the market. The market, gaining momentum, is now comprised of three types of participants:

1. happy and comfortable "old" longs, slow to sell, and ready with new-found resources to buy on set-backs;
2. potential buyers not yet in the market, fearful of missing the move and anxious to buy, set-back or not; and
3. the now nearly panic-stricken shorts, ready to buy if the market goes up "just one more tick."

With this buying pressure both above and below the market, a major trend emerges from what may have been a rather innocuous news item. Of course the same snowballing occurs in a down-trending market, in which fear drives out the longs, while greed and complacency holds in the shorts. A good example of a fear-driven downtrend occurred at the bottom of the interest rate market in 1994. In that market, mortgage-backed derivative players held short positions even when short-term rates brushed an unsustainable level of 2%. They stayed in too long due to greed, complacency, and the apparent feeling that the good times would just keep on rolling, and they absorbed tremendous loses.

Contrary Opinion

Trading guidelines can be based on market conditions that seem to precipitate changes in market sentiment. For example, one trading maxim is to always follow the trend. Another is to never follow the "crowd," which is almost always wrong. The "crowd" is defined as the majority of the market participants, including all non-professional traders and some professional traders. Presumably, the remaining professionals are bucking the crowd. The contention that the crowd almost always loses is well supported by the evidence. According to research done by John Walsh, the foremost commodity broker sales trainer, seven out of ten commodity speculators cease trading after losing money.

Trading against the crowd has been developed into a trading strategy called "contrary opinion." The psychological dynamics of this method are much the same as those producing the trend behavior described above. Traders must constantly guard against the tendency to get carried away in a ground swell of optimism that leads to the "speculative bubble," or unmaintainable movements. When speculative bubbles burst, greed turns to fear as everyone tries to get out first. Fear soon turns to panic, and profits turn to losses. Following the crowd has given us Holland's "tulipmania," the "South Sea bubble," and the stock market tops before the crashes of 1929 and 1987.

Driven by mob psychology, the crowd tends to be either overly optimistic or overly pessimistic, and thus trades rather poorly as a rule. One of its trading flaws is a lack of awareness of market efficiency. The crowd acts on what it knows (things that have happened) rather than on what it does not know (things that can happen), while the market changes on expected events and has already discounted actual events. Another trading flaw of the crowd is its low tolerance of loss. Once losses accrue, risk aversion quickly replaces risk acceptance. This flaw is fatal to profitable trading, because the market awards risk-taking and punishes risk-avoidance.

Nevertheless, history shows that the majority of traders with recent losses nurse their wounds. They play it exceedingly safe. They will not re-enter the market until a trend is firmly established and solid economic reasons justify the trend. Then they wait for a correction with a quick end to signal that the correction is not a major turnabout. Finally, they commit their money near the top of the market. The risk-takers have already built up substantial profits while the market was still "iffy." Now they get out as the crowd gets in.

"Contrarians" have developed analytical tools for trading against the crowd. One popular tool uses a simple survey of market gurus. Contrarians closely monitor market newsletters and commentary because the "crowd" tends to follow that advice. When most analysts recommend buying, the market is overbought, and contrarians sell. Conversely, when pessimism abounds, the market is oversold, and contrarians buy.

Strong and Weak Hands

Another trading technique involving market sentiment makes use of a survey of who is buying and who is selling. This survey, called the *Commitments of Traders Report*, is published periodically by market data vendors. It categorizes three types of position holders: large speculators, small speculators, and large hedgers. According to the theory, these participants either hold "strong hands," or "weak hands." The concept comes from poker. "Strong hands" have a lot of backing and are less fearful of adverse moves than other market participants. "Weak hands" are smaller players, minimally financed, who cannot stand much loss.

Large speculators can ride through adverse moves without being forced out. They are considered to be holding strong hands. Large hedgers hold the strongest hands and will not normally get out of a position under any circumstances. Market conditions must be dismal before positions in either of these two categories are liquidated to stem losses.

Small speculators, on the other hand, do not have unlimited funds. Because of previous market losses, many are already under-capitalized. They epitomize the "risk-averse" crowd. The poker game analogy explains the obvious result. Assume the strong hands are short, and the weak hands are long. The longs are very ready to sell out. This selling pressure drives the market lower. The shorts are not ready to buy back, so there is little buying pressure to drive the market higher. The market, like water, takes the path of least resistance and moves lower as more longs than shorts liquidate their positions.

However, someone taking quick losses does not necessarily hold a weak hand. Successful floor traders are always quick to get out of trades going in the wrong direction. The first rule of speculation is to take losses quickly and let profits run. The *Commitment of Traders Report*, therefore, is limited to so-called *position* traders: those who are building a position over a long period of time rather than trading back and forth for smaller gains.

R. Earl Hadady, publisher and researcher, has developed a model based on a mathematical relationship between contrary opinion and financial strength. In zero-sum games, there is a buyer for every seller, and one would expect the bullish consensus of the buyers and the bearish consensus of the sellers to be always equal. However, bullish (or bearish) consensus may be as low as 20% or as high as 80%, since there is not a *separate* buyer for every *separate* seller. Some traders carry single contracts. Others carry hundreds. So there may be one buyer for a hundred or more sellers, and vice versa.

When bullish consensus is 80%, 80% of the individual participants with open positions are bullish and long and only 20% are bearish and holding short positions. Therefore, one participant is short for every four participants who are long. In other words, the average 'short' participant holds four contracts for every one contract held by the average 'long' trader. Apparently, the shorts are larger traders with deep pockets that can finance multiple-contract positions. Since they hold the strong hands, the longs must be holding the weak hands. The contrarian would conclude that bullish sentiment has produced a market that is vulnerable to a sell-off, with the top close at hand. And conversely, when the crowd is overwhelmingly bearish, the contrarian would conclude that the market is near the bottom.

Technical Analysis

Measurements of market sentiment are not the only ways of explaining market performance. Some researchers, known as technical analysts, rely on past price moves to forecast future price moves. They rarely concern themselves with the reasons behind the move. A technical analyst does not care whether the price of the Canadian dollar dropped because of an increase in the Canadian producer price index or because the shorts squeezed out the longs. He is only interested in the move *per se*. He is interested in the chart pattern that the rising and falling prices leave behind. In short, he is looking for structure.

The school of technical analysis embraces the efficient market hypothesis. Like the trader who avoids yesterday's newspapers, the technical analyst feels that everything outside the market should be ignored. At best, fundamental variables are useless bits of information. At worst, they bias the reviewer's perception of real market conditions. Although this analysis accepts instantaneous discounting of information by efficient markets, it definitely does not accept randomness as the consequence. Markets *seem* to have structure. After all, a few traders consistently take profits out of the market. This would be statistically impossible if the markets moved completely at random at all times.

According to technical analysis, predictable sequences and patterns emerge repeatedly from the price movement itself. These patterns emerge in every currency market—in fact, in every market of any type and across all spans of time. Technical analysts have recently found an explanation for this coincidence. The new and still developing field of chaos theory suggests that natural patterns exist and repeat themselves endlessly, one within another. The patterns range from the minute to the grand in scale, from the moment to years in duration. They give structure to the chaotic directions taken by weather systems, flows of turbulent water, financial markets, and other "non-linear" systems.

Virtually every market expert interviewed during financial news programs relies on technical analysis or at least understands it and incorporates its findings into his forecast. "Trading on the technicals" is used because it beats trading on fundamentals every time, in the short term; however, forecasts six months or more into the future by either method have an equal chance of being right. It is not so much that fundamental analysis predicts better in the distant future, but technical analysis loses its ability to predict at all. Using technical analysis to predict market movements is like predicting the path of a spark in a column of smoke: the farther the smoke drifts from the chimney, the more difficult prediction becomes.

The experts' dependence on technical analysis is not widely known to the public, partly because of the image they try to maintain. Market gurus are esteemed for the knowledge they have amassed. Supposedly, they draw upon years of experience to make predictions that one with less knowledge cannot hope to match. Financial wizards command large fees because they are "in the know."

Compare that image of the TV personality with a technical analyst who does not know what a balance sheet is or how to read one and who is concerned only with lines on a chart. Pattern recognition is not complicated and can be learned in a matter of hours. The basic tools required are a price chart, a pencil, and a ruler. With these, a rookie analyst can probably forecast as accurately as fundamental analysts with years of experience. What does the simplicity of technical analysis do to the expert's image?

In fairness, experts hide technical analysis for another reason. Just as the public demands commentary along with prices in the financial journal, it demands reasons for market activity from the guests of *Nightly Business News*. Viewers do not want to be told that the market crashed because prices over the last month completed a "head and shoulders" pattern. Most would not be satisfied with that explanation, even if they understood it. They want to know the "real" reason, the reason *behind* the move. The wizards give the public the information they want and do the technical work in the closet.

Chart Analysis

Technical analysis measures a variety of internal market variables. Each particular study is described by what is analyzed. Studies analyze momentum, divergences, stochastics, moving averages, waves, trends, patterns, and so forth. Some forms of analysis take place in a computer, some with charts and rulers. The bulk of technical analysis involves charts and is sometimes referred to simply as chart analysis.

According to chaos theory, the price patterns found in financial markets are defined as *fractals*. Benoit Mandelbrot, a pioneer of fractal geometry, first discovered fractals in the annual records of cotton prices. He describes fractals as irregular geometric patterns that repeat themselves without regard to scale in dimension or duration.[3] These patterns are ubiquitous in nature. The lobes and veins of a leaf, for example, form the same pattern that stems and twigs form on the branch. The forks of the branch follow the same pattern, as do the trunk and branches forming the entire tree. From the tiniest lobe of a leave to a towering oak tree, a single geometrical pattern of development prevails. It is repeated from microscopic to cosmic scale without any significant variation. Fractal geometry is found in geology, microbiology, cosmology, and economics, to name just a few areas. It is evident in the records of price movements of cotton, long-term bonds, plywood, Fortune 500 stocks, orange juice, currencies, and everything else that trades in haphazard fashion.

Fractal geometry is best disclosed by charting the movements. It unfolds in the price history. Just as leaves and oak trees display the same pattern of development, price moves display repeating patterns occurring over periods of minutes, hours, days, or years. Without a time scale, the chart's individual marks might represent hourly moves or annual moves. After all, patterns in fractal geometry do not maintain consistent time trends. However, fractals repeat themselves. What is repeatable is predictable. And what is predictable is tradable.

Various types of charts record price movement. The most common is the *bar chart*. Here, the price range for a specific duration of time is displayed as a vertical line or bar. The duration charted may be five minutes, one day, one week, one month, and so forth. Cross marks are used to designate the opening and closing price on each vertical bar. Currency charts found in the Appendix are in bar-chart form.

A variation, known as the *candlestick* chart, is a bar chart that outlines the area between the cross marks. The outline is left empty or shaded dark to designate whether the market closed higher or lower for the day. The candlestick chart gives more visibility to market action and the otherwise inconspicuous patterns formed by the opening and closing prices.

A third chart is called the *point and figure* chart, constructed with columns of (*x*)s, used to designate up moves, and (*o*)s, used to show down moves. New columns are constructed only when the market turns. The passage of time is disregarded. Point and figure charts factor out the 'noise' of time lapse and emphasize price patterns otherwise distorted by the varying amounts of time involved in their formation.

All three chart types are shown in Figure 7-1.

Figure 7-1: Various Types of Price Charts

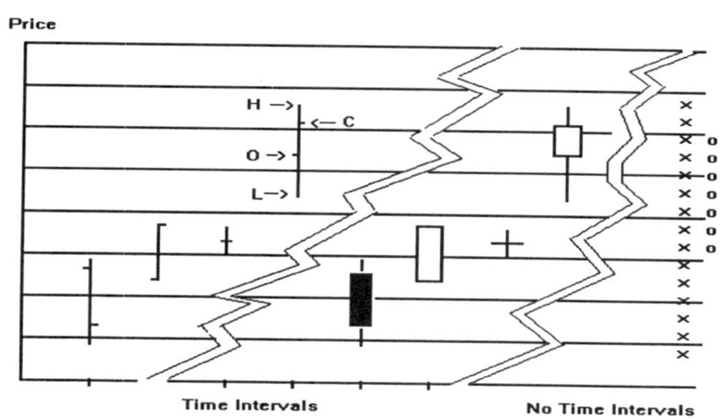

Three types of charts are shown, each displaying the same price move over four days. The first four prices are displayed as a bar chart, with the vertical line showing the range between the high (H) and low (L) of the day. The left cross mark represents the opening price (O). The right cross mark is the close (C). The next price series represent the same prices on a candlestick chart. Here the cross marks are extended across the vertical line, with the space between outlined as columns, or "candlesticks." Empty columns represent up moves, shaded columns are down moves. When the open and close are the same (third in series), no candlestick is formed. The two columns at the right are from a point and figure chart. The column of (x)s. continues as long as the market is going up. Here it accounts for the four-day up move. If the market reversed on the fifth day, with a new low near the third day's low, the column of (o)s would be added as shown.

Support and Resistance

Chart analysis also reveals support and resistance areas. Markets tend to turn back at the same general price level repeatedly. These reversals become self-fulfilling as market participants locate support and resistance price levels and place buy or sell orders at or near them. Buy orders accumulate near support levels; sell orders accumulate near resistance levels. Absent other influences, these orders are usually sufficient to turn the market (see Figure 7-2).

Figure 7-2: Support and Resistance lines on Bar Chart (open and close not shown)

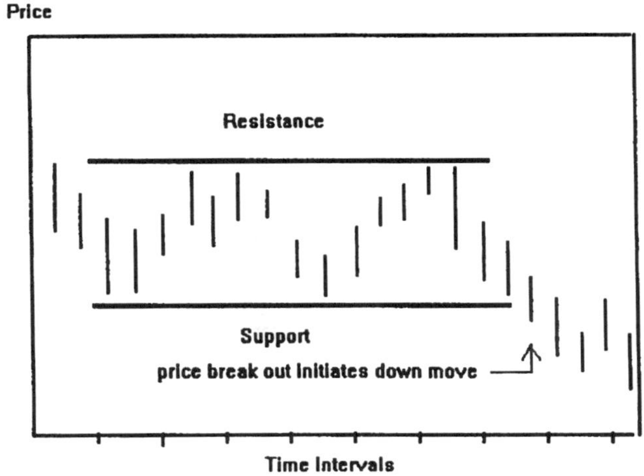

Trends

Fundamentalists study trends related to market sentiment because trader psychology may help explain the feed-back mechanism inherent in market trends. The technical analyst, however, requires no such explanation. From a technical viewpoint, the trend is simply one of a number of natural patterns inherent to the market. There are a number of other factors that regulate market movement. The regulator involved in trending markets is the propensity of a market to sustain momentum in one direction over time. Markets apparently vacillate between two states: they either trend or they "trade," meaning they move seemingly at random. Effective trading techniques for one state are often quite ineffective for the other. The trick is to figure out whether the current state will continue or whether the alternate state is eminent.

Trends can be defined by extending lines on a chart. Lines extended along the bottom of the price range identify up-trends. Lines that connect the highs over a period of time define down-trends. Channels are drawn by adding a parallel line to confine most of the price action. When the market breaks through the trend line, or leaves the channel, subsequent price action becomes less predictable. These pivot points often introduce a change of state from trending to trading, leading to increased volatility, reversals, or changes in the angle of ascent or descent (see Figure 7-3).

Figure 7-3: Up-trend with Channel Line Drawn

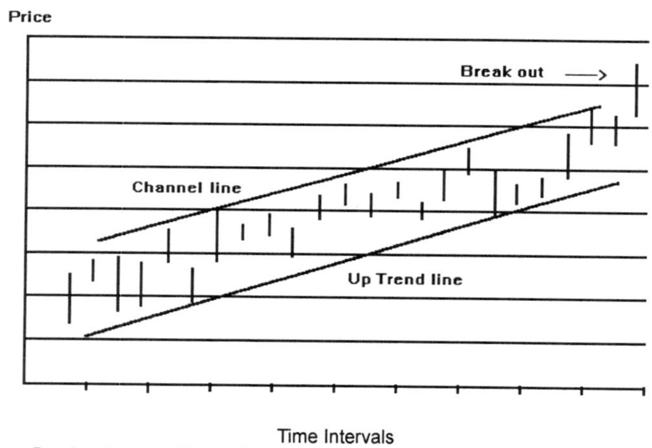

Break out on upside predicts more rapid advance and increased volatility

Price Patterns

Several other formations are used to predict future price moves. One of the most common is the *triangle*, or variations of it. As the market becomes more or less volatile, the range of prices becomes wider or narrower. These momentum changes may be traced out as triangle formations on the charts. Triangles are considered continuation patterns: prices tend to break out of the formation in the same direction they were heading when they entered it, and a trend often develops or continues from the break-out point (see Figure 7-4). Regardless of its direction, a break-out from a triangle is often accompanied by a major increase in market activity.

Figure 7-4: Continuation Patterns

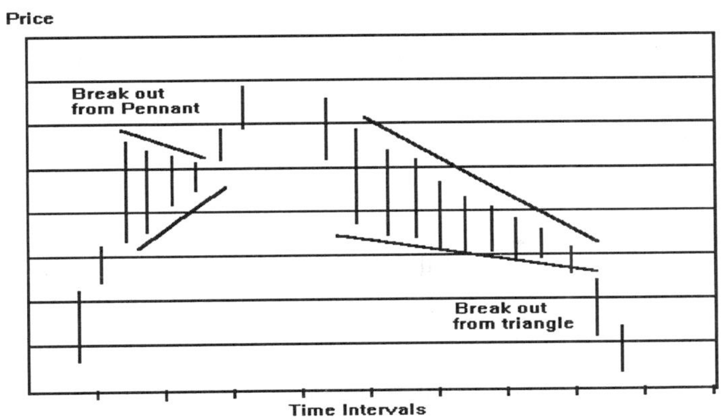

Break-outs predict resumption of trend

Another group of patterns identifies *reversal formations*, signaling a major turn (see Figure 7-5). Reversal patterns are often found at the top or bottom of the market. *Island* reversal tops are especially strong signals, comprised of a one- or two-day range (on daily charts) that marks the high of the move. The low for those days is higher than the preceding and following highs, thereby isolating these price moves as an 'island' on the chart. *Head and Shoulder* formations are classic reversal patterns that also project the minimum distance prices will move in the opposite direction (see Figure 7-6).

Figure 7-5: Reversal Patterns

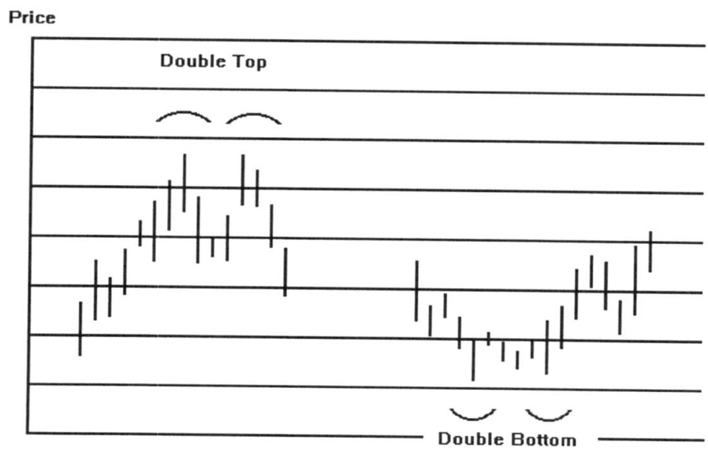

Reversal patterns predict a new trend in the opposite direction

Figure 7-6: Head and Shoulder Formation

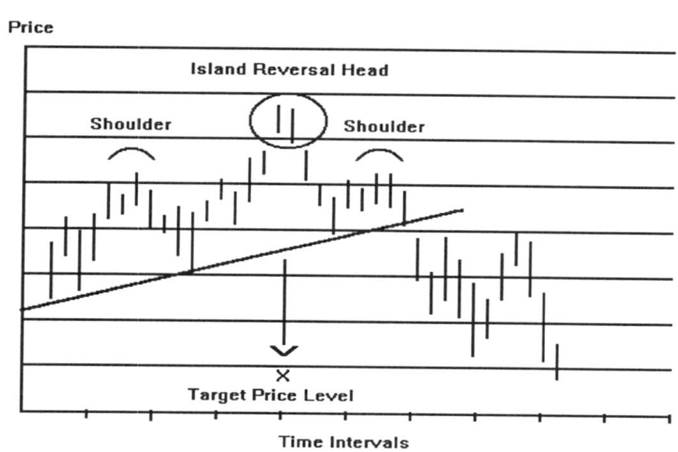

A "head and shoulders" top shown here with an "island reversal" is an especially strong indicator of a major top. A swing measurement to the target price objective (x) is drawn from the 'neckline', which is precisely midway between the high and the target price.

Elliot Wave Theory

The most fascinating property of fractals is how they repeat patterns on every scale, from the distribution of smoke particles to the distribution of stars. These patterns are thought to represent the "natural rhythm" found in non-linear, or chaotic, systems such as currency markets. Fractals include the "wave" formation that seems inherent in all systems that ebb and flow. In 1939, R.N. Elliot published a set of rules to forecast stock prices by measuring the "to and fro" movement of the market. His rules became known as the *Elliot Wave Theory*.

"Trading" markets move continuously back and forth, but even "trending" markets do not march in straight lines. Whether the trend is up or down, it usually takes "three steps forward and two steps back." Elliot proposed that stock prices actually take five steps forward (impulse waves) and three steps back (corrective waves). Proponents of the Elliot Wave Theory identify each of these waves, using the progression to predict the direction and level of future prices. Figure 7-7 shows this property of progress and retraction, found on every scale.

Figure 7-7: Elliot Wave

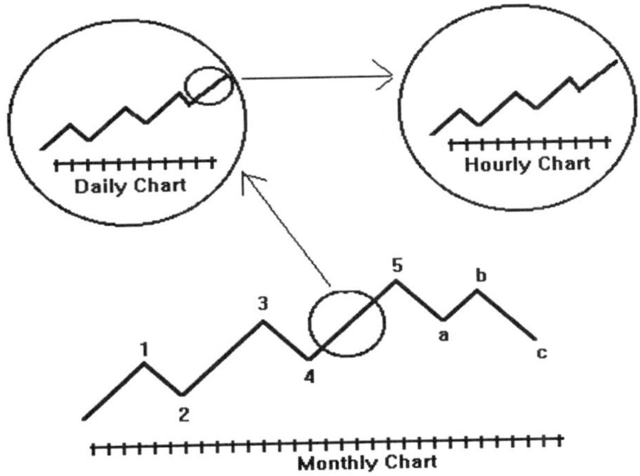

The Elliot Wave Theory predicts five impulse waves (1 - 5) and three corrective waves (a - c) across all measurable scales.

Moving Averages

A constant problem with chart analysis is the separation of predictive signals from background "noise," including variance in volatility. Sluggish trading days alternate with days of frenzied buying and selling. Unexpected events can create wide price ranges, price spikes, gaps, and blow-off tops that may drown out signals of longer-term trend change. Various 'filters' have been devised to separate the trends from the noise. The filters most commonly employed are moving averages.

Moving averages are averages taken over a specific number of observations in a series. As new information is added, the oldest information is dropped from the average. Thus, the average "moves" over time. For example, a 40-day moving average of closing prices is the total of all closing prices for the last 40 days of trading, divided by 40. The average changes each day as the newest close is added and the oldest close is dropped from the series. The average can be plotted as a line on a graph. It offers the analyst a picture of a smooth progression, moving in and out of trends, without all the confusing bumps and valleys along the way. With the noise of insignificant fluctuations removed, a clearer picture of the trend emerges.

The 40-day average, then, filters out false changes in trends. Used alone, however, it filters out all but the major market changes. By the time a new trend is indicated, the move may be halfway over. This insensitivity makes moving averages problematic for long-term traders and hedgers and useless for short-term traders. Profits quickly turn to losses before the moving average indicates the end of the previous trend. To counteract the problems, traders use two or even three moving averages taken over shorter series of closes and thus having greater sensitivity to market turns. Signals to get in or out of the market are generated when a more sensitive average crosses over a less sensitive one (see Figure 7-8).

Volume and Open interest

Technical analysts track other quantifiable market variables in addition to price. Two of these variables measure market participation: volume and open interest. *Volume* refers to the number of contracts traded in any given period of time, usually one trading day. *Open interest* is the number of open contracts in the market at any one time. Changes in these variables often indicate forthcoming changes in the direction of the market.

Figure 7-8: Moving Averages of Closing Prices

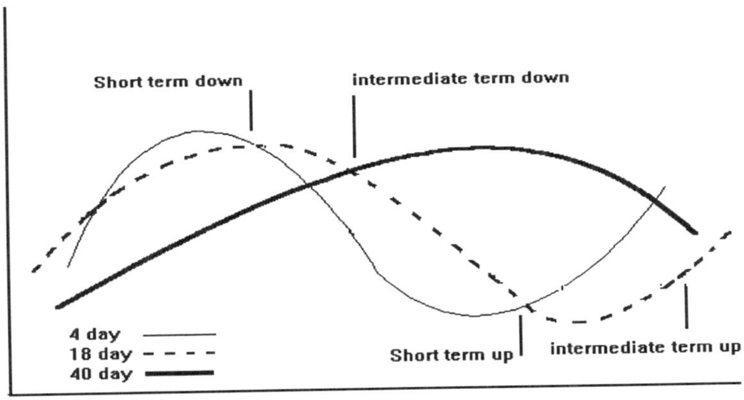

Shorter-term moving averages are more sensitive to shorter-term trends. Signals are generated when one moving average crosses another.

Volume, by itself, gives us an idea of the "popularity" of the current price move, or the degree of enthusiasm behind it. If volume increases as the market goes up and decreases as the market goes down, investors show more interest in buying than selling. Likewise, when volume increases on a down market and dries up when the market rebounds, investors show greater interest in selling than buying. Therefore, an increase in volume confirms the market sentiment for the current move.

An increase in open interest signifies new players coming into the market. Thus, changes in open interest figures are used in conjunction with volume figures to confirm price moves, or to predict an imminent top or bottom of the market. The market is strong when prices go up on increasing volume and open interest, with new longs coming in to keep the move going. If prices fall on increasing volume and open interest, the market is weak, with new shorts entering the market.

Divergence refers to changes in volume and open interest that do *not* confirm the direction of the price move but instead predict a near-term reversal. If, for example, the market is rising and volume is falling, it means that the market does not support the move. Price may be rising on thin trading, with most of the participants standing aside. They are not "buying" the up move. If open interest is also falling, it means that the market is liquidating. The move up is the result of shorts buying back their positions. No new money is coming in. The market is close to topping out, and the move will be exhausted when shorts have completed their buy-back. By the same token, falling volume and decreasing open interest during a down move is considered a negative divergence, indicating a strengthening of the market. Presumably new money is sitting on the sideline, waiting for the existing longs to finish liquidating before initiating new buying.

Talking the Talk

Whether you find technical analysis useful or not, it has contributed heavily to the language of the foreign exchange markets. The basic tool of almost every practitioner is a regularly updated price chart. The trader's world includes candlestick charts, bar charts, point and figure charts, or trend lines. The charts may show break-throughs, islands, head-and-shoulder formations, triangles, or a myriad of other patterns. They all predict probable future price movements from quantifiable data.

A knowledge of the language helps investors communicate effectively with dealers, brokers, or traders. A corporate financial manager, deciding with a dealer whether to trade and the type of order to use, does not have a lot of time to clarify terms. Knowing the language allows the manager to be direct. At a minimum, the corporate currency manager should have an updated price chart in front of him, because the individual he is talking to will be looking at one.

How might a phone conversation with a technical analyst sound? The following excerpts from the *Commodity Trend Service*© refer to the signals of various futures contracts over several weeks. Note that the terms are universal. They are used in all trading markets, not just currencies. Although every financial and commodity product has its own unique nature, the same formations of patterns, trends, waves, etc. are scrutinized in every commodity and financial futures pit.

"The uptrend appears to be running out of gas. Divergences in volume, open interest, and momentum indicators are raising a yellow flag." (silver)

> "Prices are testing the 40-day ma at the time of this writing. A close at new four-week highs would register a shift in intermediate term momentum."(Japanese yen)
>
> "A major bottom appears at hand. However, the clear five-wave advance from the (lows) warns a correction is imminent." (copper)

"The five-wave advance from the (lows) and potential double top forming on March keep us alert for a reversal." (Eurodollars)

"A daily stochastics (a moving average filter) crossing will signal another setback, probably to the 7800 support. If long, protect with stops just below (uptrend) line." (Swiss franc)

"After breaking above key resistance, prices have fallen back into the trading range. Treat as a trading range...until a weekly breakout occurs." (British pound)

"Prices are trapped dead in the middle of the triangle from hell. We'll remain sidelined until a definite breakout occurs..." (Swiss franc)

Analysis as a Trading Tool

Although technical analysis has consistently outperformed fundamental analysis, its success may also lead to its demise as a trading tool. The efficiency of the market has erased much of the advantage to technical traders. Since the trading world discovered reliability in such patterns as Elliot waves and head and shoulders, predictive patterns have been commonly traded upon while they are still forming. In other words, traders now predict the completion of predictive patterns and trade accordingly. Those who wait for confirmation trade just in time to be on the wrong side as the market turns. Just as the researcher of sub-atomic particles changes the outcome of an experiment by the act of observation, the technical analyst changes the outcome of the market by observing patterns and making them known to the average trader. Since the crowd is always wrong, common knowledge that a market will *probably* drop sharply when it penetrates a certain support area prevents the drop from happening. Technical analysis works best when practiced by just a few "in the know." Once a method is exposed, its reliability begins to dissipate, and the markets veer toward a new "random walk." Perhaps they begin new patterns that discount the effects of popular forms of technical trading.

In choosing whether or not to use technical analysis, the objective of the analysis is also important. Trading currencies as an investment ("speculative venture" might be a better term) involves a very simple goal: making money. The trader usually determines how that objective is met. The client often shows no more interest than reading a quarterly report to track his investment.

Currency hedging, on the other hand, seeks to identify, analyze, and reduce exposures. Trading systems, each with its own brand of analysis, each with its own risk and reward characteristics, concern the corporation. Hedging objectives change with the corporation's exposures, goals, and financial and operating circumstances. Hedging requires more input than investment management. The currency manager may need to provide market forecasts, enter the market, and trade on a moment's notice. Above all, his analytical information must be reliable.

Conclusion

All forecasting techniques invite skepticism. If *they* work, why do *analysts* work? Why are they not sailing on yachts in the south seas instead of hawking nuggets of wisdom purported to unlock the mysteries of the market and enrich traders with untold wealth? The answer, of course, is that not one of the techniques works *consistently.* Some techniques work well for a while, then inexplicably stop working altogether. For example, certain changes in economic variables should increase or decrease the value of a currency. But with a constant deluge of changing fundamental data, the net result for a particular exchange rate at a particular time is extremely hard to predict with any degree of certainty.

Technical analysts struggle to show that market action alone determines market action. However, in chaotic systems such as contract markets, prices do not move in an orderly fashion. Patterns do suddenly emerge, and then just as suddenly disappear. The market seems to move erratically back and forth between trends (somewhat orderly) and trading ranges (very disorderly). Each type of market requires a different trading strategy, and the type may change in minutes.

Fortunately, the currency manager can ignore market moves as long as a well developed hedging program is in place. Still, for most hedging programs, the administrator must have an idea of whether the general market trend is up or down in the long run. Though fundamental analysis has inherent problems, it is probably necessary for developing an intelligent long-term outlook.

On the other hand, technical analysis and market sentiment analysis are highly useful for deciding exactly where, when, and how to position trades. But with a viable hedging program, errors in timing should not be a problem. Hedging, after all, means reducing risk regardless of market direction.

Currency managers do not make trading decisions every hour or every day, so they should avoid analysis that requires frequent decisions. Thus, quote machines, real-time data-stream subscriptions and the satellites dishes to download that data, short-term analytical programs, black boxes, and day-trading systems are all unnecessary. Many excellent long-term hedging programs run with only a subscription to price charts, updated every morning from the quotes in *The Wall Street Journal*, *Barron's*, or another daily financial publication.

Some forecasting services cost thousands of dollars a month for hot lines, software, hardware, subscriptions, and so forth. There are alternatives; the sections following this one describe excellent currency management programs, well tailored for any operation and requiring only yesterday's financial section of the newspaper, a chart or two, and a kitchen table.

CHAPTER 8

Exposure and Risk

In this chapter, the currency used for corporate reporting of financial results is referred to as the "home currency." Home currency is used to denominate figures in the balance sheet and income statement. Unless otherwise specified, the home currency is the U.S. dollar. The generic terms "foreign currency" and "local currency" are used to describe currencies used for reporting by foreign operations, but not by the parent corporation. Some of the abbreviations used in this section and their meanings are as follows:

HC	Home currency, designating the reporting currency of the business. Unless otherwise noted, home currency is the U.S. dollar.
FC	Foreign currency
LC	Local currency, designating the foreign currency used to report financial results of foreign operations
TC	Third currency, used by a foreign operation that deals in other than the local currency.
X/R	Exchange rate between two currencies
F/X	Foreign exchange, or foreign currency markets

Defining Exposure

A company has exposure if there is a currency mismatch in some aspect of the business such that a shift in foreign exchange rates, nominal or real, affects performance either adversely or beneficially. By definition, a business sensitive to a change in currency *value* (whether or not it is reflected in the price) has a foreign currency exposure. Effects of a currency mismatch are not limited to gains and losses on the financial statement but may show up anywhere in the company. These effects are quantifiable, not qualifiable.

Risk and Volatility

When a company has a "foreign currency exposure," it has incurred a risk that the price of the currency will change. The actual risk is due to the uncertainty involved. In the world of foreign exchange, a price move of any magnitude in either direction can occur without warning. Fortunately, the magnitude of the move is not totally random, although the direction of the move may be. It is possible to make an educated guess concerning the probability that a move will occur and by how much.

The *probable* range of a currency's move is its *volatility,* calculated as the historical *standard deviation* of its price. A standard deviation, by definition, is the "dispersion of observations from the mean observation." In other words, in any time period, a currency price can be expected to move back and forth from its last point (the previous market close) by a unit of standard deviation calculated for that amount of time.

Foreign currency is managed by identifying the exposure and quantifying it in terms of volatility. However, bear in mind that past volatility of currency is only a rough estimate of its *probable* future risk. Overnight volatility of the British pound can change tomorrow, perhaps from two cents to three cents, four cents, or more. Currency must be managed dynamically, with allowance for variation in exposure and variation in the risk associated with the exposure. (For an example see Figure 8-1.)

Analyzing Exposure

The first step in developing a currency management program is to *identify the exposure* and *try to quantify it in terms of risk.* How much risk is there, as measured in units of standard deviations? How much risk would the exposure have generated over the last year or over the last five years?

Figure 8-1: Volatility of British Pound Assuming Random Price Movement: Hypothetical Example

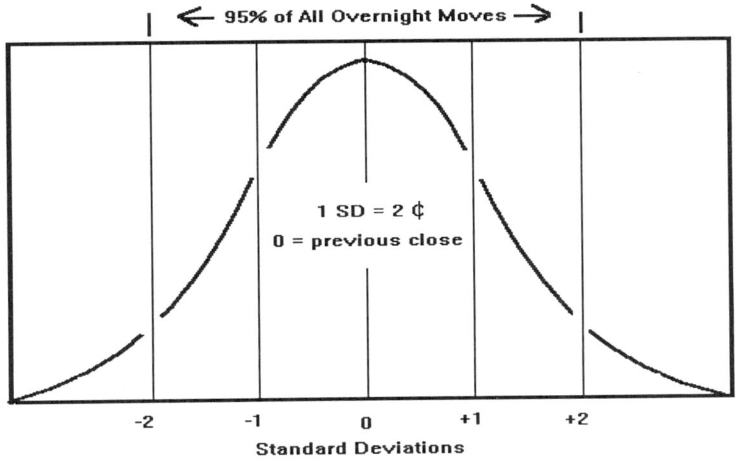

How much risk will there be over the next one, five, or ten years? Obviously, volatility can only be measured in historical terms, whereas risk management must focus on the future. Knowledge that the pound moves less than four cents 95% of the time is irrelevant when the UK pulls out of the European Monetary System, and the pound goes down 18¢ overnight. So a measurement of historical risk is only a guess of future risk.

The second step in developing a currency management program is to *review company's objectives and priorities, and then determine how each might be exposed to a particular change in a currency exchange rate.* Under various "what-if" scenarios, exactly how much damage can the exposure really do? Are only 6% of projected revenues exposed to a shift in exchange rates, or is the company's entire sales program at risk? The real risk of exposure goes unnoticed much of the time. A specific change in exchange rates can have a positive effect on one corporate objective, a neutral influence on a second, and, simultaneously, a negative effect on a third. The company may only be aware of the positive effect. A business enterprise seeking to reduce currency risk may actually increase risk by focusing on exposure from the wrong angle.

Lack of a common language to describe risk exposure hampers those who try to manage it. Foreign currency management is still developing, and the terminology is unsettled. One hears of accounting exposure, economic exposure, operation exposure, anticipatory asset and liability exposure, contingency exposure, net income exposure, and so on. Very often, the definition of the term depends upon the speaker and the context in which it is used.

This book uses the terminology and the hierarchy of definitions developed by Christine R. Hekman.[1] She categorizes exposures by duration, the business functions that are affected, and the performance measurements that will be protected by their management. The categories are arranged from the most narrowly focused, such as short-term risk to the balance sheet, to the broadest, such as risk as it affects the goals, direction, and mission of the organization. In these categories, *short term* is from the present to one year forward, *medium term* is one to five years in the future, and *long term* is more than five years into the future. The various categories of exposure are outlined in Table 8-1.

Each form of exposure may result from the potential for change in a single foreign currency. Sometimes, these different exposures may require different management techniques. In foreign currency management, it is possible to *create* a new exposure, simply by managing an existing exposure. Subjecting the company to new exposures—as hedging sometimes does—may be the only effective method of reducing existing ones.

Accounting Exposure

Accounting exposure is the risk of foreign exchange rate changes affecting current period financial statements. Accounting exposure concerns current period assets, liabilities, revenues, and expenses. Consider the example of accounting exposure that was presented in the first section, where a U.S. manufacturer records in U.S. dollars a liability payable in Dutch guilders. Initially, a kitchenware fabricator buys production machinery from a Dutch company for 1,000,000 Dutch guilders. The amount is due upon shipment, in about six months. The U.S. company makes the entries on its books as seen in Table 8-2.

Table 8-1: Categories of Exposure

	Accounting	**Cash Flow**	**Operational**	**Strategic**	**Value-Based**
Duration of effects measured:	short-term	short-term	short- to medium-term	short- to long- term	short- to long- term
Rates in which changes are analyzed:	nominal rates	nominal rates	real rates	nominal and real rates	nominal and real rates
Focuses on:	visible risk to assets, liabilities, and contractual arrangements	visible risk to current and short-term cash flow, balance sheet adjustments, and variances in short-term operating performance	hidden risk to short- to medium-term cash flow, operating margin, sales volume, and market share	risk of cash flow exposure and operating exposure	risk to corporate value, stock price, future expectations and future growth
Forms in this category are:	-transaction (or (or balance sheet) exposure -translation (or net asset/liability position) exposure		-margin exposure -competitive exposure -conversion exposure		
Manages risk to protect:	current period financial performance	short-term profitability short-term profitability	operating income, flexi-bility, and short- to medium-term operating	short- to long-term profitability and performance and and long-term strategic options	all aspects of business from account performance to longer-term strategic options
Consider these other forms of exposure:	none	none	cash flow	cash flow, operating	all others within their relevant time frames

Table 8-2: U.S. Company Ledger

Liability booked when *f*/$ = 2.00	**Translation**
Account payable - *f*1,000,000	$500,000
60 days later - *f*/$ = 2.10	$476,190
90 days later - *f*/$ = 1.80	$555,556
180 days later - *f*/$ = 1.60	$625,000
Liability covered when *f*/$ = 1.60	
Account paid - *f*1,000,000	$625,000

The transaction generates an accounting exposure. The risk to the manufacturer is the uncertainty of the dollar amount that must actually be paid. The manufacturer is exposed to the possibility of both foreign exchange gains and losses. The exposure is created by a mismatch of currencies, in this case between the dollar-denominated account payable and the requirement to make payment in guilders. The final actual result is a loss of $125,000, which is the increase in dollars required to buy the necessary guilders.

A hedge could effectively counteract the exposure above. Managing the risk of a one-time transaction is fairly straightforward. But, for the corporate treasurer involved with ongoing foreign operations, the solutions are much less clear-cut.

FASB Standards

The Financial Accounting Standards Board publishes guidelines on how to treat accounting exposure. Until December 15, 1982, FASB 8 guidelines were most often followed; after that date, FASB 8 was superseded by FASB 52. Both standards, taken together, illustrate the direction of the accounting profession in foreign currency management. Both FASB 8 and 52 recognize that currency mismatches originate from two areas: *foreign currency (FC) transactions, and home currency (HC) transactions concerning foreign operations*. The areas are defined as follows:

- A *foreign currency transaction* is a contractual agreement in which an asset is acquired or a liability incurred in a foreign currency. Transactions include (1) buying or selling using a foreign currency or (2) borrowing or lending with subsequent payables and receivables denominated in a foreign currency. If the corporation is a single unit or operates solely within its country's borders, any business denominated in foreign currency falls within this area. If the corporation is consolidated with a foreign subsidiary or other types of operations outside its country's borders, only the foreign currency transactions directly generated and booked by the domestic or parent corporation are included in this definition.
- A *foreign operation*, on the other hand, is a separate business conducted in another country. The foreign operation may be a subsidiary, a division, a branch, or any other form of overseas operation. It transacts business from day to day in the local currency (LC) of its country. Its assets, liabilities, revenues and expenses are denominated in the LC. It normally produces its own income statement and balance sheet, which is consolidated with the parent corporation's statement at the end of the fiscal year. Note that a foreign operation may also engage in foreign currency transactions, if it denominates transactions in either the home currency of its parent corporation (HC) or in a third currency (TC).

According to both FASB 8 and FASB 52, all items in the financial statement must be denominated in a single currency, called the reporting currency. (The reporting currency used here is the U.S. dollar, or HC.) Foreign-currency-denominated items must be translated into HC denominations. One of two rates of exchange are employed for translation: the *current* rate or the *historical* rate. The historical rate is the one in effect on the first day the asset or liability was entered on the books. If the item is translated at this rate, it remains unchanged from one period to the next. The current rate, on the other hand, is either the one in effect on the date the balance sheet is prepared or the average rate between the last and the current preparation dates. Since this rate changes from one preparation date to the next, current rate translations recognize gains and losses associated with currency fluctuations. FASB 8 and 52 differ in deciding which rate to use for translations.

FASB 8

FASB 8 determines which rate to use for translations based on the *character* of the item. With FASB 8, all assets, liabilities, revenues and expenses to be translated, whether arising from transactions of the parent company or its foreign operations, are divided into *monetary* and *non-monetary* items. Monetary items are translated at current exchange rates, and non-monetary items are translated at historical rates of exchange.

A *monetary item* is one with a known price. If 5 billion lire were borrowed to purchase machinery, for example, the debt remains fixed at 5 billion lira, regardless of the lira's worth in dollars; therefore, the dollar value of the debt changes every time the dollar/lira nominal rate changes. The current value in either currency can always be ascertained. For this reason, FASB 8 requires monetary items to be translated at current exchange rates.

Non-monetary items cannot be readily priced. Intangible assets such as good will, fixed assets such as land, plant and equipment, and long-term liabilities such as pension fund obligations are all examples of non-monetary items. Because non-monetary values appreciate and depreciate to compensate for changes in inflation rates, their translation *value* is influenced by both the real and nominal exchange rate. Real rates of exchange are never known with any degree of certainty. Therefore, repricing of non-monetary items in each reporting period is quite difficult. For this reason, FASB 8 requires *non-monetary items to be translated at the historical rate of exchange*.

Foreign Exchange Transactions vs. Foreign Operations Accounts

"Foreign currency transactions" on the books of the parent corporation are usually monetary in nature and must be translated at current rates. *Foreign operation accounts*, on the other hand, can be either monetary or non-monetary and must be translated at the "appropriate rate." Non-monetary items, carried at unchanging historical rates, generate no visible accounting exposure until they are liquidated. However, carrying long-term assets at historical exchange rates may significantly understate or overstate the net worth of the corporation. The day of liquidation can become a day of reckoning. Under FASB 8, many corporations carrying long-term assets at historical rates began hedging such "hidden" exposures.

On the other hand, monetary items that must be translated at current rates each reporting period generate visible accounting exposure. Each reporting period, after monetary assets and liabilities are netted, the exchange gain or loss is included in net income as a translation adjustment.

With FASB 8, exchange rate fluctuations were recognized in the income statement and impacted profitability for the first time. During periods of high currency volatility, the earnings fluctuated between profit and loss, depending on which day exchange rates were translated. To make matters even worse, the translation adjustments to balance sheet items sometimes distorted profits. For example, a foreign operation may receive revenues in a currency that is either appreciating or depreciating relative to the home currency. Those revenues are translated at the current rate; however, inventory, whose consumption offsets revenue, is considered a non-monetary item under FASB 8 and is carried at historical rates. Thus, the profit margin expands or contracts as inventory is consumed and replaced, simply because revenues are translated at current rates and expenses are translated at historical rates. In addition, the mismatch affects the corporation's tax liability, budgeting, and the calculation of costs of manufacturing and other measurements used to determine utilization and profitability.

FASB 8 allows a limited form of hedging for balance sheet exposure. The exposed net asset or liability can be hedged only if it is an identifiable commitment. In other words, it must involve a purchase, sale, or loan that commits to a specific amount over a specific length of time. The hedge must be a forward contract with expiration at or beyond the date the commitment is to be liquidated The forward contract must be in the same currency as the commitment. With these limitations, tailoring appropriate hedges to fit the FASB 8 standard is difficult. The following example illustrates the problem:

Assume that the international treasurer of Bakerfield Corporation notices the following items in the balance sheet of one of their foreign operations that transacts business in LC:

LC Subsidiary Balance Sheet

Assets		Liabilities	
Acct. receivable	10,000,000	Acct. payable	20,000,000
Inventory	30,000,000		

If the receivable and payable are netted out, and inventory (carried at historical rates) is ignored, the operation has an exposed net liability position of 10,000,000 LC. The treasurer buys a 10,000,000 LC forward contract to hedge the liability. Now the balance sheet looks like this:

LC Subsidiary Balance Sheet

Assets		Liabilities	
Acct. receivable	10,000,000	Acct. payable	20,000,000
Forward contract	10,000,000		
Inventory	30,000,000		

The monetary assets and liabilities now net out to zero. But if inventory is taken into account, the exposure actually increased from 20,000,000 LC to 30,000,000 LC. FASB 8 created a great deal of conflict between treasury managers, who try to hedge accounting exposure, and operation managers, who want to protect operating income. For some managers, accounting exposure, with its limitations, has fallen behind operating exposure on the list of priorities. Some hedge inventories, even though the hedges do not conform to accounting standards. In that case, hedging economic (operating) exposure creates accounting exposure. Sometimes the company performs a sensitivity analysis on how much "operating hedging" treasury management can tolerate.

FASB 52

FASB 52 was adopted in recognition of some of the problems of FASB 8. This new standard change the treatment of foreign operation exposure and uses the current rate to translate all financial statement items. As before, a foreign operation is defined as a subsidiary, division, branch or joint venture of the parent corporation. However, FASB 52 further qualifies an operation that is "relatively self-contained and integrated with a foreign country"[2] as a *net investment* of the parent corporation. The investment has its own "functional currency" defined as "the currency of the economic environment in which cash is generated and expended by the entity."[3] All assets and liabilities for the entity, including inventories, are translated at current rates. In a major departure from FASB 8, the functional currency gain or loss does not flow through to the income statement of the parent corporation. Instead, it is recorded as a foreign exchange translation adjustment in stockholder equity on the balance sheet. The rationale is that a foreign operation is an asset that increases or decreases in value without impacting current cash flow, just as any other net investment does.

Translation Exposure

The net asset or net liability exposure in functional currency is called "translation exposure" in FASB 52. As a balance sheet item in the equity section, it does not impact tax liability or substantially impact financial analysis. However, the adjusted gain or loss may be very significant in a volatile currency environment, and, if the operation is liquidated, the gain and loss affects income. Hedging the translation exposure may be justified. Hedge gains and losses are netted against the exposure account, and do not impact current income or tax liability or significantly affect financial analysis.

Transaction Exposure

FASB 52 defines foreign currencies that are not functional as "non-functional." In general, non-functional currencies are foreign currencies that denominate individual *transactions* of either a foreign operation or the parent corporation. The non-functional currency transactions of FASB 52 are similar to the foreign currency transactions of FASB 8. Purchases, sales, loans, payment of dividends, and inter- company payments and receipts are examples of non-functional currency transactions that may affect the parent corporation's balance sheet. Just as in FASB 8, non-functional currency exposures flow through to the income statement and impact cash flow. All such assets and liabilities are marked to the market at current exchange rates, just as translation exposure is.

Transaction exposure is more visible than translation exposure and thus gets more attention from currency managers. To allow more flexibility, FASB 52 expanded the accepted methods of hedging exposures. Hedges are no longer restricted to forward contracts or to the same currency that creates the exposure. Futures, swaps and options are allowed, and a related, more liquid, currency may be used. However, FASB 52 does not expand the types of exposure that may be hedged. To be considered a hedge, a transaction must:

- offset an identifiable foreign currency commitment,
- be designated as, and effective as, a hedge; and
- be a firm commitment in its own right.

Current Rates

According to FASB 52, *all* assets, liabilities, revenues and expenses reported on the financial statement must be translated at the current rate. The date of the current rate used varies by accounting category as follows:

- •Assets and liabilities are translated at the rate in effect on the data of the balance sheet.
- •Revenues, expenses, gains, and losses are translated at the rate in effect on the date the items are recorded.
- •Allocations such as depreciation are translated at the rate in effect on the date the allocation is included in revenue or expense.
- •Income statement items that flow over the reported period, such as revenue streams and salaries, are translated at the average rate in effect over the reporting period.

Translation of all financial statement assets and liabilities at current rates takes care of the hidden reserve/liability problem that was inherent in FASB 8. Recall than, in FASB 8, translation of long-term assets and liabilities at historical rates could result in huge unrecognized liabilities if FC is appreciating, or hidden reserves that distort the reported net worth of the company if FC is depreciating.

As troublesome as historical translation might be, however, carrying long-term liabilities at current exchange rates may be even less attractive. Boris Antl shows what may happen to a 1,000,000 FC obligation carried at current exchange rates.[4]

Date	FC	XR (HC/FC)	HC	gain(loss)
12/31/89	1,000,000	1.0	1,000,000	
12/31/90	1,000,000	0.9	900,000	100,000
12/31/91	1,000,000	1.1	1,100,000	(200,000)
12/31/92	1,000,000	1.0	1,000,000	100,000
12/31/93	1,000,000	1.0	1,000,000	

(Net effect of FX change = 0)

The back and forth swings are recorded in the equity account by marking the obligation to the market each year. Although no net foreign exchange gain or loss remains on the liability at the end of the period, either one or the other was reported in three years out of the five. If the liability had been carried at historical rates, there would have been no reported gain or loss over the five-year period.

Hyperinflation

Certain foreign operations are excluded from using a functional currency designation. According to FASB 52, operations in hyperinflationary environments must be translated as non-functional currency transactions. The rationale is that the local currency is too unstable to be functional. The more stable currency of the parent corporation (U.S. dollars) must be substituted. Hyperinflation is defined by FASB 52 as a "three-year inflation rate of approximately 100% or more."

Hedge Accounting

Hedges must adhere to the FASB 52 standards to qualify for deferred accounting. The gains and losses produced by a bona fide hedge can be deferred, along with the unrealized gain or loss from the exposure being hedged, until the transaction is completed. Thus, the hedge and the transaction exposure do not impact cash flow while the transaction is on the books and the hedge is in force. Although the hedge may be terminated before the transaction is completed, gains and losses on the hedge may still be deferred until foreign exchange gains and losses generated by the transaction are realized. The Financial Accounting Standards Board continues to scrutinize hedge accounting, so this provision is subject to change.

Inventory

Inventory exposure shows up immediately with FASB 52, while FASB 8 defers it. Marking inventory to the market per FASB 52 might create an asset exposure in foreign currency on the books, which can be hedged by selling a foreign currency forward contract for the same amount. On the other hand, FASB 8 allowed companies that denominated records in a non-functional currency to carry assets such as inventory and equipment at historical rates. That practice eliminated the above current rate asset and created a net liability exposure, which was sometimes hedged by buying a foreign currency forward.

The accounting method used for inventories also directly affects the earnings statement.[5] Table 8-2 shows inventory exposure based on the functional currency method of accounting used in FASB 52. The exposure is marked to the market at the current rate. Table 8-3 is based on the monetary/non-monetary method used in FASB 8 in which inventory is carried at historical rates. Assume that in both cases the sales revenue is applied against the payable.

Table 8-2: Current Rate—FASB 52

Item	LC	XR	HC
1st quarter			
Inventory (asset)	100	1.0	100
Payable for inventory (liability)	100	1.0	100
2nd quarter			
Payable	100	0.9	90
Net Sales	100	0.9	90
Cost of Goods	100	0.9	90
Profit(loss)	0		0

Table 8-3: Historical Rate—FASB 8

Item	LC	XR	HC
1st quarter			
Inventory (asset)		100	1.0
100			
Payable for inventory (liability)	100	1.0	100
2nd quarter			
payable		100	0.9
90			
Net Sales	100	0.9	90
Cost of Goods	100	1.0	100
Profit(loss)	0		(10)

In Table 8-3, there is no exposure from one quarter to the next when inventory is carried at current rates. The loss in inventory value is offset by the gain in the reduced payable. The earnings statement remains unaffected. When inventory is carried at historical rates, however, an exposure is created. It produces a gain on the balance sheet, because the reduction in the payable is not offset by a corresponding drop in inventory value. However, it also creates a corresponding loss in earnings.

In actuality, the *net* result under either method is the same, since assets and liabilities eventually offset each other. The difference between the methods, of course, is in perception, since many creditors and shareholders concentrate on the profit and loss statement without further analysis. Deferring exchange rate translation of inventory (per FASB 8) can create earnings swings that are hard to justify to outside interests. However, the practice of carrying inventory at the lower of replacement cost or market value could compensate for the higher historical value and prevent an exchange rate loss from flowing through to the earnings.

Summary

Accounting exposure refers to gains and losses resulting from the translation of foreign currency balances. The gains and losses might appear on the balance sheet, the income statement or, in the case of foreign operations, on the consolidated statement.

The monetary/non-monetary convention of FASB 8 created a different area of exposure than the functional currency approach of FASB 52. Under the functional currency guidelines, accounting exposure is divided into transaction and translation exposures. The FASB 8 standard impacted the income statement. The FASB 52 standard impacts the consolidated statement when the foreign operation conducts business in FC currency rather than HC currency.

Accounting exposure is static. It pertains only to numbers in a financial statement at one specific moment: the balance sheet date, for example, or the date the exchange rate is translated. The exposure is revealed after netting out the currency mismatches of that particular moment. What remains is the "exposed net asset position" or the "exposed net liability position." These positions are managed by *balance sheet hedging*, a form of *hedge accounting* that is also somewhat static. The hedge is limited to the establishment of a firm, identifiable commitment that (1) generates gains and losses recognized in a narrow accounting fashion and (2) effectively reduces currency risk to another identifiable financial commitment.

Cash Flow Exposure

Whereas accounting exposure measures the impact of risk at a specific date, cash flow exposure views risk in motion. Cash flow exposure deals with ongoing changes, not just the divergence from one accounting period to the next. Measurement of cash flow exposure not only compares current results with past performance, but also anticipates future revenue streams, sales, costs, and other budgeted items. While accounting exposure is static, cash flow exposure is dynamic.

The impact that cash flow exposure can have on profitability is staggering. At RJR Nabisco, for example, revenues worth over one billion dollars arrive annually from sales in more than 160 countries, all denominated in local currencies. With exposures in exchange rates between Deutsche marks, Italian lira, French francs, and Japanese yen, a reshuffling of the European Monetary System can translate into millions of dollars gained or lost overnight.

Accounting exposure and cash flow exposure are just different ways of looking at the same foreign currency risk. Because foreign currency inflows and outflows generate new mismatches in assets and liabilities, today's cash flow exposure is tomorrow's accounting exposure. Cash flow exposure results in an *operating variance* between accounting reporting periods. In other words, operating income increases and decreases in direct response to currency price moves, but the changes do not appear as translation adjustments until the end of the quarter.

Boris Antl describes four scenarios showing the relationship between operating variance and translation adjustment.[6] This relationship can be seen in Table 8-4. In each case, the reporting period begins with a current FC/HC rate of 1.00.

Table 8-4: Relationship Between Operating Variance and Translation Adjustment

		Total Revenues		
			In HC	
Item	**In FC**	**1st day of reporting period**	**Average throughout period**	**On balance sheet date**
Case # 1	10,000	10,000	10,000	10,000
Case # 2	10,000	10,000	10,000	9,000
Case # 3	10,000	10,000	9,000	9,000
Case # 4	10,000	10,000	9,500	9,000

Table 8-4: Relationship Between Operating Variance and Translation Adjustment *con't.*

Item	Operating Variance	Translation Adjustment	Total Impact on Profitability
Case # 1	0	0	0
Case # 2	0	(1000)	(1000)
Case # 3	(1000)	0	(1000)
Case # 4	(500)	(500)	(1000)

- Case # 1 - FC remains stable. FC10,000 in revenue is derived from sales over a one-year period. This revenue is exposed to changes in the FC/HC exchange rate. In this case, since the exchange rate does not change over the year, there is no impact on the financial statement. Foreign exchange risk goes unnoticed.
- Case # 2 - FC devalues on the balance sheet date. The FC10,000 is recorded as an asset of HC10,000 until the balance sheet date. A devaluation on that date results in a translation adjustment of (HC1000). The loss appears as the result of recognition of accounting exposure.
- Case # 3 - FC devalues on the date revenue begins. On that date, revenues are recorded at an exchange rate of HC0.9. The rate does not change during the period, and no translation adjustment is recorded. However, there is an operating variance of (HC1000) from the previous period. The decreased profits are attributed to cash flow exposure.
- Case # 4 - FC devalues gradually over the reporting period. In this case, revenues are recorded at declining HC values over the period. The portion of devaluation before a specific revenue amount is recorded shows up as an operating adjustment. Once the revenues and expenses are booked, further devaluation is identified as a translation loss and adjusted as such. The losses are examples of both accounting and cash flow exposure.

Actually, all four cases have the same exposure and the same risk. Since cash flow exposure measures variances in operating income, it surfaces when making comparisons between two financial performances. Whereas accounting exposure is found on the balance sheet and income statement, cash flow exposure is found primarily on the statement of consolidated income, where foreign operation performance of the current year is measured against the previous year. Or it may show up in the letter to shareholders, where financial results are analyzed against past performance and future expectations.

Since cash flow exposure results in operating variances, it is often identified by *variance analysis*. Variance analysis isolates the causes of changes between current and previous periods. After the changes are analyzed, they can be properly accounted for, with gains and losses due to exchange rates recognized either as translation adjustments or as operating variances. Variances due to factors other than foreign exchange—changes in management policies, for example—are also addressed in the analysis.

Management of cash flow exposure is still in development. Cash flow exposure is managed by hedging *anticipated* operating variance, and thus falls outside the accounting standards for hedging. In addition to sorting out assets and liabilities to find a net exposure, the hedge for cash flow exposure must use projections of operating income. If the projection is wrong, and the actual amount of mismatched currency does not equal the amount of the hedge, a foreign currency manager may actually be speculating in currency markets. Thus, the Financial Accounting Standards Board is reluctant to establish accounting standards for cash flow exposure.

Static hedges work for accounting exposures, where the risk is contractual and unchanging. However, hedging for cash flow exposure requires continual review as the revised actual and projected numbers flow in.

Operating Exposure

Just as in accounting exposure, cash flow exposure is limited to measuring the impact of changing exchange rates on financial statements; however, cash flow exposure moves beyond accounting exposure by looking to the future risk. *Operating exposure* takes cash flow exposure one step further; it considers the market place. The focus in operating exposure is on production, sales, and marketing, rather than on treasury management. Whereas accounting exposure impacts the financial statement, and cash flow exposure impacts near-term profitability, the effects of operating exposure are mostly felt in terms of long-term profitability, customer base, and market share. Thus, operating exposure is more of a concept than a measurement.

Currency mismatches that create operating exposure are less visible and sometimes harder to identify than those discussed previously. Basically, two mismatches, individually or together, constitute operating exposure:

(1) the mismatch between the *currency of sale* (in which revenues are denominated) and the *currency of production* (in which cost of goods, selling, or administrative expenses are denominated); and

(2) the mismatch between an enterprise's currency of production and the currency of production of a second enterprise competing in the same market.

The first mismatch affects profit margin. The primary impact of the second mismatch is on sales performance and market share. The yen exposure suffered by the Chrysler Corporation, which allowed Toyota to increase its share of the U.S. small car market, is a good example of the second type.

Operating exposure is the hardest to manage of the three types discussed so far because it considers real exchange rates rather than nominal rates. For example, operating exposure exists where a company sells in a country with a stable currency, but produces in another country wracked by inflation. If nominal rates do not keep pace with real rates, cost of goods increases, but competitive pressure holds sales prices steady. Margins narrow and profitability suffers. Let's look at an example. ABC Company produces stereo components in its home plant. Four years ago the company opened a distributorship overseas, which functions in LC. The company ships components to the foreign distributor, which it invoices in HC. When this foreign distribution operation started, the LC/HC exchange rate was 1.00. One of the components manufactured by the company is a head phone set. Based on a unit production cost of 10 HC, the company invoiced its distributor 12.50 HC for each unit shipped. The cost to the distributor, therefore, was 12.50 *LC* per unit. It stocked retailers' shelves at a consumer price of 25 LC per unit, which was competitive with head phones produced in that country.

Soon after, the company's home country began to experience a greater degree of inflation than the foreign country. Cost of labor and parts rose 10% annually for two years running. In response, ABC Co. attempted to raise its distributor price to 15 HC, representing a 20% increase; however, the nominal exchange rate had not changed. One HC was still one LC. With the inflation rate in country LC remaining relatively stable, almost the entire 20% increase in HC costs translated into changes in the real exchange rate.

To profit at a cost of 15 HC per unit, the distributorship, in turn, would have to raise the retail price to 30 LC. But the LC competitors were still retailing units successfully at 25 LC. ABC Co. had no option but to absorb the increased cost.

ABC Co. was impacted by foreign exchange exposure even though there was no visible currency mismatch on the books reflecting accounting exposure. The foreign exchange exposure was an operating exposure, which remains hidden. In this case, operating exposure appeared as decreased operating margin because of the inability to pass on cost increases. If the company invoiced the distributor in local currency (LC) rather than its home currency (HC), the hidden operating exposure would emerge as accounting exposure. In this case, hedge accounting would not help because the nominal rate remained unchanged.

Sometimes, of course, the cost cannot be absorbed. An earlier example discussed an export manager whose company (XYZ Co.) lost the UK market because of the British pound depreciation (or the U.S. dollar appreciation). As for the example with ABC Co., the invoice currency was the home currency. ABC Co. experienced changes in relative inflation rates, with no compensating change in nominal exchange rates. XYZ Co. experienced changes in nominal exchange rates that did not reflect changes in the relative inflation rates. In both cases, it was a change in real exchange rates that created operating exposure. For XYZ Co., if the devaluation of the British pound corresponded to an equal increase in the rate of inflation relative to the United States, the real exchange rate would have remained unchanged. The company could have maintained its sales price in U.S. dollars and remained competitive, regardless of the price increase in British pounds.

A comprehensive study of operating exposure was published by Donald R Lessard and John B. Lightstone.[7] They identified the following characteristics as common to this type of exposure:

- Operating exposure bears no necessary relationship to accounting or contractual exposure.
- It is determined by the structure of the markets in which the company and its competitors source inputs and products. The measurement of operating exposure must accordingly take into account the nature of the company and its competition. (Accounting and cash

flow exposure are limited to measurements from the financial statement.)

- It is not necessarily associated with the country in which goods are sold or inputs are sourced (i.e., the Chrysler Corporation exposure to yen/dollar exchange rates).
- It is not necessarily associated with the currency in which prices are quoted.
- Operating profit varies with changes in the real exchange rate.

Sensitivity to operating exposure varies by industry and by the company's position within the industry. Industries producing products for which demand is fairly inelastic are less susceptible to operating exposure. Companies that sell price-driven commodities such as automobiles, cotton, or computer chips, are susceptible to extensive operating exposure. Within any industry, price leaders have less exposure than price followers who must fall in line.

Monsanto, a major producer of fertilizers and herbicides, is an example of a multi-national company with extensive overseas operations. Monsanto's exposure to currency risk emerged when the appreciating dollar pushed the price of its products out of reach of farmers in developing countries.[8] At the other end of the economic spectrum are Jaguar and Porsche. Unlike manufacturers of more prosaic automobiles, they do not normally see dramatic swings in sales volume due to price fluctuations (i.e., demand for their product is relatively inelastic). Nevertheless, both of these companies saw U.S. sales plummet with the U.S. dollar because of quickly climbing sticker prices.[9] Eastman Kodak, Atari, Commodore International and other consumer product companies also suffered financially within the last few years from operating exposures.

Technology still drives the computer industry rather than price. "But that's going to change," according to Abraham George, of MCM Consultancy Services, Inc.[10] "Everyone will have equally good products, and the battle for market share will be fought on price. That means foreign exchange will be critical." These remarks were made in 1989, and appear to be accurate now. Today, the computer industry looks more and more like a commodity industry, with chips priced daily at the market at so much per MB and IBM clones assembled in shops around the world.

The highly profitable, research-driven business of pharmaceuticals is not considered a cost-sensitive industry. Smithkline Beckman is an international player in this arena. Its sales, for the most part, involve contracts, patents, and licenses. Smithkline saw no market risk involved with currency swings. In fact, managing currencies was viewed more as a way to maximize dollars, rather than to protect earnings.[11] However, at one point within the last five years, the entire sector of drug industry stocks was downgraded by securities analysts from "buy" to "hold," primarily due to adverse currency moves. As health care costs increase world-wide, along with demand for access to advanced technology and bioengineered products, price rationing is becoming much more of a factor. Currency moves can ration some pharmaceutical products out of the reach of individuals or even nations.

The types of currency mismatches that result in operating exposure concern the currency of sale, the currency of production, or competitive pricing. These combine to produce three major forms of operating exposure: *margin* exposure, *competitive* exposure, and *conversion* exposure.

Margin Exposure

The mismatch between sales price and production costs, each denominated in a separate currency, causes operating margins to vary with the exchange rates. "Sales price" may be the cost to the end user, the shelf price, the dealer price, or any other value that goes into the measurement of sales performance. U.S. corporations selling overseas in U.S. dollars almost certainly are at risk from margin exposure. The mismatch occurs at the point where someone converts the local currency to dollars. The converter may be the subsidiary, the jobber, or the end user. Margin exposure is not dependent upon direct competition, though it may be affected by competition between markets, such as when the demand for food competes with the demand for cars. Margin exposure *is* very dependent on the elasticity of the demand curve, plotted against price. For example, prestigious European car makers like Jaguar and Porsche do not compete by price with GM, Ford or Mitsubishi for market share. However, their sales were very sensitive to relative currency values above a certain level. There are, after all, other prestigious goods to be acquired.

Producers of agricultural products, such as fertilizers, pesticides and herbicides, have a margin exposure, especially in developing countries. Shifts in real exchange rates can put these products out of reach of farmers, who simply go without. Again, demand is more a function of price than of direct competition. Advanced technology is another area often subject to margin exposure. Industry leaders in telecommunication technology, such as Motorola, can penetrate new markets only to the degree that the market economy has sufficient funds to install the equipment.

Russia presumably would be very interested in a nation-wide telecommunication network by Motorola if it could be acquired in rubles priced Soviet-style, say at $3.00 per ruble. In another area, niche industries with unique products or services often encounter margin exposure. Laker Air, which carved out a niche in air flights between New York and London, was a prime example.

Competitive Exposure

Competitive exposure emerges when a currency mismatch in production costs between two competitors impacts the sales volume and market share of both (in opposite directions). The auto industries are replete with examples of this type of exposure. Detroit was buffeted by Japanese auto imports when the yen was 200 to the dollar. More recently, Detroit exports are surging and the Japanese companies are reeling with yen at 100 to the dollar. Who would imagine ten, or even five years ago, that General Motors would halt the importation of its Japanese model into the United States because it cost too much to produce in a yen-based economy?

The U.S. and Japanese computer chip manufacturers and other commodity-type businesses are subject to pervasive competitive exposure. An overseas governmental purchasing agency has the option of buying Brazilian soybeans or U.S. soybeans or Canadian wheat or U.S. wheat. Its decision, when not politically driven, depends almost totally on the price. The progress toward removing world trade barriers will make this exposure much more of a factor in the future.

Finally, consumer products that compete for shelf space provide good examples of this type of exposure. Comparative U.S. sales figures of Heineken, Molsen and Coors beer in the U.S., for instance, are directly impacted by changes in the real exchange rates of the U.S. dollar, the Canadian dollar, and the Dutch guilder.

Conversion Exposure

Currency mismatches between consumer pricing and revenue streams, such as sales-generated fees, produce conversion exposure. This exposure is very similar to cash flow exposure, though on a different scale. Here, the risk is to income such as royalties and license or franchise fees.

For example, hamburger and pizza chains are opening new restaurants daily in almost every country. The product is produced, sold, and consumed locally in local currency. Competitive exposure due to currency fluctuation is probably non-existent. Patrons flock to the counters, regardless of the exchange rates. These patrons do, however, produce revenue streams that flow back to the parent as franchise fees, calculated as a percentage of sales. Changes in the nominal rates used to convert LC revenues to HC revenues show up as operating variance over the short term. Changes in inflation rates and real exchange rates impact the conversion of LC revenues to HC revenues over the long term and affect overall profitability.

Pharmaceutical firms, such as Merck, and consumer product companies, such as the Amway Corporation and RJR Nabisco, sell high-margin consumer products world-wide under licensing agreements. This type of marketing is especially sensitive to conversion exposure.

Summary

A diagram of the relationship between the three types of operating exposures can identify a company, or an industry, by its exposure composition. Most often, the company is positioned between the points, subject to a combination of the three basic exposure types. Only one or two types may be prevalent in any particular case. Figure 8-2 illustrates the approximate exposure positions of nine companies.

Figure 8-2: Exposure Positionsof Nine Companies

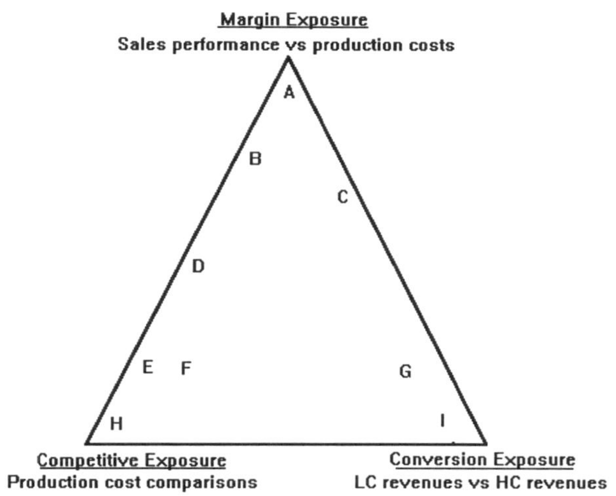

Figure 8-2: Exposure Positions of Nine Companies, *con't.*

A- Motorola, providing high cost telecommunication products to consumer and governments in developing countries, depends on stable currencies to keep products affordable.

B- Laker Air depended on a strong British pound to keep the price of air fares to the United States in line with vacation budgets. Also dependent on comparative prices of goods between New York and London.

C -Monsanto's sales volume of agricultural chemicals depends on their affordability overseas. The company is also exposed to large revenue streams of foreign currencies converted to dollars.

D- Jaguar auto sales to the United States are dependent on discretionary income available to the luxury car market. Jaguar competes to some extent with other makes in this market niche.

E- Heineken U.S. sales are directly dependent on price comparisons with premium beers from domestic and Canadian breweries. The local (LC) economy also affects percentage of sales between premium and regular beer.

F- Intel pricing policy for computer chips is heavily influenced by cost comparison with Japanese chip manufacturers, as well as differentiation in technology.

G - Amway markets a large consumer product line to countries world-wide. Competes well in a high volume, high margin market, but subject to conversion exposure from revenue streams of various currencies. Also exposed to margin variability due to its U.S. dollar production costs.

H - Chrysler and other U.S. car manufacturers have experienced several changes in an ongoing battle for market share with yen cost-based automobiles. Chrysler had the largest exposure in the 1980s because its operations were almost completely U.S.-dollar denominated.

I - McDonald's franchises ring the globe. McDonald's has no significant margin exposure, since it produces and sells in local currency. Moreover, volume and market share are largely insensitive to competitive pricing. It does, however, have a high degree of exposure in conversion of foreign currency franchise fees to home currency income.

Strategic Exposure

Strategic exposure focuses on cash flow exposures and operating exposures to protect short- to long-term profitability and performance and long-term strategic options; however, definitions outside accounting exposure are imprecise. Strategic exposure may be just another name for operating exposure. After all, protection of market share and competitive position are certainly strategic objectives. In an attempt to define strategic exposure, Helmut Hagemann offers a scenario that emphasizes forecast and planning.[12] He looks at long-term exposure.

Hagemann uses an example of a hypothetical Japanese auto company. This company plans to export a new model line to the United States. The first step is to design a car and build a factory, so investment funds are allocated for that purpose. Then distribution in the United States must be set up and the cars exported. As the cars sell, U.S. dollar revenues are generated in U.S. bank accounts. Finally, these deposits are converted to yen and repatriated. Accounting exposure is created at the time of conversion, cash flow exposure is introduced when dollar revenues begin to accumulate, and operating exposure occurs when the company begins to actually compete in the export market. Strategic exposure starts when the company first begins to plan the operation.

Quantification of strategic exposure requires forethought and time and includes "what if" scenarios. Just as for operating exposure, strategic exposure measures the long-term effects of changes in real exchange rates. But the focus for strategic exposure is more on trends in macroeconomics than on microeconomics and currency fluctuations. Forecasting changes in exchange rate *systems* is more important than predictions of exchange rates *per se*.

Operating exposure involves measurements of the competitor's pricing structure. Strategic exposure involves measurements of the overall corporate competitive position. All corporate assumptions that go into operations are analyzed from the bottom up, including assumptions about production, primary markets for products, secondary markets for by-products, and demand sensitivity for raw materials and their sourcing. The analysis also includes tax implications, financing, and involvement with equity and debt markets. When foreign operations sell in different foreign end-user markets, the analysis will also cover third currency regimes. The analysis is also applied to the competition and to the industry.

Again, the major difference between operating exposure and strategic exposure is one of scale. In the case of a tractor manufacturer, for example, knowledge of operating exposure will help determine how to price the tractors. Knowledge of strategic exposure will help decide where to produce them and where to sell them.

Value-Based Exposure

In one sense, a company has only one currency exposure: the exposure to the volatility of currency exchange rates. However, this exposure can be segmented and measured from different angles, in different exposure categories. This procedure is necessary for effective management. Value-based exposure pools the measurements, and views them as one complete variable, subject to an overall business management approach.

One cannot focus only on balance sheet exposures or earnings or even market share and competitive position. Effective currency management starts with the corporate mission and the long-term corporate objectives. A foreign management program should further corporate objectives and enhance the value of the corporation for the stockholders and the community.

Managing exposure in one area may either offset or augment exposure in another. The relationships between both visible and hidden exposures must be identified before decisions can be made on how and whether to manage them. Also, as the concept of strategic and value-based exposure develops, the companies that stay in touch with the developments will be the most prepared to compete in the twenty-first century market place.

CHAPTER 9

Principals of Hedging

In many quarters of the trading world, the activity known as "hedging" still conjures up images of corn or cattle more often than Swiss francs or Brazilian reals. This perception of hedging as only an agricultural business practice is rapidly changing: commercial entities are now turning *en masse* to the markets to manage their financial exposures. As a concept, hedging encompasses much more than simply buying and selling futures or forward contracts; however, no matter which form it takes, certain core principles are involved, including long-short relationships, parallel markets, risk transference, and basis correlation.

The Long and the Short of it

In very simple terms, life can be divided into long, short, and neutral positions, or "longs," "shorts," and "not-longs." *Longs* refer to the things a person has—the assets on life's balance sheet. Neutrals, or *not-longs*, are the things a person does not have and does not feel obligated to acquire. Neutrals do not appear on life's balance sheet. *Shorts* are obligations to be fulfilled. The obligation might be something owed which the holder is contractually obligated to acquire in order to discharge a debt (including money). The obligation might be a desire to acquire something to further the person's objectives or maintain his or her course.

Thus, a "typical suburbanite" might be long a spouse, children, a house, two cars, and a backyard barbecue. They might be not-long a vacation home: they do not own or want one. They might be short a sailboat, if they felt they just had to have one. Chances are they are also short cash. In a business example, a car distributor starts out long cash and short cars. After purchasing inventory from the distributor, he is long cars and short cash. He gradually goes long cash and short cars again, and the cycle begins anew.

Values of life's long and short positions continually change, and people are not indifferent to those changes. The suburbanite with a spouse and children finds value in "being long" a family, and looks forward to this value increasing, along with the value of his home, cars and the opportunity to cook out in the backyard. On the other hand, people hope values will decrease in their short positions. The suburbanite wants the sailboat to drop in price so he can buy it and become "long" the boat. Once he is long the boat, he hopes it will go up in value. A person who is short cash, and needs to borrow, wants money to decrease in value (defined here as the rate of interest). A person who is long cash and intends to invest will want the value of cash to increase.

By expanding on these concepts, the definition of longs and shorts can be simplified as follows:

> *A long position (or long exposure) is anything that benefits the holder by an increase in value and adversely effects the holder by a decrease in value.*
>
> *A short position (or short exposure) is anything that benefits the holder by a decrease in value and adversely effects the holder by an increase in value.*

The concept is not limited to tangible positions. For example, a U.S. company competing in the domestic market against an import produced in Canada has a long Canadian dollar exposure, even though it does not own a single Canadian dollar. The company's long exposure arises because it holds a competitive position that benefits from a rise in the value of Canadian dollars. The Canadian firm, of course, has a long U.S. dollar exposure for the opposite reason. The U.S. firm is "long Canadian dollars," and the Canadian firm is "long U.S. dollars."

The positions of the two companies, then, are mirror images of each other, illustrating an important principle of long and short positions. Any short position in *foreign currency* is the same as a long position in *home currency*, and a short position in the *home currency* is a long position in a *foreign currency*. One cannot exist without the other. The U.S. company, therefore, has a short U.S. dollar, long Canadian dollar position. The Canadian company has a long U.S. dollar, short Canadian dollar position.

"Long" and "Short" as Trading Terms

The three types of positions discussed relative to life also apply to currency trading. A "*long*" position implies ownership, and in this case, the asset is a currency contract. With a position that is "*not-long*" or neutral, the trader does not own the contract in question and is not obliged to acquire it. With a "*short*" position, traders are obligated to acquire a contract or a long position because they *owe* it to someone else. Obligations in this example could take several forms, not all legal obligations; however, a short position in a currency contract is a contractual liability, in the sense that the holder legally owes currency to the counterparty of the contract.

For example, assume that on February 1 the ABC Company calls its bank and simultaneously buys 4,000,000 Swiss francs 30 days forward and sells 2,000,000 Canadian dollars, also 30 days forward. On February 15, ABC Company buys 1,000,000 Canadian dollars 15 days forward, sells 2,000,000 Canadian dollars 30 days forward, and sells 2,000,000 Swiss francs 30 days forward. The corresponding entries in the company's foreign exchange account can be seen in Table 9-1.

Table 9-1: ABC Company FX Account

Date		buy	sell	value date
1-Feb.	Canadian dollar		2,000,000	1-Mar
1-Feb.	Swiss franc	4,000,000		1-Mar
15-Feb.	Canadian dollar	1,000,000		1-Mar
15-Feb.	Canadian dollar		2,000,000	15-Mar
15-Feb.	Swiss franc		2,000,000	15-Mar

At the close of business on February 1, ABC Company has a *short* position of 2,000,000 Canadian dollars, and a *long* position of 4,000,000 Swiss francs. Note that nothing in this example indicates whether or not the company possesses the Canadian dollars that it now owes. The short position is in this account only. Though the company may have Canadian dollars elsewhere, in this account it owes contracts that are *not* in the account. The company is therefore obligated to acquire a long position in the account to discharge the obligation.

After the additional transactions of February 15, the company has short positions of 4,000,000 Canadian dollars and 2,000,000 Swiss francs, and long positions of 1,000,000 Canadian dollars and 4,000,000 Swiss francs. The long and short positions in Canadian dollars for the same value date offset each other, leaving the company *net short* 3,000,000 Canadian dollars. However, since there are no opposing positions with the same value date in Swiss francs, the company remains long 4,000,000 and short 2,000,000 Swiss francs. Using market terminology, the account shows a net long position of 2,000,000 Swiss francs and a "foreign exchange swap" of 2,000,000 Swiss francs. With forward contracts, unlike futures contracts, all positions, including those that are offset, stay on the books until the value date.

This action of offsetting illustrates another principle concerning long and short positions. The word "equal" refers to positions that are identical in value and in duration (i.e., value dates), and the following is true of equal positions:

Equal but opposite (long and short) positions offset each other, creating an overall neutral position in which changes in value are balanced out.

Unlimited Short Risk

"Equal" long and short contractual positions are equal in every respect except one: the amount of risk that the position holder assumes. For example, consider counterparties' obligations on both sides of a given contract. Assume that the bank acts as an intermediary between ABC Company and XYZ Company in the 3,000,000 Canadian dollar short position. Thus, XYZ Company has a long position in 3,000,000 Canadian dollars that corresponds to ABC's short position. (The bank still acts as a dealer, but transfers the contractual obligations to both parties.) If the Canadian dollar was worth $.80 when the positions were contracted, what are the risks to both companies?

Assume the Canadian government undergoes a major calamity, and the Canadian dollar becomes worthless, dropping to zero value. XYZ Company's contract becomes completely valueless. It paid $2,400,000 for the long position (3,000,000 X .80) and has lost all $2,400,000. Still, $2,400,000 is the maximum loss that can be incurred.

Compare XYZ Company's risk to the risk assumed by ABC Company. The Canadian dollar may rise drastically in value. By the value date, the Canadian dollar could theoretically have a U.S. dollar value of $8.00, or $80.00 or $800.00. In short positions, the risk is virtually limitless. ABC Company must buy the currency, whatever the price, to discharge its liability. (If the example appears preposterous, substitute the Russian ruble for the U.S. dollar.) This high risk for short positions means they are not suitable for all investment portfolios. Long option positions can fit in a retiree's income-producing portfolio, where preservation of principle is the main objective. However, a short option position that is not "covered" by the underlying asset does not belong in such an account. Known as "naked writes," uncovered short positions are reserved for only the most aggressive and affluent investors. A little ditty, recited now and then in the currency pits, makes the point:

He who sells what isn't his'n, buys it back or goes to pris'n.

Definition of Hedging

Hedging may be concisely and simply defined as follows:

A hedge is the offset of a given position by an equal and opposite position, in which the effect of the offset reduces or eliminates the effects of a value change in both.

Convoluted positions and transactions must be reduced to their long and short components to more easily analyze the bottom line in any type of hedge program or proposal.

Laker Air, discussed earlier, was the charter travel service that flew British vacationers to New York until its demise when the British pound dropped sharply against the U.S. dollar. Laker Air had a short U.S. dollar position, which included the transaction exposure of a dollar payable for the purchase of airliners and a cash flow exposure. After all, the British pound, strong relative to the dollar, provided an incentive for British vacationers to fly to New York and shop. Perhaps Laker Air should have managed this position with long dollar hedges in the currency market against the payable. It could also have taken a 'long dollar' cash flow hedge position by marketing its service to American tourists visiting Europe. With this strategic hedge, dollar revenues would increase as the dollar strengthened, making trips to England more affordable to Americans. Whether such actions would have kept Laker Air solvent is unknown, of course. The point to remember is that long and short positions can be hedged in many ways, not just with activity in the currency markets.

As another example, Japanese yen exposures at one time wreaked havoc in the U.S. automotive industry because of the operating exposures that continue to affect competitive positions in this industry. The big three domestic auto companies have a continuously overhanging long yen position that influences their markets. The higher the yen in value, the more competitive the U.S. companies are and the less price pressure is exerted by Japanese imports. Conversely, the Japanese manufacturers grapple with a long dollar position in their U.S. export operations. For them, stronger dollars translate into higher profits when converted back into yen. Also, a stronger dollar creates a more receptive market for Japanese cars because yen-based products are cheaper in dollar terms. Operational hedges for the U.S. manufacturers should involve short yen positions. Chrysler, for example, began importing Mitsubishi engines. The Japanese hedge their operating exposures with short dollar positions, most notably by building assembly plants in the United States to obtain a dollar-denominated cost of goods sold.

Locking in Current Values

Classic hedging has been used only to lock in the *value* of a position that is in effect when the hedge is initiated. By definition, the hedge reduces the effect of possible value change by creating an opposite change in value to counterbalance it. The following examples, shown in Figures 9-1 and 9-2, illustrate classic hedging. On April 2, ABC company acquires a 1,000,000 Canadian dollar payable, due in four months. It hedges by purchasing ten contracts of September futures, each equivalent to 100,000 Canadian dollars. The payable and the futures contracts are opposite positions, equal in amount. The positions are also equal in duration, since ABC will liquidate the futures positions (by offset) on the same day that payment is made. The spot exchange rate on April 2 is $.7270. The forward rate (and futures price) for the third Wednesday of September is $.7210, reflecting the fact that the Canadian dollar is then a discount currency.

Figure 9-1 shows the result of the hedge in an up market. The loss from the exposure is more than offset by a gain in the futures. Figure 9-2 shows the results of the hedge in a down market. Clearly in this instance, the company would have been better off by not hedging, as the loss, or "hedge burden" reduces the cash market gain by more than half. Undoubtedly, the company would not have hedged if it had known that the market would go down. The company did not know what the market would do, of course, and decided to give up the opportunity of market gain to protect itself from potential market loss.

Figure 9-1: UP Market

Action	Cash Market	Futures Market
Book Payable; Buy Futures	Short C$ 1,000,000	Long 10 Contracts of Sept Futures
	April 2 spot at .7270	*Sept futures at .7218*
4 mo. later ...		
Exchange US$ for C$; Make Payment; Sell Futures	Long C$ 1,000,000	Short 10 Contract of Sept Futures
	August 4 spot at .7370	*Sept futures at .7362*
Gain (loss)	($10,000)	$14,400

Figure 9-2: Down Market

Action	Cash Market	Futures Market
Book Payable; Buy Futures	Short C$ 1,000,000	Long 10 Contracts of Sept Futures
	April 2 spot at .7270	*Sept futures at .7218*
4 mo. later ...		
Exchange US$ for C$; Make Payment; Sell Futures	Long C$ 1,000,000	Short 10 Contract of Sept Futures
	August 4 spot at .7170	*Sept futures at .7162*
Gain (loss)	$10,000	($5,600)

Thus, reduction of risk comes at a price: the loss of opportunity to realize a gain on the exposure. As in any game of chance, the amount of reward is tied to the risk taken. Hedging takes away risk and, with it, the opportunity to profit by chance. The effects of increasing and decreasing values disappear along with the exposures.

An Imperfect Hedge

Another problem with hedging is the imprecision involved. Hedging, regardless of the form, hardly ever results in complete offsets. If the examples shown here were perfect hedges, the $10,000 loss would be offset exactly by a $10,000 gain; however, the positions were placed in markets not completely identical. In this case, both the up market and down market resulted in a gain. The gains are phantom profits, however, occurring because the hedge involved a short spot, long forward position in a discount currency. A discount currency pays higher short-term interest rate yields than the U.S. dollar. Because of its relative currency positions, the company pays out additional interest on the liability that almost exactly equals what it gains from the hedge. If the hedge were against a long exposure, in which a short forward position would result in a net loss, the company would have realized an offsetting interest rate gain. What if the company does not have to pay the interest difference because its terms of agreement for the liability do not provide for such payment? It does not matter. The liability was contracted in a "costlier" currency, no matter how favorable or unfavorable the terms were. Both losses and gains due solely to interest rate parities should be thoroughly understood and communicated in advance to everyone involved in currency management.

Transferring Risk

Another basic principle of hedging is the transference of risk. Hedges do not eliminate exposures and the risks: they transfer them. The failure to understand this principle is the major cause of recognized exposures being transformed unknowingly into unrecognized exposures. The hedging strategy determines where the exposure is transferred.

Hedging, by definition, is synonymous with risk transference. Assume ABC Company has a long position of 1,000,000 in Swiss francs. The position is unhedged, so any change in the value of Swiss francs affects ABC financially. ABC eliminates this "value change effect" by changing their long position into a "not-long" position—the only position that insulates them from changing values. ABC obtains a "not-long" position by eliminating Swiss franc ownership risk: they give the currency away or convert it into something else (a Swiss Chalet, for example, or a short Swiss franc contract that converts to an equivalent amount of dollars). If ABC buys the Chalet, they pay the currency to another party. If they go short in the futures or forward market, another party must go long to create the contract.

Therefore, any action taken to divest oneself of a currency ownership position will result in another party acquiring that position. In any form of transaction, the counterparty will go from short to not-long, or from not-long to long, or from long to "longer." If the counterparty had a risk in Swiss francs before (a short position, perhaps) she may or may not have a risk after the transaction. If she had no risk before, she most definitely does now, since we transferred the risk to her. If we hedge Swiss francs in the currency market, the counterparty may be a floor broker or another hedger. If we hedge in other markets, the counterparty could be our supplier, our customer, or even our own market place.

Transferring Risk to the Market

In discussing transfer of risk to a market, the term "market" refers to the market in which the company sells its product or service. The market may be the local economy at large or the segment that includes the end user. Toyota and Honda build automobile plants in the United States to transfer their long dollar exposures and the attendant risks to the U.S. economy. If the dollar drops in value against the yen, the American consumer pays cheaper dollars (relative to the yen) to own the car, but also receives cheaper dollars (relative to the yen) to build it.

Consider what happens in the sale of an export with the price tag payable in FC. The price paid is directly influenced by the exchange rate between the home currency of the exporter and the local currency of the purchaser. Until the item is paid for, the would-be purchaser assumes a short foreign currency exposure. The purchaser is "short" the car, or the tuna, or the camera until cash (FC) is paid. It is to the purchaser's financial advantage to see HC lose value.

Technically, if a foreign manufacturer starts to produce its product in this country, the U.S. consumers transfer their short exposure to the manufacturer while it transfers its long exposure to them. All parties are now hedged with offsetting positions. The price of a Mazda out of Flat Rock, Michigan no longer depends on the price of tea in Japan. It now depends on the price of labor and parts in the midwest. Risks have been exchanged by transference of exposure in both directions.

Transferring Risk to the Hedger

Assume ABC Co. has a payable of 100 million Mexican pesos, due in two years. Since ABC has no pesos, it is short 100 million Mexican pesos. They can transfer the risk several ways. They can enter the over-the-counter market and swap pesos for dollars on a two-year contractual basis. The swap would be structured so that ABC buys pesos from a counterparty in exchange for dollars. Two years from now, when ABC pays off the liability, they return the pesos and retrieve the dollars. In the meantime, any gain realized in the exchange rate of the pesos offsets their liability exposure.

Here, ABC initiates the swap by buying pesos from the counterparty; therefore, the counterparty "goes short" pesos. In essence, ABC transferred the risk of their exposure to the counterparty. A transference of risk with currency swaps is normally an exchange of positions between hedgers. In this example, the counterparty may be a U.S. company with a 100 million peso asset to be liquidated and repatriated in U.S. dollars in two years. The U.S. company has a long exposure in pesos and accepts ABC's short position to offset it. In the process of accepting ABC's short position, it transfers the risk of its long position to ABC.

Transferring Risk to the Speculator

Consider another liability: a payable of 10,000,000 Canadian dollars due in six months. ABC transfers the risk of this short position with futures contracts. They enter an order on the CME to buy 100 contracts of September Canadian dollars at the opening. The order will give ABC a long futures position that is equal and opposite to their cash market exposure. The market opens and immediately begins to move higher. ABC's order stipulates that the transaction must take place on the opening, and a floor trader takes the other side of the order by selling the contracts to ABC. Even though the market is strong, the trader feels it will back off, allowing him to cover his new short position with a profit. The futures market is an ideal arena for "hedger to speculator" risk transference. The speculator accepts the risk in the attempt to make a profit, and the hedger (ABC) gives him the risk. The trader may turn around and repurchase the contracts from some other party five minutes later. His later actions are irrelevant to ABC.

Speculators provide a vital economic service, by accepting risk. Periodically, an industry involved in commodities or securities will label the speculator as the "problem with prices." Certain members of the Cattle Producers Association, for example, sought to ban speculation in cattle futures a few years ago. According to this group, the speculators were driving down the prices and thus driving cattlemen out of business. Speculators were also blamed in the aftermath of the 1987 stock market crash. Detractors argued that the speculators' reckless program trading with baskets of stock and stock index futures, without regard to the economic well-being of the marketplace, caused the market to collapse. Thus, many corporate financial officers avoid foreign exchange markets and the speculators running them.

Now consider the Canadian dollar hedge without the speculator. With no floor traders, no one in the pit would take the other side of ABC's order for 100 contracts in the opening. Hedgers, after all, are busy running companies, not trading currencies. In this scenario, brokers would look for counterparties (other hedgers) and match up open orders. Hedgers, however, are risk averse, and would not have sold into a strong market. Consequently, ABC could not have transferred its risk until prices were higher.

Actually, without speculators, the futures markets would probably be too thin to trade at any price. Hedgers might not be able to close out positions in a market with too few participants; with no currency funds, pools, partnerships or other trading accounts.

Even the interbank dealer, who buys and sells for his own account and matches orders, would avoid ABC's order in a market with fewer players. If speculation was disallowed, he could not afford to "make a market" in the currency until it settled down. Unquestionably, the speculator is essential to the liquidity of the foreign exchange markets. Hedging would be extremely expensive and burdensome without it.

Transferring Risk to the Supplier

Financial hedges may not be necessary in a hedge program. Even the most carefully planned currency trading is never risk-free. Without careful management, exposure risk may translate into even higher trading risk. Other ways to reduce exposures should be considered. One possibility is the transfer of short exposures, such as deferred payables, to the supplier. For a U.S. company, if purchase orders can be denominated in U.S. dollars, the risk of the exposure automatically transfers to the supplier.

Of course, this type of hedging is not always the most desirable, even when it is available. The supplier may not be willing to assume the exposure. The price he demands for assuming the risk may exceed the cost of hedging in the foreign exchange markets. The supplier may agree to contract provisions that allow for a *sharing* of the risk; however, some escalator clauses create larger exposures than the foreign currency itself.

Even if the supplier will accept the exposure risk, it may not be wise to allow the transfer. A furniture manufacturer was contracting to buy an annual supply of lumber from a Canadian mill. During a corporate policy meeting, the company tried to get a handle on the resultant Canadian dollar exposure. Various suggestions were tossed about. The majority present began leaning toward denominating the contract in U.S. dollars, thereby avoiding foreign exchange exposure altogether. There were assurances that the supplier would agree; he was not in a position to object. At this point, however, one of the principals made a rather insightful observation:

> "We know how to hedge," she said, "and we know how to do it right. (The supplier) has never hedged and doesn't understand it. If he tries, he may lose control of it, and get into deep financial straits. If he doesn't hedge, he may lose his shirt on the deal. Either way, we lose our supplier."

Transferring the risk to the supplier in this case would only serve to exchange transactional exposure for less manageable operating exposure. The decision was made to contract in Canadian dollars, and to develop a hedge program toward that end.

Transferring Risk to the Customer

By far the most common method of transferring risk for U.S. companies, and by far the riskiest, is to give it to the customer. Companies using this method send their products overseas with catalogs and price sheets denominated in U.S. dollars. This method does not work as well as it once did. The international customer today does not have to buy American—or Japanese, or German, or British. The bazaar is replete with competing products from every corner of the globe. Some competitor will almost always supply the right product at the right price in the right currency. Transferring risk to the customer trades visible (accounting) exposure for hidden (operating) exposure. Hidden longs and shorts are easy to ignore, and may cause damage before they are found. The long and short accounting positions disappear when a company transfers exposure risk to the customer, but their markets are in jeopardy of disappearing along with them.

Parallel Markets

Hedging works because parallel markets exist.* A parallel market may be defined as follows:

> *Given a market in which an item is valued at a price that correlates significantly with the price of the same or related item in a different market, the two markets are considered to be parallel markets.*

Many parallel markets exist. Market pairs can be differentiated from each other by almost any imaginable criteria as long as they are, indeed, separate markets and their prices correlate. For example, U.S. treasury bills and Eurodollar contracts trade in parallel markets. Prices correlate because both are based on short-term U.S. interest rates. Other examples of parallel markets are treasury notes and treasury bonds (both priced in accordance with longer-term U.S. interest rates); crude oil and its distillates; soybeans, soybean oil, and soybean meal; the S&P 500 futures index and the underlying stock; the Swiss franc spot market and several Swiss franc option markets; the spot market for a currency peg and the spot market for the currency pegged to it; the gold bullion market and the London fix; the cash market for bacon and the futures market for pork bellies; corn markets and sorghum markets; the Kansas City wheat market and the Chicago wheat market; and the U.S. automotive labor market and the U.S. automotive consumer market. Though some of these parallels stretch the boundaries of the definition, the list is undeniably long.

Why are parallel markets important to hedging? All hedges take place in parallel markets, with one "leg" in each market place. For example, what happens if a company attempts to hedge 1,000,000 Swiss francs in a single market? Assume that the Swiss francs are in the form of cash. Thus, the company has a long cash market position. It hedges with a short cash market position, a Swiss Franc payable. A long cash position and a short cash position equals no cash position. The company is "not long," but it is not hedged either. Figure 9-3 shows that the definition of hedging presented above (page 187) is somewhat incomplete. A more precise definition follows:

> *A hedge is the offset of a given position by an equal and opposite position in a separate, but parallel market, in which the effect of the offset reduces or eliminates the effect of a value change in both positions.*

*Not to be confused with "Black Markets" as defined in chapter two.

Foreign currency hedges are not restricted to the financial markets. There are parallel currency markets in cash (spot), forwards, futures, options, and over-the-counter agreements such as swaps. A financial hedge is in place whenever two equal and opposite positions exist in any two financial marketplaces. Other hedges are possible in non-financial markets. For example, assume that "Wearforever," a European outdoor wear manufacturer, sells to the Australian consumer market. Wearforever is long Australian dollars: its cash flow is denominated in the local currency, and its profits increase when the Australian dollar strengthens against its home currency. But the long position is also an operating exposure, since a weaker Australian dollar can price the company's products, which are cost-based in home currency, out of the market. The company hedges by forming a manufacturing venture with an Australian partner, thereby creating a short Australian dollar position in the labor and/or raw materials (wool) market. Now a declining Australian dollar will lower production costs and increase sales, thus maintaining profit margins.

Figure 9-3: Hedges are Produced by Opposite Currency Exposures in Parallel Markets

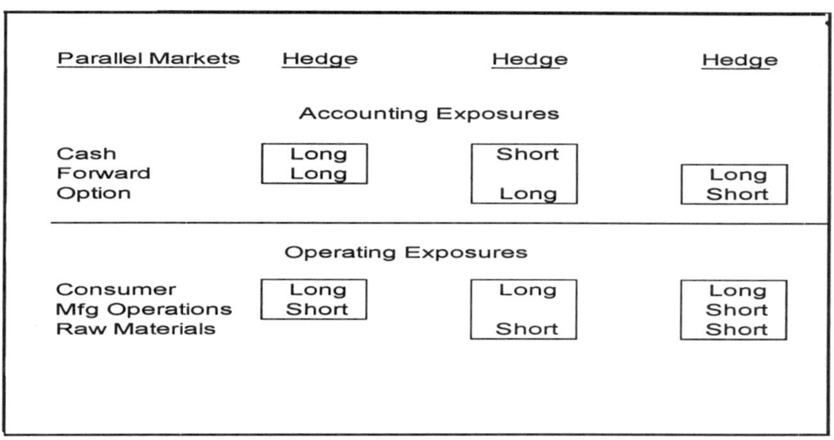

Basis

The terms *basis* and *spread* both refer to differences in prices, but each is used in a slightly different context. "Spreads" in foreign exchange markets are the difference between the offer and the bid quoted by the dealer. Price spread may refer to the difference in price standards for the same item. A price spread might be the difference between the retail and wholesale price, or between the consumer price and the cost of production. Price spreads also refer to spreads in price between related items in the same or parallel markets, such as the spread between spot Canadian dollars and September Canadian dollar futures, or the spread between cash market wheat and wheat futures contracts. The term "spread" implies significant price correlation between the two values, just as the term implies significant price correlation between the two markets.

The term *basis*, on the other hand, does not *necessarily* imply a price correlation. For example, in the basis between Swiss francs and Deutsche marks, or between Chicago wheat and Kansas City wheat, or between the S&P 500 index and the value line index, the prices of the two items show significant correlation. On the other hand, in the basis between Deutsche marks and Japanese yen, or between gold and British pounds, or between coffee and copper, or between cabbages and kings, the prices of the two items are not significantly correlated. The basis is simply the difference in prices between any two marketable items.

Obviously, the price basis can be volatile: narrow one day and wide the next. If two markets are completely unrelated, the basis is random and not useful for hedging. However, a correlation between prices identifies parallel markets. Correlation may be spotted by charting historical price data and finding evidence of *predictability.* If two items' prices move together in highly predictable fashion over a significant amount of time, the markets are *parallel* and *hedgeable.*

Basis, Correlation, and "Substitutability"

"Price correlation" in parallel markets means the two prices follow each other in predictable fashion. The more closely prices move together over time, the higher the correlation. One unit of measurement often used to describe correlation is the coefficient of correlation. The coefficient of correlation is the change in price of one item for every one unit change in the price of the other item.

If the coefficient equals 1.00, correlation is perfect: if price "A" moves up one, price "B" moves up one; if price "A" moves down two, price "B" moves down two; if price "A" moves up three, price "B" moves up three. In other words, the two prices move as one price. An example of basis correlation with a coefficient of 1.00 would be the basis between Japanese yen spot and 30-day forwards, in a situation where the short-term interest rates for both yen and U.S. dollars remained absolutely fixed. On the other hand, a coefficient of zero means the prices have no relationships to each other and the basis is random.

Just as for any price movement, the historical basis between two prices can be plotted, measured, and predicted. The higher the correlation, of course, the more reliable the prediction of future correlation; however, a prediction is merely a guess; two prices that have moved together historically will not necessarily move together in the future.

For example, consider the trading history of gold and silver. For centuries, these two metals substituted readily with each other. Gold coins and silver coins were exchanged for trade goods in every port. In fact, the first U.S. dollar coin minted by congress could contain either 371.25 grains of gold or 24.71 grains of silver, since each had equal value. This mutual property of "substitutability" continued to hold in modern times. Just as now, gold was considered to be the ultimate inflation hedge, the currency of choice in difficult times. Silver was thought of as "poor man's gold," and could be hoarded just as easily at a much lower cost. The two were interchangeable to investors.

Now the historical relationship between gold and silver appears to have broken down. The ratio of gold to silver mandated by congress for coinage (371.25 to 24.71), no longer describes the basis between them. Recently, gold traded around $370 an ounce, and silver was about $4.00 an ounce. The basis is both wider than before and much less predictable. Gold traded from just over $280 in 1985 to over $480 an ounce in 1988, a $200 increase. In the same time period, silver traded mostly flat between $6.00 and $5.50, with a temporary spurt up to almost $10.00 during 1987. At this point silver may be more an industrial metal whose price changes with the economy than a "precious" metal whose price moves with gold. In any event, because of the currently low correlation coefficient between the two markets, they are probably no longer parallel.

Effective hedges depend on the degree to which the hedge substitutes for the item hedged. A financial hedge in the currency market is a temporary substitute purchase and sale, to be terminated as soon as the "real" purchase or sale takes place. This principle is illustrated in Figures 9-1 and 9-2. ABC company has a 1,000,000 Canadian dollar payable, due in four months. It *temporarily substitutes* the upcoming purchase of Canadian dollars required for the payment with a long futures position. Four months later, when the "real" purchase of Canadian dollars takes place, the company terminates the substituted purchase by liquidating the futures position. If the exposure resulted from a Canadian dollar receivable rather than a payable, the company would "sell" the Canadian dollars received in four months. ABC hedges this position with a temporary sale, by going short in the futures market, then terminates the "substituted sale" by closing out the short position when the "real" sale takes place.

If hedges are simply substitutions, the market in which the hedge takes place must serve as a substitute for the market in which the exposure takes place. For this substitution to be effective, the two markets must be parallel: their prices must move together predictably. The basis is suitably predictable when the coefficient of correlation is 0.70 or higher. This additional condition belongs in the definition of a hedge, as follows:

> *A hedge is the offset of a given position by an equal and opposite position in a separate, but parallel market, in which the effect of the offset reduces or eliminates the effect of a value change in both positions. Markets are parallel if their price basis correlates at a coefficient of 0.70 or higher.*

Figure 9-4: A Parallel Market Hedge

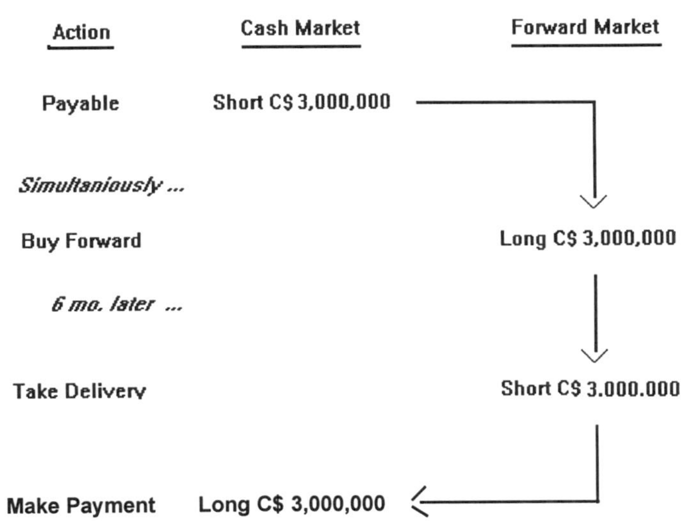

Taking delivery is equivalent to initiating a short position, making payment is the same as going long. Long and short positions in parallel markets offset each other. Long and short positions in the same market cancel each other out.

Figure 9-5: Charting the Basis

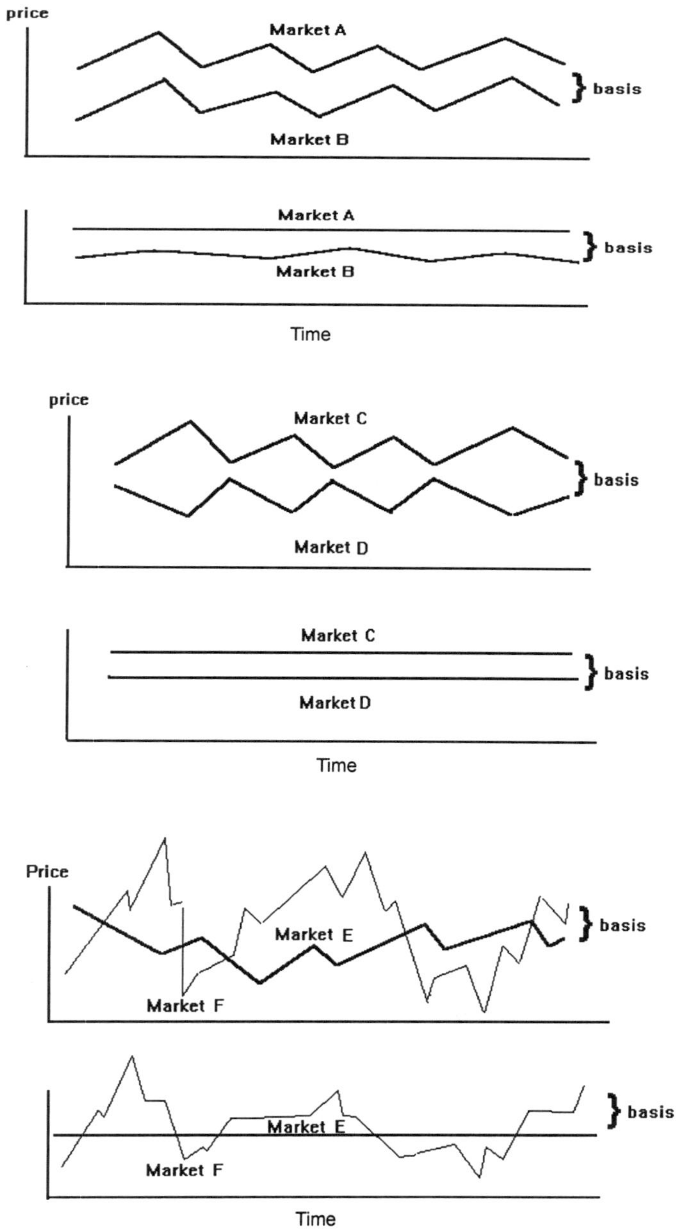

Figure 9-5: Charting the Basis, *con't.*

Two price charts are illustrated for each pair of markets. The top chart in each grouping shows individual price moves for each market. In the second chart of each pair, the prices of one market are held constant at "0" value and the price *differences* of the second market are plotted against this "base line" to show the correlation. This type of chart is known as a "basis chart." Basis is often referred to as a premium or a discount. In these examples, the price basis of Markets B and D are at a discount.

The basis between Markets A and B shows a high degree of correlation, with a coefficient well above 0.7. These two markets are therefore considered parallel for hedging purposes. Note that there can also be a high degree of *negative* correlation, such as with Markets C and D. Mirror images of each other, the correlation is perfect, with a coefficient of -1.00. These markets are also well suited for hedging.

Reverse hedges are used for negatively correlated markets. Assume, for example, that Market C represents the *yield* of a U.S. T-bill in the cash market, and Market D represents the price of a futures contract for the same bill. The two markets maintain a perfect negative correlation: an uptick in yield is a downtick in price. If a hedger were *long* short-term interest rates, he would *go long* T-bill futures. This strategy appears to be the opposite of a normal hedge; however, in this case, the loss caused by a decline in interest rates is offset by a gain from the higher futures *price*.

Basis charts can be drawn for any two markets. If the two prices are of vastly different scales one can be plotted as a percentage of the other. In the price relationship between cabbages and kings, Market E might be the value of a room full of gold (a king's ransom) over time, and Market F might be the price of a head of cabbage over the same length of time. Presumably the correlation coefficient of these two markets is zero.

The Hedge Triad

High correlations can generally be found in the currency markets. When cash market exposures are matched with hedge positions in forwards, options, or futures, the parallel market movements practically guarantee the results of the hedge, but financial markets are not suitable for all types of exposures. Swiss franc futures may parallel the gains and losses from Swiss franc cash accounts, but they may correlate very weakly to variances in cash flow from operating a Swiss ski lodge. Strategic, operating, and cash flow exposures may have to be eliminated, reduced, or otherwise managed outside the currency markets. For these types of exposure, currency management may not include currency hedging except in the broadest sense of the word.

Three methods are used to "hedge" foreign exchange exposure: (1) *operating strategies*; (2) *financial adjustments*; and (3) *transactional hedging*. The first two are often referred to as "natural" hedges. Natural hedging may involve the offset of opposite positions, though sometimes it means only eliminating the source of exposure or shortening the duration of the exposure position. A natural hedge may be as mundane as adjusting payment and invoice schedules or as far-reaching as relocating a manufacturing plant. Operating strategies, especially, involve changes in business practices and may encompass new approaches or business goals. For this reason, application of natural hedges is often referred to as "strategic hedging," regardless of the type of exposure managed.

The third hedging technique, transactional hedging, includes both long-term and short-term hedges. It entails opening foreign exchange or futures accounts and transacting in currency market contracts. Transactional hedging is the most flexible of the three techniques. Positions can be put on and taken off at will, something nearly impossible with strategic hedging. Most transactional hedging is short-term. For this reason, it is well suited for most accounting exposures and some cash flow exposures. It is not as suitable for longer term operational and strategic exposures. Following is a short summary of the various techniques.

- *Operating Strategies*: These usually involve changes in the course of business. Thus, they are most appropriate for long-term, pervasive or future currency risk, such as that involved in strategic and value-based exposures. They offer permanent, or at least very long-term, solutions. They often require months or years of planning. Operating strategies are most often considered during strategic planning.
- *Financial Adjustments*: This method of hedging is usually suitable for operating and cash flow exposures, for non-specific exposures, or for exposures where the value exposed is conditional, in the future, or otherwise uncertain. This method offers more flexibility than operating strategies. Financial adjustments can be changed or reversed when the situation changes-an important consideration in the choice of hedging techniques.
- *Transactional Hedging (Long-Term)*: This method works best with accounting exposures, which are contractual in nature; however, certain derivatives used in transactional hedging, such as long forwards, forward roll-overs, and currency swaps are sometimes suitable for long-term cash flow and operating exposures.
- *Transactional Hedging (Short-Term)*: This method is used for hedging accounting exposure of less than a year in duration. The

hedging results become immediately apparent with such short-term actions. Transactions in short-term financial instruments relate more to day-to-day management decisions than to long-range planning.

Currency Derivatives

The complexities of derivatives are manageable to anyone comfortable with the concept of parallel markets. Derivatives are the contracts in the various foreign exchange markets: forwards, futures, options and swaps.* The markets for these instruments all closely parallel the spot currency market. A currency derivative is defined as follows:

> *A currency derivative is (1) a contract or financial agreement to exchange two currencies at a predetermined rate, or (2) a contract or financial agreement whose value is derived from the rate of exchange of two currencies at spot. In either case, the exchange of currency may be actual or implied.*

Currency derivatives trade in markets that parallel the spot market, so spot (cash) market exposures can be hedged with currency derivatives. The spot rate is the price of the "underlying currency." One advantage of derivative hedging is the number of markets available, all moving parallel to the underlying currency. Geometry teaches us that when two lines are parallel to a third line, they are parallel to each other. Thus, all derivative markets of a particular currency parallel each other, allowing a wide variety of hedging tactics (See Figure 9-6 for examples of currency derivatives).

Following are six diagrams that review derivatives with an emphasis on their interrelationships. Figure 9-7 portrays a simple spot currency exchange between a corporate customer and its bank, based on a spot rate of exchange of FC/HC = 2.00. Spot transactions settle in two business days.

Non-spot transactions take longer to settle. The delivery, or exchange, of currencies can take place on any "good" business day. A "good" day means the banks are open that day in both countries to effect delivery. Figure 9-8 shows delivery scheduled for a date one year in the future, making the transaction a one-year forward contract. The one-year forward rate, then, rather than the spot rate, is used to determine the amount of HC in the exchange. The amount of HC in the exchange changes daily as the forward rate changes. The spot rate plus interest debt determines the forward rate. The forward rate, in other words, is a function of the changing spot rate. Consequently, the forward contract value is derived from the underlying currency value on any given day, making the contract a derivative of the currency.

Figure 9-6: Examples of Currency Derivatives[1]

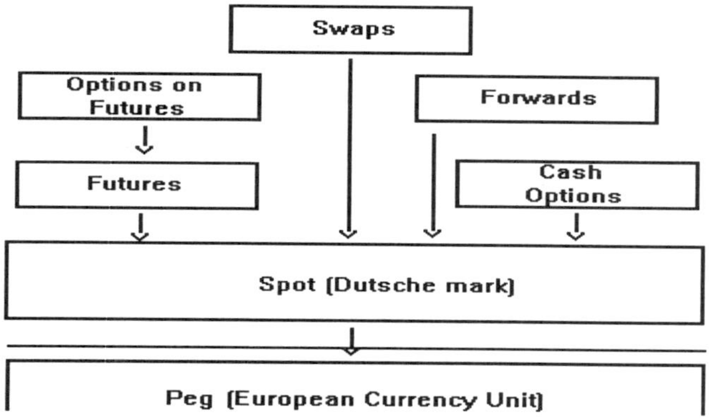

Derivatives are financial instruments, usually designed with hedging in mind. Markets in currency derivatives closely parallel the spot currency market. Note that the currency itself can be considered a type of a derivative if it is pegged to something of underlying value: precious metal, for example, or another currency or currency basket. Hedges can be placed in any market that correlates well with the exposure market. Derivatives themselves can be hedged with other derivatives. For example, a futures option can be used to hedge a forward contract, or a currency swap can be hedged with forwards. A pegged currency, such as the Deutsche mark, can be hedged with its peg, the ECU.

Figure 9-7: Spot Transaction

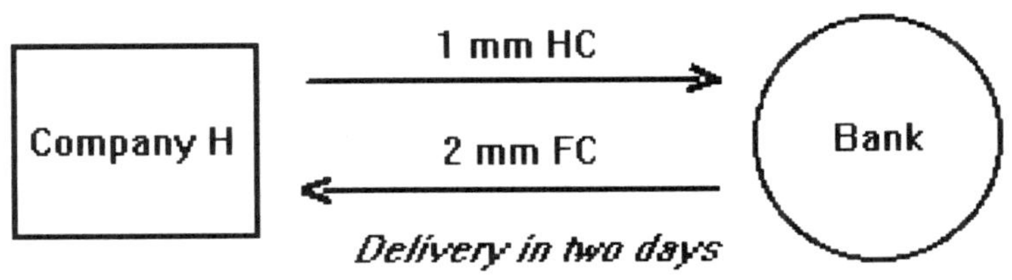

Figure 9-8: One-Year Forward Contract

Figure 9-9 shows a similar transaction, except that the company does not have to accept delivery. At the last moment, it can choose to walk away from the contract. This transaction depicts a one-year, over-the-counter cash option. The company paid a premium for the right to change its mind; it will exercise that right if the exchange becomes unprofitable. However, the value of this option is the same as the forward contract value at any given time, except that it carries an added charge for the "option" to back away from the exchange. Therefore, the option value, like the forward contract value, is derived from the underlying currency value.

Figure 9-9: One-Year Cash Put Option

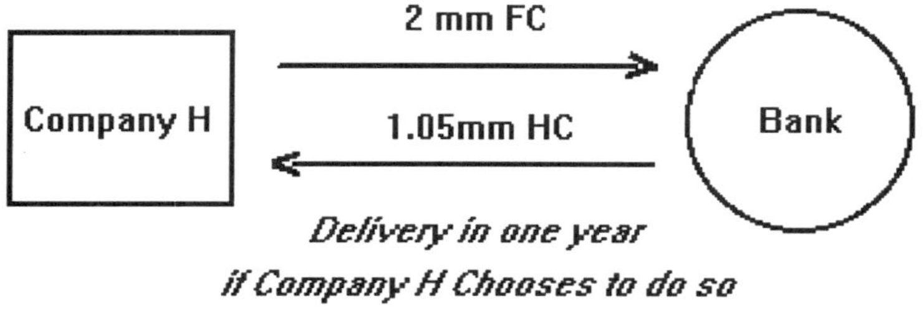

Now assume that instead of a wide choice of "good" delivery dates, there are just four: the third Monday of March, June, September, or December. Also, the counterparty is now an exchange rather than a bank. The forward contract with those changes becomes a futures contract, shown in Figure 9-10 Some cosmetic differences also exist between futures contracts and forward contracts: the futures contract amounts are standardized, so company H may deliver somewhat more or less than 2,000,000 FC; the accounting procedures are somewhat different; and the method of computing transaction costs are different, but the forward and the futures contract are priced identically in the market. The value of either one is a function of spot.

Figure 9-10: One-Year Futures Contract

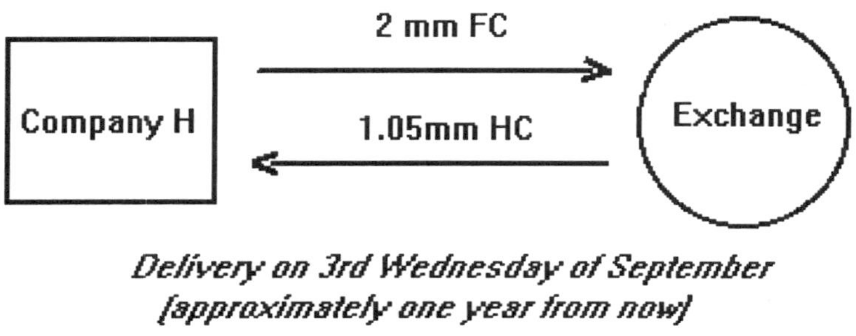

Figure 9-11: Put Option on One-Year Futures Contract

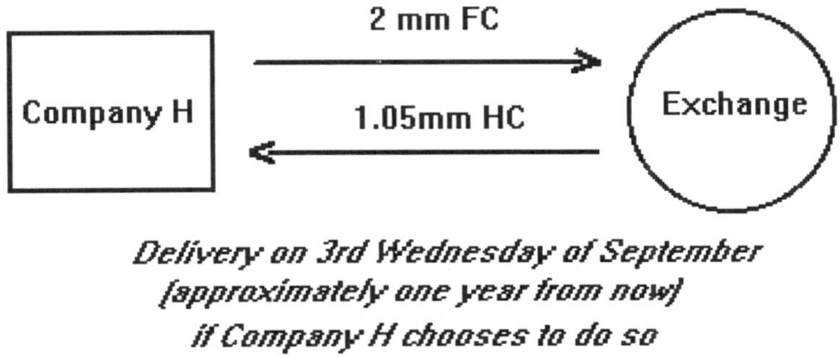

The cash option in Figure 9-9 and the option on a futures contract in Figure 9-11, are essentially the same. One converts to a spot transaction. The other converts to a futures contract that, in turn, converts to a spot transaction. To reiterate, the term option simply refers to the additional right granted to one of the parties to cancel the contract. This right is sold by the "option writer" and purchased by the "option buyer." When the cost of this right is ignored, the intrinsic option value is determined the same way as the futures, the forward, or the spot transaction-it is derived from the underlying currency.

A two-party swap (Figure 9-12) is no more complicated than any of the above derivatives. Instead of using a bank or an exchange, Company H transacts with a private party. The swap consists of two spot transactions. One takes place immediately and the other at some later time, such as five years from now. The rate of exchange is the rate in effect at the time of the first transaction. A payment from one party to the other at the end will compensate for the rate change over the five years. In the interim, the exchanges are considered to be interest bearing loans between the parties, and interest payments are exchanged periodically. The value of the swap at any given time is derived from the value of the spot currency.

Convertibility

Each of the derivatives discussed can be converted into the underlying currency. Some, like forwards, are always converted. Others, like futures, are almost never converted, but contain provisions allowing conversion to take place at the holder's option. This convertibility produces the high degree of correlation found in foreign exchange derivatives. They were designed to convert expressly for this reason.

Figure 9-12: Currency Swap

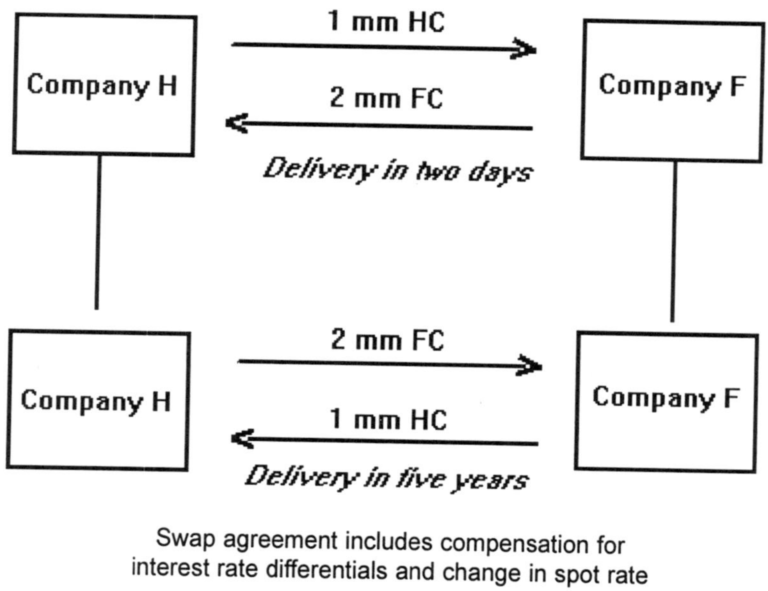

Understanding the relationship between convertibility and price correlation is crucial to the concept of hedging with derivatives. Consider what would happen if a currency derivative could not be converted. Assume that positions in Australian dollar futures are held to the last trading day, at which time they expire. The last traded price is used for settlement purposes to establish equity balances for the longs and shorts still remaining. On this day, the spot rate for Australian dollars is .7347. What is the settlement price of the futures contract?

Unless the futures can be converted into actual Australian dollars, the last price traded could be virtually anything: .7320, for example, or .6950, or even $130 or 13¢. There is absolutely no reason for the price to have any relationship with the underlying currency. Obviously, a non-convertible futures contract is worthless and untradeable.*

*Convertibility may be actual or implied. See discussion of "cash delivery" contracts on page 209.

On the other hand, if the last price for the futures contract is .7320, and spot is at .7347, the difference would be eliminated in a market where the future can be converted. All long positions would be converted into cash, which would then be exchanged at the spot rate for a 27-point profit. Currency traders around the world would quickly buy contracts just before the close and make the conversion. Of course, all the buyers would quickly drive the price up from .7320 to .7347. The ability to convert derivatives is what keeps their values in line, maintaining parallel market conditions. Mispricing rarely occurs with convertible contracts, and, when it does, it lasts only a few minutes before being swiftly arbitraged away. Still, exchange-traded derivatives are rarely converted into deliveries. They are simply offset by the initiation of an opposite position. Forwards and cash options are often offset the same way. Remember, it is the *ability* to convert that matters, not the actual conversion.

Some futures contracts are "cash delivery" contracts. The S&P 500 futures, for example, is a derivative of the Standard and Poor index. Its price is derived from the individual prices of the 500 stocks that make up this index. The futures contract, however, cannot be converted into 500 individual shares of stock. The settlement price is the actual value of the underlying S&P 500 index base on the close of the New York Stock Exchange on that day, not the last price at which the contract trades. The long positions remaining are valued *as if they were* 500 individual shares of the underlying stock.

"Soft" currencies that are subject to exchange restrictions are like non-convertible currency futures contracts. The primary reason a government erects exchange restrictions is to prevent free conversion of its currency, and its flight from the country. Who knows what that currency is really worth?

Convergence and Basis Trading

The price basis between a currency derivative, such as a forward or futures contracts, and spot currency equals the interest rate differential. The forward rate moves toward spot over time as the remaining amount of interest diminishes. Thus, in any forward versus spot market, the passage of time wrings out the basis—the difference in interest rate values—as the derivative moves toward its value date. The narrowing spread between the spot and derivative price is known as *convergence* (see Figure 9-13). The two prices gradually converge into one price, the spot price. The timing and amount of expected convergence is important in hedge determinations. If the *actual* convergence at any time differs from the *expected* convergence, hedge unpredictability increases. This variability occurs because derivative traders often focus on factors other than the spot market price, such as all the news, rumors, and sentiments that go into anticipatory trading. Convergence is rarely a smooth transition. Convergence is usually "wobbly," with temporary under- or overvaluations of a derivative.

Figure 9-13: Trading Deviations Along Path to Convergence

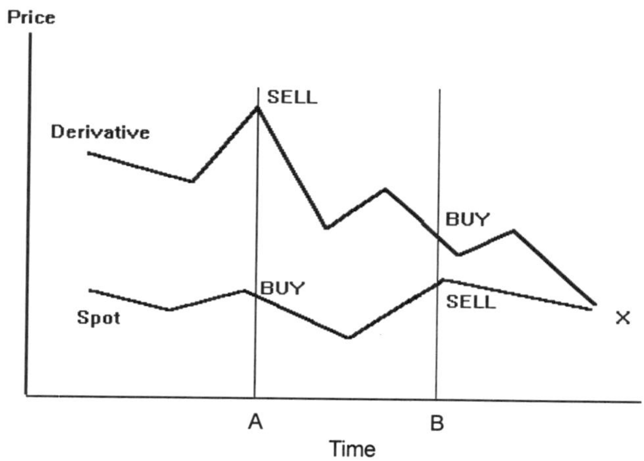

A spot currency and its derivative are priced against each other, showing the converging of the basis. The two prices converge when the derivative is convertible to spot (point X). The basis often deviates from its "norm" along the way, providing opportunities for spread traders, as well as hedgers. When the basis is at a premium, as shown here, the rule is to "sell the basis when it is wide (point A); buy the basis when it is narrow (point B)." The opposite rule applies when the basis is at a discount: sell when narrow, buy when wide.

Both hedgers and speculative traders take an interest in these "wobbles" from the normal convergence. "Spread" traders, like hedgers, take equal and opposite positions in parallel markets; for example, a trader may buy treasury bill futures and sell Eurodollar futures. (This is the popular "TED spread.") He may buy July corn futures and sell December corn, or buy options in British pound futures through his broker and sell

British pound forwards through his banker. Spread traders look for markets in which the basis deviates from the norm, then "lock in" the apparent misprice by going long one market and short the other (see Figure 9-14).

Figure 9-14: Trading the Basis

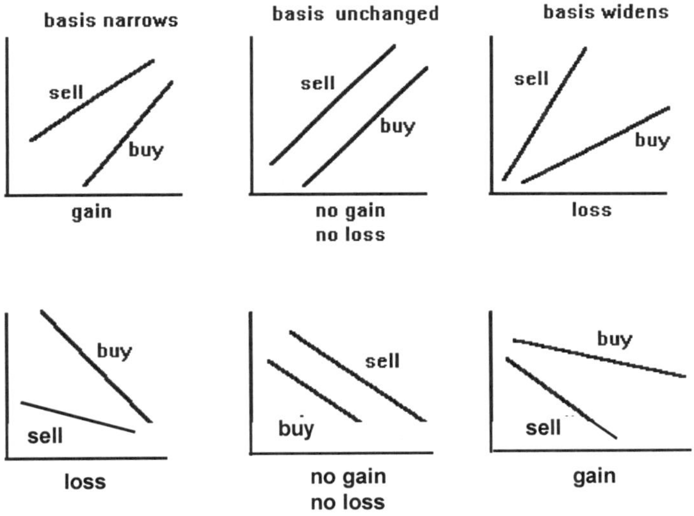

Spread traders are less concerned with the market direction than they are with variations in the basis between two markets. Profits and losses are determined by the direction of price differences, not the direction of the market. In the same manner, hedges "lock out" the overall market move. A derivative hedge can be viewed as a spread trade and will produce gains and losses in exactly in the same manner. For this reason, the continuing price correlation between two markets is a major consideration to the hedger.

Locking in prices, of course, is what the hedger also does. The difference lies in the objective. The hedger offsets positions to eliminate risk. He accepts the basis variations from the norm as unavoidable imperfections in the hedge that are small enough to be tolerable. The spread trader also offsets positions to eliminate overall market risk. He actively seeks basis deviations, however, and enters the market hoping to profit from them.

Trading Derivatives—What's the Risk?

The pitfalls of derivative trading have been dramatized in the media. In 1994, mortgage-backed derivatives, which generated huge losses when interest rates turned around, were the target. Before that, stock market derivatives—index futures and options—bankrupted many traders. One of the earlier reported booby traps for unwary investors was the commodity option.

Sensationalism aside, derivative trading certainly involves risks; however, most risks in derivative markets are the same as risks in all types of markets, such as the risk of the market changing direction unexpectedly. All risks in derivative trading are manageable.

Still, the risks of derivatives have received a lot of attention recently. In July 1994, a committee of international banking and securities regulators issued a series of guidelines regarding the subject.[2] The guidelines were published in a joint statement by the *Basel Committee on Banking Supervision* and the *International Organization of Securities Commissions*. The statement lists six major classes of risk involving derivatives:

1. *Credit risk* is the risk of default by one of the parties to a contract. Forwards transacted through the interbank are two-party contracts, with each party maintaining required equity through a credit line. The bank, as an intermediary, is the actual counterparty in the majority of forward trades undertaken by corporate hedgers. Default of forwards is almost unheard of, due to the capital reserve requirements in the international banking industry and the short-term characteristics of the forward market. The futures market is even safer. By utilizing a clearinghouse concept, in which the entire brokerage industry stands behind each contract, defaults in U.S. futures markets have been eliminated in recent history.

   The swap market, however, is one with a significant amount of credit risk. Because currency swaps are unregulated, not subject to clearing, and arranged between private counterparties, the agreement stands only on the credit worthiness of each party. Good credit is rewarded in the swap market. Companies with strong credit ratings are able to command good swap prices. Those whose credit history is weaker pay premiums as compensation for the added risk accepted by the counterparty.

2. *Market risk* is the risk of a long or short position losing value due to adverse moves in the overall market. In a true hedge, market risk can almost be ignored, since it simply determines which side of the hedge provides the gain and which provides the loss. Of course, some corporate decision makers pay serious attention to their hedge "burdens," more because of corporate philosophy than because of corporate trading strategy. Of course, market risk is all-important if the corporation finds that it is speculating rather than hedging. Since the difference between speculation and hedging is not always obvious, it is critical to correctly identify long and short positions before placing hedges.
3. *Liquidity Risk* is the risk that a corporation must unexpectedly liquidate a position (perhaps because the exposure prematurely disappears) and cannot do so because of a lack of available counterparties to take the other side of the trade. Illiquidity can be a significant risk in all markets, but it is easily avoidable by not trading in "thin" markets. For example, if open interest in a futures market is bunched up in the first two contract months, do not take a position in the third or fourth month out. The same rule applies to forwards: do not trade out twelve or fourteen months; stay in the nearby contracts and roll the positions forward as necessary. Liquidity is a major risk in customized swaps and other complex hedging arrangements. These non-standardized contracts may be illiquid most of the time, since very few counterparties would have identical hedging or investment needs. One way to eliminate an illiquid position is to customize a second hedge position, which offsets the original one, and carry both of them until maturity.
4. *Settlement Risk* is similar to credit risk, and is handled in the same manner. The risk is that a party fails to provide the required currency or instruments at the agreed-upon time. Again, the risk is most prevalent with customized, "off-exchange," two-party agreements, and is familiar to any company that books receivables. The rule here is to "know your counterparty."
5. *Operations Risk* is one of the biggest risks in trading derivatives. It is the risk of human error. The markets move so quickly and in such huge dollar amounts, that an error in order entry can be ruinous if not caught immediately. The most common of all errors is confusing a buy order with a sell order, or vice versa. This type of error occurs constantly, because orders are given verbally over the phone, often during very chaotic market conditions. Three rules reduce operations risk to a minimum:

   a. Insist that the broker or dealer repeat to you the transaction order you just gave him.
   b. Tape record all conversations with a broker or dealer when there is a possibility of an order being issued.
   c. Review all order confirmations for accuracy as soon as they are received from the broker or dealer.
6. *Legal Risk* pertains primarily to counterparties of currency swaps that go into receivership while the swap is in place. Swaps often involve exchanges of interest rate payments between the parties, with each liable to the other for interest on the currency received. The risk is that the receiver will "cherry pick" the payment schedule, demanding those payments due the receivership and ignoring the counterpayments it owes. In some cases now, this problem is avoided by netting out all balances before calculating payments. Another legal risk involves legal changes in the country issuing the currency being hedged. Delivery of currency is always subject to the foreign exchange laws of the country, which may change overnight.

One major risk, absent from the list, is *basis risk*, covered previously. Apparently, the agencies consider basis risk to be a part of market risk; however, basis risk is the potential of a change in correlation between the value of a derivative and the underlying currency, which should be considered separate from market risk. When the basis moves in an unexpected direction or ceases to correlate to the degree it has previously, the best laid hedges can fail. Watching basis is as important as watching the market.

Leverage

Option contracts are purchased for cash, just like securities in a cash account. Most other types of financial instruments are purchased on credit. Investors purchase these instruments by putting down a portion of the purchase price, known as margin, or, in the case of forward transactions, with nothing down. A holder of a long position has to pay the full dollar value only if the currency is actually delivered; however, delivery does not always occur with forwards and cash options, and it almost never occurs with futures and futures options. Acquisition requiring little or no front-load or back-load makes derivatives highly leveraged instruments. Table 9-2 shows the leverage available with various types of derivatives.

Table 9-2: Derivative Prices as of April 12, 1994*

Derivative	Value	Cash Up Front	Gains & Losses
Japanese yen			
Forward	**Any Amount - usually in** $mm increments		**credit acct**
buy		0 with credit extended	credited & debited daily
sell		0 with credit extended	credited & debited daily
Cash option (PHLX)	**$60,438** [1]		**margin acct**
buy		$1250 pmt in full [2]	priced daily
sell		$453 to $2418 [3]	credited & debited daily
Futures (CME)	**$120,956** [1]		**margin acct**
buy		$2,000 [4]	credited & debited daily
sell		$2,000 [4]	credited & debited daily
Futures option (CME)	**$120,956** [1]		**margin acct**
buy		$2500 pmt in full [2]	priced daily
sell		$2500 max [5]	credited & debited daily

Notes

(1) Option and futures price reflects the delivery value of currency based on spot rate of .0097 as of April 13, 1994.

(2) Premium for at-the-money June call. This payment allows holder to purchase and receive yen in the dollar value amount shown, based on a rate of .0097.

(3) Seller collects premium in exchange for delivery obligation above (2). Cash down is performance bond of 3/4% to 4% of total value of contract. Premium remains unremitted as part of performance bond until obligation is due.

(4) Initial margin requirement for hedge purposes. Speculative margins may be higher. Spread margins (for simultaneous long and short positions in parallel markets) are substantially lower.

(5) Same as (3), except maximum performance bond normally equal to initial futures margin. Like cash options, premium remains unremitted until obligation ends.

*prices approximated or rounded for sake of illustration.

A comparison of derivative values with cash up front requirements shows the amount of leverage involved in financial hedging programs. Also, the "down payment" may be securities instead of cash. Note that all except the option buyer can leverage the transaction.

The above amounts are the *initial* requirements for funds to be placed in a margin account the day the position is taken. Gains on the positions are credited to holder, and losses are *collected* from the holder, or from his account, on a daily basis. If the additional required funds are not in the margin account, or if credit limits are exceeded, a call for more money goes out immediately. This call must usually be satisfied within 24 hours or even sooner. The leverage involved in trading derivatives can produce major unfunded losses in a very short time.

The Leverage Problem

The advantage of using leverage is obvious. A $10,0000,0000 asset exposure does not require $10,000,000 allocated for a hedge. By using forwards and other derivative strategies, this exposure can be protected with virtually no initial outlay of funds. Since the actual values of the derivatives almost never have to be funded, a very small amount of money can hedge a very large exposure.

On the other hand, relatively small amounts of money get less attention than larger figures. So a senior manager might readily sign off on a margin call of a few thousand dollars. Few senior managers, however, would be as cavalier with a $10,000,000 margin call. But the purchase of forwards with no significant money changing hands can put a company at risk for many millions of dollars, though the risk may be slight. Leverage may be even higher for interest rate derivatives, which are often incorporated into currency management strategies. Consider that one contract of treasury bill futures, a $1,000,000 obligation, can be bought or sold for $250. Also, the complexity of hedging with derivatives means this activity is often delegated down the line to someone who has time to figure it out. Many times a banker or broker outside the firm becomes the *de facto* hedge manager. Thus, to manage risk, the company may become obligated for huge financial positions without being fully knowledgeable. Many individuals at higher management levels are unaware that a corporate liability exceeding last quarter's earnings can be contracted verbally with a casual two-minute phone call to the broker.

Delegation of authority to manage hedge programs should be carefully considered. When outsiders trade corporate funds, the quality of hedging decisions can suffer. Quick, reactive decisions over the phone with millions of dollars at stake take on an unreal quality. Many traders, whether brokers, dealers, or private speculators, find the massive amounts of money flowing back and forth hard to grasp. After a while, a person becomes desensitized to the emotional impact of big wins and bigger losses. Trading decisions, no matter how well planned, may still produce more hedge losses than hedge gains. To avoid the paralysis of knowing that an amount equal to ten years of salary is being put on the line, a trader sometimes retreats into a make-believe world of "Monopoly" money, where nothing "really serious" happens. The same individual who deliberates long and carefully when choosing between the $14 prime rib and the $7 roast chicken while sitting in a restaurant might make million dollar decisions with the flip of a coin while sitting at his desk. (One trading system that makes the rounds now and then consists of a coin with "buy" on one side and "sell" on the other. Its results are mediocre.) Whether you are a floor trader or a corporate hedger, your buy and sell decisions are the opposite of someone else's decisions in a zero-sum game.

There are moments when senior management is made very aware of what is happening. This is when it's time to pay off the hedge burden. The "hedge burden" is not called a "hedge loss" because, theoretically, it is not a loss. The hedge, properly applied, creates equal debits and credits. Theoretically, which side of the hedge shows the debit and which side shows the credit should not matter.

Of course, losses from hedges do matter. Few managers, few directors, and practically no shareholders look at large losses in derivative trading and think about the offsetting gain. As far as they are concerned, only one side matters: their hedge. Hedging was a good idea if the "hedge" made money; it was a mistake if the "hedge" side lost money. Countering this perception takes planning, knowledge, and *an in-depth, effective presentation of the program to senior management before trading starts.*

CHAPTER 10

Currency Management Considerations

Developing A Program

Developing the program to manage foreign currencies is the most difficult step of currency management. Many questions must be addressed. Where is the company at risk? Which currencies should be managed? Which exposures should be managed? How? Who manages them? Does he or she manage alone, or should this be a team effort? Is hedging to be centralized or decentralized? What, exactly, are the goals? A good place to start when planning a program is to analyze how the company is impacted by foreign exchange. To achieve this, exposure may be redefined as follows:

> *Foreign currency exposure is the sensitivity of some corporate objective variable to changes in foreign exchange rates.*

In other words, each exposure type measures the impact of exchange rate changes on a specific variable, such as performance or cost. Recall the description of exposure types, as discussed previously:

- **Accounting exposure** involves the impact of foreign exchange fluctuations on financial accounts, such as reported earnings, receivables, payables, and other long- and short-term assets and liabilities that have a determinable value and can be translated from one currency to another. Accounting exposure can be divided into *transactional exposure* of foreign currency transactions and *translation exposure* of long-term foreign currency assets and liabilities, such as those held by a foreign subsidiary.

- **Cash flow exposure** involves the anticipated impact of foreign exchange fluctuations on financial accounts. Projected revenues and expenses, bonuses, performance fees, anticipated inventories of parts, and materials still unpriced are examples of items impacted by cash flow exposure. Once these transactions change from anticipated to actual, the risk is to the balance sheet instead of cash flow, and so it converts to accounting exposure.
- **Operating exposure** concerns the supply and demand variables that affect sales performance, production costs, and responsiveness to customers and competitors. Identifying operating exposures involves answering several questions. Is the product still affordable (after a change in rates)? Has product substitutability changed? Is it still competitive? Has cost and availability of components changed? In which currency does the competitor sell? In which currency does the competitor produce?
- **Strategic exposure** relates to the impact of foreign exchange on operations and cash flow. However, though operating or cash flow exposure are normally measured in weeks and months, strategic exposure can endure for years. For this reason, near-term accounting exposure is essentially disregarded in analyzing strategic exposure.

  Strategic exposure takes into account both real and nominal exchange rates, trends in buying, trends in inflation, and current and potential competition. Strategic exposure focuses primarily on the company's competitive position on a short- to long-term basis.
- **Value-based exposure** focuses on the impact of foreign exchange on corporate values. This exposure affects the value of the corporation as perceived by its shareholders, creditors, customers, and community. Value-based exposure is a composite of all other exposure types.

Managing the Right Exposure

For some companies, the exposures that are detrimental to the company and require management are obvious. For example, an exporter might only sell leather goods produced in Australia to U.S. merchandisers. It books receivables in U.S. dollars and payables in Australian dollars. The firm is clearly at risk of accounting exposure and maybe at the risk of cash flow exposure.

Contrast the above example to a farm implement manufacturer who produces and sells only in the United States. Its policy does not permit transactions in foreign currency, and it never has a currency mismatch on the books. Assume that its biggest competitor is a Japanese firm selling the same machinery in the same market. This competitor prices aggressively, and the U.S. manufacturer often cuts margins in order to compete. This is an example of operating exposure: it should be managed either near-term, or on a strategic level, or both.

Problems arise when a company is subject to more than one type of exposure. Corporations who operate internationally often experience simultaneous risk in two or more categories. Quite commonly, marketing strategy will be jettisoned suddenly by a change in operating exposure, while at the same time accounting exposures come and go as price agreements and contracts are initiated, fulfilled, and completed.

As more and more businesses obtain an international presence, multiple risks are becoming the norm. Often, several currencies impact the company with rate changes, each reflecting a different type of exposure. Sometimes management of one exposure allows another exposure to increase. The currency manager must decide which exposures to manage and with what priority.

The function of currency risk management is to help the company reach its overall goals and objectives. To function effectively, a currency manager must identify, measure, and manage the individual exposures and the *interactions* between them. He must also set priorities among the corporate objectives. By reviewing exposures in light of corporate objectives, he can determine which objective is most sensitive to which exposure. The findings of this *sensitivity analysis* determine the objectives of the currency management program.

The program planner doing a sensitivity analysis must: (1) measure corporate "values;" (2) identify exposures impacting those values; and (3) measure the sensitivity of a particular value to a particular exposure. Thus, the planner studies the interrelations between corporate functions to measure exposure *in toto*. The findings determine the objectives of the program and the hedging vehicles or tools for achieving them.

Defining Objectives by Measuring Value

The above three steps embody the concept of value-based exposure.[1] Value here refers to *the value of current and future cash flows*. A business enterprise may be concerned with much more than just cash flow. Indeed, many corporate assets, such as good will and employee satisfaction, and corporate liabilities such as responsibility to the environment, are non-monetary. But value-based exposure concerns only measurable cash flow or anything else of perceived monetary value that enters (thereby increasing net assets) or exits (thereby shrinking net assets).

By focusing on current and future cash flows, value-based exposure touches on most areas in a corporation. All aspects of a corporate environment—its procurement policies, its manufacturing processes, its sales and marketing endeavors, and its support functions—affect current cash flows, both incoming and outgoing. Also, all strategic decisions concerning future events such as new product design, capital expenditures for new machinery, upgraded facilities, and new marketing strategies, affect future cash flows, such as sales revenue, cost of goods, cost of customer service, and so forth. In effect, value-based exposure concerns the same factors weighed by security analysts, creditors, and stock holders when they determine the worth and potential of the company.

The value of any cash flow is classified in one of two ways: nominal or perceived (see Figure 10-1). *Nominal value* is the units of currency that reflect an item's monetary value. *Perceived* value is the importance of one cash flow, dollar for dollar, compared to another. Perceived value can rise and fall with changes in the environment and goals of the company, even though nominal value remains static. The following examples illustrate perceived cash flow value:

Example # 1: "Mr. Dig," a private U.S. excavation contractor, is bidding on a project related to the construction of a power grid in Canada. The firm has no other contracts, and the success or failure of this bid will determine the company's viability. The general contractor is a Canadian firm and requires that all bids be submitted in Canadian dollars. The cash flow with the highest perceived value to Mr. Dig is obviously the revenue to be received from the awarded contract.

Example # 2: Soya Do Sol, a Brazilian soybean processor, gets most of its income by buying soybeans locally and selling soybean products internationally. The company serves markets in the United States, Europe, and Asia. Soybean purchases are denominated in Brazilian reals, and sales of oil and meal are denominated in U.S. dollars, Deutsch marks, and other major currencies. The company sees little flexibility in changing its operations, which are heavily weighted by fixed costs. The cash flows with greatest perceived value to the company, therefore, are its current streams of payables and receivables.

Example # 3: Druck Industries, a German die caster of aluminum auto components, sells to customers in five countries. Senior management decides it will invest heavily to expand its world market. The company must totally restructure manufacturing processes to change a traditional line operation into several manufacturing cells. In keeping with this new philosophy, all employees are currently being trained in Total Quality Management (TQM) procedures. The cash flows of greatest value to this company are its reduced *future outflows*, which will come from lower production costs and a lower volume of rejects, and increased *future inflows* from increased customer satisfaction.

Figure 10-1: Cash Flow

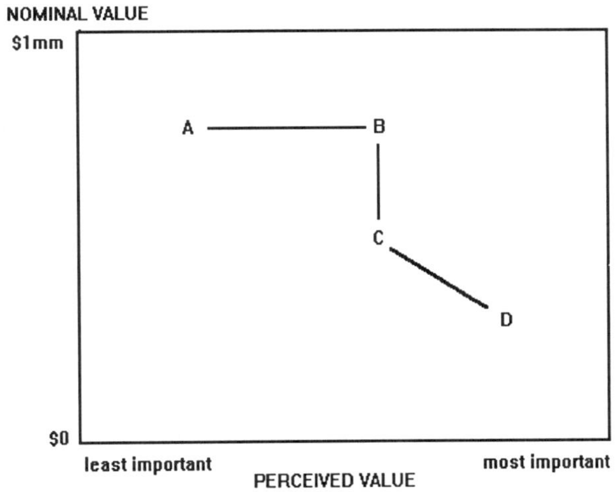

Cash flow can be evaluated two ways, nominal and perceived. A combination of the two views creates total corporate value, which identifies value-based exposure. In this case, cash flow B may have more value to the corporation than cash flow A. In like manner, cash flows A, C, and D may all have equal value.

Capturing Value-Based Exposure

Value-based exposure readily lends itself to currency management programs. Using comparative cash flow values as a measuring devise, program objectives can be formulated as follows:

1. Identify relevant cash flows.
2. Measure total value of each cash flow (the "corporate" values).
3. Identify factors that produce or contribute to high values (for example, product quality contributes to sales revenue).
4. Determine sensitivity of these factors to currency exposure.
5. Focus management on the exposures having the most impact on the selected factors.

Graphs may be used to view the relative values of current and future cash flows (see Figure 10-2). A particular cash flow can be considered either *contractual* or *non-contractual*, depending on whether its nominal value, either now or in the future, is known. For example, a 2,000,000 Deutsche mark bank loan taken out to defray operating expenses represents two current contractual cash flows: the loan proceeds and the repayment schedule. In the same manner, a 2,000,000 Deutsche mark bank loan planned for next year represents future contractual cash flows. *Non-contractual* cash flows, both current and future, are those that are anticipated, or included in the budget, but do not yet have a known nominal value. Current operating income is a current non-contractual cash flow. Next year's payout of sales bonuses would be considered a future non-contractual cash flow.

Because every business is unique, each solution to its exposure must be custom tailored. All successful risk management programs are developed "on-site" and tailored to fit the company and its specific operation. The above five-step process for finding value-based exposure takes into account the company's current position, its mission, and its chosen path for fulfilling the mission. Only when these considerations are known can priorities be assigned for exposure management. The relative importance of selected cash flows depends on the company's situation, as illustrated in Figures 10-3, 10-4, 10-5, and 10-6. The letters (A) through (F) refer to the cash flow designation in Figure 10-2.

Figure 10-2: Cash Flows

Current	Future	
0 to1 year	1 to 2 years	2 to 10 years
Contractual [a] A	Contractual [a] [o] C	Contractual [s] E
B Non-contractual (c)	D Non-contractual (c) (o)	F Non-contractual (s)

Current and anticipated future cash flows from different sources make up the total value of a business enterprise. Each cash flow is most sensitive to the specific type(s) of exposure as shown in parentheses. Possible factors influencing cash flows shown here are:

(A) Sales and operating income and expenses currently "booked;"
(B) Anticipated revenues and expenditures for the current reporting cycle;
(C) Pending sales and supplier contracts, projected capital investments and debentures;
(D) Market and sales projections, targeted operating expenses, targeted cost of goods;
(E) Changes in plant and equipment, new manufacturing sites, acquisitions or joint ventures; and
(F) New product development, long-term changes in product mix, new or changing markets.

Accounting exposure - (a) Cash flow exposure - (c) Operating exposure - (o)
Strategic exposure - (s)

Figure 10-3: MR. DIG

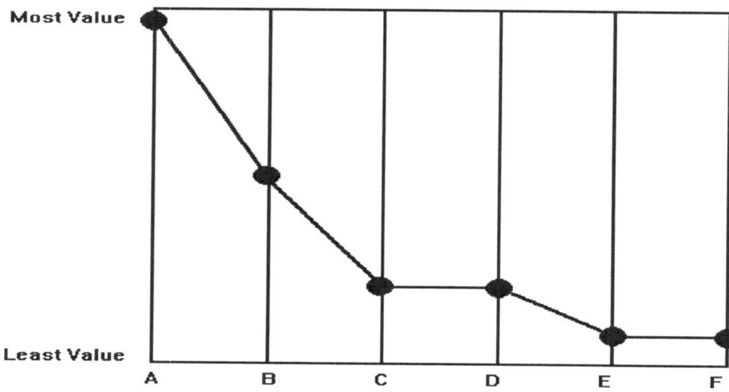

The survival of Mr. Dig in example #1 above depends upon the award of the project at hand. The resulting current contractual cash flow is by far the most valuable to the contractor. Any currency management program will focus almost exclusively on near-term transactional accounting exposure. The letters (A) through (F) refer to cash flow designations in Figure 10-2.

Figure 10-4: SOYA DO SOL

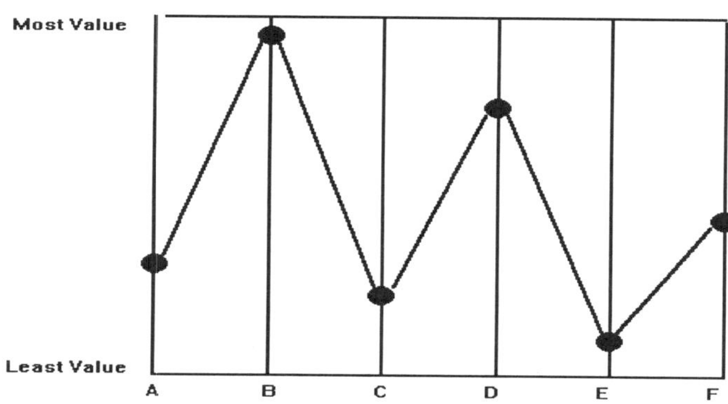

Soya Do Sol in example #2 finds little flexibility in its contractual operating costs, either current or future. Its cost of goods and revenue streams are strictly market-driven. Profits depend on successfully predicting market prices or locking in the spread with soybean complex futures contracts. Current and near-future anticipated sales revenues and cost of goods are the cash flows of highest value. These values are most sensitive to cash flow exposure. The letters (A) through (F) refer to cash flow designations in Figure 10-2.

Figure 10-5: BRUCK INDUSTRIE

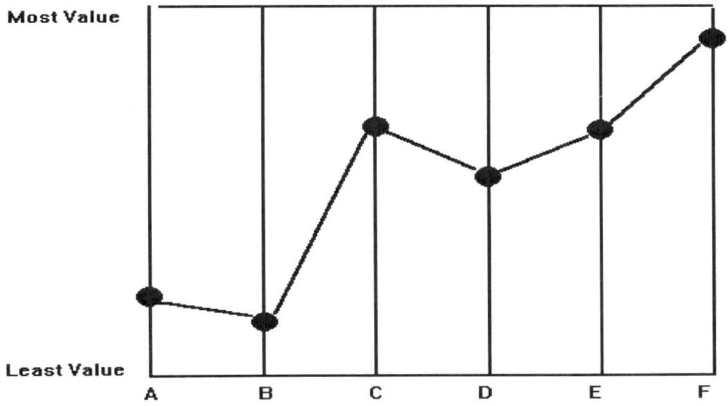

Bruck Industries is willing to plow positive cash flows back into the business for future growth. It focuses on revenues and expenditures 5 to 10 years in the future. These values are most sensitive to strategic exposure. Also, a high value is placed on contractual cash flows 1 to 2 years forward, representing anticipated infusions of capital for new processes and equipment. If foreign operations or borrowing are involved, management of near- to medium-term accounting exposure is required. The letters (A) through (F) refer to cash flow designations in Figure 10-2.

Figure 10-6: MR. DIG

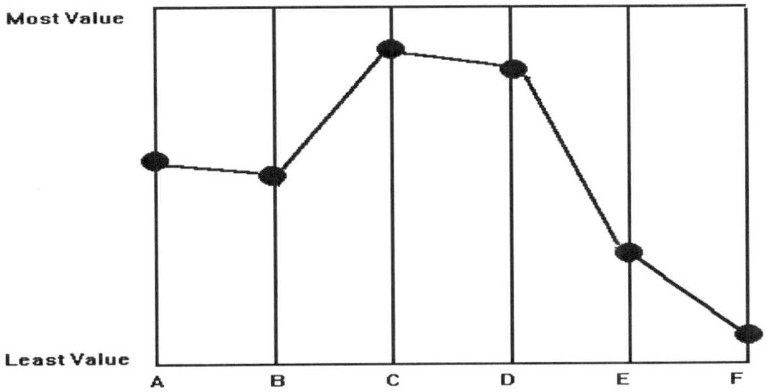

With the current project nearing completion, Mr. Dig shifts its focus to upgrading skill levels and technical and marketing capabilities, in order to bid successfully on future projects. Therefore, higher values are now placed on future non-contractual cash flows such as salary, training and promotional efforts, and revenue flow from the future contracts that result from these efforts. The letters (A) through (F) refer to cash flow designations in Figure 10-2.

Note that these graphs do not represent static positions: they are valid only for the moment. If Mr. Dig was awarded the project, it would regain solid financial footing as it neared completion of the project. As management starts to focus on future prospects and on upgrading its performance capabilities, its relative values change to those shown below. Thus, value-based exposure is a dynamic concept that must be reviewed regularly.

Working within the Corporate Culture

The experience and personal opinions of the corporate decision makers largely determine the *corporate culture*. A new employee quickly learns that "we do things certain ways around here." Cultural perceptions have a major impact on the continuing success of a currency management program. A director or senior manager may have fairly strong viewpoints on foreign exchange rates: he may be absolutely convinced that the dollar is going up, or down, or nowhere. If he is a key decision maker, a program that runs counter to his view has little chance. Another executive manager may have strong opinions on how a hedge should be constructed. The following syllogism applies:

Many managers are ex-commodity traders.
Many ex-commodity traders have been burned trading commodities.
Many managers have been burned trading commodities.

A manager with bad previous experiences may view currency hedging as far riskier than the exposures it is meant to protect. Getting that manager to accept hedging with derivatives as part of a currency management program might be difficult, particularly because the difference between hedging with derivatives and speculating with derivatives is not well recognized; however, even if the manager cannot be convinced, several unleveraged hedge vehicles, such as short-term bank borrowings or options, can replicate the results of derivative hedging fairly well.

On the other hand, many other senior managers are over-eager to hedge with derivatives. In agribusiness, many CEOs rose to power buying and selling livestock, grain, or lumber and other commodities. To them, taking a chance with currency derivatives is a natural adjunct to the business. In fact, they often feel hedging can be quite profitable. As experienced traders, they may want to call the shots on a day-to-day basis, which may sabotage a program.

The program developer must therefore be aware of the culture in which the program is taking form or his efforts may be wasted. Corporate culture involves perceptions and mis-perceptions, not measurable variables such as cash flow. One perception that deserves particular attention is what senior management expects the program to accomplish.

Defining Objectives by Expectation

The purpose of a management program can be determined by identifying the most important corporate values and the corresponding value-based exposures. Another way to define the program objectives is to simply ask senior management what it expects to accomplish.

What should a currency management program do? Many programs quickly fall apart because the purpose is left muddled or changes. If the program is to *protect* profits, then all hedging procedures, tools, and techniques must be developed with that focus in mind. If, on the other hand, the program is to *produce* profits, an entirely different set of management techniques is required, with more attention to the market than to the exposure. The main objective may be neither protecting profits nor producing profits. Instead, the purpose may be to identify and lock in a dollar amount, with hedging used to discover price. Or perhaps the program's function is to coordinate far-flung receivables and payables under one roof. Each of these objectives dictates a specific program development.

Imagine a meeting between a currency program planner and senior managers of a manufacturing firm. The firm is a progressive company with substantial operating revenue and growing international sales. First, the program planner asks the CEO and CFO what they want to accomplish with a currency management program. The CFO replies,

> *"We want to eliminate any effect of foreign exchange in both U.S. and foreign sales and operating earnings. All transactions involving another currency should be insulated from exposures of all types. The balance sheet should be protected against both contractual and anticipated transactional exposures. We want it to predict inflation, and account for it in all reported reevaluations of fixed assets and long-term liabilities."*
>
> "*Especially as they pertain to future expansion plans*," says the CEO, jumping in. "*And near-term currency fluctuations should be predicted with enough accuracy to be budgeted into next year's projections*."

Realistically, can management's objectives for the program be achieved? The program, unfortunately, will be limited to less grandiose objectives. For example, all current and future transactions cannot be isolated from foreign currency movements. However, a program can compensate automatically when the effects of currency movements on earnings become evident. Future rates cannot be predicted with any degree of certainty. However, the program can be structured to follow well-defined price trends.

In short, no currency management program can fully protect a business enterprise against every exposure. In fact, hedging against some types of exposures often creates others. If, for example, the program is designed to eliminate balance sheet exposure, the most effective strategy is to invoice and purchase solely in dollars, but, as mentioned previously, that technique may produce even more costly operating exposures. If, on the other hand, the program is to protect against real exchange rate operating exposure brought about by competitive pressures, the planner might order that all catalog sheets be reprinted to reflect local currency pricing, yet this strategy creates an ongoing cash flow exposure. Thus, major decisions in planning a program will determine which risks to allow, which to eliminate, and which to maintain at manageable levels.

Adopting Basic Principles

Fortunately, some principles are true for every currency management program. The program should:

- effectively protect profits;
- promote continuity of business;
- enhance competitiveness both at home and abroad; and
- promote good citizenship both at home and abroad.

These principles can be incorporated into the charter or the mission statement for the program. Next, the developers create a prioritized list for how to achieve the mission. With this basic momentum and direction, all further progress can be directed to "secondary" objectives. The selection of the secondary objectives depends greatly on how the perceptions underlying the cultural environment were addressed. Perhaps the most important perception to understand is how the company views risk and reward.

Developing a Risk Profile

Postmortems on failed programs often reveal that the program did not fail because the risk was too high, but because tolerance for risk was too low. In some cases, unexpected losses prompted orders for immediate liquidation, erasing any possibility that the hedge would eventually offset the loss. Understanding a company's tolerance for risk during the early stages of program development is critical.

How can risk tolerance influence the purpose and objectives of a currency management program? First, the act of hedging involves a forfeiture of opportunity. After all, hedging eliminates possible gains as well as possible losses. This risk of lost opportunity for profit may not be tolerable to management, especially to senior managers who felt that the currency was heading in a favorable direction and hedging was not necessary.

Identifying tolerance of risk helps to clarify management's expectations for a currency management program. If the risk of opportunity loss outweighs the risk of exposure, currency management may not be appropriate. However, some hedging techniques, such as option hedging, protect effectively against exposure loss *and* hedge loss. Of course, the company must pay a premium for the additional protection. When cost margins can absorb this premium, however, option hedging is appealing.

At the other extreme, some enterprises have a very high tolerance for market risk, but are intolerant of exposure risk in any degree. A company with this cultural attribute is an ideal candidate for the classic form of hedging, in which all exposure is hedged all the time.

What kind of program would be suitable for a company that tolerates some degree of exposure loss and is also fairly comfortable with hedge burden? The list of achievable objectives can be greatly expanded; for example, the program could: (1) reduce cost of goods (sourcing); (2) reduce cost of production (siting, labor); (3) compete more effectively (trade finance); (4) augment a new product marketing effort (foreign distribution); (5) better coordinate far-flung foreign currency cash flows (cash management); and (6) buttress an international presence (foreign currency invoicing). Dynamic hedging—meaning that exposures are hedged or not hedged, depending on factors such as timing, market trends, price levels, and so forth—can be effective in all of these endeavors.

Sometimes management expects trading activity to improve the bottom line, in addition to protecting it. Here, currency management is considered a profit center. In this case, forecasting consistency must be included in the hedge or speculative trading model. Forecasting models are available to assist in this attempt.

The Risk Profile Questionnaire

When managers are asked directly about corporate risk policy in foreign exchange, they often fall silent, searching for an answer. There may be no policy because management is not knowledgeable about currency and hedge risks. Investment portfolio managers often measure market risk tolerance of individual investors with a questionnaire. This method can also be used to determine the risk profile of a particular manager or company. Questions can be direct or indirect, as the situation warrants.

The most effective questionnaires measuring market risk are individually tailored. One effective questionnaire utilizes a graph based on the concepts of modern Portfolio Theory (see Figure 10-7). According to this theory, the level of risk and the potential for reward are directly proportionate for any fairly priced investment. Given this fact, an investor selects a portfolio that contains what he perceives to be the most attractive risk/reward characteristics. For a corporate profile, each senior manager would be asked to construct a hypothetical portfolio, first using personal funds and then using corporate assets. The assumption is that the senior manager's personal risk tolerance levels are imbedded in the corporate culture, and the managers' personal tolerance levels are the corporation's tolerance levels. The currency management program is then developed accordingly.

Benchmarking

The initial gathering of data to identify currency management goals can be daunting: it may take six months or more. Data is gathered, assimilated and interpreted to identify corporate values, management expectations, and cultural perceptions. In addition, the program development must identify the company's current position in its industry, its product, its market, and its competition. Knowing the company's mission, without knowing the company's current position, does not give the program adequate direction.

One way to identify the current position is by *benchmarking*, a technique employed in TQM[1]. Benchmarking is a process of evaluation and comparison. Various functions, operations and values within the company are compared to recognized standards, both inside and outside the industry. Often, "world-class" standards are chosen as the ideals. For example, a manufacturer may recognize a competitor within its industry as a "world-class" innovator, meaning that the competitor's quality is recognized internationally. Product engineering performance is subsequently evaluated against that particular level of innovation. Other standards might be found far afield from the industry. The same manufacturer could determine that a major bank is the standard bearer for quality customer service, and thereafter it measures its own customer service to the bank's. Benchmarking means finding an ideal, then constantly striving to attain the ideal by continually improving and measuring the progress.

Figure 10-7: RISK-REWARD RELATIONSHIPS

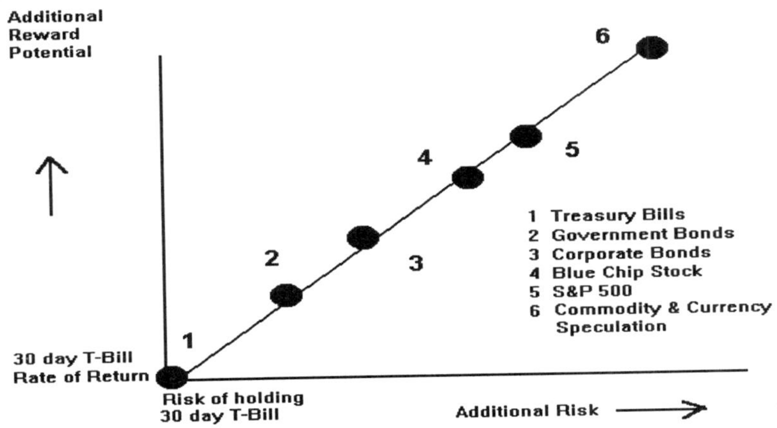

Modern Portfolio Theory focuses on the relationship between risk and potential rate of return. According to the theory, any rate of return above that derived from guaranteed short-term investments represents additional reward for the additional risk taken. Here, the standard is represented by 30-day treasury bills, considered the safest investment available. They offer low return, with no reward for risk. At the other extreme, the potential rate of return from commodity trading is quite high. A rate of 20% to 35% is certainly not unreasonable, but the return is certainly not guaranteed.

This relationship can be used to identify market risk tolerance, by determining if more weight is given to reward in spite of risk, or to risk in spite of reward. Tolerance for risk can be measured by a questionnaire or survey, in which senior managers are asked to devise a hypothetical portfolio for investing personal and corporate assets.

Defining Objectives by Benchmarking

Benchmarking works particularly well for currency risk management, because performance can often be improved by reducing exposure to risk. Of course, not every corporate objective variable is sensitive to changes in foreign exchange rates. Which ones are? What is their importance to the company? How do they change through benchmarking? If a company wants to improve a high-value operating variable and that variable is sensitive to changes in foreign exchange rates, it is a prime area for exposure management.

Figure 10-8 illustrates possible performance and objective variables that make good candidates for benchmarking. They are grouped under the exposure types that generally have the most impact on them.

The path from benchmarking to defining currency management objectives involves the following steps: (1) the variables subject to performance improvement are ranked based on their importance to the company; (2) the current performance of selected variables is measured through benchmarking; (3) the sensitivity of each variable to one or more currency exposures is measured; (4) when a variable exhibits a high degree of sensitivity to a particular exposure, that exposure is earmarked for management purposes. Compare these variables to the cash flows shown in Figure 10-2.

The Information System

An integral part of any currency management program involves how data is gathered, processed, reported, and utilized. Data handling requires development of an information system, which evolves in stages. The first stage is the initial analysis of the corporate position and its goals, as previously discussed. The second stage involves handling the ongoing flow of information that drives the currency management program toward meeting its objectives.

The Ongoing Report

Analysis of a company's position is not a one-time event. Once the initial findings are completed, performance within selected areas is periodically re-evaluated against the standards or objectives. Therefore, an ongoing reporting process to identify performance changes caused by foreign exchange variations must be incorporated into the program.

Figure 10-8: Variables Subject to Benchmarking

Current Exposures	**Future Exposures**
Accounting	**Cash Flow, Operating and Strategic**
Treasury and Finance Income Statement Balance Sheet	Industrial facilities engineering new, upgraded sites new material handling methods
Accounting and Cash Flow	**Cash Flow, Operating and Strategic**
Current products and services price delivery guarantees, warranties	Product engineering New design innovations cost reductions competitive features
Cash flow and Operating	**Operating and Strategic**
Sales and Marketing Meeting customer expectations	Sales and Marketing Meeting customer expectations
Accounting, Cash flow and Operating	**Operating and Strategic**
Manufacturing Processes Production cost, quality Current suppliers Support functions Labor costs	Manufacturing Processes Process engineering changes Manufacturing changes Labor changes Supplier partnerships Materials inventory costs Parts inventory costs
Operating and Strategic	**Strategic**
All functions Customer satisfaction Employee Satisfaction	All functions Customer satisfaction Employee Satisfaction

The nature of the reporting process depends on the program objectives, as follows:

1. What information needs to be reported?
2. Who needs to report it?
3. How often should it be reported?
4. How will it be transmitted?

The type of information to be reported and its value depends on the types of exposures being managed. If the program concentrates in the areas of accounting and cash flow exposure, information relevant to cash management and asset management is pertinent. The following list contains some of the items that might be included in a biweekly or monthly report to the currency manager:

- Payables and receivables
- Information on payer or payee
- Invoicing dates and currency of invoices
- Bank balances in all countries
- Currency deposits and ready assets in all countries
- Borrowing and lending fees and services in countries of operation
- Ready methods of repatriating funds
- Latest valuations of fixed assets and long-term liabilities
- Latest budget projections
- Pending sales and purchases
- Inventory denominated in foreign currency

Fundamentals affecting the foreign exchange markets should also be reported regularly. Again, the specifics vary depending on the program, but reports should certainly include data from the following areas:

- Exchange rates
- Interest rates
- Updated price charts (daily, weekly, and monthly)
- Current price trends

- Economic indicators and econometric input
- Fundamental and technical market analysis

Support of an information system can be time-consuming and may drain already overloaded employees. Date must be updated daily, weekly or monthly, depending on the information. The company may need to use either consultants or hire additional staff to maintain the system. Fortunately, the job is not complicated. Much of the information gathering is clerical. It can be reviewed by the department supervisor for accuracy.

The broker or dealer used for currency transactions should be expected to help report, or at least help analyze the information. The currency manager should insist that the broker or dealer schedule time for analysis and reporting weekly. This value-added service might be a fifteen-minute phone conference once a week to review the latest circumstances influencing foreign exchange.

The method for transmitting information must be simple. Try to keep transmittals to a single page. Constantly look for ways to simplify the procedures and forms used to transmit data. Any extra time or difficulties in the transmittal process may create a bottleneck that collapses the entire system. An all-purpose form could be developed to be filled in and forwarded by e-mail. A standard software spreadsheet form, such as Microsoft Excel® works well (see Figure 10-9 on page 236).

Price Charts

Currency price charts must be part of the reporting system. Currency price charts allow the client, the broker, the dealer, and the analyst to talk with common terminology. Price charts are available on a subscription basis from various commercial charting services. Bar charts, point and figure charts, and Japanese candlesticks are just a few of the charts available. Some of these are mailed weekly to subscribers. Computer data services are also available after trading hours for downloading price information, which can be converted into charts. The grid size for any charting service should be large enough to permit penciling in daily price ranges until the next issue arrives, usually the next Monday morning.

With a little practice, anyone can update a chart. Updating is a purely mechanical task, done with a pencil and a ruler. Charts should reflect daily information, even if new data is received only weekly. Many corporate hedgers and traders delegate this task to a secretary, but *the currency manager should update the charts personally* as a daily routine. Updating charts normally takes less than ten minutes per day and gives the manager a "feel" for the market. Convert price data received through a computer to hard copy for the same reason. Draw in the trend lines, consolidation patterns, and reversals yourself. (See Figure 10-10.)

Figure 10-9: Standard Information Form

British Pound

Date: 8/17/95 **by**: GDS

Range (basis 30 day)

Long-term	*med-term*	*short-term*
16500	16250	16000
15000	15300	15500

Upcoming reports

CPI (UK)	7-Sep
employ (US)	31-Aug
trade (UK)	10-Sep

Trend

Long-term	*med-term*	*short-term*
sideways	down	down

Interest Rate differentials

BP vs USD		change
ST	1.5	-
MT	2.7	up
LT	3.9	up

Near-term technical outlook Bob B, Analyst

downside breakout from symmetrical triangle turning nt and mt trends down. No clearcut lt direction. Watch market sentiment—near 4-year bear extreme indicates poss nt rally to resist of 16000 (30-day) support still at 15000.

Near-term fundamental outlook Clora J, Analyst

specs selling $ without central bk intervention. Floor feels fed support underneath. Job report 8/31 to tell if mkt expects US Int rates drop. Bundesbank still sending out warnings regarding ECU success. Large British Bank takeover rumors supporting BPD. Call nt up to mid Sept.

The form shown in Figure 10-9is created on a software spread sheet program and contains the type of information a currency manager might receive on a weekly basis for managing near-term accounting exposure. The headings in bold remain the same; the data changes for each new report. Dialog boxes are kept small because dialog often expands to fill available space.

Figure 10-10: Price Chart of British Pound

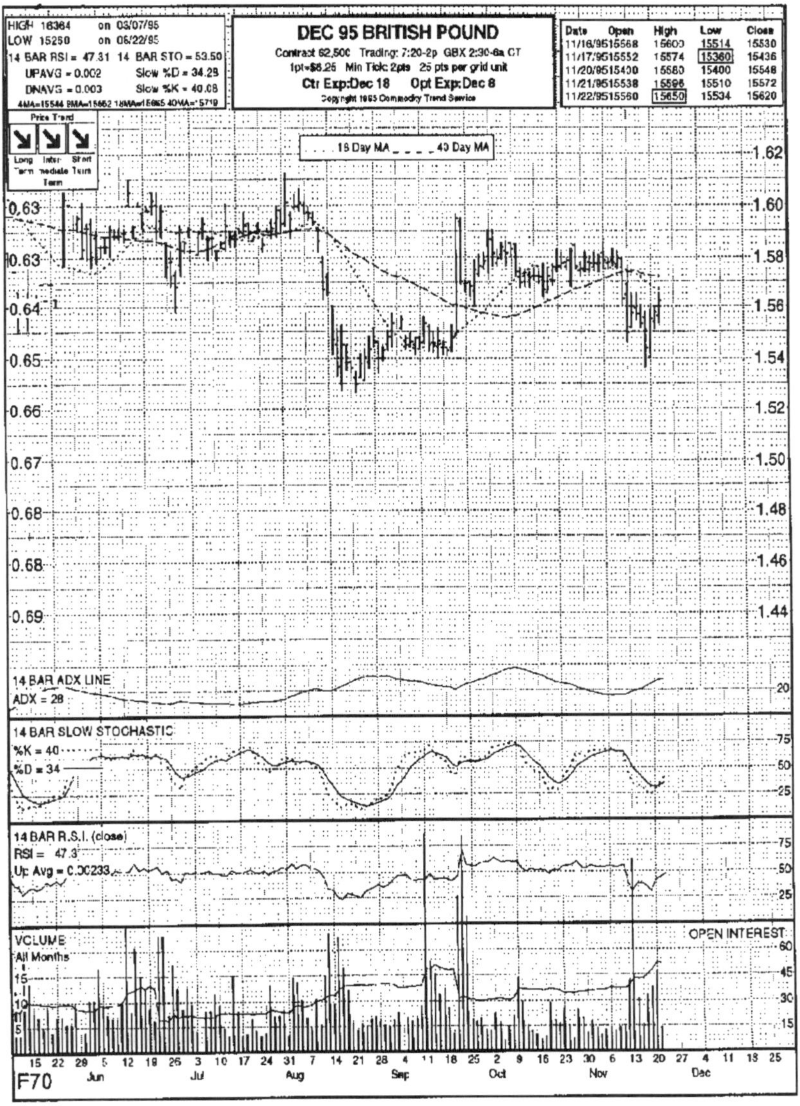

Charts should be in front of you whenever you are on the phone with your broker or dealer. The person on the other end of the line will certainly be using a chart. Find out which ones he uses and subscribe to those. Or, better yet, ask your broker or dealer to subscribe to ones you are using. He probably will make constant reference to it during your meetings. You will find that the price chart is the common tongue of all currency traders.

The Currency Management Team

Who is the currency manager? What is his or her function? His or her responsibilities? A few years ago, the currency manager would have been the treasurer (or controller, or VP of finance), and his function would have been to hedge currency exposure. He would have hedged by buying and selling contracts in the foreign exchange market. He would have been responsible for the outcome. Today, however, a growing number of business enterprises have currency managers that do not meet this description.

Two things have changed. First, the concept of currency management has evolved to much more than simply hedging transaction exposures by buying and selling currency contracts. Today's currency management function and the hedging techniques used by it are much broader and more complex. Functional decisions range from finding the ideal site for a new industrial facility to purchasing a 30-day put option.

The second change involves the business enterprise itself, particularly in product manufacturing and marketing. The new environment is a "global economy," and producers find that they must cut response time considerably in this sphere to remain competitive. Competitors from around the world flood the market daily with new products providing greater benefits at lower costs. Almost overnight, product life cycles in some industries have gone from years to months, and being first to the market is now critical. Also, product quality is constantly improving. Components that comply with machining tolerances considered unattainable a few years ago are rejected and scrapped today. Zero-defect tolerance has become the standard. The customer no longer has the time or patience to drop the kitchen blender off at the service center. Today, if an appliance fails, the purchaser trashes it, vilifies it, and never purchases any other appliance carrying the same brand name again.

To reduce time to market and cost while increasing customer satisfaction, fundamental changes are required. Corporate functions, which operated traditionally as independent, non-communicative "silos," must now merge and flow together. Managers, employees, financiers, suppliers, distributors, and even the customer have become partners in the company's goal of staying in business. The old concept of each function standing alone, to be managed "top down" in hierarchical style, has given way to the "level organization," to manufacturing "cells," and to product task forces. Today, everyone must be a team player (see Figure 10-11).

Figure 10-11: Currency Management Team

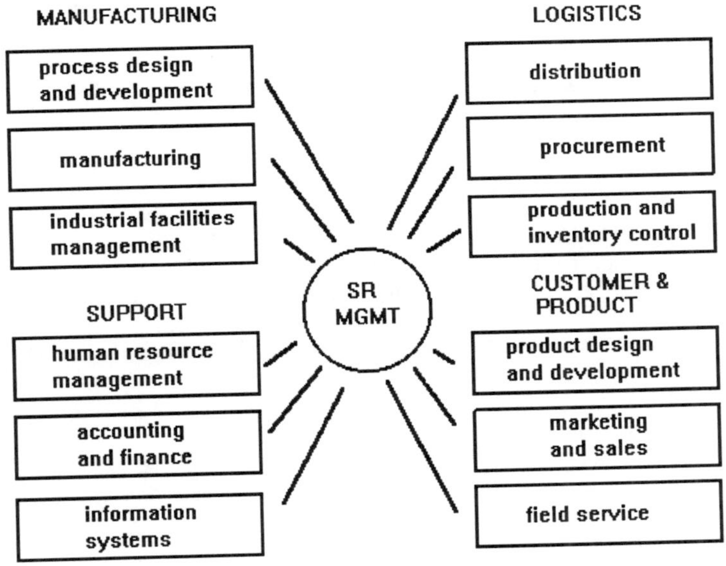

Manufacturing functions were traditionally divided into "silos" with little ongoing dialog or communication among them. The silos were managed in hierarchical fashion from top down.

Figure 10-11: Currency Management Team, *con't.*

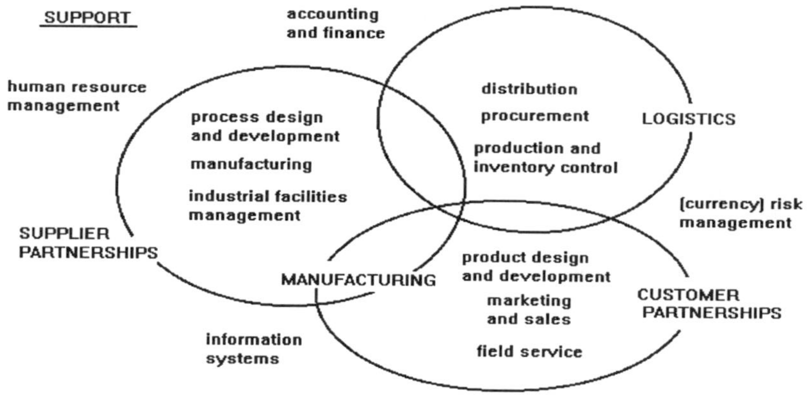

Today's global market requires much shorter lead times and continuously improved product features. This can be best achieved by inter-functional partnership between employees, management, suppliers, and customers. Such "level" organizations without boundaries have been developed to take advantage of Total Quality Management and Just-in-Time manufacturing techniques.

Source: CIRM Support Functions Student Guide, APIC

The Currency Manager, a Team Player

No operation is more suited for management by team effort than currency management. Currency exposures cross functional lines, as do the impacts of managing them. As discussed previously, management techniques that reduce exposures in one area can easily create new exposures in another area. Consequently, the "currency manager" today is only one member of a team. As before, the treasurer or controller is often the currency manager. Now, however, the currency management team has members from other operating and support functions, such as cost accounting, product engineering, procurement, manufacturing, marketing, and customer service. The function of the currency manager may include currency trading, but his major role is to facilitate, communicate, educate and accumulate opinions. The currency manager cannot make decisions alone.

Seven Reasons for the Team

Many so-called "hedge programs" are still just standing instructions to a banker or futures broker to "call us whenever the dollar needs buying or selling." The calls come in and the orders go out. More and more, however, corporate management realizes that foreign exchange movements affect every aspect of the organization, not just the treasury department. New ideas for hedging exposures come from various fields. Some of these methods are simply more sophisticated ways of trading. Others are adjustments in areas such as receivables, payables, marketing and trade finance. Still others involve changes in industrial facilities management, product design, and manufacturing; thus, currency management in most cases must be developed and monitored by a team, for a number of reasons, including the following:

1. Value-based exposure management involves the impact of foreign exchange in all areas of a business enterprise. No single individual can know or understand the impact of currency moves in each area. In addition, risks to one area influence exposure in other areas.

   Since fluctuations in the exchange rates affect operations in so many areas, the managers and employees in these areas will also be affected by the management of the fluctuations. Affected employees must be made aware of shifts in currency and the steps being taken to counteract shifts as they occur. They should know the options available to reduce exposure, and they should help decide which option to use.

2. A currency management program that covers foreign exchange operations needs a wide range of expertise. No one person can be an expert in all areas: transaction costs and procedures, order entry techniques, record keeping, hedge accounting, tax implications, impact of exchange rates versus interest rates, the latest economic indicators, market and technical analysis, and exposure analysis. Furthermore, new hedging procedures and financial instruments are constantly offered by the exchanges and banks. Hedging is a dynamic enterprise, continuously undergoing revisions in outlook and methodology. Experts, inside and outside the corporation, are necessary to keep abreast of changes. At the very least, the broker, the banker, the foreign exchange consultant, and decision makers

from operations and treasury should be on the roster of any currency management team.

3. Developing a currency management program requires coordination and cooperation. If futures or options will play a part, risk disclosure statements and account forms must be signed and notarized. Updated financials will be required. The brokerage firm or bank will probably review a copy of the corporate charter. A board resolution may be necessary to amend the charter, permitting the corporation to use derivatives for hedging purposes. Brokerage firms opening futures accounts require names of at least two people, one to enter the orders and one to receive the order confirmations.

4. Exposures change continuously, so both current and future exposures must be constantly addressed. Departments must exchange information so the team will be aware of what sales are pending, what investments are under consideration, what purchase contracts are being negotiated, and what new marketing plans are being formulated.

   In addition, forecasting of future currency rates, though imprecise, is integral to currency management. Individuals active in a country often have a better feel for what its currency might do than the distant foreign exchange experts do, particularly for currencies of developing countries. Analysis based strictly on market conditions or technical patterns suffers greatly when markets for the currency are thin. One can predict the direction of the Brazilian Real better by knowing what is going on in São Paulo than by studying a price chart. Even in the more developed countries, regional sales managers and distributors may have insight on near-term economic conditions that is not available to foreign currency analysts in U.S. banks or brokerage firms.

5. In the end, senior management must "buy into" the program's concepts and actions. If they are on the team, corporate decision makers will have an understanding of what they are being asked to buy. Until senior management or the board understands the program, it will not be launched.

   The initial response of directors or senior management to a hedging program is often "we'll take a look at it." Too much negative publicity has made hedging suspect to the uninformed. The most common response is, "We manufacture products. We don't gamble in the currency markets." Time and patience are required to demonstrate that, by not hedging, the company is gambling in currency. Team members understand that concept.

One knowledgeable risk manager claims that it usually takes up to a year to obtain approval after a hedge program is put in front of the executive committee.[2] Getting senior management involved initially with a team concept improves the chances of a quick acceptance. The highest levels of management must be involved in the program anyway, but the team concept encourages their participation and agreement sooner.

6. Hedging often produces losses, since hedges shield the company from foreign exchange losses *and* profits by offsetting them with profits *and* losses. Hedge profits are universally accepted; hedge losses are not. Consider the difficulties of telling a product manager that his performance over budget will not result in bonuses after all, because the excess was due to shifts in foreign exchange that were hedged away.

   Currency managers need support. Hedge losses must be accepted *before* they occur, not explained afterwards. Support for the program is enhanced by a team approach to hedging, in both the developmental and operational stages. Decision makers in the various departments should know the hedging concept employed, the objectives, and the possible results.

7. The team concept increases disclosure. One way for a company to make headlines in the financial news is to assign an individual the task of hedging (trading) currencies, furnish him with a desk, a quote machine and a phone, and then leave him alone. Soon, no one inside the company except the trader knows what is going on in the market, the net position on a day-to-day basis, or the amount of profits or losses accruing. Trading currencies is an extremely intensive activity. Traders cannot share the elation or misery of trading with anyone except another trader, because no one else understands. Therefore, close friendships often develop between the corporate hedger who approves the trades and the person who advises him almost daily, usually the broker or the dealer. If they trade in reaction to the market, in lieu of using a programmed approach, they will often be trading under pressure.

   This method of trading often leads to a we-versus-them mentality, where "we" are the traders and "they" are everyone else. Traders can easily rationalize losing trades or justify hiding losses "until the market turns around." Fear plays a role. The broker or advisor fears the loss of the account, and the corporate trader fears the loss of his standing, or even his job. This type of management program may end with the CEO standing miserably in front of the cameras describing a multi-million dollar loss in derivative trading and vowing "never again."

The best security against an unexpected major hedge loss is disclosure. The person charged with buying and selling must disclose all open positions, along with their unrealized gains and losses, on a daily basis. Positions should be scrutinized by *at least* one other person. A senior manager should be responsible because he will be the one explaining the normal and inevitable hedge losses to outsiders.

Writing Policy

Guidelines for implementing risk management strategies emerge as the program develops. These guidelines should be written down in a policy manual, especially guidelines for financial hedging that involves market transactions. Guidelines and rules must be developed to work in all market conditions. The market at the time trades are entered will almost certainly be different from the market during development of the program. Market perception changes, and large hedging gains and losses affect corporate attitude. Fear and greed can alter program objectives. Long-term trading plans can be easily deferred, or simply forgotten, as the market churns. Trading strategy should therefore be committed to writing. The policy manual should be widely distributed or at least available to all members on the management team. In addition, the manual should be distributed to anyone who may have to explain hedging results.

The policy manual should address actual and potential conflicts of interest, such as those suggested by the questions below:

1. Will bonuses and incentives be based on local currency or on translated dollars?
2. Will performance measurements be based on exchange rates at the beginning or end of the reporting period?
3. Will performance measurements be based on hedged or unhedged exposures?
4. Will the upcoming budget consider currency management decisions?

5. If market forecasting plays a part in the program, whose forecast will be used?
6. Who will be responsible for overseeing trading activity?
7. Who will be responsible for understanding the intricacies of a complex hedge position?
8. Will hedging be centralized as a treasury function with exposed positions consolidated, or will the program be handled on a local basis by each division?

These and other interdepartmental decisions should be resolved at the start of the program to avoid conflicts later on. When conflicts arise—and they will—policy must dictate that senior management arbitrate the disputes. Many currency programs fall into disarray because of interdepartmental squabbles.

Other Considerations

Much of the information a currency manager receives concerns the currency itself. When the manager wants an update on a particular currency, he will normally call the banker or broker. He is told the current rate and, if he asks, the price range for the day. He might be briefed on market conditions and any pertinent news events. But the manager must know more.

First, he must recognize the rate of primary importance to him. The *nominal* rate represents the number of currency units equal to one dollar, and is the rate quoted. The *real* rate is the dollar amount of a particular currency in terms of purchasing power. These two rates are rarely the same. Knowing the difference is essential when dealing with any exposure other than accounting exposure.

For a soft or illiquid currency, the manager should know how the nominal rate is determined. The value of a currency is either the market price or the price dictated by the authorities of the country. Such values can be transitory. Virtually overnight, governments have flooded the world with their currencies or withdrawn them completely. The market will re-value the currency, but the market is only efficient if currency trades are unhindered.

Any analysis of currency must look forward. The market price of a currency belonging to a major industrialized country and trading at a floating price is the best indicator of the country's direction; however, for many developing countries, the currency markets may not yet be liquid enough to reflect the latest economic situation accurately. On the other hand, currencies in less developed countries are often very predictable. Without the vast, daily overflow of news (or "noise") characteristic of the liquid currency markets, the future sometimes seems clearer. In soft or exotic currencies, the most reliable foreign exchange forecasts come from an out-of-the-way distributor, agent, or consulate. For best results, talk to people who do business in the currency daily.

Locking in the exchange rate for six months in a country with hyperinflation does not help much. Also, in a hyperinflationary economy, currencies are not considered functional from an accounting standpoint,[2] and they are not hedgeable. The dollars paid for the currency today may not be retrievable tomorrow at any price. Currency management in hyperinflationary countries should consider counter trades, commodity swaps, or other barter techniques. At times, it might be better to avoid the currency altogether.

Summary

Development of a currency management program starts by defining objectives, establishing priorities, and developing guidelines. The actual hedging activity happens after specific exposures are analyzed in great depth. Initially, no particular trading or hedging expertise is required. Conceptual knowledge is required, though, and trading expertise must be acquired later to manage accounting and cash flow exposures as necessary. Initially, managers must only analyze the company, the inter-relations between exposures, and the currencies themselves. While engaged in this process, consider three principles:

1. Foreign currency management must be consistent with the philosophy, goals and objectives of the company.
2. Foreign currency management must be a team endeavor that crosses functional boundaries.
3. Foreign currency management must be a written policy, with emphasis on oversight, education, and disclosure.

CHAPTER 11

Managing Strategic Exposure

Strategic exposure, discussed in this section, includes both long-term and short-term operating exposure, as well as cash flow exposure. In fact, it embodies all but accounting exposure. This section, then, discusses from a strategic point of view the management of foreign exchange risk as it impacts operations and cash flow.

The Fordoche Company

Consider the example of "The Fordoche Company," a U.S. manufacturer of hydraulic pumps, valves and related equipment. It serves the chemical process, food and beverage, and pharmaceuticals industries. It is a growing company, with annual sales approaching $300 million. Fordoche enjoys a solidly based domestic market and has recently started "seriously" exporting to Canada, Europe, and the Middle East.

In order to augment its product mix, The Fordoche Company is distributing a line of filtration equipment manufactured in England in addition to its own product lines. Also, it is currently negotiating with a small German producer of large flow hydraulic rotary motors to either acquire the firm or engage in a joint marketing venture. Its major competitor, both domestically and in Canada, is "Vortex," a Canada-based manufacturer with sales throughout North America.

The Fordoche Company has developed a long-term strategic plan to achieve its major objective of becoming a global player in the international market.

Areas of Operating Exposure

The corporate officers, Bob, the Chief Executive Officer (CEO), Sally, the Chief Financial Officer (CFO), and Jim, the Chief Operating Officer (COO), have identified four areas in which they feel the company is at risk for adverse currency moves. The areas are:

1. *Industry*: The manufacturing of materials handling equipment is exposed to long foreign currency, short home currency positions. This exposure exists regardless of the location for production. The industry is price-driven, since little else differentiates competitive products. Certain U.S. companies have located abroad, seeking low production costs. Fordoche produces in the United States and competes domestically primarily against Vortex, the Canadian-dollar-based manufacturer, and against other foreign manufacturers internationally.
2. *Marketing*: In this area, Fordoche is also exposed to long foreign currency, short U.S. dollar positions. Fordoche denominates its price sheet in U.S. dollars, both at home and abroad. This practice protects against transactional exposure, but puts the company at a disadvantage when selling against a competitor that prices locally, especially if the dollar strengthens. Competitive pricing is a major factor in products that have little else to differentiate them.
3. *Manufacturing*: The same long foreign currency, short U.S. dollar exposure is found in manufacturing. Fordoche produces in dollars. A strong U.S. dollar increases cost of production relative to foreign producers. Margins are constantly under pressure in the effort to maintain market share. Specifically, a weak Canadian dollar puts Fordoche at a competitive disadvantage domestically, where it sells against the Canadian manufacturer.
4. *Cash flow*: An opposite exposure exists for cash flow. Here, Fordoche is short British pounds and long U.S. dollars because of a continuous cash outflow of pounds to buy the British line of products that Fordoche distributes domestically. Also, if the company decides to either join with or acquire the German producer, it may acquire a short Deutsche mark exposure by importing German products to sell in the United States, offsetting a long Deutsche mark exposure due to its foreign operations.

The Fordoche officials analyze the company and its goals and then conclude that the greatest risk is in areas affecting future growth: the long-term operating exposures in industry, marketing, and manufacturing. These areas of operation produce the exposures that most affect the value of Fordoche Company, and they will get the most attention in an exposure management program. The exposures in all these areas are a result of the corporate goal to become a global player in the industry.

The first decision is to allow the exposure in the fourth area, cash flow, to continue unabated since it is a short foreign currency exposure that *reduces* risk to the company. The short position offsets, at least partially, the long operating exposures. The offset is only partial, because the British pound and the Canadian dollar do not normally move in parallel markets; however, if the U.S. dollar strengthens sharply against foreign currencies *in general* the two are likely to move in the same direction against U.S. dollars, resulting in a more complete offset of long operating exposure.

Operating Strategies

Bob, Sally, and Jim review the methods available to deal with Fordoche Company's strategic operating exposures. The Fordoche Company officials look to eliminate long-term operating exposure where they can and hedge it where they cannot. The act of hedging may simply push the exposure into short cash flow positions; however, these newly created short positions would help offset long operating exposure, assuming the currencies affected trade in parallel markets. The three types of hedging techniques available are *operating strategies*, *financial adjustments*, and *transactional hedging*. Operating strategies are most commonly employed against operating exposures because they offer the most effective long-term solutions. All operating strategies must be considered carefully, as they often change business practices permanently. Here are the five strategies most often considered:

- *Retrenchment*—The most effective way to avoid risk of exposure is to eliminate it. The strategy is simple: get out of the market creating the exposure. The question of whether the market potential is worth the foreign exchange risk is always legitimate. If the company is already exposed in a foreign market, has the situation changed? A change in the political or social climate is often decisive. Companies pull out of markets all the time for any number of reasons, including the elimination of currency exposure.

- *Siting*—One method of hedging foreign exchange exposure involves siting of manufacturing facilities. If a new foreign market looks promising, can some of the production be shifted to that country, either by constructing a new facility or buying an existing one? This hedge matches the revenue with the cost of goods and inventory.
- *Changing the Mix*—Exposures might be reduced or offset by changing the mix of marketing and production in domestic and foreign markets. This technique works especially well for a growing company that is acquisition-oriented. For example, Fordoche Company, which produces in the United States and markets in Germany, might decide to acquire the German firm that makes a complimentary line of products. These products would then be imported into the U.S. market. In this way, long exposures resulting from Deutsche mark revenues and U.S. dollar costs are offset by short exposures resulting from U.S. dollar revenues and Deutsche mark costs.
- *Product Modification*—Modification of the product line can help reduce exposure from foreign currency. This technique works best for operating exposure due to competitive positioning. A product line, such as a low-cost consumer item with little or no competitive differentiation, may be very sensitive to price change. If the company competes only on price, the item may be priced out of a foreign market where it competes against a product based in a weaker currency. The company could promote the item in a different market segment that is less price-sensitive or modify the item to differentiate it from the competition.
- *Sourcing Flexibility*—If starting an entire manufacturing facility in a foreign country is not feasible, smaller adjustments can be made that also reduce exposure in cost of goods and inventory. So-called "screwdriver" facilities, used to assemble components with little capital investment, might be located in countries where labor is relatively cheap. Such facilities are inexpensive to start up, shut down, and move around, relative to full-scale manufacturing units. A company could open several such facilities and then shift production among them based on currency strength and weakness. This method reduces exposure and takes advantage of shifts in the strengths of currencies to obtain a competitive edge in new markets.

After considering these options, Fordoche rejected retrenchment out of hand. After all, Fordoche was using foreign currency management to grow internationally. The siting option seemed to have potential and would fit into their plans of acquiring or joining up with the German pump manufacturer. This technique would help reduce general exposure in the European market, as long as the Deutsche mark and other regional currencies maintained some degree of correlation within the European Rate Mechanism. The subsequent expansion of imports would also change the product mix at home, making it less susceptible to a stronger U.S. dollar.

Jim, the COO, came up with a "product modification" that would help Fordoche expand internationally. Fordoche's product lines were difficult to differentiate from competitor's lines. However, Fordoche could improve customer service and make their product information more "user friendly" to build a competitive advantage. An obvious way to be more customer-oriented is to denominate price sheets in the customer's local currency rather than in U.S. dollars.

Publishing price sheets in local currency meant pushing a large amount of exposure into cash flow. But the company officials felt that they could handle exposure in cash flow better than in sales operations. They started the change in their Canadian market where local currency revenues produced long Canadian dollar exposures that directly offset some of the competitive exposure at home. They followed with British pound and Deutsche mark pricing strategies in the European markets. They also acquired the German manufacturer outright with Deutsche Marks rather than entering a joint venture

The program was successful. As the U.S. dollar rebounded from recent lows in the world currency market, Fordoche maintained its growing share of the Canadian and European markets by moving some of the production to its new facilities in Germany. It was able to increase its margins on U.S. sales of German and British imports, offsetting some of the higher U.S. production costs. Fordoche reduced its U.S. dollar costs further by shifting some of its domestic sourcing overseas: it purchased parts and built subassemblies through its German subsidiary and British supplier, which also had international sourcing ability.

Cash Flow Exposure

With these changes, Fordoche's direction was permanently altered. It participated in additional joint ventures abroad, in regions where it wanted to establish a presence in both marketing and manufacturing. It now strived to maintain flexibility in both sourcing and sub-assembly, based on exchange rates, interest rates, and tax considerations. The focus began shifting to cash flow exposure. Fordoche, by now, was handling cash outflows as well as inflows in Canadian dollars, British pounds, Deutsche marks, French francs, and Australian dollars. The company needed to manage these cash flow exposures more actively.

Financial Adjustments

Cash flow exposure can be managed with several techniques, including financial adjustments and long-term transactional hedges. The various adjustments and transactions usually considered for the management of cash flow exposure are listed below. They should not be used as permanent solutions. Flexibility is important in managing cash flow exposures, and the degree of flexibility in each method is a major consideration when matching exposures to solutions.

- *Home Currency Invoicing*—One common financial adjustment is to invoice customers in home currency instead of foreign currency. The company simply prices everything in the home currency, such as the U.S. dollar. This method is most effective when the product line is unique and not price-driven. Pharmaceuticals and other high-tech items are good examples. Home currency invoicing should be monitored continuously, since it invites competition from countries with weaker currencies. Also, if demand elasticity changes, the market may simply disappear.
- *Strong Currency Invoicing*—Sometimes a choice of invoicing currency is available, but the home currency may not be used. The best hedge in this situation is to invoice in the strongest currency, because gains are more likely. For example, if invoices can be denominated in either ECUs or Deutsche marks and the Deutsche mark is the strongest currency in the ECU composite, that should be the invoice currency.
- *Home Currency Sourcing*—Whenever possible, inventories of components should be paid for in the home currency if the finished product will be sold in the home currency. The purchasing department of a U.S. corporation would favor the foreign vendors who agree to invoice in U.S. dollars. This practice transfers the risk to the supplier and works as long as the supplier agrees to accept the risk. However, marginally profitable vendors cannot afford the

additional burden, and vendors who accept the risk will probably add the potential cost to their quotes.

- *Same Currency Sourcing*—An alternative is to find suppliers in the country producing the revenue exposure and purchase from them in the local currency. This hedge is a shorter term version of the sourcing methods described above in operating strategy.
- *Long-Term, Fixed Rate Borrowing*—Perhaps the most common method of hedging long-term, translational exposures is to finance the activity with long-term, fixed rate loans in the local currency. For example, a firm that constructs a plant or distributing facility abroad finances the construction and operation in local currency from a local bank. Resulting revenue in local currency is then offset with principal and interest payments in local currency over a number of years, thus hedging the exposure to nominal exchange rate changes. Risk of change in the real rate of exchange remains, however, since fixed interest rate loans do not compensate for changes in inflation. The greatest long-term exposure for fixed assets is to the real rate of exchange, so this method is only a partial hedge.

  Long-term foreign currency borrowing can hedge cash flow exposure as well if the proceeds from the loan are converted into the home currency. Repayment is made by reconverting the currency at higher or lower rates, offsetting risk to future foreign currency revenue. Borrowing funds from foreign banks to convert the funds to another currency and take them out of the country may cause difficulties with foreign exchange regulations. Two viable strategies are to pay out the proceeds as dividends, or to use them for paying off existing debt.
- *Leading and Lagging*—When multinational organizations consolidate their exposures by having a central organization net out internal transactions of foreign subsidiaries, exposures may be hedged by adjusting timing of internal payments depending on the strength of the currency. Subsidiaries in strong currency countries receive prompt payment on invoices submitted to the netting unit, but they are given surplus time to pay off their internal debts. Subsidiaries in weak currency countries receive the opposite treatment: payment is withheld for 30, 60 or 90 days after they submit an invoice, but when they buy internally, prepayment or cash on delivery is required.

> This method, along with the others that differentiate between "strong currency countries" and "weak currency countries" are really just ways of trading the market. The method will succeed only if strong currencies continue to strengthen and weak currencies continue to weaken. "Leading and lagging" is a sensible approach, however, for currencies that are rapidly changing in value. This adjustment to scheduling may also be used with a single foreign operation and external cash management. After allowing for differences in credit, it makes sense to pay certain vendors more quickly than others and to bill certain customers more quickly than others.

A cursory glance at these financial adjustments illustrates why hedging one exposure can create another. Perhaps the most effective of the above methods for hedging cash flow exposure is to invoice in the home currency. In the case of the Fordoche Company, however, invoicing in HC would be a step backwards, since U.S. dollar invoicing produced much of its operating exposure. Introduction of foreign currency invoicing was the first, most important step in establishing a currency management program. Reliance on home currency sourcing has no appeal to the Fordoche managers for much the same reason.

"Same currency sourcing," on the other hand, has already been started by moving some assembly operations overseas to offset operating exposure. The Fordoche Company is less dependent on the competitiveness of the U.S. dollar when it sources in Deutsche marks and British pounds. Same currency sourcing allows it to price its products competitively in foreign markets whose local currency remains in line with the currencies denominating its costs. After reviewing the methods available for managing cash flow exposure, the Fordoche Company initiates a policy that any consideration of market expansion in other countries will include an analysis of sourcing possibilities in those counties.

Long-Term Forecasts and Short-Term Trading

The Fordoche officers also decided to permit more flexibility in the handling of payables and receivables, where feasible, to conform with exchange rate predictions. They are aware that the success of *leading and lagging* and *strong currency invoicing*, a possible solution in Europe, is dependent on their ability to predict that a currency will increase in strength. Because the officers do not consider themselves currency traders and realize that consistently accurate predictions are impossible, they look for a method of forecasting the market without having to call each turn. The difference between trading and market forecasting, they feel, is a matter of magnitude and duration of market moves. "Trading" consists of market predictions on a daily or weekly basis. Bob, the CEO, defines "market forecasting" as the act of identifying the *major* market trends over a longer term, such as quarterly. His approach is practical, since major trends are easily identified and less susceptible to sudden, unanticipated changes than shorter term trends (see Figure 11-1). The price charts can be reviewed daily and the forecast revised over time if the trend appears to be changing.

Figure 11-1: Testing the Major Trend

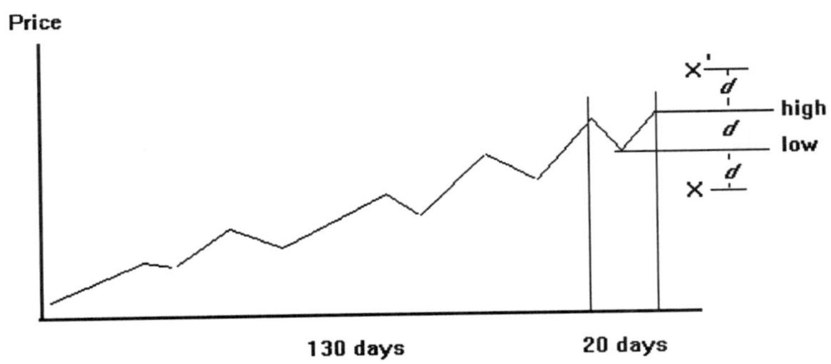

A number of technical systems identify and trade the major trend. One, called the *Babcock Long-Term System*, uses 130 days of price history as its starting point.[1] After a new 130-day high or low is made, the price range of the previous twenty trading days is measured. This distance (d) is added to the high or subtracted from the low to establish two targets (X and X'). If an uptrending market touches X', the major trend is continuing, or resuming, upwards. If it touches X, the major trend has reversed. A downtrending market is measured the same way: with the X target marking a continuation or resumption of the down trend, and the X' target placed at the point of reversal.

Note that any trading system may or may not continue to be valid or profitable. In order to trade this system as intended, orders must be entered under certain prescribed conditions. This example summarizes the major points only.

Another method of protecting long cash flow exposure (resulting from the company's new Deutsche mark revenues from its German subsidiary) is to establish short Deutsche mark long-term liabilities for that operation. Deutsche marks can be borrowed from a bank and converted into dollars. The loan would be repayed with the revenues generated in Deutsche marks. Sally quickly determines, however, that the company has insufficient credit history internationally to qualify for favorable bank loan terms. Therefore, she explores the feasibility of long-term transactional hedging rather than borrowing from a bank. Certain transactional hedges are legitimate management tools for cash flow, if they replicate long-term fixed rate borrowings. Two such transactions are the forward roll-over and the currency swap.

Forward Roll-Over

Remember that fixed rate borrowing from a local bank in a foreign country is a financial adjustment form of hedging. Forward exchange swaps from the interbank can replicate such borrowings. A *forward exchange swap* is two simultaneous forward positions (or a spot and a forward position): one long, the other short. Essentially, a forward exchange swap amounts to borrowing the foreign currency for a fixed time at a fixed rate of interest. Foreign currency proceeds are received on the value date of the long position and paid back on the value date of the short position. Interest on the loan is calculated as the difference between the two rates.

With a forward exchange swap, the holder may pay back the currency to fulfill the short position. The holder may also simply take a new long position to offset the existing short, while simultaneously taking a new short position for a value date even further in the future. This new pair of positions is called a *roll-over*. A forward position can be maintained indefinitely with a continuous series of roll-overs. The only practical difference between forward contracts that are rolled over and a traditional long-term fixed rate loan is the interest rate adjustment. The interest rate changes each time the forward is rolled over, since each newly established short forward will reflect the rate of interest in effect when the position is taken.

The Anatomy of a Swap

Currency swaps and interest rate swaps are based on the concept of the foreign exchange swap, but the construction of currency swaps is much different. The following example describes a currency swap based on an illustration offered by Satyajit Das.[2]

Assume the following :

FC / HC = 2.00 (spot)
FC / HC = 1.90 (1-year forward)
Eurorate for HC = 10% per annum
Eurorate for FC = 5% per annum
(transaction costs are ignored)

Company H requires 2,000,000 units of foreign currency (FC) to loan to its foreign subsidiary for capital improvements. It needs the 2,000,000 FC immediately, so it calls the bank with which it has established a line of credit for foreign exchange and initiates a spot transaction (see Figure 11-2).

Figure 11-2: Spot Transaction

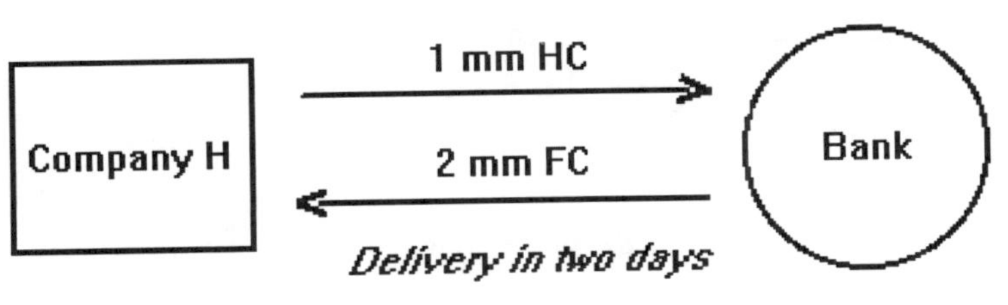

The company knows that its subsidiary will pay the loan back in one year; therefore, it has an exposure for the next twelve months. The company decides to hedge this exposure by selling FC one year forward (see Figure 11-3).

Figure 11-3: One-year Forward Contract

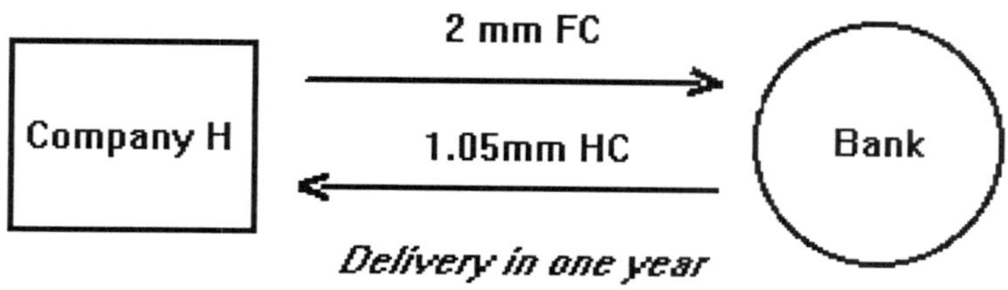

These two transactions may be combined in one as a foreign exchange swap between Company H and the bank (see Figure 11-4).

Figure 11-4: Foreign Exchange Swap

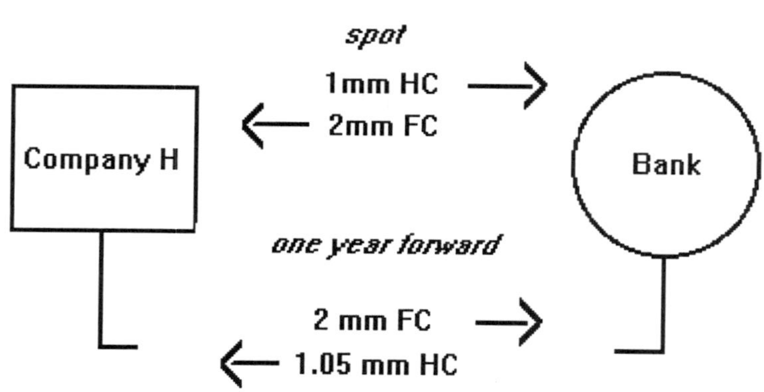

So far, Company H has dealt directly with its bank, just as retail customers usually do. The bank, however, wants to offset its exchange transactions with other dealers or other clients. The bank becomes an intermediary, "passing through" the transaction by taking the opposite sides of the bid/offer spread with Company H and another counterparty. The bank finds Company F located in the FC country with requirements that mirror those of Company H. Company F needs 1,000,000 HC for one year. Company H and Company F become counterparties but are not aware of each other. As far as each is concerned, they are dealing only with the bank (see Figure 11-5).

Figure 11-5: Foreign Exchange Swap

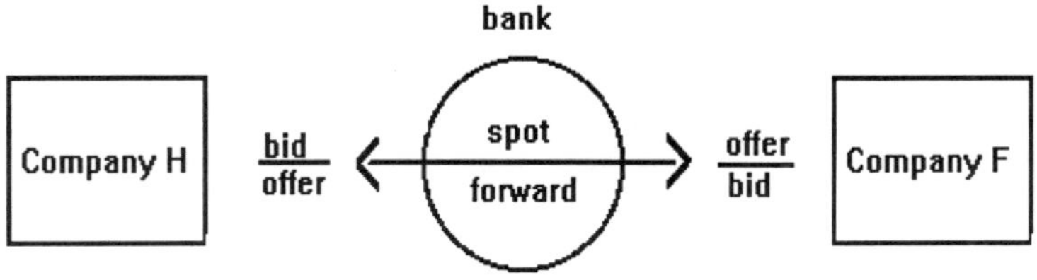

Forward contracts work well for managing individual accounting exposures a year or less in duration. They are less effective for uncertain or variable exposures, such as cash flow, or for durations of more than a year. The currency swap market evolved for risks poorly managed with forward contracts. The swap consists of a written contract or agreement between two counterparties with opposing exposures. The bank may act as a matchmaker, finding a counterparty and facilitating the agreement, or it may act as a principal and assume one side of the swap. If the bank acts only as an agent, it brings Company H and Company F into direct contact.

At this point the companies are no longer dealing with a simple, verbal foreign exchange swap. The transaction now becomes a currency swap, supported by a written agreement. Currency swaps differ from forward contracts in (1) duration (currency swaps typically are for one to ten years); and (2) in their terms and payment schedules (currency swaps are contracted with customized terms and considerations that may vary from forward contract terms.)

Currency swaps also allow counterparties to take advantage of each other's credit rating in financial markets. For example, if Company H does not have strong lender relations in country FC, it would have to pay a premium in order to borrow FC from a foreign bank. In its own country, however, it has a strong credit rating, allowing it to borrow at a favorable rate there. The reverse situation applies to Company F. The swap allows each to take advantage of the other's borrowing power.

Assume the above transaction is a one-year currency swap and the bank only facilitates the swap as an intermediary. The contract terms are the same as for a regular spot/forward swap, but the written terms are binding on both counterparties. The bank introduces the parties, brokers the deal, and then drops out of the picture (see Figure 11-6).

Figure 11-6: Currency Swap

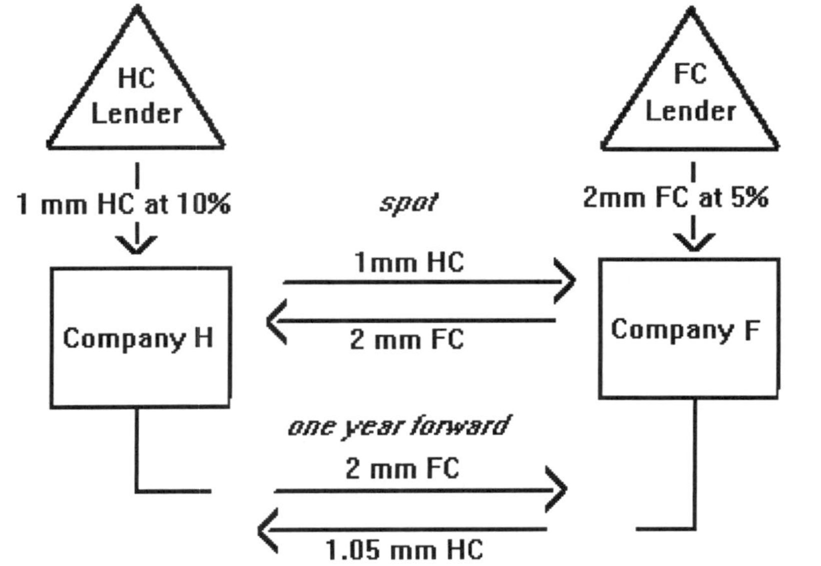

Now, assume the duration of the swap increases to five years. The "swap rate", defined as the difference in value between spot and forward rates, is now more difficult to determine, since the longer yield curve is more subject to unpredictable change. The type of exposure moves from trade flows to capital flows. Multi-year swaps involve management of long-term interest rate risk and credit risk, in addition to exchange risk.

Since future forward rates are difficult to calculate with any certainty, the counterparties usually do not try. Rather, they simply exchange currencies at the spot rate and service each other's debt. At the end of five years, they re-exchange the same amount at the original spot rate. The difference between spot and forward rates is, after all, the difference in interest rates. As long as the holder of the currency pays the interest which that currency earns, he is automatically compensating for the differences between spot and forward rates (because of interest rate parity). There is a credit risk involved in doing this, since each counterparty services the other's debt by making periodic interest payments to the other party, rather than to other party's lender. The loan obligation remains the borrower's. The lender—be it a bank, a buyer of commercial paper, or an investor in corporate debentures—is often not even aware that the swap has taken place.

Any two interest rates can be used for the swap. The rates can be fixed or floating, or fixed for one party and floating for the other. One counterparty may have a higher or lower credit rating than the other. To equalize the rating, either the more highly rated company pays interest, less a discount, or the company with the lower rating pays interest plus a premium. Options can be included (*embedded*). For example, a party paying a floating rate may want to put a ceiling on the rate. He can purchase an interest rate call option, written by the counterparty and made part of the agreement, with a strike price corresponding to the interest rate ceiling. Both calls and puts can be embedded to establish a "collar," or a ceiling and a floor on the rate. No matter how structured, the swap vehicle can provide an agreement tailored to work best for both parties. Diagrams "A," "B," and "C" of Figure 11-7 show examples with loans made at a floating Eurorate, by which the coupon yields of the 10-year Eurobond denominated in each currency are swapped periodically over a period of 5 years.

Figure 11-7: Swap of Eurobond Yields

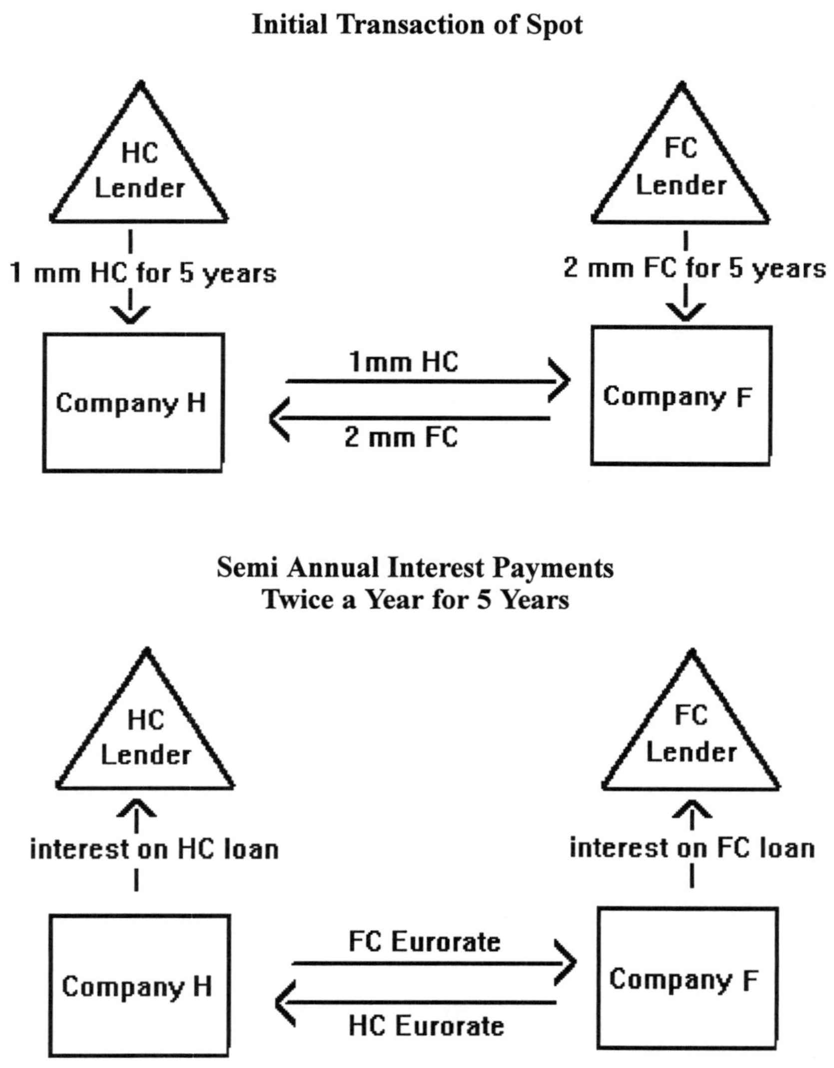

Figure 11-7: Swap of Eurobond Yields, *con't.*

Final Transaction at Initial Spot Rate

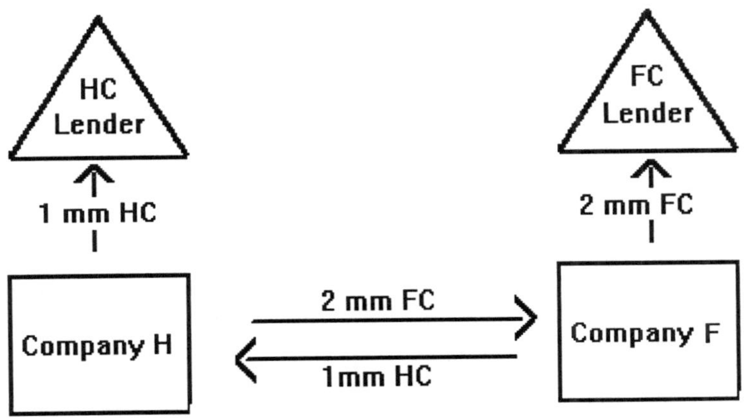

As experience in structuring swaps accumulates, new techniques are introduced for the sake of efficiency. For example, both counterparties do not necessarily have to "keep crossing checks in the mail." If the amounts that each owes the other are perfectly equal, the payments will cancel each other out. Very likely, one party will owe more than the other on each payment due date. Only one must send a payment for the difference.

The swap can even be accomplished without an initial currency exchange between parties. Each party may go directly to the interbank and make the exchange as a spot transaction. Then only the debt service is swapped, not the currency itself. In the same manner, the final re-exchange can also be eliminated and the parties can reverse their initial spot transactions in the interbank. The swap agreement might stipulate a spot rate that both parties agree to for the initial and final swap, though the rate is usually the same for both swaps. Such an agreement requires an interest payment on a periodic basis by the one who owes the difference at each remittance date (see Figure 11-8). In addition, a final payment from one party to the other compensates for the difference between the actual market rate at which the final exchange takes place and the agreed-upon rate.

Figure 11-8: Currency Swap

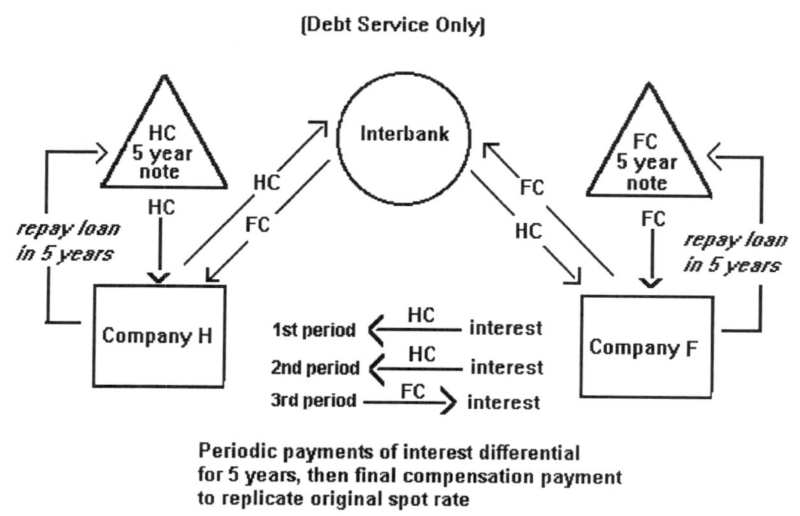

The Fordoche Company decides to use a currency swap to borrow Deutsche marks as a cash flow advance. Once it obtains the Deutsche marks, Fordoche will exchange them for U.S. dollars and pay off debt, pay bonuses or dividends, invest, or whatever. Note that the currency *must* be exchanged to provide a hedge. Left as Deutsche marks in a cash management account in Germany, the swap would simply constitute a new long and short position in the cash market, an asset and a long-term debt, each offsetting the other. Instead, because the currency must be converted back into U.S. dollars, Fordoche does not need physical possession of the Deutsche marks. Thus, the company takes the swap one additional step by skipping the initial interbank spot transaction. Fordoche initiates a swap consisting of an interest payment schedule and a compensation agreement with settlement five years in the future.

The Deutsche mark debt repayment at fixed rates anticipates future cash inflows. The primary reason to enter into a currency swap with a counterparty, instead of borrowing from the bank, is to take advantage of the more favorable credit terms available to the counterparty.

Multinational Cash Flow

So far, strategic exposure has been discussed on a relatively small scale. Fordoche Company initially has only one foreign operation, its German subsidiary. True, it also distributes for a British manufacturer and is open to additional overseas ventures in the future, but at this point its foreign exchange exposures are quite manageable. Yet, for large consumer-oriented multinationals that source, produce, and market in many local currencies, simply finding and tracking cash flow exposure can be quite a job.

When confronted with foreign currency flows from all directions, the first thing to consider is whether to manage them together or separately. Some good arguments support separate management of cash flow. A multinational may have several foreign operations or subsidiaries each with foreign currency exposures of its own. The financial manager of each operation is responsible for payables and receivables that are mailed out, transferred out, collected, and financed. Each transaction takes place in a local currency through a local bank and requires a local banking relationship. The subsidiary must often deal in three or more separate currencies: its own, its parent's, and one, two, or more of its customer's. So, theoretically, the financial officer of the foreign operation will know the financial and economic dynamics in his region better than someone in a home office will.

Argument for Centralized Management

Nevertheless, centralized management appears to be increasingly favored for dealing with multinational cash flows. Although management at a distance certainly has some drawbacks, compelling reasons support centralizing hedging activity. Normally the central location is the parent's headquarters, though another location may be preferable. The reasons to centralize management are as follows:[3]

- Centralization gives currency managers an overall view of the corporate position that is not available to each foreign operation.
- By pooling all exposures, central currency managers can get better prices for exchanges, deposits, and borrowings.
- Timing with a centralized program is more flexible. Management is not dependent on timing of operational cash flows, such as receivables and payables.
- Centralized functions have direct access to more financial marketplaces.
- Centralization reduces duplication of functions and may make it easier to justify hiring people with greater experience.
- Cross-conversion, in which one subsidiary is buying a currency at the same time another is selling it, can be eliminated.
- Funds for hedging are more readily available to centralized functions
- Policy disputes are more quickly resolved with centralization because communication to senior management is more direct.

Consolidating Exposures

Centralizing management does not necessarily mean consolidating exposure. Exposures disbursed throughout the organization might be effectively managed from one location, especially with a good cash flow reporting system. But managing exposure on a consolidated basis is easier.

Figure 11-9 diagrams the cash flows of a multinational corporation. In this example, the parent corporation is located in the United States, and its home currency is the U.S. dollar. It has several manufacturing facilities abroad. Product is shipped from manufacturing to marketing subsidiaries located in the region serviced by that particular manufacturer. These regions might be Europe, Southeast Asia, and Latin America. In turn, the marketing subsidiaries sell to independent distributors, both within the country and in the surrounding nations. The parent corporation and the manufacturing units invoice and remit to each other in U.S. dollars.

Figure 11-9: Multinational Currency Flows

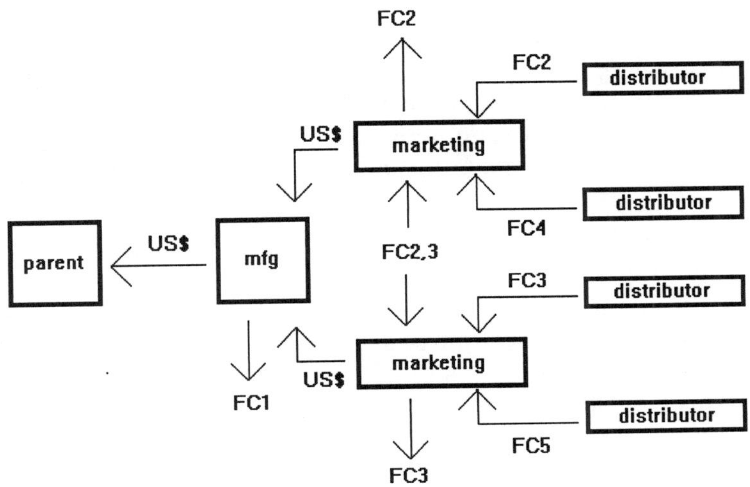

Figure 11-9 illustrates the following cash flows:

- The manufacturing unit submits dollar-denominated invoices to marketing and transfers dollar-denominated receivables to the parent corporation. Otherwise, it conducts business in its local currency (FC1).
- Marketing units within the region remit the transfer price in dollars to manufacturing and pay operating expenses in their local currencies (FC2 and FC4).
- The marketing units invoice domestic distributors in their local currency, but invoice foreign distributors in the distributors' currencies.
- In addition, all units buy and sell between each other, each invoicing in its local currency. As shown, cash flows are denominated in at least six currencies.

There are several ways to manage these exposures, but first they must be consolidated. Exposure can be consolidated in several ways, as follows.

- *Netting*—A netting unit can be set up to consolidate the exposures. Every corporate operating unit informs the netting unit of pending intercompany transfers when they are booked. Netting consolidates the transfers into net balances. It then gives each operating unit a list of amounts to pay and the names of the recipients. Netting vastly reduces the number of redundant currency mismatches and the resulting cross-conversions where one unit sells a currency while another buys it.
- *Centralized Settlements*—Whereas netting consolidates only internal cash flows, a centralized settlement unit collects all receivables and makes all payments for all operating units of the corporation. This method comes closer to achieving the main purpose of hedging - protecting the corporation's bottom line. Netting on this level reduces the foreign exchange exposures between the corporation and the outside world, not just those between operating units.
- *Multi-currency Billing Systems*—Multi-currency billing systems reduce exposure at the marketing level by transferring it to manufacturing. The manufacturing unit simply invoices marketing in the local currency of the marketing unit (or in the currency of the distributor) rather than in dollars. The exposure then transfers to the manufacturing level, which still remits in dollars to the parent corporation.
- *Factoring*—Once a multi-currency billing system is in place, manufacturing can also hedge exposure by transferring it. For example, the company might create a factoring unit that buys foreign currency receivables from manufacturing or any other operating unit in dollars and then invoices in the foreign currency. The factoring unit accepts the receivable and any currency or credit exposure. As compensation, the unit buys the receivable at a discount from face value. The amount is also adjusted for time, by purchasing at a forward rate that corresponds to the anticipated date of collection.
- *Reinvoicing*—A second way of transferring exposure risk from manufacturing is with a reinvoicing unit. A reinvoicing unit is similar to a factoring unit except that it only protects manufacturing against the risk of exchange rate changes between when the product is shipped and when it is paid for. The manufacturer ships

product to marketing and bills the reinvoicing unit in the marketing unit's local currency. Reinvoicing, in turn, sends the bill to marketing. Manufacturing is given a fixed rate of exchange when the invoice is issued. The exposure between the date of the invoice and the date of the currency conversion following payment belongs to the reinvoicing unit.

Exposure Management as a Cost Center

The unit retaining most of the corporate exposures usually will be the one to manage them. A reinvoicing unit, which fixes the exchange rate for manufacturing and lives with the exposure until it receives the payment, should certainly be allowed to transfer that exposure to the marketplace by selling the currency forward and locking up a known rate of exchange. The corporation should not expect trading profits from the unit. As a cost center, the unit should measure its success by the margin between what it pays and what it collects for receivables, not by how well it can do in the market.

Currency management should be centralized at corporate headquarters; however, tax implications often suggest that exposure and currency accounts should not be held at the parent's physical location. A currency netting or consolidating unit could be established virtually anywhere and, given today's communication technology, could be directed as easily from a separate continent as from a separate desk. Companies might select an existing subsidiary or set up a special financial subsidiary to consolidate exposure.

Offshore locations in low tax regions should be considered, particularly in countries that offer liberal regulation of foreign exchange remittances and conversions. In most countries, foreign exchange and movement of currency across borders is regulated by banking authorities. Financial companies established just to exchange and move money may come under special scrutiny. As an alternative, selecting a manufacturing unit for this type of operation is often politically advantageous. Manufacturing units can carry a lot of weight with regulatory officials, especially units that are both exporters and major employers.

CHAPTER 12

Managing Accounting Exposure

Accounting exposure is the most visible, the most quantifiable, and perhaps the most troublesome of the currency exposures. Accounting exposure is readily managed by currency hedging. Developments in foreign currency management are heavily concentrated in this area. This chapter reviews and expounds on some accounting exposure concepts mentioned previously. Later chapters will discuss the mechanics of contract hedging and specific trading strategies.

General Perceptions

Accounting exposure is the possibility of changes in the rate of exchange affecting the company's assets, liabilities, revenues, and expenses. Accounting exposure may be *transactional* exposure or *translation* exposure. Transactional exposure, as the name implies, refers to risk in specific transactions or contractual commitments that are denominated in foreign currency. Transactional exposures are specific in amount and duration and are guaranteed by a contract. Examples are: a loan of 1,000,000 British pounds by a U.S. company, repayable in five years; a purchase order from a Canadian customer with deferred payment in its local currency; a six-month inventory of parts, purchased in Danish krone for a European subsidiary; and a 90-day note from a German manufacturer to finance a shipment of parts.

Contractual commitments that are conditional can also result in transactional exposure. A fairly common example is that of tendering or bidding in foreign currency for a job. An entity such as a governmental agency may ask for bids denominated in its local currency that must be submitted months before the contract is awarded. The company is at risk from the time the bid is submitted until the job is finished.

Translation exposure, on the other hand, refers to the impact of foreign exchange on the net assets and liabilities of a foreign operation such as an overseas manufacturing subsidiary. Translation exposure is less visible than transactional exposure and, consequently, does not cause as many problems. Translation exposure is produced because the foreign operation's values are translated into the home currency on the consolidated statement. Foreign exchange gains and losses appear in the equity portion of the balance sheet and have no effect on earnings or taxes until the operation is sold or liquidated. Of course, a foreign operation may have its own *transactional* exposures, from conducting business either in the local currencies of third countries or in the parent's local currency. Such currency exposures can be managed with the parent's transactional exposures on a consolidated basis.

Implications of Accounting Exposure

Strategic exposure differs from value-based exposure in that it does not consider short-term foreign exchange impact on the financial statements (i.e., accounting exposure). Strategic exposure ignores accounting exposure because the act of reducing risk on a strategic basis often creates a new accounting exposure. Either strategic or accounting exposure can be reduced or eliminated, but not both, or at least not both at the same time from a strategic management perspective.

Nevertheless, accounting exposures do impact the company, and, because they are visible, they must be considered when analyzing the impact of foreign currency on the overall value of the company. Earning reductions (and taxable increases) caused by currency fluctuations are apparent to all, including securities analysts, creditors, and shareholders. The impact falls heavily on the CFO or the treasurer, and so individuals in these positions try to understand accounting exposure before all else.

Quantifiable Results

Operating and cash flow exposures are managed at the conceptual level over the long term. Strategies are devised, policy enacted, and long-term solutions are implemented. Immediate results are not expected. Indeed, the results are often difficult to quantify. There is no way to measure the precise effect on revenues of invoicing in local currency rather than home currency, or of siting the new manufacturing facility in Seoul rather than in Glasgow or Houston; however, results of managing accounting exposure are always quantifiable.

Hedges of an accounting exposure have a much shorter time frame than the techniques for managing strategic exposure do. The outcome produced by an operating strategy may not be evident for months, years, or even decades. For this reason, the price forecasts that influence strategic solutions and adjustments tend to focus on major, long-term trends.

The result of a transactional hedge, on the other hand, is recognized immediately as it changes with every up-tick and down-tick in the market. This immediacy and rapid-fire changeability requires a new set of management rules. A new factor is central to the success of a transactional hedging program: human emotion. For example, visualize two very different scenarios. In the first, a strategic operating decision is required on whether to site a new assembly facility in Mexico or Malaysia. Foreign currency exposure is one of a number of factors to consider. The CEO makes the final decision to locate in Mexico.

In a second scenario, the same company is carrying a Japanese yen receivable valued at $10,000,000, and the treasurer is facing a dilemma. A G-7 meeting is currently in process, and the representatives may reach an accord to strengthen the U.S. dollar. The dollar is on the edge of a support shelf and, if the accord takes place, will most likely skyrocket. On the other hand, if no agreement is reached, the dollar will probably break support and drop precipitously. A public resolution is expected the following morning. The treasurer decides to enter the market and go short yen contracts valued at $10,000,000. Which of the two decision makers—the CEO or the treasurer—will sleep more soundly that night?

Obviously management of accounting exposure can be stressful. The remainder of this section will show how to set up a management program that allows the treasurer or the currency manager to sleep at night *because he makes the correct decision regardless of what happens in the market.* Objective, dispassionate decision-making lies at the core of every successful management program, whether it involves selecting a future plant site or taking an overnight position in the currency market.

The Hedge Model

Managing accounting exposure, especially transactional exposure, is more about day-to-day decision-making than long-range planning. Currency managers must get in and out of market positions that may last no longer than a few days. There are two methods of currency trading. Each defines a particular process for making decisions. Each determines the manager's actions at critical junctures during the market's twists and turns during the day.

The most popular method seems to be the "omigosh" trading strategy. This method is best illustrated by the currency manager who walks into his office, turns on his real-time quote machine (most managers using this method require up-to-the-minute quotes), and loudly exclaims, "Omigosh! The yen is through the roof!" He immediately picks up the phone, punches a button to get the broker on the line (most corporate traders have their broker's number on speed dial) and shouts, "get me in!" or "get me out!" The hedging decision is a function of adrenaline overflow, and the trading technique is to make knee-jerk reactions to unexpected events.

A different approach involves an "if-then" analysis and uses a model. A wide range of potential market moves is tested in advance with a spreadsheet. Each possibility is considered and an appropriate response determined. The manager (and his broker or dealer) know in advance that *if* such and such occurs, *then* they (buy, sell, do nothing). With this method, as many decisions as possible are made prior to the market move. The decision-making process is devoid of emotion. The advantages are obvious: when judgment calls are reduced, the quality of trading increases immeasurably. The currency manager may still be shocked to see the yen going through the roof, but his reaction is predetermined—*if* yen trades above *x* price, *then* we (buy, sell) y number of contracts.

This trading method starts with a model constructed to conform with corporate policy and currency management objectives. Trading with a hedging model approved by senior management has another advantage for the currency manager. The manager whose trades are predetermined is never wrong. The hedge may lose money, the model may be seriously flawed, or the decision may seem wrong later. But since the trading model has been approved and the rules governing the model rigorously adhered to, the decision to transact or not to transact is mechanical. No one can be blamed for making the wrong call. The treasurer goes short yen because the model dictates a short yen position.

Yet, even with all its advantages, mechanical trading appears to be the exception, rather than the rule. Presumably, novice currency managers, who are eager to be "traders," have definite opinions about the market's direction and relish calling the shots; however, many of those who obtain the authority to trade soon wish they had not. Anyone making emotion-driven decisions in a fast-moving market soon finds himself wrong with large amounts of money. Soon the trader feels his ego, or perhaps his job, is on the line. Cycles of elation and fear replace objectivity. It is not long before the entire currency management program spirals downward toward recrimination and failure.

Trading models start with the data gathered during program development. What exactly is the objective of *this* particular company in hedging *this* particular exposure? How does the company perceive exposure risk? Market risk? Basis risk? Leverage? What about the economics of the hedge? Which dynamics should be considered, and which have little importance? Although the following models are quite basic, many variations exist, providing a framework for a well tailored program to fit every corporate situation and risk profile.

The Classic Model

The model for the classic hedge has the following characteristics:

Objective:	Locking in an existing profit margin
Risk profile:	High aversion to exposure risk
Hedge dynamics:	Exposure-driven

The concept is simple: all exposure is hedged at all times. It is the banker's favorite hedge: he pushes for its adoption by his loan customers because no one using it will be playing the market and thus speculating with the company's assets. Farmers, traditionally a conservative lot, were the first to embrace the idea of classic hedging over three decades ago. Classic hedging was a sound idea then and is still a sound idea today. The rationale for this model is that no one can predict the market accurately enough or consistently enough to make a difference, so why try? Market conditions are ignored. Current price level and direction are ignored. If the margin produces a profit, the profit is locked in, regardless of the market's position or direction.

The classic hedging model often takes an "all-or-nothing" approach: the exposure is either hedged totally or ignored; however, the classic model can be adjusted for some fixed, predetermined percentage of the exposure. For example, the model could be set to always hedge 50%, or 75%, or 35%, etc., of the exposure. The percentage used reflects the company's attitude toward market risk compared to their attitude toward exposure risk. (see Figure 12-1.)

Figure 12-1: Classic Hedge Model

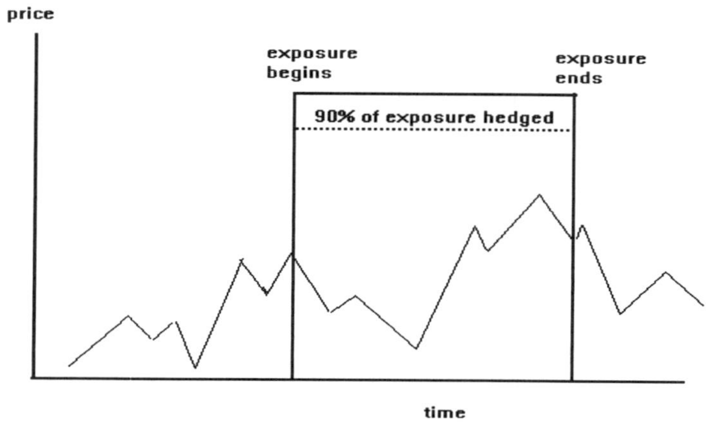

The Timing Model

A timing hedge model has a different objective than a classic model, as shown:

Objective:	Competitive pricing
Risk profile:	Moderate to high aversion to exposure risk
Hedge dynamics:	Time- and price-driven

This model does not reduce exposure when the exposure appears. The company utilizing a timing hedge model is indifferent to the exposure until a particular point in time. Then a window of perhaps a few weeks opens up, in which "price setting" takes place. When this window closes, the cost of goods, the exchange rate, and, consequently, the margin on sales must be locked in place. Timing hedges are often used for seasonal products that are priced competitively in the marketplace (see Figure 12-2).

Agribusiness uses timing hedge models. A company that sells seed corn internationally will wait until just before planting season to establish prices. They will fix their cost of goods (the price paid to growers) with a commodity futures contract. The company then determines the spread between the distributor's price and cost of sales, and fixes the exchange rate for foreign sales. The company tries to delay price fixing as long as possible. The last company to set a price has a competitive advantage. Also, changes in factors, such as planting intentions, commodity prices, weather, farm subsidy programs, and stocks in storage, influence futures prices and price strategy up until the minute the hedge is placed.

During the period for price setting, companies pay very close attention to the competition and the commodity and currency markets. They try to lock in the most competitive cost of inventory and exchange rates by taking advantage of market opportunities. *It is important to note that the exposures will be hedged during this time, regardless of market price.* In this regard, the hedge model is classic in form. Usually the entire exposure is hedged at one time. Once the hedge is established, the model reverts completely to the classic form of hedging. Margins are locked in place, and hedge positions are not liquidated under any circumstance, except to balance disappearing inventory.

Figure 12-2: Timing Hedge Model

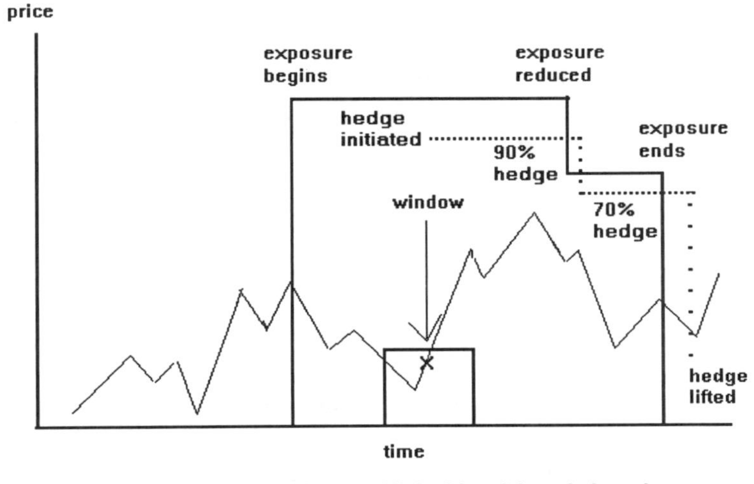

90% long hedge position established in pricing window after market turns up. Hedge reduced along with exposure.

The Range Model

The major difference between the previous models and a range hedge is that a range model is dynamic. Market conditions dictate whether an exposure will be hedged and to what degree it will be hedged. Therefore, the hedge is continuously adjusted. A range hedge model has the following characteristics:

Objective:	Locking in the top (or bottom) third of the range
Risk profile:	Moderate aversion to exposure risk
Hedge dynamics:	Price-driven

Price levels, rather than exposure, drive the range model. Market analysis and forecasting are necessary for it to succeed. The first step in setting up this model is to determine a time span for forecasting. The time span will probably be within three to nine months, since forecasts beyond that time are generally useless. Range hedges rarely exceed one year.

The second step is to forecast the most probable price range for the timeframe chosen. Since forecasting is imprecise, most hedges allow prices to exceed the predicted range 10% to 15% of the time. Therefore, the range is defined as the ceiling and floor between which the (spot) currency trades 85% to 90% of the time. This flexibility allows room for the sudden price "spikes" characteristic of volatile markets (see Figure 12-3).

In many cases, the management team determines the price range. The team should consider all factors that could conceivably affect prices. Committees, being committees, are inept at making day-to-day decisions for trading, but can be a prudent forum for range setting. Range predictions determined without group acceptance are too easily abandoned in chaotic market conditions. If it becomes evident that the predicted range is no longer accurate, a new floor and ceiling should be established by the group, and the hedge should be adjusted accordingly.

Once the range has been determined, it is subdivided into, segments, such as the top 20%, the second 20%, and so on, down to the bottom 20% of the range. The amount of exposure hedged at any moment in time depends upon which segment of the range contains the current price. The objective is to have the greatest amount of an asset (liability) exposure hedged in the top (bottom) 20% of the range, and the least amount hedged in the bottom (top) 20%.

The mechanics are fairly straightforward. Assume that a foreign currency (FC) has been trading between 60 and 70 for the last six months. The current price is 65. Recently, a moderate upward trend has emerged. The consensus is that FC will now trade between 62 and 72 for the next six months. The management team decides that the exposed asset is to be 100% hedged at 72 and 10% hedged at 62, with the percentages increasing or decreasing accordingly as the market moves through the various levels. It is apparent that the positions must be "actively traded" to keep the hedge in line with the market.

Figure 12-3: Range Hedge Model

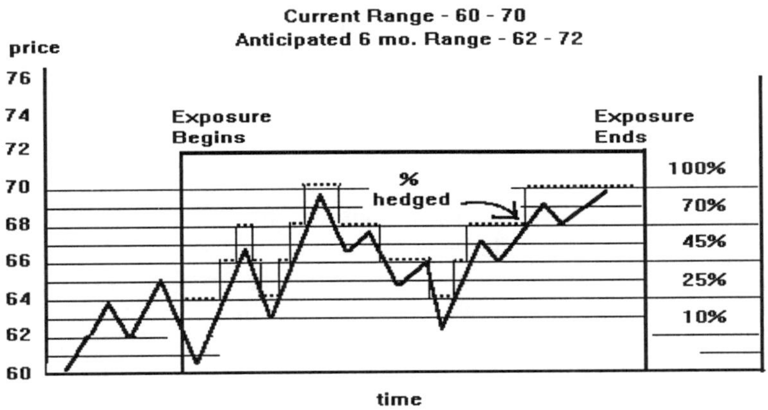

A tradable range is one that contains the price 85% to 90% of the time on a short- to medium-term basis. After forecasting a range, it is subdivided into 4 or 5 segments, each identifying the percentage of exposure to be hedged. Ideally, the average hedge price falls within the upper (or lower) one-half to one-third of the predicted range. One advantage of the range model is that hedge losses cannot be taken unless the range forecast changes. To illustrate, assume that a short position covering 25% of the exposure is placed at 65. Prices rise, and the position becomes a loss. The hedge is not liquidated, but *added to*, since a larger percentage of the exposure must now be hedged. Conversely, when prices drop, say from 70 to 65, the individual hedges are liquidated at a profit in compliance with the decreased percentage stipulated by the model.

For the model to work, the range must be *tradable.* In this example, a 6-month range prediction of 10 to 100 would have an almost perfect chance of being accurate, but is worthless for hedging purposes. Likewise, a very narrow range prediction, 66 to 70 for example, would very likely allow hedging opportunities from top to bottom, but would fail to contain the price 85% to 90% of the time.

The range model operates exactly the opposite of many hedging "strategies," which dictate getting out of losing positions when the losses become unbearable. In these cases, the loss often is taken just before the market turns around, requiring that the hedge be reinstated at a less favorable price.

Once the range is established, the hedge becomes price-driven, not market-driven. As with the classic hedge, no day-to-day forecasting is required. The hedge position is determined by where the price is, and market direction is not considered. (By contrast, in a market-driven model, positions are based upon the predicted direction of the market.) The range model, does not permit trading decisions based on judgment, news, current conditions, or “gut feelings.” The currency manager must follow the model in making a trading decision.

An obvious problem with the range hedge is that the range prediction may be incorrect. Thus, the program must be flexible enough that new ranges can be established when the range appears to be off. When ranges are adjusted, the hedges must be adjusted accordingly. Adjustments usually mean that losing positions are liquidated and realized. The company might not tolerate realizing losses on one side of the hedge before realizing profits on the other side, especially since ranges might have to be adjusted several times during a hedge. Therefore, company policy might dictate that hedge loss may not be realized until the relevant exposure are terminated. In these circumstances a miscue in range prediction converts the hedge to a classic form, in which positions are simply left in place until the exposure disappears.

Another problem with the range hedge involves transaction costs. A flurry of trading activity can occur if the price hovers near the line dividing two range segments. Positions are continuously taken and then liquidated as the market vacillates back and forth. To counteract this tendency, a ‘filter’ can be added to the model. For example, the model could include a stipulation that no position can be added or liquidated until the price moves a certain distance away from any dividing line.

The range hedge model does not offer perfect results every time, but it is quite appropriate for certain types of exposures. For example, if a company is already carrying an unrealized loss due to a change in exchange rates, a classic hedge would simply lock in the loss. A range hedge, however, may allow the company to recover its loss, and even turn the transaction into a profit.

How can loss be turned into profit? Assume that the predicted range is 62 to 72, as in the above FC example. Short positions equal to 70% of an asset exposure are placed at 69. The market then drops to 64, which requires only a 25% hedge. In compliance with the model, profits are taken by liquidating positions equal to 45% of the exposure. The remaining 25% of the exposure remains hedged. The market then returns to 70, and the shorts are re-established. Prices would not have to traverse back and forth very many times before significant trading profits accrue.

Range hedge models can also work for other types of risk, including cash flow and short-term translation exposure. Whenever exposure persists, or cannot be precisely determined beforehand, or is subject to ongoing changes in duration, a dynamic hedge permitting price flexibility usually out-performs a static model.

Selective Hedging

Some practitioners claim, with justification, that selective hedging is really speculation. A currency manager uses hedging positions that are opposite the exposure, but a selective hedger takes a position only to make a profit. If the exposed position appears to have high profit potential, the hedge is not placed or an existing hedge is liquidated (see Figure 12-4).

Objective:	Increasing profits
Risk profile:	Low to moderate aversion to exposure risk
Hedge dynamics:	Market-driven

Unless a model is adopted in the program development stage, the currency manager ends up with the selective hedging model by default. With no formal hedging policy or written guidelines, he trades the market with the help of his dealer or broker and hopes that their decisions make money rather than lose money for the company. Because they are trading without a plan, they will almost certainly lose money for the company.

When selective hedging is adopted by default, profitable trading is critical. The manager may be instructed to "do your best," with an implication that "your job may depend on it." Of course, some managers thrive on the challenge. They do not like guidelines or trading constraints, especially those formulated by a committee that "can't trade its way out of a paper bag." And the committee is inept at trading, because trading involves intuition; however, intuition's drawbacks are apparent from recurring statistics showing that seven out of ten trades result in losses—statistics that include very seasoned and sophisticated traders. Thus, unless you are prepared to slavishly follow a set of specific trading rules, do not use selective hedging.

A selective hedge model is a legitimate technique and may be the most suitable technique if the objective is to increase profits or the company feels comfortable speculating part of the time. Companies may adopt this model to speculate with the cash exposure under the right conditions and to hedge the exposure when a loss will otherwise ensue.

In this case, the "right" conditions for speculating are indicated in "specific trading rules."

Figure 12-4: Selective Hedge Model

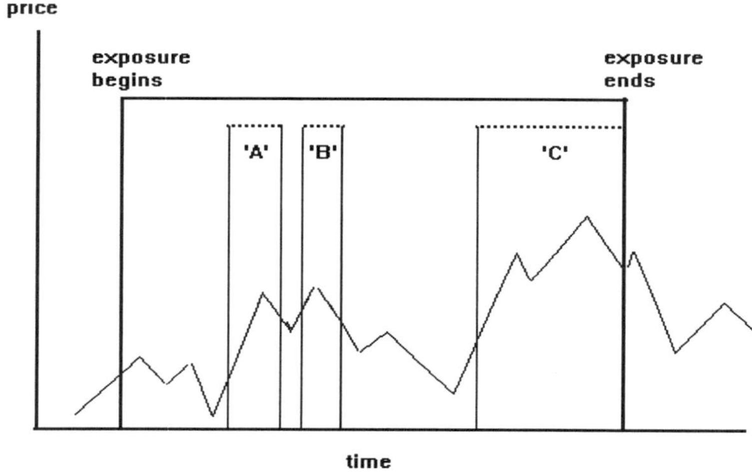

This exhibit illustrates the selective hedge model for enhancing profits. The exposure is only hedged when the predicted market move would result in a loss on the exposed position and a profit on the hedge position. When the market reverses, the hedge is lifted. Selective hedge positions may be initiated and liquidated a number of times during a single exposure period. The results are often mixed. In this example, the hedge is for an exposed liability and consists of long forward contracts.

Position 'A' is liquidated at a profit, position 'B' at a loss, and position 'C' is terminated when the exposure disappears and ends in a profit. Compare this model with the classical hedge model above.

Trading Systems

A trading system is an intricate part of any hedge model. The trading system is a set of "trading rules" that determine how and when to put on and take off positions for profit. Through the years, trading systems have become quite sophisticated. Computers now have supplanted people in generating buy /sell signals. One of the latest advances in technical analysis is the prediction of short-term price moves by a neural network, a sort of Boolean-algebra-driven microprocessor that discovers previously hidden price patterns and relationships. Still, none of these technologically advanced systems can consistently out-perform an old-fashioned trend line analysis—drawing lines on a price chart with a ruler and pen.

The major advantage of a simple, straightforward system is that everyone can understand it. Simplicity makes the hardest part of currency management—selling the concept to nonbelievers-that much easier. Corporate directors tend to shy away from derivative trading when the trading rules are mysterious. Any selective hedge model must therefore include a systematic, understandable trading system, whether it follows trends, recognizes patterns, or studies econometrics or fundamentals.

Trend-following systems are very popular among selective hedgers. The basic objective in a trend-following system is to find a trend and trade on it before it is well under way. Misidentified trends—as when the market is just going back and forth in a range—usually become apparent just *after* you have committed to a position and just *before* prices reverse. Numerous systems have been devised to identify major trends. In most of them, buy or sell signals are triggered after significant evidence supports an emerging trend. They make no attempt to capture the very top or bottom of the market.

An example of a trend-following system is illustrated in Figure 12-5. Welles Wilder, a pioneer in commodity trading systems, developed this *Directional Movement Indicator*,[1] which identifies trends by the highs and lows in a series of daily (weekly or monthly) trading ranges. An uptrend is marked by progressively higher highs, and a downtrend is marked by progressively lower lows.

Even the best trading systems do not prevent hedge losses. Hedge losses most often occur in trend-following systems when false signals are generated and an emerging "trend" suddenly aborts and reverses. The frequency of false signals reflects the amount of sensitivity built into the system. A system that is highly sensitive to the market will catch trends very early and may realize large gains, but sensitive models also generate more false signals, piling up relatively small individual hedge losses into larger cumulative losses. On the other hand, a system that holds out for absolute proof and does not respond until the trend is established, will be too late in establishing hedges.

Figure 12-5: Directional Movement Indicator

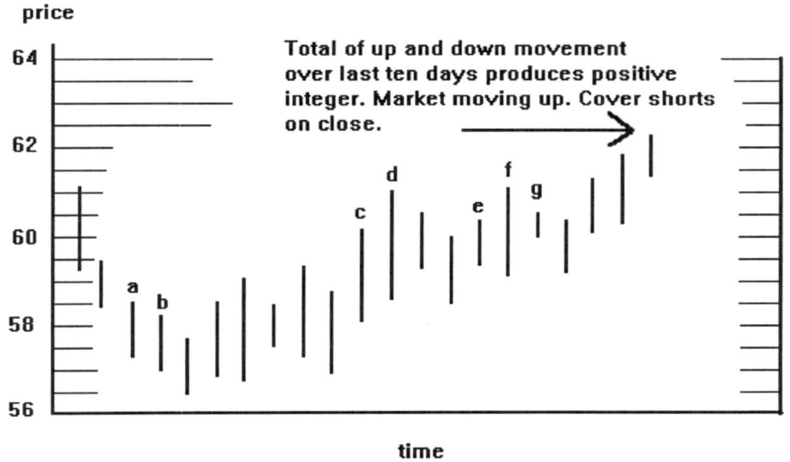

This diagram depicts a bar chart, with each bar representing the price range in one day of trading. The directional movement from one day to the next is established by a two-day pattern. Measurements specifically pertain to the two highs or two lows.

For up-moves, the ticks between the two highs are positive integers. For down-moves, the ticks between the two lows are negative integers. The number of ticks for each movement over a specific period of time, such as 10 days or 28 days, is totaled. If the number is positive, the market is in an uptrend. If the number is negative, the market is in a downtrend. A position is then established that goes in the direction of the market. The patterns are as follows:

- (A & B): The low of price range (B) is lower than the low of price range (A). This signifies downward movement.
- (C & D): The high of price range (D) is higher than the high of price range (C). This signifies upward movement.
- (E & F): Price range (F) has both a higher high and lower low than (E). The largest directional movement is significant. The other is ignored; therefore, (E & F) display upward movement.
- (F & G): Price range (G) contains neither a higher high nor a lower low; therefore, no directional movement is indicated.

Source: Welles Wilder's system adapted from the Dow Jones-Irwin *Guide to Trading Systems*

Other available systems generate signals based on fundamental analysis or econometrics, rather than on market activity. These systems analyze the current state of the domestic economy, the foreign economy, the political situation, and so forth. Such information is essential for analyzing the currency situation during the development of the program. But the values of these systems for timing trades is questionable. Invariably, half of the incoming fundamental data conflicts with the other half. If you feel that you can sort it all out and consistently and accurately predict future currency moves, read this book again.

Texas Hedging

The infamous "Texas Hedge" is an option that is not recommended. When cattle futures were first used to lock in the market price of yearlings before they were shipped to the feed lots, many ranchers became convinced that speculators lay in the bushes, waiting to short the market. Ranchers thought that speculators rushed in and pushed prices down, then bought up the ranchers' contracts for a song. To offset perceived actions of speculators, ranchers starting buying futures rather than selling them. They justified this "reverse hedge" by the fact that they also raised cows, and going long futures amounted to the same thing. In fact, they claimed, holding futures was even better than holding live cattle because "futures eat less." These positions became known as "Texas Hedges," a term now applied to any market position that increases rather than reduces exposure. Since this strategy was used, the Cattlemen's Association has tried repeatedly to ban speculative trading in cattle futures altogether. More than likely, Texas hedging is behind most stories about the farmer who "lost the farm by hedging."

The Trading Unit

Accounting exposure is managed most effectively from within a "trading unit." The trading unit is a function created to manage accounting exposure and is directed by a "currency trading manager," operating in conjunction with a support staff and outside service providers. With strategic or operating exposure management by the team, the CEO, or perhaps the CFO, would be a good candidate for currency manager. However, the daily task of hedging accounting exposure belongs with a different person: the "currency *trading* manager." His function, first and foremost, is trading currencies (see Figure 12-6).

Figure 12-6: The Trading Unit

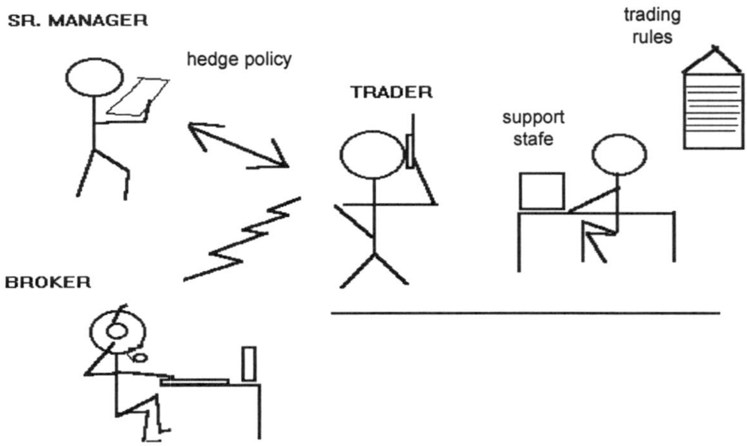

The trading unit consists of an individual trader with support staff, outside service providers, a hedge policy manual, an accounting system, an information system, oversight management, and a hedge model that includes a system of trading rules.

One currency management principle should be carved into the executive officer's desk for constant review: "committees cannot trade." Perhaps more hedge programs have failed because trading decisions were made by consensus than for any other reason. In this regard, management of transactional accounting (and, sometimes, short-term cash flow) exposure stands alone. "Real-time trading" is a one-person activity. A committee cannot be convened each time a decision is required.

Advocating a one-person trading responsibility may seem inconsistent with the previously advocated team approach to management and with hedge models that preclude on-the-spot decision-making. A hedge model does eliminate many individual decisions. But a model that provides for every possible situation would be impossible. Assume, for example, that the Canadian dollar market turns down, and the model requires a new short futures position. The trader is on the phone to the floor. Should he sell now or at the close? Should he go with a market order or a with limit order? How about a stop order? Is there enough activity to ensure a fair entry price or should he wait a few moments and allow the volatility to settle down? Responses to these questions have a lot to do with intuition and "market feel," and very little to do with consensus-building.

The position of currency trading manager often falls to someone in finance, probably the treasurer. The treasurer or his equivalent can handle the job when the exposures are only periodically scheduled transactions. The treasurer can easily enter the trades personally whenever necessary. The most time-consuming activity might be updating price charts daily.

When accounting exposure is pervasive and volatile, such as for a multinational involved in a number of foreign markets, the treasurer should probably delegate the trading to a full-time currency trading manager. Only by continuously keeping abreast of the market can any individual competently make the day-to-day decisions required. The treasurer should, however, retain close supervision of the trading.

In many cases, currency management takes only a few moments out of the day; however, some hedge models require trades to be initiated the moment a target price is hit during trading. With such a sensitive system, the manager must always be "on call" in case the broker or the dealer needs to contact him to approve a trade. Systems that are that sensitive are fine for speculation, but usually unsuitable for hedging purposes. As a trader enters and exits the market more frequently he increases the opportunity for trading errors and increases transaction costs. Consider changing the model to generate signals based only on the closing price. Orders can then be entered, carefully and deliberately, before the opening the next morning. Watching the market's every more is unnecessary and can even be dangerous to the company's financial health.

In addition to personnel, a "trading unit" consists of the company's hedge policy, the accounting system for tracking account activity, the information reporting system, the oversight system of checks and balances, the hedge model, and the trading system employed. The unit also includes the information sources available to the currency trading manager and the required transactional and advisory services.

Hedging Considerations

Trading units often deal solely with accounting exposure, specifically short-term transactional exposures. The exposures they protect may be the primary concern of the company or a minor part of the overall currency management program, depending on the value-based priorities identified during program development. The Fordoche Company, studied in the last chapter, would assign this unit the residual mismatches after all operating or cash flow positions have been netted. Other companies, of course, might see accounting exposure as the *only* problem, to be hedged without regard to other types of exposure. Whatever its importance in the overall scheme of things, accounting exposure is managed in much the same way. The considerations are as follows:

1. *Identification of the Specific Exposure*: What is the *net* exposure, after all assets and liabilities have been netted against each other?
2. *Analysis of the Currency*: What is the risk to the company of this particular currency? Does it move in conjunction with the home currency, as the Hong Kong dollar does with the U.S. dollar? If so, the currency generates little or no exposure. Does it move in conjunction with other currencies that denominate offsetting items, thereby creating a natural offset? For example, an unmatched 5,000,000 guilder short position does not constitute a risk if there is also an unmatched 10,000,000 Deutsche mark long position on the books. Assume the guilder is worth $0.60, the Deutsche mark is worth $.065, and they move parallel to each other. The real exposure, then, is not a guilder short position but a 5,000,000 Deutsche mark long position.
3. *The Risk Tolerance Level*: How much exposure risk is the company willing to tolerate? How much hedge burden (hedge loss) is tolerable? The answers will help determine the type of hedge model to use, as well as the types of derivatives used. Must derivative trading be part of the program? Hedge models are normally strategies for trading derivatives, but these models can be used almost as easily without using derivatives or leverage. Long classic hedges, range hedges, and selective hedges can be put on and taken off simply by purchasing and reselling money market instruments denominated in the appropriate currency. Short hedges can be established by borrowing and repaying foreign funds through an international bank account.
4. *Transferring Leverage*: Still, most financial managers will use leverage by trading currency derivatives. Which ones? The risk profile of the company will determine which derivatives are used. Market transactions may be separated into three risk groups. The first contains futures, forwards, and option *writing* strategies and provides maximum leverage.

The second group consists of option *buying* strategies. These long option strategies still involve leverage, but the *risk* associated with leverage is transferred to someone else at a cost known as the option premium.

The third group includes the long-term transactional hedges of bank borrowings and currency swaps. As the name implies, these are techniques for managing long-term risk, such as transactional exposures over a year in duration, long-term translation exposure, and ongoing cash flow exposure.

5. *Security*: Disclosure is paramount in derivative trading. The huge losses experienced by companies hedging in the currency markets are very often the result of senior managers delegating trading authority and then not maintaining vigilance over the accruing gains and losses. The best way to build security into the program is with a check and balance system. For example, the transacting dealer or broker should be instructed to submit copies of all order confirmations, fills, and account statements directly to an individual whose function includes fiduciary responsibility to the company. This overseer, ideally the senior manager on the currency management team, should not be involved in the day-to-day trading activity. Both overseer and trader should review and account for all information received immediately upon receipt.
6. *The Desired Results*: Currency programs are best developed "bottom up." In other words, the desired results are first identified, and then the methods for achieving the results are developed. The desired results might be a complete elimination of all accounting exposure risk, reduced exposures during times of volatility, or even the acquisition and exploitation of transactional exposure to increase profitability. Whatever the objectives, they will help determine the model, the derivatives, the guidelines, and the currency manager's role as a trader.

CHAPTER 13

Hedge Transactions

Any operating system works best when the operator follows an established set of instructions or a "rule book." For traders, the "rule book" consists of communication protocol, contract obligations, order entry rules, and, finally, a list of trading "do's and don'ts."

The Broker/Dealer

All futures contracts, exchange-traded forward contracts, and exchange-traded options on either futures or spot are effected through a broker. Forward contracts and most over-the-counter derivatives, such as options and swaps, are dealer products, available through a bank that provides customer service in these areas. A "broker/dealer" is a person who can be a broker or a dealer, depending on the circumstances. The term here refers both to the bank foreign exchange dealer who transacts for the bank's customers and to the futures broker, trading for his customer's account.

Finding a Dealer

A currency manager may contact a foreign exchange dealer, establish an account or a line of credit, begin trading, and build a long-term relationship without ever meeting that person face-to-face. In fact, this procedure is a normal way to initiate a currency trading relationship with a bank. The currency manager calls the local branch office. The lending officer, or customer relations officer, then sets up an appointment to obtain pertinent information about the company, either by phone or in person. Credit history is checked, and hedging requirements are reviewed. Documents are signed. Trading limits are determined, and a line of credit is set up. The currency manager is given access to the bank's foreign exchange desk, which may be located in a distant city, and is invited to call whenever he wants to make a trade or obtain a quote. Normally, there is a "bank" of dealers within a foreign exchange trading unit, and the currency manager deals with whoever answers the phone.

Not all banks offer market research and hedging guidance. Dealers may or may not offer insight regarding current market conditions. Basically, the relationship between the corporate manager and the dealer is one of buyer and seller, rather than one of client and advisor. Often, the currency manager will set up foreign exchange credit lines at more than one bank. Obviously, the currency manager will need to find research and advisory services from some source other than his foreign exchange dealer. Fortunately, a wealth of services are available, mostly on a fee or subscription basis.

The Client-Broker Relationship

Relationships between clients and futures brokers are often closer that those between clients and banks, but obtaining independent research is still advisable. Brokerage firms often supply abundant market research and trading advice, but the advice may not be *appropriate* for the company. The broker/client relationship is often a friendship between two individuals rather than a supportive structure between two business enterprises. Trading is conducted mostly one-on-one between client and customer. For this reason, brokers who switch firms often take their customers with them; those who have built a sizable customer "book" may be pirated by competing firms. Understandably, a client will not take the trouble of closing an account with one firm and opening an account with another firm unless a strong client-broker bond exists with the second firm.

Because of this bond, brokers want to produce winning trades for their clients. Whether the clients wants it or not, the broker becomes personally invested in the account. However, unless the broker specializes in currency or in hedging, he may give advice that is unsuitable to the account. His outlook is usually very short-term. Currency trading, like any other commodity trading, tends to compress long-term outlooks into weeks and short-term outlooks into hours. This compression is fine for speculation, but not for hedging. The currency trading manager must realize that the broker's perception of a winning or losing trade may change every five minutes or so, and his advice often reflects that fact.

A Conflict of Interest

Another pitfall inherent in the client-broker relationship is conflict of interest. This conflict exists regardless of how professional or how customer-oriented the broker is. The conflict stems from the brokers' compensation, which is based on account *activity* instead of account *profitability*. The more the account trades, the more income the broker receives, regardless of the amount of dollars gained or lost on the trades. Also, brokers tend to focus on the present, where they have opportunities for compensation, thus giving them a short-term outlook that is inappropriate for most hedging strategies.

Face-to-Face Meeting

Thus, brokerage accounts should be set up with a personal, face-to-face meeting. One purpose of the meeting is to fill out and sign the necessary documents and to establish the ground rules. The broker must be aware of the company's objectives and trading goals. He should fully understand the hedge model behind the trading decisions. He should be informed that any advice he provides must be appropriate to the model and that the currency manager is not interested in receiving urgent phone calls to "sell now because someone says the peso is going to break this afternoon." The manager should clearly establish *what* he wants to hear from the broker and *when* he wants to hear it.

Negotiations

The meeting before an account is established is also a time to negotiate. If volume warrants, a discounted commission structure may be available. Minimum exchange margins should be requested. Determination should be made whether collateral such as treasury bills can be used instead of cash for initial margins. Interest earnings on margin account balances may be available. A commitment of time from the broker for market updates, such as ten or fifteen minutes on the phone at the beginning of each week, should be included in the terms.

During the initial meeting, potential conflicts of interest should be addressed. Some managers use the broker only for transactions and obtain market research from another source. Others use more than one broker if the trading volume permits. In any event, establishing the ground rules early on and face-to-face avoids costly misunderstandings later.

Forward Contract Specifications (A Review)

In general, foreign exchange contracts in both the interbank and futures market are created by verbal agreements to transactions. The contracts are irrevocable and non-assignable, and they govern how, when, and at what rate the currencies will be exchanged. Credits and debits that reflect the unrealized profits and losses of open positions are booked daily. If a position is not offset with a reverse position, the delivery and receipt of both currencies are obligations to be fulfilled by the counterparties involved.

Interbank Participants

The interbank is primarily a corporate and institutional dealer market, involving transactions between a central bank and a commercial bank, between two commercial banks, or between two foreign exchange dealers, etc. Corporations and other entities without direct access to interbank can buy and sell currency though an account with a bank that enters into contracts on the client's behalf. Depending on size, the bank may pool or batch client orders before effecting transactions in the market to offset their orders.

The terms of the corporate client account with the bank closely conform with the transaction terms between members of the interbank network. The amount of currency that can be exchanged is not subject to a maximum. Normally, the interbank deals in amounts of currency valued at $1,000,000 or more. Anything less than $1,000,000 lots would be similar to an "odd lot" on a securities exchange and priced at a premium. Actually, anything less than a 5-lot or 10-lot order is often subject to higher spreads as well, depending on the dealer.

Value Dates

Currency contracts can be for spot (two-day delivery)[1] or for forward value dates. Any value date can be contracted as long as it is a "good" date in both countries. A good date is when the banks in both countries are open to effect deliveries. Normally, trading activity will center around spot, 30 days forward, 60 days forward, and 90 days forward. Trading volume is heaviest for spot and diminishes as the value date extends further into the future.

Quoting Forwards

Prices are quoted indirectly as the number of foreign currency units in one U.S. dollar (though the British pound and a few other British commonwealth currencies are quoted directly). The rate of exchange charged to a corporate client represents an "all-in" price, which means all transaction costs are figured in. There are no charges added to the all-in price, such as commissions for dealer/client or bank/client trades. Dealers may give three quotes for any particular value date: the bid, the offer, and the mid-price. The bid and the offer include a mark-down or mark-up to compensate the dealer. The mid-price is quoted only as an "informational" rate, not one at which a transaction will take place. Trading occurs only when one person's bid equals another person's offer.

Spreads and Compensation

The bank increases the market spread to compensate for its service. For example, a corporation buying Canadian dollars will pay the bid price quoted by its bank. This price includes the current bid quoted in the market plus a mark-down. The amount of the mark-down or mark-up can vary widely, based on size of transaction, competitive pressure, whether or not the bank is aggressively seeking the business, volatility in the market, etc. Normally, the quote is not broken down for the client: the transaction cost is hidden.

Delivery and Offset

Delivery terms for both forwards and futures are essentially identical; however, the two markets differ in their intents. The interbank is geared toward delivery. Almost all forward contracts are undertaken with the intention to make or receive delivery. The contracts are irrevocable, so they must be delivered unless offset. The only time delivery does *not* occur is when two counterparties (the bank and the customer) have contracts that offset each other. For expediency, the parties may simply agree to net out the contracts and adjust the difference with a cash payment.

Trading on Credit

Dealers establish reciprocating credit lines for transferring credits and debits back and forth with other dealers. The transfers correspond to daily gains and losses incurred on open positions. None of the principal in either currency changes hands until delivery is made. Banks also extend credit lines to corporate clients involved in interbank transactions. Each bank may establish its own procedures regarding client accounts, and some may require maintenance of additional security or compensating balances.

Futures Contract Specifications (A Review)

The futures contract is between the exchange member (broker or trader) and the exchange clearing house. The clearing house takes the role of counterparty in every contract traded. Non-members (such as the Fordoche Company) access the futures market through a brokerage account. The regulations governing activity in these accounts conform to the exchange rules governing members and contract terms.

Standardized Size and Date

Futures contracts are standardized at a minimum number of currency units (such as 100,000 Canadian dollars, 12,500,000 Japanese yen, etc.) that can be traded. However, transactions may involve any number of contracts. Futures, like forwards, have settlement dates, or value dates. A number of value dates fall within a 12- to 15-month period, but only four dates trade actively: the third Wednesday of March, June, September, and December. The *last trading day* for a value date is two business days before the value date.[2] The first two contract months in the future are usually the heaviest traded, and trading volume in the more distant months can be very thin, making fair market prices difficult to obtain.

Spot trading with contracts of one week duration for British pounds and Deutsche marks is continuous. These contracts are referred to as *rolling spot* contracts. The CME, in a bid to capture some of the interbank business, has also introduced forward contracts, which combine the unlimited value dates of the interbank market with the trading procedures of the exchange. These "future forwards" are quoted indirectly as is the custom of the interbank.

Quoting Futures

All futures contracts besides the future forwards are quoted directly as the number of dollars in a unit of foreign currency. Trades usually take place at the so-called "mid-price." In slow trading with little volatility or in markets trading within a narrow price range, a bid and offer market can form. In these conditions, floor traders act as dealers, selling and buying the spread (or "hitting the bids and offers," as they say). This type of market quickly disappears when either volatility increases or trends begin to emerge.

Commissions

Transaction costs for futures contracts are commissions. As mentioned above, commissions are based on the number of contracts traded, not on the value of the contracts. Commissions vary greatly, depending on customer trading volume and competition. Commissions costs are always broken out in the account, so the transaction cost is visible.

Offset and Delivery

Offset is the rule rather than the exception with futures contracts. Although currency can be delivered for futures contracts just as for forwards, delivery occurs less than 5% of the time. Brokers and traders are often inexperienced in deliveries and actively discourage customers from making or receiving delivery. Instead, the futures market has developed efficient offset methods. Offset occurs as it does in the interbank: a long position is transacted and entered in the account to match a short position, and vice versa.

Clearing House as Counterparty

For interbank positions, the counterparties must be identified and in agreement before offsetting positions can be netted out. In the futures market, however, the exchange clearing house is the only counterparty. Therefore, every position can be netted out. Unlike positions taken in the interbank, which remain on the account until the delivery date, offsetting futures positions are closed out immediately. The clearing house matches buy and sell contracts at the end of each day and keeps track of the credit and debit flows. It automatically closes out any position when an offsetting trade is posted in the same account. Attendant profits and losses are realized and available to the customer the next day.

Margin is not Credit

No credit lines are used in the futures market. Instead, margin accounts are established between and their clients. When a client takes an open position in a currency, he places funds into the account that equal or exceed the initial margin required. Initial margins required are quite small, perhaps 1% of the value of the contract. Gains and losses from positions are credited and debited to the margin account daily. If the net balance in the account falls below a certain minimum requirement, additional funds (called *maintenance or variation margin*) must be added to bring the balance back to the initial margin amount. Cash or cash equivalents such as U.S. treasury bills may be deposited as initial margin. Only cash may be used to satisfy maintenance calls.

Minimum, Maximum, and Limit Price Moves

A unique feature of the futures exchange is the maximum daily price limit. The limit is based on the minimum price movement for a currency. Contract prices move in increments of "tics." Prices can move 5, 10, 100 tics or more at a time, but a registered change in price requires a move of at least one tic. The value of one tic is 1/100 of one cent of the currency price expressed in U.S. dollars ($.0001). Japanese yen is the exception. A tic move on a yen contract is worth $.000001. So the value is $6.25, $10.00, or $12.50, depending on the number of currency units in the contract (i.e. 62,500 BP; 100,000 CD; 125,000 DM; 12,500,000 JY; etc.). One tic equals one *point*, except for the British pound, where it equals 2 points. Prices can only move a certain number of *points* in one direction during one trading session. This number is the "daily price limit."

Currently, the daily price limit for all currencies is 200 points from the previous closing price (400 points for the British pound). Remember that the limit concerns moves in one direction only. For example, if a Deutsche mark contract trades at 5325 (53.25¢), a drop to 5324 or, conversely, a rise to 5326 is a one-point move. If the contract closes at 5325 on Thursday, on Friday it is allowed to trade up to 5525, which is 200 points higher than its previous close. On the same day, the contract may reverse direction and is allowed to trade as low as 5125, which is 200 points lower than its previous close. It cannot be traded beyond those price limits. If it hits its upper limit of 5525 and buy orders are still unfilled at that price, trading is suspended until sell orders enter the market in sufficient numbers to satisfy the outstanding buy orders and push the price down. If insufficient sell orders enter at the maximum allowed price, the market remains "locked limit up" until the following Monday morning. Then, when the market opens again, new limits from Friday's limit up close will be in place. The market can lock limit down in exactly the same manner.

Limits for Cooling Off

Price changes can occur on rumor or on late-breaking news. The market does not wait to "get the facts," but responds immediately to any stimulus as traders and dealers try to avoid potentially damaging losses. The purpose of daily price limits is to allow a "cooling-off" period. The exchange controls the amount of these limits (with approval of the

Commodity Futures Trading Commission, or CFTC) and can expand, contract, or eliminate them to compensate for market conditions.

The effectiveness of this cooling-off period is debatable. Originally, limit moves worked as planned. Today, however, the currency futures market is large, efficient, and mindful of the much larger interbank, and so prices do not trade "out of line" for more than a few moments. Some evidence suggests that limit moves actually increase volatility by creating a panic as unfilled buy or sell orders pile up and persons trapped in the market try to get out at any price. This type of panic trading sometimes spills over from one market to another.

Entering the Order

Many corporate hedging strategies come apart with the first order to the broker or dealer. Giving the wrong order at the wrong time can result in a very bad price or in no price at all.

Basically, orders are either (1) *day orders* or (2) *GTC* (good 'til canceled) orders. A day order is valid only during the day it is entered: if it was not filled by the end of the day, it is automatically canceled. GTC orders, on the other hand, remain in the market until they are filled or canceled (sometimes for days or weeks).

Other ordering procedures depend on the market or on market conditions; for example, brokers in exchange markets and dealers in the interbank give quotes differently. When the customer calls a bank's foreign exchange dealer for a price, the dealer gives a one-way quote. In other words, the customer is asked whether he wants to buy or sell, and *then* the dealer quotes him a price. The customer usually has about 15 seconds to make a decision, and, in volatile conditions, the decision may be required "right now." When the allotted time is up, the dealer gives a new quote, and the customer has another few seconds to accept or reject it. If the quote is acceptable, the order is filled immediately. Some banks and dealers may accept orders for specific prices that are "away from the market" either on a GTC or a day basis. Many do not. This practice depends on the dealer's operating procedures and his relationship with the customer.

On the other hand, when the customer calls a broker, the broker gives one price, which is the last traded price. The broker works on a per-trade commission and does not factor a mark-up or mark-down into the price. Thus, the price quoted is not affected by whether the customer buys or sells.

In a typical transaction, the customer asks the broker where the market is, and the broker responds with the last price traded. If queried, the broker also gives the high and low of the day, the last 5 prices traded, whether the market is strong or weak, and probably a "guesstimate" of where prices are heading in the next 15 minutes or so. The broker offers information to help the customer get a feel for market volatility, current trend, and sentiment. Armed with this information, the customer places an order. The order tells the broker whether to buy or sell and how to buy or sell.

Acceptable trading instructions are limited because of the tremendous number of orders that flow onto the exchange and the number of hands the orders must pass through before reaching the pit. For expediency, all participants write and talk in a common, stylized shorthand. Orders are distilled to three basic instructions, shown in Table 13-1.

Table 13-1: Order Designation

Designation	Implied Instructions
Market	Fill this order immediately at the best price available.
(Specific Price) OB	Fill at the specified price, or better (OB), if possible. Hold the order and wait for the price if the price is not currently obtainable. This type of order is a *limit order*. It is used when the market is trading above the specified buy price or below the specified sell price. "Or better" means a lower buy price and a higher sell price.
(Specific Price) Stop	Fill immediately as a market order if and when the market trades at the specified price. Stop orders are used when the current market is below the specified buy price or above the specified sell price. In other words, the price used to fill the order is *worse* than the current price.

There are a number of variations to these basic forms. For example, a *market close* order instructs the floor broker to hold the order in his "deck" until the closing minutes of trade, then fill it as a market order. A *stop limit* order converts into a limit order rather than a market order when the stop price is hit. A *FOK* order (fill-or-kill) is a specific price order that does not allow for partial fills. If it is impossible to fill the entire order immediately, the order is canceled. An *OCO* (one-cancels-the-other) order is actually two separate orders. As soon as one is filled, the other is canceled.

Entering the "Best" Order

Some order specifications work better under some conditions than others. The guidelines listed below work most of the time. Still, choosing an order type is often a judgment call. The advice of the broker can be invaluable for determining the best type of order. However, solicit his advice only when you are confident that he is working in your best interest. Remember, both dealers and brokers have a potential conflict of interest. Dealers buy and sell *to* you (read "against" you.) Brokers buy and sell *for* you, but are biased toward market orders, because they guarantee the fill and the commission, while stop orders and limit orders may not be filled; however, the vast majority of brokers operate ethically. Ethical behavior is also required by law for the brokerage industry. Almost all brokers and dealers realize that working in your best interest is also in their best interest.

Order Entry Guidelines

- **Market orders** are appropriate for:

  (a) *liquidating a hedge*. The primary objective when liquidating a hedge is to get out of the market. Trying to get out at a specific price may result in missing the market completely. Remember that as soon as the exposure disappears, all hedge positions immediately become speculative positions.

  (b) *an active market confined to a narrow range*. Here, trading takes on the characteristics of a bid-and-offer market, with a narrow spread between the two prices. Using limit orders to try to buy the bid or sell the offer is playing the floor trader's game without his advantages. This practice is a good way of missing the market, since active, liquid markets can break out of the range anytime, leaving your order unfilled.

  (c) *an orderly trending market*. "Orderly" means that the market is not trading wildly, with wide gaps between prices. The order should fill somewhere near the current price. Market orders in run-away markets, however, should be avoided if possible, because they may remain unfilled for several minutes, only to be transacted at the worst price of the day. In some cases, such as to liquidate a hedge, you must use a market order in volatile conditions. In those cases, consider market close orders, or OCO orders consisting of a limit and a market close. Or, if possible, have the broker watch for a break in the action and then fill your order when it occurs. Again, as long as conditions permit, use market orders when prices are trending up or down. Any other type of order risks being unfilled.

- **Limit (or OB) Orders** are appropriate for:

  (a) *volatile markets*. Most of the time, a very volatile market leaves large gaps between prices traded. Eventually, these gaps are filled (barring a run-away market), and a limit order resting in the market will be filled as the market returns to it.

  (b) *large orders*. Especially in quiet markets, an order of 100 or 200 contracts can move the market against you. Often, after the order fills, the market returns to where it was originally. Consequently, the average fill price is way off the market. The best way to handle large orders is to trickle them into the market as limit or market orders. Hide large pending orders by entering them in an irregular fashion, or by instructing your broker to use more than one floor broker.

  (c) *thin markets*. In illiquid markets, an order of *any* size can easily move the market, since there is minimal competition between traders to take the other side. As a result, floor traders take the other side of market orders only on their terms.

  (d) *critical pricing*. If the hedge strategy depends upon precise market prices, you must use a limit order. Even in a quiet market, the price quoted by the broker will probably not be your price for a market order. The last trade may have taken place several minutes ago, and no orders may currently rest in the pit, so the next trade may be at a much different price. Market orders guarantee transactions, but not prices. If pricing requirements are critical, however, your hedge model may be too price-sensitive.

- **Stop Orders** are appropriate for:

  (a) *capping losses*. A stop order is usually used to cap losses. In fact, a stop order is often referred to as a 'stop loss' order. With a stop order, the position is liquidated at the market if the market worsens to the stop price. The specified price acts as a cap on the amount of loss accruing in a trade; *however, hedge policy often prohibits capping a loss*, because caps can defeat the purpose of the hedge. Nevertheless, some circumstances or strategies may include placing ceilings on hedge losses, and stop orders are a good way of doing so.

  (b) *improving upon the price*. If the model permits stop orders, they can be effective for placing hedges. A stop order acts somewhat like an option. As long as the market is going sideways, or in the "right" direction, the hedge is not placed. When it starts to go in the "wrong" direction, the stop order is there to trigger the hedge transaction. A *trailing stop*, which moves over time just under a rising market or just over a falling market, is normally used.

  For example, assume that the company has a long Deutsche mark receivable. The currency manager is required to hedge this exposure by going short September futures. September is currently at 6500 and rising. The currency manager might place a sell stop order at 6470, risking 30 points. If the market drops down and trades at 6470, the order fills. Instead, the market continues to rise, reaching 6550. The manager "trails" the market by canceling his 6470 stop and re-entering a 6520 stop, still risking 30 points. As long as the market does not back off and trigger the stop price, the manager will continue to trail the market by canceling and re-entering orders at ever higher levels. (No transaction costs are involved in doing this.) Eventually the sell order is filled but, with luck, at a significantly higher level than the starting price of 6500.

  (c) *trend following systems*. Stop orders can be used as a selective hedging technique. Almost all trend following systems trigger buy and sell signals after the market confirms the trend. The market must move higher to trigger the buy, lower to trigger the sell. GTC stop orders, placed at the signal price, are quite appropriate for trading these systems.

  Note that since stop orders become market orders when triggered, they entail the same risks. Many traders make the mistake of putting stop orders at "obvious" turning points in the market, right beneath support, for example. Consequently, they end up with market orders just as volatility picks up dramatically. Often the fill price is far different than the stop price. Selecting a proper point in the market for placing a stop order is extremely important. Unfortunately, proper placement relies more on intuition than on mathematics. Also, existing stop orders must be monitored, canceled, and repositioned as changing conditions warrant.

An example of market, stop, and limit orders is illustrated in Figure 13-1.

Trading Rules

Obviously, the corporate currency manager and the currency speculator have much more in common than either are willing to admit. Each will risk financial loss in unpredictable markets. The cash exposure carried by the corporation is no different than the market exposure of the speculator, since they are managed similarly. Paradoxically, the risk disappears for both when the currency manager gets into the market and the speculator gets out.

Thus, one currency manager and one currency speculator could enter into a trade, each hoping to profit from a position in which only one will. If the speculator is seasoned, he is probably trading as mechanically and impassively as he knows how, aided by a system that is calling the shots. He pre-plans the trade and then trades the plan. The currency manager should do the same.

The currency manager must therefore, know the rules, listed below. Most were developed by speculators and validated by painful experience. Others pertain specifically to hedging. With a little modification, they all serve the currency manager equally well.

1. *Do not Texas Hedge*. Obviously, unless the market exposure is an opposite position to the cash exposure, the company is speculating, not hedging. To the extent that the exposure is over-hedged or under-hedged, the company is also speculating, either in cash or derivatives.
2. *Be sure of your position*. Forward, future, and option contracts are obviously long or short, but as the hedge becomes more complex, the direction in which it faces may become less obvious. Convoluted option strategies and option-embedded counterparty agreements may be difficult to unravel into component longs and shorts. *Thoroughly* pick apart all hedge strategies and identify each component by amount, duration, and position.

3. *Calculate your equity balance daily.* Foreign exchange accounts and futures accounts should be marked to the market daily to prevent huge losses from accruing undetected until too late to salvage the program.
4. *Do not over-leverage.* Figure out the worst case scenario, and make sure funds are available to back up the market position if necessary. If you cannot meet margins in time, the broker or dealer has standing instructions to liquidate your position immediately, at the market and with or without your approval .
5. *Do not lift hedges prematurely simply to stem a loss.* If the hedge is sound, liquidating it to cut a loss will leave the exposure vulnerable to a price reversal. There is nothing worse than getting out of the market with a realized loss only to see additional losses accumulate in the exposed position as prices suddenly reverse.
6. *Do not lift hedges prematurely simply to take a profit.* Taking profits can be tempting, especially after agonizing through a string of trading losses. Profit taking may be rationalized by saying that the market has gone too far, too fast and an opportunity will emerge to re-establish the hedge at a better price. Too often, no better price emerges. A characteristic of market trends is that they go much further than anyone expects. Hedge profits can quickly dissipate as the now-unhedged exposure continues to generate losses.
7. *Do not carry futures contracts into the last trading day*, and do not carry options to expiration unless you intend to exercise them. Liquidity dries up rapidly during the last weeks before contracts go off the board. Illiquid markets can be very difficult to get in or out of at a fair price, since very few traders will transact the other side. If you carry the position into the last moments, you may not be able to liquidate at any price, but will be obligated to exchange the underlying currency, with added trouble and expense.
8. *Stress test your model.* Design a "what-if" spreadsheet, and try various "worst-case" scenarios. Scenarios should test for changes in liquidity, volatility, price extremes, and basis correlation. With advanced preparation, unusual conditions will not result in panic.
9. *Do not subscribe to real-time quote streams.* Watching price fluctuations throughout the day does not improve either hedging techniques or decision making. It *does*, however, bring on adrenaline rushes, outbreaks of emotional trading, and stupor. Leave

real-time quotes to the day traders and scalpers. They are useless for most hedge programs. Instead, download end-of-day price data, or simply review *The Wall Street Journal* the following day.

10. *Update price charts daily.* Daily, weekly, and monthly price ranges should be charted. Together, they provide a short-term, intermediate-term, and long-term view of the market, thus permitting an excellent "feel" for the market. Daily price charts should be updated before the next trading session. Update these charts *personally* to stay on top of the market.
11. *Trade only liquid positions*. Whether transacting futures, options, or forward contracts, stay away from distant or illiquid months if possible. Obviously, some derivatives, such as long-term swaps and forwards, are illiquid by nature. Look for ways of offsetting these hedges with derivatives or currency positions in parallel markets, if necessary. The ability to quickly liquidate all positions at a fair price should be built into every currency management program.
12. *Liquidate with market orders*. After the exposure disappears, get out of the market. Doing anything else is simply speculating.
13. *Shop around.* When phoning for a dealer quote, have another dealer on another line and let each one know you are getting simultaneous quotes. The spread will usually narrow in your favor. Shop brokerage commissions as well. The range is from $125 per round turn to $12 or under if you are willing to accept very spartan transactional services. Needless to say, commissions on the high end are probably negotiable if you trade in any significant volume.
14. *Avoid conflicts of interest*. Your broker or dealer may be the most knowledgeable person on your team. But remember that his compensation is based on the number of trades. Keep this conflict of interest in mind when considering delegating trading authority to the broker/dealer.
15. *Avoid Order Miscommunications*. The second leading cause of financial loss in trading the currency markets stems from errors in communication. The only source of greater loss is market risk itself. "Buy" and "sell" orders are often inadvertently turned around during a phone conversation with the broker/dealer or later in the transmission of the order. For example, when your broker is told to "buy ten contracts of March Swiss francs," he

normally writes down those instructions exactly and forwards them to the floor, where the contracts are purchased for your account. If, however, he has been selling Swiss francs for customers all morning long and has sell orders scattered across his desk, he may write "sell ten contracts" by mistake.

Sometimes the confusion results from differences in the markets. Compare the function of the broker with that of the dealer. If you call your broker and instruct him to "buy 50 contracts of March Swiss francs at the market," he knows your intent. On the other hand, if you call your bank and instruct the foreign exchange dealer to "buy 600,000 Swiss francs for March 21," the instructions are not as clear. Do you mean that the dealer is to buy francs *for* you, or buy francs *from* you? The first constitutes a buy, the second a sell.

The best way to avoid order entry errors is to always have the broker/dealer repeat your instructions back to you. They are instructed to always repeat the order, but sometimes neglect to do so during active market conditions. You should also tape all conversations with the broker/dealer to protect yourself in disputes, just as they do for their protection. Also, scrutinize all order and trade confirmations as soon as you receive them.

16. *Keep Track of GTC Orders*. A forgotten order may also cause losses. Of course, day orders are automatically canceled at the end of each trading session. But for GTC orders, the loss occurs when a limit or stop order is placed and not filled. The market moves away, and the order is re-entered at a different price. If the original order is forgotten and left uncancelled, it remains valid until filled. The forgotten order is discovered when the manager receives an unexpected confirmation of a trade weeks or even months later. (However, the exchange or the broker usually cancels GTC orders automatically after 30 days, requiring their reinstatement by the customer.)

17. *Support the trader*. Whether you or someone you authorize makes the day-to-day trading decisions, never second-guess the decisions. Trading is difficult in any case and very ego deflating when it produces losses. Intense pressure to always make a profit can lead to paralysis, recklessness, or hiding of losses—all roads to financial disaster. The best way of preventing recriminations is to use the mechanical style of trading advocated in this book.

Figure 13-1: Market, Stop and Limit Orders

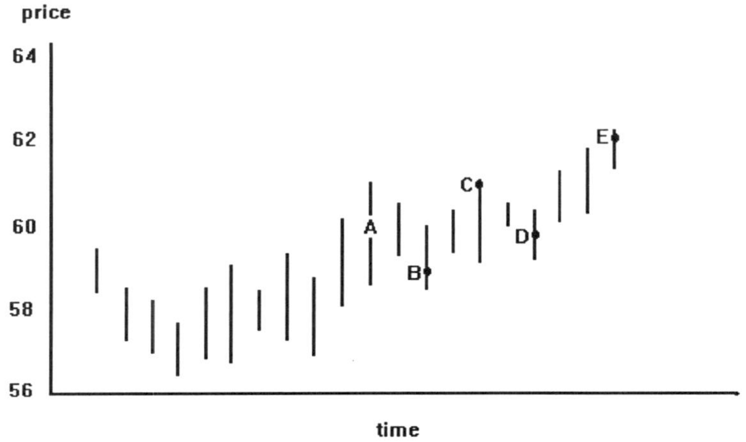

Assume for this example that the FC market is trading in a range between 56.50 and 61.75. The following sequence of orders takes place:

Market at 60.00.

A- market order is entered to buy, and fills at 60.10.
B- limit order to buy at 59.00 OB is entered. It fills at 59.00, establishing a second long position.

Market at 59.00

C- limit order is entered to sell at 61.00 OB. It fills at 61.00 for a 90 point profit on the first position.

Market at 61.00

D- The remaining long position is protected by placing a stop order to sell at 59.50 stop. The market drops, and the order fills at 59.30, for a 30-point profit. (Market and stop orders are subject to price "slippage" in fast markets.)

Market at 61.00

E- No positions remain. In order to catch the market if it begins trending upward, a stop order to buy at 62.00 stop is entered. The order fills at the market when that price is hit.

CHAPTER 14

Trading Forwards and Futures

This section looks at specific currency hedges and their effects on specific transactional exposures. Each hedge will be constructed step-by-step. Their differences and their similarities will be discussed. Three examples will be studied, involving forwards, futures, and options on futures.

Derivative Pricing

All exchange-traded currency derivatives are quoted in points. If the contract is quoted directly, the points refer to the number of dollars in a unit of foreign currency. If the contract is quoted indirectly, as a forward is, the points refer to the number of foreign currency units in one U.S. dollar. In either case, each point translates to a fraction of a cent. The fractional equivalent of a point depends on the currency quoted. If the Canadian dollar is quoted directly at .7502, for instance, the Canadian dollar is worth $0.7502. One point is equivalent to .01 cent ($0.0001.) The same price, quoted indirectly, is 1.3329, or C$1.3329 to be precise. One point more is $C1.3330, which is equivalent to .75018, or approximately .002 cents less.

The full value of a forward, futures, or option contract can be calculated in two ways. For a direct quote, multiply the price by the number of foreign currency units in the contract. (There are 100,000 Canadian dollars in a futures contract. Therefore, $0.7502 x 100,000 equals $75,020.) For an indirect quote, divide the number of foreign currency units by the price. (i.e., 100,000 /1.3329 = $75,024. The four-dollar difference is due to rounding.) Consider a December Swiss franc futures contract trading at .5949, almost 60¢. There are 125,000 Swiss francs in the contract, so the contract has a value of $74,362.50 (125,000 x $0.5949).

As you read through the examples below, convert the quotes from direct to indirect, or vice versa, to improve comprehension. To go from one quote to the other, simply divide 100 by the first quote.

Consider the Fordoche Company again. Senior management has given Mary, the corporate treasurer, the responsibility to oversee a trading unit for accounting exposures. Any foreign currency transactions that are not offsets to the strategic exposures of the company are to be hedged in the market. Policy calls for management with a classic hedge model, modified to take advantage of near-term range predictions with appropriate option strategies. As Mary sets up the unit, she is given a specific transaction for management.

The Fordoche Company has just been awarded a contract by a major food distributor in the Netherlands. This contract is for the installation of a complete production line to produce and package a new chocolate bar. Payment is denominated in Dutch guilders (symbolized here as *f*) with an exchange value of $1,200,000. The terms provide for *f*400,000 paid up front, *f*1000,000 paid at the time the installation begins (scheduled in six months), and *f*1,000,000 upon completion, approximately six months after installation begins. The payment amounts are based on the current spot rate of the guilder, which is *f*/$2.00. The Fordoche Company, therefore, has an exposure of *f*2,000,000, equivalent to $1,000,000 for the first six months, and *f*1,000,000, equivalent to $500,000, for the second six months (see Figure 14-1).

Figure 14-1: Contract of May 15 for Sale and Setup of Production Unit Based on Spot rate of ¦/$ 2.000

		Dutch Guilder	*U.S. Dollar*
Sale price:		2,400,000	1,200,000

Terms of Sale

	Now May 15	**6 months** November 15	**12 month** May 14
Payment Due:	*f*400,000	*f*1,000,000	*f*1,000,000
Exposure amount (after initial pmt)	*f*2,000,000	*f*1,000,00	0
Duration of Exposure	12 months	6 months	0

The Forward Contract Hedge

Mary decides to hedge this exposure with forwards. She phones the local bank with which the company does business and ascertains that it deals in foreign exchange. She makes an appointment with the loan officer. Upon reviewing the company's requirements, the bank sets up a line of credit for foreign exchange. The initial limit on the line is $1,000,000. Note that this limit does not refer to the amount of the exposure, but to the maximum allowable debit. Since unrealized gains from foreign exchange trades are credited to the line and unrealized losses are debited, the Fordoche Company would have to incur an unrealized loss of $1,000,000 before exceeding the limit.

With the credit line in place, Mary phones the foreign exchange trading desk, intending to short forward contracts for *f*2,000,000. In keeping with the timeframe of the exposures, this hedge would consist of a *f*1,000,000 six-month forward and a *f*1,000,000 twelve-month forward. She asks the dealer for an indication of spot. ("Indication quotes" do not commit the dealer. They are for information only.) Finding that spot guilders are exactly 2.000, she asks for *firm* bids on *f*1,000,000 six months out and twelve months out. Mary does not know the exact date on which the payments will be received, and therefore stays with the easier-to-price "even date" forwards (30 days, six months, twelve months, etc.) rather than asking for specific value dates. She is quoted 2.008 and 2.040, respectively.

Mary considers the six-month quote to be in line, but questions the dealer on the wide spread for the twelve-month forward. He informs her that European interest rates are "in flux" and, besides, very few trades are done that far out. Because the market is so illiquid at twelve months, the dealers protect themselves with the wider spreads. Mary decides not to accept the twelve-month bid and hedges the entire exposure by selling a single *f*2,000,000 six-month forward. The dealer confirms the price of 2.008 and informs her that the contract value date is November 15th (see Figure 14-2).

A written trade confirmation is faxed to Mary the following morning, and a copy of the confirmation is faxed to Jim, the chief operations officer, in compliance with the company's check and balance system. A debit entry also appears on the account the following morning, along with the trade, reflecting a rise in Dutch guilders overnight. From that morning until the forwards are liquidated, credits and debits will be entered daily. Balances are not due and payable in either direction until the value date, even if the position is liquidated in the meantime.

Figure 14-2: Forward Contract Hedge

Mary establishes line of credit: $1,000,000

	6-month contract	**12-month contract**
Ideal Hedge	*f*1,000,000	*f*1000,000
Forward Rates	2.008	2.040
More Practical Hedge	*f*2,000,000	0
Value Date	Nov. 15	May 15

Nearly six months later, on November 7, the first payment of *f*1,000,000 is received. By this time, the guilder has fallen in value a full cent, and the receivable is converted at the spot rate of 2.041. Mary now has a short *f*2,000,000 eight-day-forward position (since the value date is still November 15). She phones the dealer, and *buys* a *f*2,000,000 eight-day forward at the current offer. These two positions, a short and a long, completely offset each other. Although both continue to be carried until the value date, further gains and losses on the two cancel each other out, essentially terminating the hedge (see Figure 14-3).

Figure 14-3: Hedge Liquidation

	November 7	**November 15**
Payment Received	*f*1,000,000	
Existing forward		short *f*2,000,000
New forward		long *f*2,000,000
Rate of exchange (mid-point)	2.0410	2.0415

Remaining exposure—Second payment due in 6 months (May 14).

Note that the date on the offset must be the same as the date on the initial contract. When Mary initially shorts the even-dated forward, she does not know the *exact* value date: she simply sells a "six-month" forward. Once a position is on the books, however, it is very important to liquidate it by buying a forward for the exact value date as the one being offset. Mary does not enter an order to "buy an eight-day forward." The order reads, "buy guilders for November 15" and thus ensures that she does not end up with two value dates with neither liquidating the other.

On November 15, the offsetting positions convert to spot. The *f*2,000,000 short converts to a guilders payable at the spot rate, the *f*2,000,000 long converts to a guilders receivable at the same rate, and the two cash items cancel each other out, leaving a credit or debit dollar balance. Mary does not oversee these conversions. They are done automatically by the bank. Mary only sees the disappearance of the forward positions and a credit or debit in the account to reflect the realized gain or loss.

Rolling the Hedge Forward

The company is still exposed to the *f*1,000,000 receivable due six months later on May 14th; therefore, when Mary buys the eight-day forward to offset the hedge, she *simultaneously* sells another six-month forward for *f*1,000,000 to hedge the remaining receivable. Note here that she is not forced to sell a forward six months out, but only does so after finding the bid acceptable. If the spread were too wide, she could sell a three-month, or even a 30-day, forward and *roll it over* before the value date. When the second receivable is paid, Mary again liquidates the hedge by buying an offsetting forward contract (see Figure 14-4).

One point in particular should be emphasized about this transaction and its hedge. At no time did the transaction that generated the exposure use "hedge currency". Each payment from the Dutch company to Fordoche was deposited in an account domiciled in the Netherlands. Once the deposit was made, the bank, following the Fordoche Company's instructions, exchanged the guilders for U.S. dollars and credited the resulting dollar balance to the company's U.S. bank account. The payment transaction used different banks and different accounts from those used for the hedge transactions. The only connection between the payment of the receivable and the offsetting hedge transaction is timing: they take place on the same day and, presumably, close to the same exchange rate. This total segregation between cash and hedge markets is the norm. It allows the individual transactions in each to be done most efficiently, without the added paperwork, time, and trouble involved in taking or making currency deliveries on derivative contracts.

Figure 14-4: Rolling Forward

On November 7:
Mary rolls hedge by buying *f*2,000,000 for Nov. 15 and selling *f*1,000,000 for May 14

	Value Date **November 15**		Value Date **May 14**	
Existing forward	short *f*2,000,000			
New forward	long *f*2,000,000 (first leg of rollover)			
New forward			short *f*1,000,000 (second leg of rollover)	
	Initial	1st pmt	1st leg	2nd leg
Rate of Exchange:	**May 15**	**Nov 7**	**Nov 15**	**May 14**
	2.000	2.0410	2.0412	2.0496

In summary, by dealing in near-term contracts at the onset, Mary avoids paying the additional spread on the twelve-month forward. Rather, she took the opportunity to re-transact at a later date, after the interest rate market had more depth. In Figure 14-5, we show a gain on the November 15 forwards that is realized on that date. Normally, any gain or loss on the portion of the hedge rolled over is simply deferred until the final offset. The exchange rate exposure is completely hedged from the time Mary first enters the market until the final payment is received. A rollover *does* allow for an interest rate exposure, however, because, initially, only the first six months of interest are locked in on the one-year (second) receivable. The second six months of interest are not locked in until the rollover takes place.

Figure 14-5: The Fordoche Company-Forward Hedge Results

Terms of Sale

	Date	Cash Market	Forward Market
Initial payment	5/15	*f* 400,000	
Receivable due 11/15		*f* 1,000,000	
Receivable due 5/14* (*the following year)		*f* 1,000,000	
exchange rate		*f*/$ 2.000	
$ equivalent		$1,200,000	
less initial payment		$ 200,000	
$ exposed		$1,000,000	
Hedge Activity			
Short 11/15 forwards	5/15		*f* 2,000,000
exchange rate			*f*/$ 2.0080
$ equivalent			$ 996,000
Collect 1st receivable	11/7	*f* 1,000,000	
exchange rate		*f*/$ 2.0410	
$ equivalent		$ 490,000	
Buy 11/15 forwards	11/7		*f* 2,000,000
exchange rate			*f*/$ 2.0412
$ equivalent			$ 980,000
Gain (loss)		**($10,000)**	**$16,000**
Short 5/14 forwards	11/7		*f* 1,000,000
exchange rate			*f*/$ 2.0496
$ equivalent			$ 487,900
Collect 2nd receivable	5/14	*f* 1,000,000	
exchange rate		*f*/$ 1.9608	
$ equivalent		$ 510,000	
Buy 5/14 forwards	5/14		*f* 1,000,000
exchange rate			*f*/$ 1.9608
$ equivalent			$ 510,000
Gain (loss)		**$10,000**	**($22,100)**

The Spot-Forward Swap

What happens if the value date occurs before the payment is received? Let's assume that November 13 arrives, and the first receivable is still outstanding, although payment is expected at any time. In this case, Mary simply rolls over the *f*2,000,000 forward, day after day, until the payment is made. For example, on November 13, she buys a November 15 *f*2,000,000 forward to offset the original position, and simultaneously sells a November 16 *f*2,000,000 forward. The next day, on November 14, she buys a November 16 *f*2,000,000 forward and simultaneously sells November 17. She continues rolling over the hedge until the payment is received, then she simply "buys in" the hedge to liquidate.

In this case, the term *forward* is somewhat inaccurate. Since spot settles in two business days, the November 15 forward becomes a spot contract on November 13. Mary is actually buying *spot* guilders to offset her short obligation to deliver, while selling the *next day forward* to maintain the hedge. You may recall that this procedure describes a swap. Mary simply does "spot-forward" swaps on a daily basis. Spot-forward swaps are routine procedures, and some banks, if instructed, will continue to roll the position automatically until notified otherwise.

As you probably suspect, there are costs involved in spot-forward swaps, such as a slight interest penalty. Buying the spot and selling the next day forward is the same as lending dollars and borrowing foreign currency overnight. If the foreign currency pays a higher interest rate, as it does in this example, the purchase price is always higher than the sale price. Of course, the reverse is true if the dollar pays the higher rate. In any case, the overnight interest rate differential is relatively slight unless substantial sums are involved. A more significant cost is the bid-offer spread, which gives the dealer a cut in every swap.

Notes on Figure 14-5

The Fordoche Company contracts *f*2,000,000 of receivables on May 15 that it hedges over one year by initially selling six-month forwards for the entire amount. Six months later, on November 7, it offsets 50% of the position and rolls the remaining portion ahead for another six months. At no time do they actually deliver or receive guilders, since the long and short contracts cancel out both obligations.

The losses and gains are due to the Dutch guilder falling the equivalent of one cent during the first six months and then rising the equivalent of two cents.

This hedge is profitable for the first six months, but loses money overall because it involves shorting discount currencies. The company would have been better off by not placing the second hedge on November 7, though it could not have predicted that result.

This example is not a perfect hedge, in which the gain and losses precisely offset each other. A perfect outcome almost never occurs. Interest rate differentials, time differences, slippage, and transaction fees can all exact a cost. Nevertheless, the resulting gain or loss from market differences is insignificant compared to the potential gain or loss of an unhedged exposure.

Does this hedge result in an absolute loss? Not really. Receivables denominated in currencies yielding higher rates of interest are intrinsically costlier than those denominated in currencies yielding lower rates of interest. Receivables, after all, represent loans to the customer. Ideally, this hedge loss should be compensated for by the interest charge factored into the customer price.

The Futures Hedge

In our second scenario, Mary uses futures rather than forwards to manage the guilder receivable. She begins with a visit to a brokerage firm. Mary interviews the futures broker and establishes a futures hedge account. The broker agrees that the initial margin requirements may be met by treasury bills, purchased and held in the company's account. Mary also negotiates that the broker will pay interest on Fordoche's free margin balances.

Why should Mary use futures to hedge Fordoche's exposures? Currently, the futures exchanges in the United States offer actively traded futures contracts for only five currencies and the dollar index. Of course, contracts are available in additional currencies on overseas exchanges, if a currency manager is willing to trade offshore. There are other limitations to futures trading as well. For example, there are only four actively traded value dates, and contracts are standardized in fixed currency units, so a precise match with the amount of currency exposed happens only coincidentally. With all these limitations, why bother with futures at all? Why not stay with interbank forwards, which are available for practically any date, in any amount, for any freely traded currency?

The answer is that futures contracts are designed expressly for retail customers. Credit risk is virtually non-existent. Price is extremely visible. Transaction costs are easily discernible and competitive. While interbank spreads are narrow between dealers and large customers, they widen out significantly in lots of less than $1,000,000. Standard commissions for futures contracts, however, are the same whether the contract is valued at $30,000 or $3,000,000, and commissions are negotiable. For these reasons, many currency managers try to use futures in their hedging programs.

The Fordoche Company's guilder exposure is a case in point. The United States has no actively traded futures guilder contract and, even if it did, the contract size would probably not match the exposure size exactly. In addition, the Fordoche Company expects payment of the guilder receivables in November and May, whereas futures contracts settle only in March, June, September, and December. Nevertheless, this exposure may be effectively hedged with futures contracts. Mary approached the problem from two directions.

First, a proxy hedge may be possible. Proxy hedging requires finding something with an active market that correlates highly enough with the exposure to be used as a hedge vehicle. The Dutch authorities have confined the guilder/Deutsche mark exchange rate to a narrow range for a long time, so Mary instructs her broker to furnish guilder/Deutsche mark correlation charts for the last five years. She also requests correlation charts between the spot Deutsche mark and Deutsche mark futures. If the combined basis fluctuations between cash market guilders and Deutsche mark futures correlate with at least a .70 coefficient, she could use a Deutsche mark contract to hedge the guilder exposure. As an added advantage, the Deutsche mark is already being managed by the company as a strategic exposure.

Proxy hedging must be considered carefully. The fluctuating basis between the parallel market and the hedged currency adds one more uncontrolled variable to the hedge. Besides, historical currency relationships may not remain the same in the future. Thus, Mary explores a second approach. Rather than fitting the futures contract to the exposure, she tries fitting the exposure to the futures contract. She ascertains that the distributor, although unwilling to denominate the contract in U.S. dollars without a change in terms, is quite comfortable dealing in Deutsche marks. It is therefore agreed that the payments are to be made in Deutsche marks rather than guilders. This solution also adds a basis risk, but the risk is transferred to the Dutch distributor.

Having solved the currency mismatch, Mary turns to the problem of mismatched amounts and value dates. Actually, value dates are no longer a problem, because she is using Deutsche marks. The CME recently introduced forward contracts in that currency that trade as futures, but with unlimited value dating. If this contract is successful, other exchange-traded forwards in other currencies may be added. This example, however, uses traditional futures contracts to illustrate hedging of mismatched dates, which is by far the most common situation.

Figure 14-6: Contract of May 15 for Sale and Setup of Production Unit Based on Spot rate of *ƒ*/$ 2.000

	Dutch Guilder	*U.S. Dollar*
Sale price:	2,400,000	1,200,000

Mary determines that the distributor who is purchasing the line is willing to pay in Deutsche marks rather than Dutch guilders. Thus, she can establish a futures hedge in Deutsche marks.

	Deutsche mark	*U.S. Dollar*
Sale Price at DM/$ rate of 1.82	2,184,000	1,200,000 (r)

Terms of Sale

	Now May 15	**6 months** November 15	**12 months** May 14
Payment Due:	DM 364,000	DM 910,000	DM 910,000
Exposure amount (after initial pmt)	DM 1,820,000	DM 910,000	0
Duration of Exposure	12 months	6 months	0

Along with the change in denomination, the amounts of the receivables are revised to retain the total contract value of $1,000,000 after the initial payment. With a Deutsche mark exchange rate of 1.82, or $0.5494 per unit, the new contract calls for two payments of 910,084 Deutsche marks (DM), each equivalent to $500,000. The timing of payments remains unchanged. Since the Deutsche mark futures contract contains 125,000 units, hedging the exposure of each receivable requires 7.28 contracts. Mary must decide whether to over-hedge each payment with eight contracts or under-hedge with seven contracts. A look at the market shows that the Deutsche mark has been relatively strong lately. She decides to under-hedge, leaving an exposure of 70,168 Deutsche marks to fluctuate with the market.

Figure 14-7: Futures Contract Hedge

Mary Establishes margin account and puts up T-bill as collateral
Receivables to hedge—910,084 DM each
Deutsche mark futures contracts: 125,000 DM

	Nov 15 receivable	**May 14 receivable**
Ideal Hedge →	7.28 Nov contracts	7.28 May contracts

Problems:
Fractional contracts—not available
November contracts—not active
May contracts—not active

Next Best Alternatives:
Use *nearest* whole contract amount (either over or under)
Use *nearest* contract month that extends *beyond* value date

	Nov. 15 receivable	**May 14 receivable**
Practical Hedge(?) →	7 Dec DM contracts	7 June DM contracts

Problem:
liquidity

On May 12, Mary reviews the current information on futures contracts and finds the following:

Month	Close	Open interest
June	5493	114,290
Sept.	5496	5,587
Dec.	5514	216
Mar.	5534	622

Since the value dates of the exposure and futures do not match, she looks for the nearest contract extending *beyond* the payment due dates of November 15 and the following May 15. These futures contracts could be offset anytime up to their last trading day. As was the case with the forward hedge, Mary has no intention of making delivery. Therefore, she has no reason to hold the contracts until they convert to spot. She should also avoid carrying contracts into the last trading day because of the anomalies of trading in the last days. In the futures market (unlike the forwards market), trading becomes very thin and volatile close to last trading day, and correlations break down. Therefore, unless actual conversion to spot takes place, trades in the last days can often be liquidated only at unfavorable prices. As a general rule, futures contracts should be offset well in advance of their last trading day.

Another general rule is to hedge an exposure with the futures contract that terminates in the next *nearest* month to the date on which the exposure is liquidated. A November exposure should be hedged with December futures, a February exposure with March futures, a May exposure with June futures, and so forth. So Mary is looking for December contracts to hedge her November receivable and June futures to hedge her May exposure. June is on the board and can be traded. It is not quoted because there are, as yet, no open positions in that contract. Even the December contract is still quite illiquid, with only 216 open contracts. We know that one of the basic trading rule is to avoid positions that are not easy to liquidate. Therefore, selling June is out of the question, and even selling December is "iffy," so Mary decides to not take the chance.

Figure 14-8: Futures Contract Hedge

	Nov 15 receivable	**May 14 receivable**
	910,084 DM	910,084 DM

Best Solution: Short 14 Sept Contracts!

Instead, Mary decides to place a temporary hedge and roll it forward later. She shorts 14 contracts of September futures. She will roll seven contracts into December futures before September goes off the board. These will maintain the hedge position for the November receivable. To cover the May receivable, she plans to roll the remaining seven contracts into next June, liquidity permitting. If June is still too illiquid, she will roll them into March, then into June later. This strategy entails several transactions, but Mary has negotiated a reasonable commission schedule with the broker ahead of time.

Figure 14-9: The Fordoche Company-Futures Hedge Results

Terms of Sale	**Date**	**Cash Market**	**Futures Market**
Initial payment	5/15	DM 364,033	
Receivable of 11/15		DM 910,084	
Receivable of 5/14*		DM 910,084	
(*following year)			
Exchange rate (direct quote)		$/DM 5494	
$ equivalent		$1,200,000	
Less initial payment ($ equiv)		$ 200,000	
$ exposed		$1,000,000	
Hedge Activity			
Short Sept	5/15		14 contracts
Exchange rate			$/DM 5496
$ equivalent			$ 961,800
Roll Forward			
(last trading day approaching)			
Buy Sept Futures	9/12		14 contracts
Exchange rate			$/DM 5460
$ equivalent			$ 955,500
Short Dec	9/12		7 contracts
Exchange rate			$/DM 5463
$ equivalent			$ 478,013
Short March	9/12		7 contracts
Exchange rate			$/DM 5480
$ equivalent			$ 479,500
Partial Liquidation			
Collect 1st receivable	11/7	DM 910,084	
Exchange rate		$/DM 5400	
$ equivalent		$ 491,445	
Buy Dec	11/7		7 contracts
Exchange rate			$/DM 5410
$ equivalent			$ 473,375
Gain (loss)		**($8,555)**	**$7,788**

Figure 14-9: The Fordoche Company-Futures Hedge Results, *con't.*

	Date	Cash Market	Futures Market
Roll Forward			
Last trading day near):	3/10		
Buy March Exchange rate $ equivalent	3/10		7 contracts $/DM 5504 $ 481,600
Short June Exchange rate $ equivalent	3/10		7 contracts $/DM 5490 $ 480,375
Remaining Liquidation			
Collect 2nd receivable Exchange rate $ equivalent	5/14	DM 910,084 $/DM 5600 $ 509,647	
Buy June Exchange rate $ equivalent	5/14		7 contracts $/DM 5598 $ 489,825
Gain (loss)		**$9,647**	**($8,400)**
Total Gain (Loss)		***1,092***	***($612)***

Notes on Figure 14-9

May 15 Fordoche initially places its entire short position in September futures. The last trading day is September 21. Fordoche covers these contracts a few days before they go off the board—a good idea because the last few days of trading can be volatile as liquidity dries up.

Sept. 12 As the company covers the contracts, it shorts 7 December contracts to hedge the November exposure, and 7 March contracts to hedge the following May exposure. June contracts would have been preferable, since they extend beyond the May exposure date, but the liquidity in June was too thin at the time.

Nov. 15 When the November receivable is collected, the company lifts its hedge on that portion of the exposure by covering December.

March 10 Enough liquidity had built up in June to allow easy trading in that contract. Therefore, the company rolls its March contracts into June.

May 15 Fordoche subsequently covers the June contracts when the second receivable is paid.

Transaction costs are ignored, but could conceivably range between $875 and $3500 for the entire hedge, depending on the commission rate negotiated. Value fluctuations represent a premium currency that first depreciates, then strengthens, with forwards going to a discount due to changes in short-term interest rates.

Figure 14-10: Calculations of Gains and Losses on Deutsche Mark Futures Hedge

An easy way to calculate hedge results is to total the number of cents gained or lost, multiply by the contract value of one cent ($1,250 in this case), and then by the number of contracts.

(Contract value of 1¢ = $1,250)	*EXPOSURE*	*FUTURES*
Receivable # 1: booked at .5494, collected at .5400=	**$8,555 loss**	
7 Sept. contracts sold at .5496, bought at .5460 =		$3,150 gain
7 Dec. contracts sold at .5463, bought at .5410 =		4,638 gain
		$7,788 gain
Receivable # 2: booked at .5494, collected at .5600 =	**$9,647 gain**	
7 Sept. contracts sold at .5496, bought at .5460 =		$3,150 gain
7 March contracts sold at .5480, bought at .5504 =		2,100 loss
7 June contracts sold at .5490, bought at .5598 =		9,450 loss
		$8,400 loss

Basis Considerations

The difference between spot and forward rates is even more of a consideration for futures than it was for forwards, since the exposure and hedge positions can rarely be matched. The spot price of Deutsche marks on May 12 is 5494, while September futures are 5496—not much different in price. What if Mary decided to use March futures, priced at 5534? What if she were hedging a liability rather than an asset and needed to buy March contracts instead of selling them? Would she be losing 40 points at the start?

Consider a liability hedge for a moment. Assume a Deutsche mark payable is due next March. Mary buys March at 5534 to hedge the exposure, intending to hold the contracts until the last trading day and then convert them to spot. By coincidence, the same day Mary places a hedge, the U.S. and German governments sign an agreement to freeze the dollar/Deutsche mark exchange rate at the current level of 5494. If she holds her March contracts until they converge to the spot rate, the contracts are worth only 5494, and she has lost 40 points. These points cannot be covered in the cash market, since the exposure began and ended with spot frozen at 5494. Is this, therefore, an unrecoverable loss? If the accounting is accurate, it is not a loss at all. The 40 points are (almost) exactly equivalent to the interest *saved* by denominating the payable in Deutsche marks instead of dollars. Deutsche marks offer a lower yield, so Deutsche mark liabilities are carried at a lower rate. The "loss," therefore, is the price of translating the exposure into the costlier dollar denominated payable, which is what the hedge does. In Mary's original case, the reverse situation applies. Hedging an asset, she shorts March instead of going long. Her gain of 40 points over spot represents the additional interest picked up by translating a Deutsche mark receivable into a higher yielding dollar receivable.

If Mary is not aware of this forward/interest rate relationship, she may be tempted to collect the premium. Assuming no problem with liquidity, Mary can use any contract she chooses. She sees that December is at 5514 and March at 5534. Attempting to capture the extra 20 points, she sells March instead of December. On November 15, the hedge is lifted. Spot falls 94 points to 5400, and Mary buys March back at 5440, realizing 94 points. But December is now at 5410. If she had sold December, she would have gained 104 points. An increase in the yield differential resulted in a widening of the basis between contract months, costing Mary 10 points on the hedge. Actually, if interest rates remain constant, both contracts should yield the same number of points for the same number of days. (See Figure 14-11 for a summary.)

Figure 14-11: Collecting Premiums Can Lead to Inappropriate Hedges

Month	May 12 Sell at:	Nov. 15 Buy at:
Spot	5494	5400
Dec.	5514	5410
March	5534	5440

Selling the higher priced March futures results in less gain as the basis widens.

Note that from day to day, if the short-term yield differential does not change, the change in the value of spot will almost exactly match the change in the value of *any* futures contract, no matter which month is chosen and no matter what the initial basis may be. Yet, interest rates do change often; therefore, the hedge should be liquidated as close to the contract's last trading date as possible. Thus, the first choice is always the *nearest* contract extending beyond the last date of exposure, as demonstrated by Mary's lost opportunity cost above.

Figure 14-12: Stiffing the Hedger?

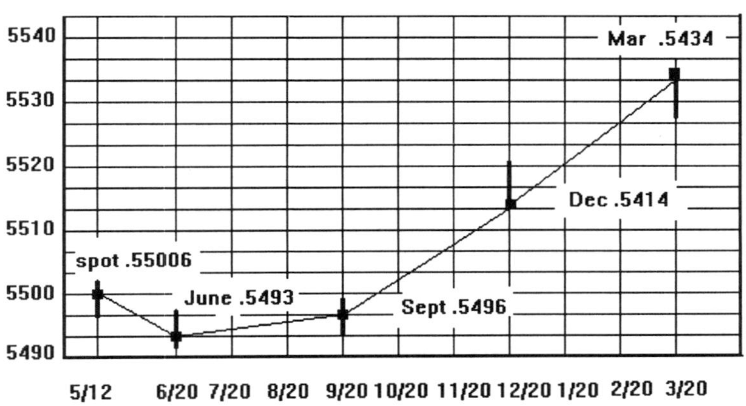

Deutsche Mark Spot and Futures at 3:00 P.M. May 12th.
Closing Ranges and Settling Prices

Figure 14-12: Stiffing the Hedger?, *con't.*

A currency manager will sometimes transact a position in futures or forwards at a certain price, only to discover the next day that it is 'out of line' with the published quote for spot. This situation often prompts an angry phone call to the broker/dealer. Actually the futures price may be away from the market for a good reason, as follows:

(1) *The daily range.* Published prices are quoted as of 3:00 EST. If the order were filled at any other time, the trade might occur anywhere within the daily range. Even the last minute of trading produces a range of closing prices. The settlement price represents an average of all trades filled within the closing range.

(2) *Intermarket "slippage."* Spot may be over June because spot and futures trade in different markets. These markets parallel each other, but not tick-for-tick. The coefficient of correlation is never 1.00. A 5 or 10 point "slippage" between markets is not out of line, especially if the markets are somewhat volatile.

(3) *The yield differential curve.* The basis between months is not always a straight-line progression. These quotes reveal a yield differential curve for short-term interest rates. Although the annual interest rate differential accounts for about a 10-point spread per month (December-March), the 90-day rate differential is much more narrow, producing about a 1-point spread per month (June-September). The differential continues to narrow as futures approach spot. Except for slippage, the 30-day rates are practically identical.

The Option Hedge

Buying and selling forward and futures contracts is not the same as exchanging things of value, such as currencies. For example, assume that you "buy" 10 futures contracts of Canadian dollars at the market, which represents C$1,000,000 spot. Your order fills at 7895. At that point, your contract is essentially worthless. It is neither an asset nor a liability. It has no current value. It is simply a transaction that gives you a market position. When the market moves away from 7895, your position acquires value. If the market moves to 7896, the value is positive. If it moves to 7894, the value is negative. Whether the position starts out as an asset or a liability depends on the first tick away from the fill price.

The Anatomy of a Currency Option

The primary difference between a currency option and a futures or forward contract is that the option contract, *in and of itself*, has value: the buyer's right of conversion. It is a "buyer demand" right, and it refers to an obligation that the option seller assumes when selling the option to the buyer. The seller must convert the option into an exchange of currency (or into a futures contract if it is a futures option) upon the buyer's demand. The buyer can demand this conversion at any market price. This distinctive right, conveyed by the seller to the buyer, is the reason the purchase and sale of options is handled more like a security than like a futures or forward contract.

The cash option converts into a currency at a specific price just as a forward contract does, if and when the conversion is made. Cash and futures options are identified by the month in which they stop trading (expire), just as futures are. Unlike futures, however, options are also identified by the price at which the exchange takes place, called the *strike* price. For example, a Swiss franc March 7600 option has a strike of 7600: it can be converted into an exchange of Swiss francs for U.S. dollars at a \$/SF rate 7600. This conversion can take place anytime before the option expires in March upon buyer demand. (Some options can be converted only on the date of expiration.)

A buyer has a right to convert the option at either a profit or a loss to himself, but he has no obligation to take a loss; thus, the buyer will *always* demand an exchange of currency (or "exercise his option") to secure a profit and *never* to take a loss. In fact, options are the only financial instruments that allow gains and prevent losses. Of course, this feature comes at a price. The buyer's price is the value of the option, called the *premium.* (A summary of option term definitions is shown in Figure 15-1.)

Figure 15-1: Definition of Option Terms

An *option* gives the buyer the right to exchange a specific amount of currencies at a specific rate sometime in the future.

A *call option* gives the buyer the right to exchange U.S. dollars for a specific amount of foreign currency (i.e., buy foreign currency) at a specific price sometime in the future.

A *put option* gives the buyer the right to exchange a specific amount of foreign currency for U.S. dollars (i.e., sell foreign currency) at a specific price sometime in the future.

The *strike price* is the rate at which the currency exchange takes place.

The *option month* is the month the option expires.

The *premium* is the market value of the buyer's currency exchange right, paid by the buyer to the seller.

The buyer effects the currency exchange by *exercising* his option (right).

The seller is called the *writer*, just as an insurer is a writer of an insurance policy.

Calls and Puts

There are two classes of options: *call* options and *put* options. A "call" is an option that conveys the right to exchange U.S. dollars for a foreign currency. A "put" conveys the right to exchange foreign currency for U.S. dollars. When U.S. residents exchange U.S. dollars for foreign currency they are, in fact, "buying" the foreign currency. Conversely, U.S. residents exchange foreign currency for U.S. dollars by "selling" the foreign currency.

Figure 15-2: Examples of Cash Currency Options

Current price of Canadian dollar—.7363

75 October call trading at 0.14

Option type:	Cash
Exchange:	Philadelphia
Underlying:	50,000 Canadian Dollars
Class :	Call
Month:	October
Strike:	.7500 (US$/CD)
Premium:	0.14¢ per C$1.00

Buyer pays writer (option seller) premium of 0.14¢ (times 50,000, or $70) for the right to *buy* C$50,000 from writer at rate of $0.75 per C$1.00 anytime before the option expires in October.

Current price of Canadian dollar—.7363

72½ Nov. put trading at 0.63

Option type:	Cash
Exchange:	Philadelphia
Underlying:	50,000 Canadian Dollars
Class :	Put
Month:	November
Strike:	.7250 (US$/CD)
Premium:	0.63¢ per C$1.00

Buyer pays writer premium of 0.63¢ (times 50,000, or $315) for the right to *sell* C$50,000 to writer at rate of $0.7250 per C$1.00 anytime before the option expires in November.

Note that the buyer would not exercise the option at the current price in either example, since he would be buying above the market or selling below the market for a loss.

Futures Options

The primary difference between the cash options trading on the Philadelphia exchange and the futures options trading on the Chicago Mercantile Exchange is that cash options convert into cash (an immediate exchange of currency) and futures options convert into futures contracts (a deferred exchange of currency).

Regardless of option type, obligations and rights flow in opposite directions. The seller, or *writer*, has the *obligation* to perform his side of the contract upon demand; and the buyer has the *right* to make such demand, but is not obligated.

Both buyers and writers can assume either a long or short position in options. The example in Figure 15-3 with futures options illustrates.

Figure 15-3: Long and Short Positions

Long Positions

- The *buyer* of a *call* is long, since he *can* acquire a long futures position by exercising his right to buy the futures contract from the writer.
- The *writer* (seller) of a *put* is long, since he *must* acquire a long futures position when the buyer of the put exercises his right to *sell* the futures contract to the writer.

Short Positions

- The *buyer* of a *put* is short, since he *can* acquire a short futures position by exercising his right to sell a futures contract to the writer (seller).
- The *writer* (seller) of a *call* is short, since he *must* acquire a short futures position when the buyer of the call exercises his right to buy the futures contract from the writer.

The Option Month

An option is the right to buy or sell at a specific price sometime in the future. Most options are designated by the month they expire, just as futures contracts are. *European-style* options can only be exercised on the day of expiration. *American-style* options, such as futures options, can be exercised anytime before they expire. As a matter of practice, however, futures options are rarely exercised before the date of expiration.

Futures option months identify the month of expiration, which may be different than the month of the underlying contract that it converts into. Only active futures contract months are available by exercise, and those are the fiscal quarters, March, June, September, and December. Options are exercised for the *next nearest active* futures month. For example, a July option expires in July, a month with no active contract. The next active contract is September. Therefore, the July option can be exercised for a September futures contract. In the same way, an April option expires in April and can be exercised for a June futures contract, and so forth.

Evaluating the Premium

A concept unique to options involves *option pricing*. The cost to purchase an option is called the *premium*. An option contract is written by one party (the writer) who sells it to another party (the buyer) in exchange for the premium. Exchange-traded contracts, such as future options, are not physically "written" every time a trade occurs. They are standardized instruments, just as futures are. Over-the-counter and customized options, on the other hand, are individually written contracts.

The premium is a composite of *intrinsic value* and *time value*. Intrinsic value is the amount by which the option is "in the money." For example, if an options trader buys a Swiss franc futures call option with a strike price of 6000, he may exercise the option when the underlying futures contract is trading at 6100. The day *before* he exercises, his futures account contains a futures option (paid for in full - options are not margined). The day *after* he exercises the option, his account contains a long futures position in place of the option, with a trade price of 6000. Since the current market value is 6100, the position has an unrealized gain of 100 points. Each point is worth $12.50 (in a futures contract of 125,000 Swiss francs). The gain, therefore, is $1,250. The buyer can immediately sell the contract and take the profit, and so the intrinsic value of the option at the time of exercise is $1,250.

If, instead, the option buyer holds a put in his account with a strike price of 6000 (also fully paid for), he may exercise it when the underlying futures contract is trading at 5900. The next day his account contains a short futures contract position in Swiss francs at a trade price of 6000. As with the call, it is marked to the current market for an unrealized gain of 100 points. The buyer can immediately purchase a contract of Swiss francs, currently trading at 5900, to acquire an offsetting long position. The two futures positions, one long and one short, cancel out, leaving a realized gain of $1,250 in the account. This amount is the intrinsic value of the put option.

Time value is the amount of the premium in excess of the option's intrinsic value, if any. It is a price determined by the market based upon how "promising" the option looks. For example, if the call has 100 points of intrinsic value today, how much more might it have tomorrow if left unexercised? Time value is influenced by four variables: interest rates, time, price, and price volatility as shown in Figure 15-4.

Figure 15-4: The Determinants of Time Value

- *Interest Rates*. The difference in short-term interest rates between foreign currency and U.S. currency is the cost of financing the underlying currency in U.S. dollars. This cost is added to the premium for call options and subtracted from the premium for put options. Therefore, the lower the yield of the foreign currency, the greater the time value of calls and the lower the time value of puts.

- *Time Remaining*. The more time remaining before the option expires, the more opportunity the intrinsic value has to increase. Time value increases with the time remaining.

- *Underlying Price*. The closer the strike price is to the underlying currency or derivative price, the less intrinsic value the option has, and thus the potential is there for a greater percentage gain. Consider, for example, two futures options. One has a single point of intrinsic value, since the strike price and current price of the underlying futures contract are only a point apart. The other has 100 points of intrinsic value. Assume the futures contract moves four points, so each option gains four points of intrinsic value. For the first option, the move represents a 400% increase in value, whereas for the second option the move represents only a 4% increase.

Figure 15-4: The Determinants of Time Value, *con't.*

Consider again the 6000-Swiss franc call. If the underlying contract is at 6001, the option is "in the money." If the contract is at 5999, the option is "out of the money." The "money" is the intrinsic value. By definition, the premium of an out-of-the money option consists solely of time value.

In contrast, options containing a large amount of intrinsic value have little or no time value, regardless of how much time remains or how volatile the market becomes. These "deep-in-the money" options are considered no more or less promising than the underlying contract. Since the option does not provide any additional opportunity over the contract, there is no additional opportunity cost. The contract and option are, therefore, priced the same.

Thus, time value increases as the market price approaches the strike price.

- *Volatility*. Assume the Swiss franc 6000 call is trading at 6010, so it has 10 points of intrinsic value. The option would not be "promising" if the Swiss franc had been virtually lifeless, hovering within two or three points of 6010 for several months. The option would be worth more if the Swiss franc were vacillating wildly. Volatility creates opportunity, and an increase in volatility produces an increase in time value.

Time value may increase dramatically when markets become volatile. Time remaining, underlying price, and volatility identify how much more "promising" the option is over its current intrinsic value. The remaining variable, interest rates, is a function of the cost of holding the option. Together they determine the amount of time value for the premium.

Visualize the premium as a "see-saw" with pointers (see Figures 15-5 and 15-6). The two values that make up the premium—time value and intrinsic value—are represented as stacks of gold coins. The "stacks" that make up the premium are pointed out. ([–] signifies no value.) The greatest time value occurs when the option is at the money (or just in or just out of the money). Time value decreases when intrinsic value increases or, going in the other direction, as the possibility of intrinsic value recedes.

Figure 15-5: The Premium See-Saw
(A + B = Premium)

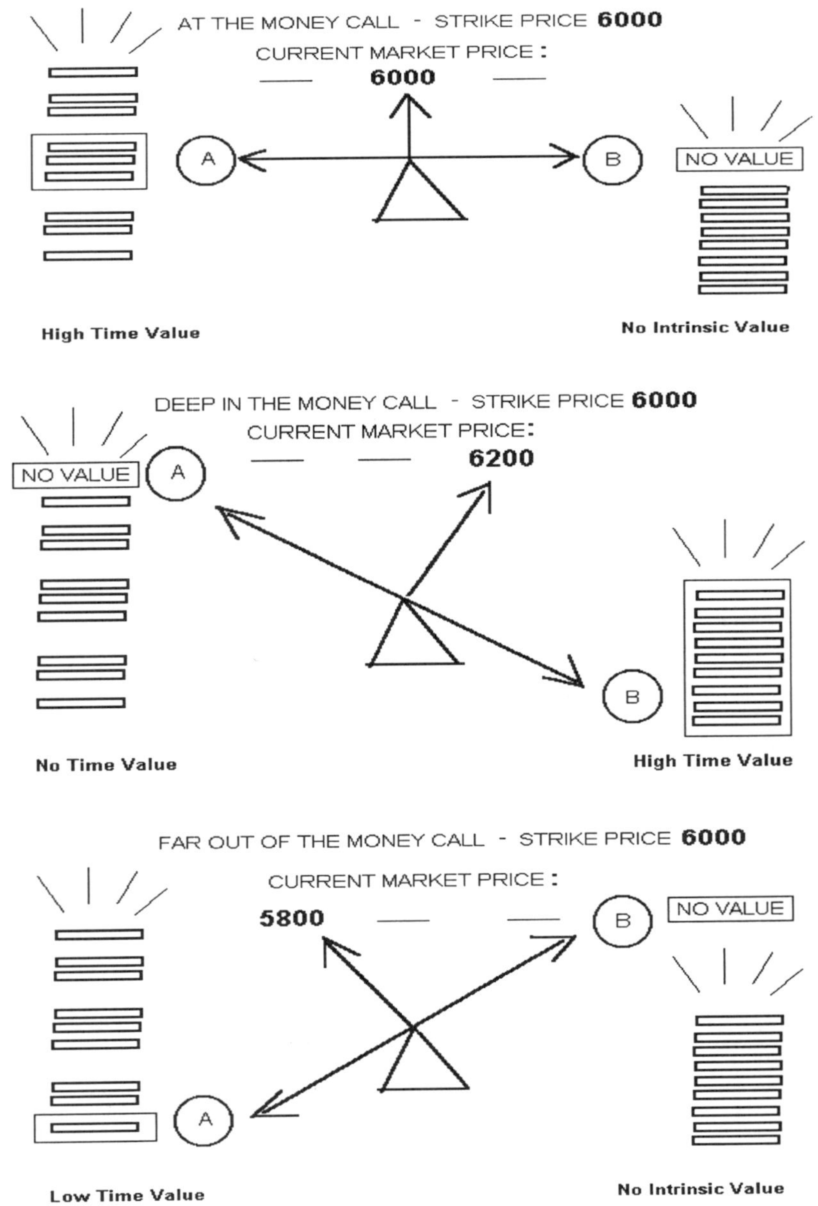

Figure 15-6: Time Value Determinants

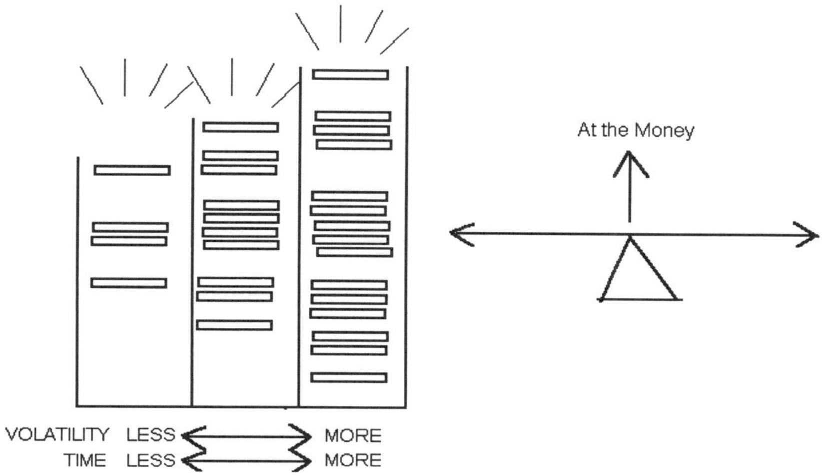

Proximity of price, volatility, and time remaining are factors that determine the amount of time value in an option. Comparative interest rate yield is also a factor, but its impact is relatively minor compared to the first three.

The Option Account

Although options have intrinsic value, just as a bond or stock certificate does, the similarity stops there. Options exist only as an entry or position in an account. Options are held in margin accounts, just as futures contracts are. In fact, futures and options on futures may be held in the same account, which is convenient for hedging strategies that use options and futures positions together. Option buyers do not deposit margin; they simply purchase the option for cash and deposit the premium in the account. Option writers, however, are required to deposit margin, just as they would with futures positions. In fact, short positions in futures options are margined as if they *were* long or short positions in the underlying futures contracts. The margin includes the premium collected by the writer, which must remain in the account until the position is liquidated. Option writers, then, utilize leverage. Option buyers do not.

Of course, both futures and cash options resemble futures contracts in other ways. They are all convertible: futures contracts convert into cash and options convert into either cash or futures contracts. But, for all of these instruments, conversion rarely takes place. Much more often, both options and futures are liquidated by offset. The balances resulting from the offset are applied against the other side of the hedge as either a gain or a loss.

Option Strategies

For hedging purposes, options may be the only practical alternative if: (1) corporate policy does not allow for losses in hedge positions; (2) the hedge is expected to *produce* profit, not just protect profit; (3) the exposure is not "locked in" contractually. An exposure that is not locked in contractually is a *projected* asset or liability, such as a bid for a contract not yet awarded.

Hedging exposures with options is similar to acquiring price insurance for the value of the exposed asset or liability. Ideally, the full value of the exposure would be insured, but insuring full value means purchasing at-the-money options, and the premiums are relatively "expensive." This cost can sometimes be as great as the potential risk of loss. A practical alternative is to purchase out-of-the money options, pay a smaller premium, and assume the "deductible." Thus, a hedger can establish a "ceiling" for a liability or a "floor" for an asset. The "space" between the exposed value and the ceiling or floor represents the deductible (see Figures 15-7 and 15-8).

Fair Market Value

Option strategies, in order to work, must incur option premium cost at fair market value. Option price models are available to precisely estimate the fair market value of any exchange-traded option under practically any market conditions.

Over-the-counter options are available for long-term hedges of up to five years and more. These options can secure the price of almost anything of determinable value for that period of time. Any derivative that sounds somewhat conditional probably includes an option or two. "Pending forward transactions" are examples, as are "deferred currency swaps" and "swaptions." Conditional clauses are the same as options, and customized financial instruments that include them are called 'option-embedded' derivatives. Some of these variations have been standardized and sell as dealer products. Financial packages such as, "floors," "ceilings," and "fences" are examples. At the other end of the spectrum, exchange-traded options are usually quite short-term. Exchange-traded options are most commonly used in currency management programs.

Figure 15-7: Covering a Liability with a Ceiling

Liability	3,000,000 FC		
Payment Due	6 months		
Price of FC (spot)	5000 ($0.5000)		
$ amount of Liability	$1,500,000		
Insurance:	Buy 3,000,000 FC calls		
Strike Price	*5100 ($0.5100)*		
Duration	*6 months*		
Premium	*50 points ($0.005)*		
Deductible	*100 points ($0.0100)*		
Deductible equals strike price minus spot price			
6 months later: FC Price Rises			
Price of FC (spot)	5300 ($0.5300)		
$ amount of Liability	$1,590,000		
Loss	300 points	(5300 less 5000)	$90,000
Deductible	100 points	(5100 less 5000)	$30,000
Option pays	200 points	(5300 less 5100)	$60,000
Cost of option	50 points	$0.005	$15,000
Net $ recovered	**150 Points**	**$0.015**	**$45,000**
6 months later: FC Price Falls			
Price of FC (spot)	4700 ($0.4700)		
$ amount of Liability	$1,410,000		
Gain	300 points	(5000 less 4700)	$90,000
Deductible	(Not applicable)		
Option pays	0 Points		
Cost of option	50 Points	$0.005	$15,000
Net $ Gain	**250 Points**	**$0.025**	**$75,000**

Figure 15-8: Underlaying An Asset with a Floor

Asset	3,000,000 FC		
Receivable due:	6 months		
Price of FC (spot)	5000 ($0.5000)		
$ amount of Asset	$1,500,000		
Insurance:	Buy 3,000,000 FC Put		
Strike Price	*4900 ($0.4900)*		
Duration	*6 months*		
Premium	*50 points ($0.005)*		
Deductible	*100 points ($0.0100)*		
Deductible equals strike price minus spot price			
6 months later: FC Price Falls			
Price of FC (spot)	4700 ($0.4700)		
$ amount of Asset	$1,410,000		
Loss	300 points	(5000 less 4700)	$90,000
Deductible	100 points	(5000 less 4900)	$30,000
Option pays	200 points	(4900 less 4700)	$60,000
Cost of option	50 points	$0.005	$15,000
Net $ recovered	**150 Points**	**$0.015**	**$45,000**
6 months later: FC Price Rises			
Price of FC (spot)	5300 ($0.5300)		
$ amount of Asset	$1,590,000		
Gain	300 points	(5300 less 5000)	$90,000
Deductible	(Not applicable)		
Option pays	0 Points		
Cost of option	50 Points	$0.005	$15,000
Net $ Gain	**250 Points**	**$0.025**	**$75,000**

Consider again the Fordoche Company and Mary, the treasurer (see Figure 15-9). Assume that the company does not yet have the order from the Dutch food distributor. In fact, Fordoche is competing with two other companies for the business. The company submits a bid in Deutsche marks, hoping to beat the competition by assuming the foreign exchange risk. To simplify things, assume the bid is equivalent to an even

$1,000,000. The Deutsche mark is currently trading at 55¢, so the quote goes out at 1,818,181 DM. The bid is good for 60 days, from May 15 to July 15. Fordoche builds a 10% margin into the quote and is willing to invest 1% to secure the exchange rate in the interim.

Figure 15-9: The Fordoche Company

Memo from Fred to Mary:

Date: May 15, 19xx
Project: Chocolate bar production line
Quote : 1,818,181 Deutsche marks

Price firm for 60 days from time quote received (until July 15)

Profit margin: 10%
Cost budgeted for foreign exchange risk management: 1%

Current U.S. dollar / Deutsche mark exchange rate: 5500 (spot)

Mary reviews the most recent price chart on the Deutsche mark, which shows the currency confined to a 2¢ range, between 54¢ and 56¢ (5400 and 5600). Currently, the Deutsche mark is right in the middle at 5500, and no near-term trend is evident. Because Mary does not want a contractual hedge commitment until she knows Fordoche has been awarded the job, she considers using put options to protect the bid. She finds that PHLX options, exercisable for spot currency positions, are liquid only for the two most current months. Even so, illiquidity in the farther out months is not a serious problem because the nearby options can be used and then rolled over as many times as necessary; but Mary recalls that CME futures options, also potential hedge instruments for this exposure, are often liquid up to four months out. Deciding to use CME futures options, she opens the daily *Journal* and finds the option quotes shown in Table 15-1.

Table 15-1:Deutsche Mark (CME)
125,000 marks; cents per mark

Strike	Puts		Settle
Price	June	July	Aug.
5400	0.20	0.51	---
5450	0.35	0.70	---
5500	0.58	0.94	1.17
5550	0.89	1.22	1.44
5600	1.24	1.53	1.75
5650	1.67		

The most appropriate options month would be July, since the job may not be awarded until then; however, the premium for the 5500 July put is .94, almost a full cent. After paying out this amount, the hedge would lock in a net price of only 5406 (5500 minus the premium of 94 points), instead of 5500. The strategy would lock in almost the very bottom of the projected range for the currency, and therefore, options do not seem to be the answer.

But Mary perseveres. After a few calculations, she devises a hedge that will cost less than 1% of the bid price, the amount the company was willing to spend to manage the exposure. In fact, it may cost substantially less if the job is awarded quickly. The hedge offsets 96% of the total exposure down to 5400, the bottom of the range. It does not protect any of the exposure below 5400, an acceptable risk in a range hedge model. In addition, the hedge retains the potential for a gain in the event that the bid is successful and the Deutsche mark strengthens. Or, once the commitment is made, it can easily convert to a futures hedge to protect 100% of the exposure. Figure 15-10 shows how this hedge is designed.

Figure 15-10: The Fordoche Company

Memo from Mary to Fred:

Think we can protect 96% of bid price for under 1%.
Protection good down to $/DM rate of 5400.
Hedge allows for upside potential of possible FX gain.
Can convert to standard futures hedge when job awarded.

Once Mary has approval for the hedge, she calls her broker and places an order to buy 14 July 5500 puts at a premium of 0.94, producing a debit in her account of $16,450 (14 x $1,250 x 0.94), payable immediately. At the same time, however, she places an order to sell 14 July 5400 puts at a premium of 0.51, giving her a premium *credit* of $8,925 (14 x $1,250 x 0.51). The credit and debit combined reduce the cost of the hedge to $7,525, which is well within the 1% budgeted for the $1,000,000 exposure (see Figure 15-11).

Figure 15-11: Option hedge against potential Deutsche mark move from 55¢ to 54¢ between May 15 and July 15

Mary's Order to the Broker

Action	#	Option	Month	Strike	Premium	Credit (Debit)
Buy	14	Put	July	5500	0.94	($16,450)
Sell	14	Put	July	5400	0.51	8,925
Total cost					**0.43**	**$7,525**

(1) Option for one futures contract of 125,000 DM
(2) 14 options equal 1,750,000 DM.
(3) DM spot rate at time of hedge = $.55
(4) 14 options equivalent to $962,500 (96% of bid price)
(5) Cost = 0.7525% of bid price

Recall that (1) the Deutsche mark is trading at 5500; and (2) the objective of the hedge is to protect against a fall in the Deutsche mark. How do these positions achieve the objective? The actual protection is the fourteen long 5500 put positions, which create a floor just under the current exchange rate of 5500. The dollar amount hedged is $962,500, or 96% of the exposure (14 x $1,250 x 55). July puts can be exercised for short September futures positions, so if spot falls, September futures will fall also, producing a gain in option value. As the price drops from 5500 to 5400, the 5500 put will gain up to 100 points of intrinsic value.

If the price continues to fall below 5400, say down to 5300, the 5500 puts will continue to gain in intrinsic value, point for point, but the hedge will not. The short 5400 puts will increase one point in value (a loss) for every additional point of gain on the 5500 strikes. In effect, the hedge stops performing below 5400, but maintains its maximum gain of 100 points. This strategy is like a range hedge, which is lifted at the bottom of the range to leave the exposure unprotected (see Figure 15-12).

Figure 15-12: Price Outcome if Deutsche Mark Declines

(1) Puts can be exercised for short September futures contracts at the strike price;
(2) Time value (premium paid) is the non-recoverable cost of hedge;
(3) Potential intrinsic value (gain) is 5500, less the September futures price, down to 5400.

Spot	September Futures	Intrinsic Value Only (Time Value Ignored)	
		Long 5500 put (Credit to account)	Short 5400 put (Debit to Account)
5500	5510	0	0
5470	5480	20	0
5440	5450	50	0
5390	5400 (protection to 5400)	100	0
5380	5390	110	10
5350	5360	140	40
5320	5330	170	70

Below 5400 September Futures: Credits = Debits.
Assume spot/September spread remains unchanged

What if the Deutsche mark strengthens from 5500 instead? In this case, the option positions gain no intrinsic value, and they begin to lose time value. The initial cost of the hedge is time value premium only. If the currency continues to strengthen and enough time passes, the options will become worthless. The $7,525 premium payment will not be recovered, but not a penny more will be lost. This strategy involves no leverage problem. The premium payment is the maximum amount at risk. Actually, if the company is awarded the job, the premium simply represents the offsetting side of a winning hedge, because the increased value of the Deutsche mark makes the bid that much more profitable. With a quote of 1,818,181 Deutsche marks, the premium can be fully recovered in the job quote if the Deutsche mark increases 43 points. Any increase in value of the Deutsche mark over that is an absolute gain to the company (see Figure 15-13).

Figure 15-13: Price Outcome if Deutsche Mark Rises

(1) Puts can be exercised for short September futures contracts at the strike price;
(2) Time value (premium paid) is the non-recoverable cost of hedge;
(3) Potential intrinsic value (gain) is 5500 less the September futures price, down to 5400.

Spot	September Futures	Intrinsic Value Only (Time Value Ignored) Long 5500 put (Credit to account)	Short 5400 put (Debit to Account)
5680	5690	0	0
5650	5660	0	0
5620	5630	0	0
5590	5600 (5543: cost recovered)	0	0
5560	5570	0	0
5530	5540	0	0
5500	5510	0	0

Assume spot/September spread remains unchanged

As yet, this example does not cover the implications of offsetting or exercising the options. Of course, only the 5500 long put position can be exercised by the company. (Under 5400, the short option position might be exercised by the exchange clearing house that represents the buyer, and it is exercised *against* the company.) Under what conditions is it advisable to exercise an option?

As a starting point, Mary will not exercise if the job is lost. Once the exposure is gone, she immediately liquidates both positions by offset, thereby clearing the account. If the job is let to a competitor fairly quickly, such as a couple of weeks after the hedge is placed, a substantial amount of time value may be recovered. The final hedge cost, then, might be markedly lower than the original premium cost. However, if the options are far out of the money, with little time remaining and low market volatility, time value may be only nominal. In any case, all positions should be liquidated when they are no longer hedging an exposure.

If the Fordoche Company is awarded the job, the hedge might be continued without any change in positions, depending on the hedge model. Mary might continue holding the option position and actively managing it if she is utilizing a dynamic model, such as a range hedge. If converting to a classic type of hedge is more appropriate, the options will be liquidated by offset or exercise and replaced with futures or forwards positions. Offset may be better than exercise; for example, time value is not recaptured by exercising an option. Liquidating and recapturing the difference in time value remaining between the two positions may be more profitable than exercising. The company can then acquire futures positions in a separate transaction. The positions should also be liquidated rather than exercised when forwards are preferred over futures for hedges.

Probably three conditions would have to be met before the company would exercise the long option position:

1. the company is awarded the job and has a contractual exposure that it wants to hedge with September futures; *and*
2. the options are in the money, so the short position is profitable, *and*
3. little time remains before option expiration or the options are deep in the money, such that no time value remains to be recaptured.

What if the 5400 put is exercised against the company? For example, Mary may arrive one morning and find the short 5400 puts replaced with a long position of fourteen September contracts, priced at 5400. The market is trading under 5400, so the position has an unrealized loss. (Remember, the buyer would only exercise if his resulting short position is profitable.) This discovery causes no concern. The account is profitable, since the long put position has gained 100 points more than the corresponding long futures position has lost. The account is protected, since the option and futures will continue to move in tandem, generating equal gains and losses. If Mary wishes to stay with the hedge, she can simply hold the options and futures positions in the account, then liquidate both at the appropriate time.

Managing Option Positions

Calculation of intrinsic values uses simple arithmetic. The gain between the strike price and the market price of the underlying asset, either the currency or the futures contract, is the intrinsic value. If the market is at 5400, the intrinsic value of a 5500 put is 100. If the market is at 5600, the 5500 *put* has no intrinsic value, but the 5500 *call* has 100 points of intrinsic value.

Calculation of intrinsic values is adequate for options carried up to expiration. But, since most options are not carried to expiration, the other component of premium price, time value, must be considered. Time value is affected by four variables: (1) interest rates; (2) the distance between strike price and market price of the underlying currency or futures; (3) the amount of time remaining before expiration; and (4) price volatility in the underlying currency or futures contract.

Three of the four variables are readily measurable, but the fourth—volatility—is not. Thus, the correlation between the time value portion of the option premium and the underlying currency is elusive. The option value will move in the same *direction* as the underlying value, but the two may change at different *rates*. Of course, the difference in rate of change between the premium and underlying currency price can be measured at a point in time, but that relationship may change. The correlation is very sensitive to market conditions and changes just as quickly and unpredictably. When planning to exercise the options, you can put on positions and forget about them. But when liquidating options ahead of expiry, you must watch for time value changes.

Since time value is a "wild card," varying numbers of options may be required for a given amount of exposure. For example, if the futures option premium move lags behind the price move of the underlying futures, more than one option is necessary to replicate the effect of one futures contract. The number required depends on the *hedge ratio* and its inverse, *delta.*

Deltas and Hedge Ratios

The problem of determining time value is volatility. For example, compare the Swiss franc during the Bretton Woods regime with the Swiss franc of today. When it was pegged, the Swiss franc moved scarcely a penny in 25 years. If the exchange rate was 6750, a 6800 call or a 6700 put with two months remaining would be virtually worthless. Today the same currency often moves more than a 100 points a day, and the same out-of-the-money option for 125,000 francs may have $1,200 worth of time value alone.

Just as time value is divided into four variables, including volatility, volatility may be divided into four measurements: *delta, gamma, theta,* and *vega.* These measurements identify how responsive the premium is to changes in the underlying price from different angles. Delta is the most commonly used volatility measurement. Delta compares the amount of price change in the option to the amount of price change in the underlying market within a given time span. It is expressed as a number from 0 to 1.00, where 1.00 signifies identical price moves between the two markets. Delta increases in direct proportion to volatility and to the percentage of intrinsic value in the option.

For example, in the option example above, September futures might move up 10 ticks, while the 5500 July puts simultaneously move 10 ticks lower. Subsequently, September moves 30 ticks lower, and the July puts move 30 ticks higher. In other words, the two move in sync; therefore, the July put has a delta of 1.00. September futures in this example must be trading much lower than 5500, because only deep-in-the-money options with no time value remaining trade at a delta of 1.00.

If, however, September goes up 10 ticks, and the put moves only 3 ticks lower, or September drops 30, and the put rises 10, then the put has a delta of 0.33. Options far out of the money, with virtually no chance of acquiring intrinsic value, trade at deltas as low as 0. In other words, they no longer respond to the underlying value changes. Because time value is constantly changing along with volatility, delta is constantly changing. If it is .33 today, it may be .20 or .75 tomorrow. Delta, like price, cannot be predicted with certainty. It can be *measured*, however, and, by extension, so can volatility, since one is a function of the other. Because the other three variables of time value are also measurable, we can estimate a "fair market" value of an option.

The delta is useful as a pricing mechanism and as an indicator of the number of options required to hedge a given amount of exposure. This number of options is called the *hedge ratio*. It is more precisely defined as the number of options required to replicate the underlying asset. (A derivative "replicates" an underlying asset if it can replace it without changing the values.) Consider a deep-in-the-money option, with 100% intrinsic value and a delta of 1.00. Only one option is required to replicate the underlying futures contract. An at-the-money option, with significant time value remaining, might have a delta of .5: it would move one tick in value for every two ticks in underlying value. Therefore two options are required for one futures contract. Determining the number of options based on delta is referred to as *delta hedging*.

Delta	Hedge Ratio	Number of Options to Replicate One Underlying Futures Contract
1.00	1 to 1	1
0.50	2 to 1	2
0.33	3 to 1	3

Figure 15-14: Time Value of July 5500 Call 60 Days before Expiration

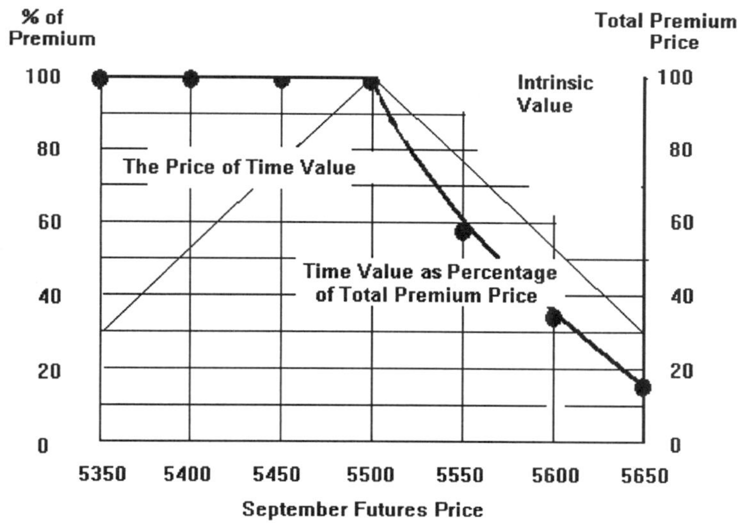

Time value is determined by how much potential of profit there is, percentage-wise, and what it is worth, money-wise. The heavy line designates the percentage and the light line shows the value in points at various market prices for September Futures. When time value is less than 100% of total premium value, the remaining balance is intrinsic value.

Although the level of volatility is not specified, it can be inferred by the dollar value, shown as points. These points moves up or down in response to volatility. The more volatile the market, the higher the value. When a premium increases in value because of rising volatility, it becomes less responsive to changes in the underlying futures contract (or underlying currency in the case of cash options). As a result of this decrease in delta, more options are required to hedge the same exposure.

Assume that Mary decides to hedge close to 100% of the potential exposure with options, just as before. But now she may liquidate the options and replace them with forwards or futures whenever the job is awarded. Thus, the options position must correlate very closely with September futures while the hedge is in place. She discovers that the total position has a delta of 0.5, meaning it will move one point in value for every two points that September futures move. To replicate a futures hedge, therefore, she must put on 28 positions instead of 14. The hedge cost doubles to $15,050. As you can see, option hedging can be very expensive.

For this reason, the currency manager should constantly look for opportunities to improve his position. The high premium costs demand diligence, especially when ratio or delta hedging is involved. Improving a position means liquidating old options and establishing new ones, replacing one strike with another, or replacing one option month with another.

Consider Mary's delta hedge for a moment. It consists of 28 long-5500 puts, and 28 short-5400 puts. Shortly after the position is established, the Deutsche mark runs up to 56¢. The news helps the bid, but hurts Mary's hedge strategy. She can improve her hedge, however, by selling off the 5500 puts and replacing them with 5600 puts, for an additional expense, of course. The 5500 puts, originally at 0.94, cost the company $32,900 (0.94 x 28 puts). Now they are trading at 0.60, for a total premium value of $21,000. Selling them here generates a realized loss of $11,900. But by "trading up," she locked in an additional 100-point margin with the 5600 puts, worth an additional $12,500 in the bid and twice that amount in her two-to-one delta hedge position. Mary also closely tracks volatility. If volatility diminishes, she can buy back the 5400 puts relatively cheaply, since they are now so far out of the money and out of favor. Liquidating the 5400-short-put position will provide unlimited protection on the downside.

Also, option positions should be monitored closely because the hedge ratio will probably change. Assume Deutsche marks are still at 5500, but volatility increases dramatically. The option delta goes from 0.50 to 0.75, so now any gain or loss on the options equals 75%, rather than 50%, of the move in September futures. If the market subsequently moves up, the loss on a two-to-one delta hedge will accumulate faster than the potential gain on the bid. In effect, the company becomes over-hedged: the risk is reversed, and the exposure has shifted to the long side of the market. In response, the option position should be reduced. Again, active management, with the ability to quickly adjust positions, is paramount in most option hedging strategies.

Figure 15-15: Option hedge against potential Deutsche mark move from 55¢ to 54¢ between May 15 and July 15

(I) *Objective*: match option position with exposure at time of option expiration. Ignore delta, since options to be held until expiration with no remaining time value to recapture. Potential hedge gain equal to whatever intrinsic value there is at expiry.

Action	#	Option	Month	Strike	Premium	Credit (Debit)
Buy	14	Put	July	5500	0.94	($16,450)
Sell	14	Put	July	5400	0.51	8,925
Total cost					**0.43**	**($7,525)**

Exposure: $1,000,000 in Deutsche marks;
Options equal to 1,750,000 DM, or $962,500

(II) *Objective*: match options position with exposure on continuous basis. Use delta hedge since potential hedge gain includes intrinsic value and recovered time value. Delta is 0.50; underlying value currently changing twice as fast as option value. Therefore, hedge position must equal two times underlying (exposure) position.

Action	#	Option	Month	Strike	Premium	Credit (Debit)
Buy	28	Put	July	5500	0.94	($32,900)
Sell	28	Put	July	5400	0.51	17,850
Total cost					**0.43**	**($15,050)**

Exposure: $1,000,000 in Deutsche marks;
Option position equal to DM 3,500,000, or $1,925,000

Subsequent change in volatility moves delta from 0.50 to 0.75. Change in hedge value now exceeds change in exposure value in either direction:

Position	#	Option	Month	Strike	Premium	Credit (Debit)
Long	28	Put	July	5500	1.50	$52,500
Short	28	Put	July	5400	0.90	(31,500)
Total asset					**0.43**	**$21,000**

Figure 15-15: Option hedge against potential Deutsche mark move from 55¢ to 54¢ between May 15 and July 15, *con't.*

(III) Objective: Reduce option position to reflect change in delta, in order to maintain equal gains and losses for both exposed position and hedge position.

Action						
Sell (liquidate)	7	Put	July	5500	1.50	$26,250
Buy back	7	Put	July	5400	0.90	(15,750)
Cash credit					**0.43**	**$10,500**

Exposure: $1,000,000 in Deutsche marks;
Remaining option position equal to 2,625,000 DM, or $1,443,750

The Customized Hedge

The hedges above are examples of hedging with standardized financial instruments appropriate for standard exposures. Each corporation, however, has its own unique challenges with foreign exchange. All situations do not fit into prepackaged hedge models or software programs. Fortunately, financial derivatives can be interconnected to form custom hedges.

Options can be combined in financial packages with other options or with other types of derivatives. Some customized options are *look backs* (buy now, choose your strike price later), *barriers* (the option appears and disappears at preset prices), *contingent premium* (buy now, pay later, but only if you want to), *alternative currencies* (pick the currency of your choice when you exercise), and *compounds* (an option to buy an option at a later date). One option even has a strike price that is the equivalent to an *average* price over a certain period of time. (This option has low premiums and real potential for cash flow exposure.) A currency manager can buy and sell puts, buy and sell calls, buy puts and sell calls, sell puts and buy calls, *ad infinitum*. Each combination achieves different results under specific conditions, but all trade exercise rights for something at a specific price to someone else for a specific amount of time.

One combination is the *covered write*. A covered write connects the best features of the futures and options hedge above. Instead of Mary taking a long put position, she establishes a short September futures position. In addition, she still sells the 5400 puts and uses the premium credit to increase the profit margin on the outstanding bid. Of course, she may have to buy back the puts, but if 5400 is truly the bottom of the range, as predicted, they will expire worthless, and the premium is a gain (see Figure 15-16). If Deutsche marks fall, the offset is the same as the long put, short put position.

Figure 15-16: Intrinsic Value on Option Hedge
at Selected September Future Contract Values
Covered Write: Short Futures at 5500, Short 5400 put

5350		5400		5450		5500		5550
	^			^			^	
	A			B			C	

A - September futures at 5400 or below: At 5400, the futures contract has 100 points (1¢) of intrinsic value. The 5400 put has 0 intrinsic value. When the market falls below 5400 - to 5350, for example - the 5400 put accumulates value, but the futures contract continues to gain, tick for tick. Therefore, net intrinsic value on the two positions remains fixed at 100 points whenever September is 5400 or below.

B- September futures at 5450: The short futures has 50 points of intrinsic value. The 5400 put has 0 intrinsic value.

C- September futures at 5500 or above: One point of loss occurs on the short futures contract for every point above 5500. The 5400 put has no intrinsic value and will expire worthless as long as the market remains above 5400. The premium of 51 points is applied against the futures loss, to provide a gain on the hedge below 5551, a break-even at 5551, and a loss over 5551 (ignoring exposure gain).

Gains and Losses at Various Values
for September Futures*

	5350	**5400**	**5450**	**5500**	**5550**
Short futures	150	100	50	0	(50)
Short 5400 put	(50)	0	0	0	0
Premium credit	51	51	51	51	51
Exposure gain (loss)	(150)	(100)	(50)	0	50
Total gain (loss)	1	51	51	51	51

*Time value ignored

We can even short September futures without using futures. Assume that Mary wants to obtain the full coverage of a futures hedge, but she also wants to profit from volatility changes, something that can only be done with options. As before, she buys 5500 July puts for 0.94, but instead of selling 5400 puts, she sells 5500 July *calls*, priced at 0.90. She collects the premium for the calls, so her total cost for the hedge is only 4 points.

Compare this hedge with a short futures position, placed when the market is trading at 5500. Ignoring time value, Mary gains one point on the 5500 puts for each point September drop below 5500. The calls have no value, nor do they accumulate any, as long as the market remains under 5500. The reverse occurs when the market trades above 5500. Mary incurs a loss for every point of gain on the short calls, and her long puts remain without value. The resulting gains and losses are identical to those of a short futures position when the time value fluctuations are disregarded; however, time value fluctuations are also producing gains and losses. Actually, with this option combination, Mary is hedging foreign exchange rates and speculating in foreign exchange volatility. If she incurs a loss in volatility, however, she can keep the options until expiration, when the loss disappears along with the time value. Again, the hedge is identical to a futures position at expiration. In fact, this option combination is referred to as a synthetic futures position. When time value is ignored, they replicate each other as follows:

Short futures = long put and short call at the same strike
Long futures = long call and short put at the same strike

The synthetic converts to the actual futures contract if it is allowed to mature. Carried to expiration, either the put or the call will be exercised (never both). In Mary's case, the option combination would culminate as a short position in September futures at 5500, regardless of the market price (see Figure 15-17).

This hedge could be designed with more flexibility. Assume the Fordoche Company has sufficient margin in the bid to tolerate a decrease in the exchange rate from 55¢ to 54¢, but Mary is concerned about a possible drop below 54¢. Yet, she still wants to take advantage of potentially higher rates. Reviewing prices, she finds July-5400 puts going for 51 points, and July-5600 calls for 50 points.

Figure 15-17: Intrinsic Value on Option Hedge
at Selected September Future Contract Values
Synthetic Short: Long 5500 put, Short 5500 call

5350	5400	5450	5500	5550
		^	^	^
		A	B	C

A - September futures at 5450 or below: The call has no value, the put has 50 points of value at 5450, representing gain on the position. The hedge gain will increase, as the market continues to fall, point for point.

B- September futures at 5500: Neither option position has intrinsic value at this price.

C- September futures at 5550 or above: The long put has no value, the short call has 50 points value. The hedge position loses as the market trades above 5500, point for point, just as a short futures position would.

Gains and Losses at Various Values for September Futures*

	5350	**5400**	**5450**	**5500**	**5550**
Long 5500 put	150	100	50	0	0
Short 5500 call	0	0	0	0	(50)
Premium cost	(4)	(4)	(4)	(4)	(4)
Exposure gain (loss)	(150)	(100)	(50)	0	50
Total gain (loss)	(4)	(4)	(4)	(4)	(4)

*Time value ignored

Mary establishes a *collar*, consisting of a *floor* on potential loss and a *ceiling* on potential gain. She purchases July-5400 puts at 51 points (the floor) and sells July-5600 calls for 50 points (the ceiling). Between these two prices, the exposure remains unhedged. In effect, the company is only hedged under 5400 or over 5600. Since the premium paid and the premium collected virtually offset each other, the hedge is placed for the cost of transaction only. If the hedge is not "delta neutral," (i.e., the hedge ratio is not the same for both the call and the put), Mary may have to buy more puts or sell less calls to balance out the moves of each position (see Figure 15-18).

Figure 15-18: Intrinsic Value on Option Hedge
at Selected September Future Contract Values
Collar: Long 5400 put, Short 5600 call

5300	5400	5500	5600	5700
^	^		^	^
A	B		C	D

A - September futures at 5300 or below: The put has 100 points of value. The call has 0 value.

B- September futures at 5400: This is the floor. Neither option position has intrinsic value, but the put will acquire intrinsic value as soon as the market falls below 5400.

C- September futures at 5600: This is the ceiling. Neither the put nor the call have any value as long as the market remains between 5400 and 5600. The call begins to acquire value above 5600, translating into a loss for the position.

D- September futures at 5700 or above: The call has 100 points of value, for a 100 point loss. The put has 0 value. Total hedge has a maximum gain or a maximum loss of 100 points.

Gains and Losses at Various Values for September Futures*

	5300	**5400**	**5500**	**5600**	**5700**
Long 5400 put	100	0	0	0	0
Short 5600 call	0	0	0	0	(100)
Premium**	0	0	0	0	0
Exposure gain (loss)	(200)	(100)	(0)	100	200
Total gain (loss)	(100)	(100)	0	100	100

*Time value ignored **nominal cost or income

This discussion has covered some features of recently popular customized derivative programs. Obviously, when you combine currency option strategies with interest rates hedges and include imaginative conditional clauses, it is not always evident whether a hedge is net long or net short, or by how much. Hedge combinations provide the flexibility required to compete in today's global market place, but no combination should be entered into before the derivative has been deconstructed, and each component thoroughly analyzed.

Presentation

Author's Note: This chapter has been reprinted in its entirety from "*Currency Risk Management: A Broker's Handbook.*"[1] The material covers techniques for successfully selling the concept of currency risk management to a prospective client. It is addressed specifically to the future broker.

If your role is that of a sales person in this industry, be it broker, banker or consultant, the reason for including this chapter is self-evident. If, however, you are a corporate manager, treasurer, accountant—in other words, if you are the "buyer"—concluding with this chapter poses a legitimate question; namely, why should you be interested in sales material better directed to the person facing you across the desk?

There are three reasons. The first has to do with *relevancy.* Having worked through the preceding chapters, you probably already have a high degree of interest in foreign currency management. You do not have to be sold on the concept. In fact, you may very well find yourself wearing the salesman's hat, since you may now be the expert called upon to present this concept to others. Remember, all the time and energy put into a risk management program is wasted if the decision makers don't buy it. Program presentation, therefore, is every bit as important as program development; and "presentation," as this chapter explains, means selling. Successful selling techniques are just as valuable, just as pertinent, whether you are selling to your prospect, your client, your executive committee, or your board of directors.

The second reason involves *competency.* The sales techniques presented here have been derived from my own experience as a broker and dealer, as well as well-known authorities in the field and the experience of my compatriots: these techniques are well grounded. If you do find yourself in a selling situation, information gleaned from this chapter can well make the difference between success and failure.

Author's Note, *con't.*

The third reason has to do with skills of *negotiation.* If you plan to sit down with the banker, the broker, the dealer, the advisor, or anyone else who solicits your currency trading business, here is a revealing glimpse into his or her thoughts and motivations. Knowing where the other person is coming from strengthens your own hand during negotiations.

Everyone in the futures business is familiar with boiler room operations. They usually go hand in hand with aggressive telemarketing. The operators dial for dollars, promising wealth to anyone who picks up the phone. Of course, deceptive selling is not confined to futures trading; it started with the first batch of snake oil made ready for bottling. This is "hucksterism," and it is based upon the belief that every sale results in a winner and a loser. If the salesman succeeds in closing the sale, he wins and the buyer loses. If he doesn't succeed in closing the sale, he loses; the buyer wins. Win-lose selling is not an enjoyable way to make a living, nor is it a successful way in the long term.

Consultative Selling

There is another method, called consultative selling. This method is used by all types of salespeople, consultants and non-consultants alike, from counter clerks to diplomats. Consultative salespeople have a few things in common. Their probability of success is high. They are professional. They probably enjoy respect. They often exhibit a sense of high self-esteem. The principle behind consultative selling is simple and basic. It is called *win-win selling*, and it involves a transfer of information from the seller to the buyer by which the buyer profits. The consultative salesperson does not try to close a sale until *both parties win*. Both must be better off after the sale than they were before. Furthermore, the win for the buyer is always apparent. The win for the seller is less so, sometimes delayed, but just as sure. The hallmark of consultative selling is "the customer comes first."

How does consultative selling work in the futures industry? John Walsh, who "wrote the book" on how to open futures accounts, states that the most important criterion by which to judge a broker from the client's perspective is credibility.[2] The size of the firm, track record, and commissions are all secondary. The client, as well as the prospect, wants to be able to believe his broker above all else. He becomes a willing buyer only after he knows the broker is genuinely looking for a way for his customer to win. At that point, he believes.

Win-win selling and credibility are two sides of the same coin. Both are absolutely mandatory in the presentation of a currency management program. Hedging currencies is too complex and fraught with its own set of risks to be an "easy sale" unless the buyer has complete confidence in the broker; however, to enjoy maximum success in this field, you must take win-win selling one step further. As the seller, you must often delay your gratification. The client must always win immediately through a reduction of risk, even if his doing so delays the "win" for the broker (generation of commissions). Often, you must advise *against* hedging when you find it is not in the client's best interest. This characteristic of immediate buyer and delayed seller wins leads to the following categorical statement:

> *Unless the broker anticipates building a long term client-consultant relationship, he or she has no business presenting a currency management program to a prospect.*

This is not a statement of ethics, although that certainly is part of it. It is a matter of practicality. For your own success, currency management must be sold as a long-term program, an ongoing policy, a program in which you intend to play a part as long as you and your client remain in business. Developing a currency management program for a one-time commission—a single foray into the markets—is simply not worth your effort.

The First Appointment

Properly nurtured, credibility develops very rapidly between broker and prospect. The first time you meet the treasurer, you will know whether or not he believes you. We've heard that first impressions are lasting. Here, they are critical. If you are found wanting in believability, there will not be a second appointment. In prospecting efforts, you may often experience that the less knowledgeable your listener is about what you have to say, the more interest he will have in *you.* You are suggesting something that can greatly impact the company's financial condition. You and your proposal will be scrutinized thoroughly.

This is why credibility is so important. Remember that you are asking the company to turn to you for help in determining which derivatives to use, which trades to make, when, for how long, and for how much. A dependency of sorts results—the company hands over to you a certain amount of fiscal control. It would not even consider doing so if your credibility was in doubt. This being the case, how do you gain credibility?

Do Your Homework

Let's start with product knowledge (in reference to your product, not your prospect's). Your role is that of an educator. During your first few contacts with the company, you probably will be talking to people with little more than a passing knowledge of what this is all about. They must depend on your expertise. Your knowledge base should include, of course, the current situation of specific currencies, as well as the dynamics of specific exposures. There is no point in speaking at length on a particular exposure in British pounds if you don't know, within a few points, where the pound is currently trading or what is presently influencing the price. Do not, for example, stand in front of a customer or an audience talking about a country when you don't know how to pronounce the name of its currency properly.

Secondly, you must know your prospect. You need to be familiar with the company's operations *before* your first appointment. Although you may not have detailed information, you should at least know the names of the officers and their positions. You should have some knowledge of the industry and the current business cycle. You should know a little about its main competitors. You most certainly should know what the company produces and sells, and, if possible, where.

Where do you learn these things? Begin with other brokers in your office. A cohort may be in contact with the company with regard to another matter such as pension planning or cash management. Check with your manager. His function is to know the local market. Perhaps your research department has data on the company. Often, however, you will have to supplement any internal information you gather by going outside. Ask the chamber of commerce about the prospect. Check the local library. You will find a wealth of knowledge in the directory section. If your prospect is a public corporation, call the public relations department and ask them to mail you the latest copy of their annual report. Call the company's marketing department and ask for a product catalog. If you are checking out a position, call the main switchboard and tell whoever answers that you are directing a letter to the person in that position. (It's the truth. If you get the appointment, you should send a follow up letter.) Ask for a spelling of the name, as well as the title. Confirm the correct mailing address, phone, and fax numbers while you're at it.

You have done the homework and set up the appointment. You are now sitting in a conference room at the company's main office, addressing three or four corporate managers whom you met just moments ago. Someone suddenly asks you about a competitive product line that you never heard of. What do you do? First, let's talk about what you *never* do. You do not fake it. If you don't know the answer to an unexpected question, say so. We have all heard the speaker trying to extricate himself by taking a stab at the answer. This is a death knell for any sales presentation at the level we're discussing. Fielding a question without knowing the answer never goes unnoticed. The speaker's credibility immediately plummets. When you don't know the answer then say, "I don't know" or, "I'll find out." It is surprisingly well accepted. When you stand in front of an audience, remember that you are not *really* expected to know *everything.*

Create an Interest

After fifteen tries, you finally convince the secretary of the CEO that you are important enough to be patched through to her boss. He answers the phone and barks "Smith!" or "Jones!" Definitely not a person given to small talk with strangers. You respond by saying (pick one):

(a.) "Good morning, Mr. Smith. This is Bob Crandell with AZ Futures. I have an idea for reducing the risk of your foreign exchange exposures. When can I stop by to explain it to you?"

(b.) "Good morning, Mr. Smith. This is Bob Crandell with AZ Futures. Your treasurer, Mr. Green, and I are conducting a foreign exchange survey to determine your company's exposure to currency risk. This entails including some information from you. When would be a good time to get together?"

Which statement do you think will get a more positive response? The foreign exchange survey is one of the best door openers for prospecting new accounts. It certainly builds credibility; however, it is not without pitfalls. You should not attempt a foreign exchange survey unless it is thoroughly thought out and well executed. It has to be of value to the company. An ill-conceived or unprofessional findings report is worse than useless. Bad advice can be very damaging to the prospect. At the very least, your credibility will take a lethal beating.

If you do not have the time or expertise to prepare a top-notch survey, call in an expert who does, perhaps an accountant or a management consultant familiar with international treasury operations. (Go with him during the interview.) If the prospective company understands the value of the survey, it should have no problem paying the expert for his time. Not only will the results appear more credible, you will also, by association. After all, it is you who presented the concept and initiated the effort.

The Follow-up Proposals

It is rare indeed to open a hedge account on the first appointment. Some risk managers claim that the average time from the initial contact to the signing of the papers is between six months and a year. During that time, you will be meeting with mid-level and senior managers. You may be asked to talk to the executive committee, the bankers, or the attorneys. Sometimes the meeting will be on a one-to-one basis. Other times you will be standing in front of an audience, flip chart beside you and pointer in hand.

The sale, in other words, is not a single event. It is a procession of appointments and meetings. Nor does the sale end with the opening of the account. Now, the company must learn how to use futures and options in a systematic manner. More selling takes place in different forums with different objectives. In fact, between the time you first initiate contact and the time the company has a detailed currency management program up and running, you will be a familiar enough figure at the company to be mistaken for an employee now and then.

Be prepared, then, to make a series of presentations. Whether they take place over lunch with just the treasurer or in front of a class of marketing and production personnel, these presentations should be consultative in nature and educational in content. Remember that imparting knowledge is the hallmark of consultative sales.

Let's review the various phases of a currency management program that may require the presentation of a proposal in one form or another.

- *The introduction.* Let's say that your first encounter is with the treasurer. You have two primary objectives. The first is to sell yourself as knowledgeable and credible in this area of expertise. The second is to learn about your future client. For this presentation, bring a blank note pad and a list of questions. Don't bring in promotional or other prepared material. You don't want to look like you're selling off-the-shelf solutions. The third objective is to be invited back. If you sell yourself successfully, the treasurer can find a reason for you to return, even if he is not yet convinced about the concept. A foreign exchange survey is one good reason for coming back.
- *The foreign exchange survey.* Depending on the scope of the operation, this may take anywhere from an hour to a few weeks of your time. Let's say the company is a mid-sized manufacturer without extensive foreign operations. A survey of this size might require

two to four appointments on-site to gather information. This is the time to ask for a tour of the plant. A tour helps you get a feel for the operation and demonstrates your interest.

- *Presentation of the survey findings and recommendations.* How you handle this depends on the circumstances. You might decide on a full-blown presentation to a group, complete with slides or overheads, or you may decide on an informal work session with your contact person. When the company accepts your findings and is ready to proceed, the way is clear to introduce other proposals or objectives such as those listed below. Any or all of these may need to be presented to the company either formally or informally:

- Forming a management team
- Policy and strategy meetings
- Developing an information management system
- Developing hedge models
- Final approval and sign off
- Instruction in trading derivatives
- Instruction in market forecasting techniques
- Monitoring the program and providing updates

To summarize, selling a currency management program is not a one time event. It is a process that advances step by step. You are introducing a number of objectives which need to be presented and accepted. No matter what you are proposing at any particular moment, or to whom, one thing never changes. You are continuously selling yourself, your firm, and your credibility.

Full Disclosure

There is more to credibility, of course, than a display of knowledge. After all, many hucksters are experts in their field. A credible presentation does not just inform; it informs *honestly.* At some point during the sale, the listeners become convinced that their interests are being fully addressed and have precedence over those of the broker. They reach this point when they realize that the broker is *fully disclosing* all the material facts.

John Walsh, in his ethics training seminars, refers to a particular broker whom he observed in front of an audience of prospective clients. "Most of my clients lose money," she intones, during her opening remarks, "and if you each open an account with me, seven out of ten of you will lose money." She is one of the most successful futures brokers in the business, opening more speculative accounts than many of her cohorts combined. Why? Because she is so believable. There is no question that she fully discloses the facts.

Putting the client's interests first means that you, the broker, not only understand, but believe in what you are saying. It means that you are as forthright with the negative aspects of hedging as you are with the positive. In the futures industry, anything less than "full and complete disclosure" is construed as an unethical, if not fraudulent, business practice. This includes not only misstatements of fact, but *omission* of facts. (There is no real distinction between the two.) A corporate decision-maker who is not familiar with hedging will be very attentive to what you say and how you say it. Any sign of holding back will almost certainly be noticed, and that will be the end of any chance of approval for your program.

Everyone has heard biased sales pitches, the ones that highlight the advantages and gloss over the disadvantages. A hedge advisor, for example, may propose to a company that it manage its liabilities with long hedge positions. Then he offers examples of hedges that only involve up markets. The examples always result in a hedge profit. Such a biased presentation almost never goes unnoticed. To achieve credibility, the presentation must illustrate examples of up markets *and* down markets. Avoid illustrations that can be construed as less than forthright. When the presentation is peppered with profitable hedge examples, the question in your prospects' minds becomes, "what *else* is he hiding?"

Make sure that everyone has a complete understanding of the risks involved. The idea, of course, is to *reduce* exposure. Explain that hedging does not completely *eliminate* exposure. Sometimes it replaces it with another type. Certain techniques substitute exposure risk for market risk, credit risk, or whatever. Discuss operation risk, basis risk, loss of liquidity, etc. It is far better to disclose these pitfalls up front. Remember that it is not just the rules of hedging you are concerned with. Corporate managers bring their own set of rules to the table. Near the top of the list is "no surprises." When surprises such as unexpected basis fluctuations or liquidity problems occur, it can get quite unpleasant all the way around.

The biggest disclosure problem of derivative hedging concerns leverage. This is totally unnecessary. I strongly recommend presenting all derivative examples as unleveraged transactions. In other words, if it takes 100 futures contracts of Swiss francs to hedge an exposure and the required margin is $290,000, don't create the impression that the company is only risking $290,000. With Swiss francs at 8550, the company would be committing $10,687,500 in francs, and it should be made perfectly clear that this is the amount, in dollars, exposed in the market.

Selling a Track Record?

You may be recommending a trading system as part of your model. Perhaps your system comes with an enviable track record. The *Commodity Futures Trading Commission* (CFTC) requires that any published track record regarding futures contracts includes a disclaimer. This is a statement that "past performance does not guarantee future results." Making a claim to the contrary constitutes fraud according to federal regulations. The CFTC also differentiates between a "real" and a "hypothetical" trading record. The latter contains results that would have occurred if the trades had actually taken place. Both are legitimate representations, but there is an additional caveat included with the use of hypothetical results. A system can be "curve fitted" to include winning trades and exclude losing ones. Whether that same curve will ever recur is anyone's guess. No system yet devised has ever performed consistently in every currency market over significant periods of time. Even if one were found, no claims could be made regarding its *future* performance.

There are a lot of past and current commodity traders around. Some may be on the corporate executive committee or in the board room listening to your presentation. They are well aware of the inflated claims surrounding trading systems. The best advice I can give you is to not even *hint* that you may have a "profitable trading system" for the program. If you do, keep it to yourself.

Some Common Traps

Never forecast the market during a sales presentation. Why? Because you might be risking the whole program on the toss of a coin. This is a major trap for brokers. It is often set while you are in the middle of your presentation. Someone around the table innocuously asks what you think the franc or the pound or the peso is going to do in the next two weeks or so. You innocently share your thoughts. It's going to continue up, or head back down, or whatever. You have at least a 50% chance of being wrong. You probably have closer to a 80% to 90% chance of being wrong because the market is going to go up *and* go down *and* go sideways over the near term. The person who queried you doesn't remember the days you are right. He remembers the days you are wrong.

When the buyer discovers that you predicted the market incorrectly, well then, where else are you misinformed? What if they had placed company funds on that forecast? "We could have lost a great deal of money," the thinking goes. "Let's take another look at this." (Translation: forget it.) On the average, seven out of ten futures trades go awry. That's 70% of all predictions. An old pro once told me of a technique he used when prospecting for commodity speculators. "Whenever someone tells me about a big position he's holding with another broker," he said, "I furrow my brow and look worried." If you are pressed on this issue, and must respond with a prediction of some sort, use the "straw man" approach. Tell them what some *other* analyst thinks. Set some one else up.

"So you're a Technician"

Once at a prospecting seminar hosted by a team of futures brokers, the brokers took turns describing their technical system to the audience for more than two hours. The brokers were quite wrapped up in the subject, and their excitement was certainly genuine. Later, as the attendees filed out the door, one elderly gentleman turned to another and remarked, "I didn't understand a word they said." Do you think he ever called them to find out?

It seems as though brokers inevitably talk over the heads of their clients and prospects. They speak in an arcane jargon trying to persuade people to open accounts. Sometimes they live with chart patterns, divergences, and crossovers so long that they forget there is another world out there, complete with another language. Sometimes they're simply trying to impress others with their expertise. It is difficult, of course, to take a highly technical subject and reduce it to everyday language. Yet, this is precisely what you must do if you hope to sell your program. You're selling to corporate executives, not floor traders or foreign exchange dealers.

Zig Ziglar, one of the most widely sought after motivational speakers in the nation, speaks on a seventh grade level. During his presentations, he limits his vocabulary to words of mostly one or two syllables. As he explains it, people may *converse* on a college level, but they *feel* on an elementary level. A presentation can be *felt* if it is delivered in simple, every day words. Take time to translate where necessary. Use analogies wherever possible. Use visual aids (overheads, slides, charts, etc.). Make them simple to understand. Stay with line diagrams and lots of white space. (Can you *really* understand those three-dimensional option charts?) If you are speaking conceptually and can get away with it, illustrate your examples in generic terms (*FC* instead of *Swiss francs*) and arbitrary values (100 instead of .86854). This way you avoid cluttering the listener's mind with yesterday's irrelevant values carried to lengthy decimal places. It also safeguards you against getting bogged down in the middle of a presentation if your math skills are less than stellar.

Chart Patterns and Tea Leaves

A further word about charts. Do not show charts plastered over with waves, wedges, triangles, etc. If you can avoid it, don't get into technical analysis at all; this can be a Pandora's box. If you start explaining the importance of the Fibonacci sequence in Elliot wave theory, for example, you could easily spend the rest of your time talking of nothing else. Even if your listeners understand it, will they buy it? The general public still needs meat-and-potato fundamentals. These are the things that make real sense, whether or not they make predictive sense. Technical analysis is too much like tea leaf reading—hardly the impression you want to create with an audience still struggling with the difference between futures markets and gaming tables.

Of course, if your hedge model is going to incorporate technical analysis as a means of predicting currency moves, you must disclose this fact to your audience. So disclose it and move on. You can get into specifics later. Remember, unless you first sell the concept, the details won't matter much.

"So you're into Derivatives"

It used to be that the word *commodities* enveloped all one needed to know about trading, speculating, and hedging, but the term took on a negative connotation after the inflationary bubble of the late 1970s was punctured and trading profits were given back *en masse*. The public, for a time, had had its fill of commodities. So *futures* came along as a replacement. This word, in turn, was replaced with *derivatives*, to separate the up-and-coming risk-management industry from its more earthy and speculative roots. Now we can read about derivatives and bankruptcies every time we pick up a newspaper. So much for image building.

It is unfortunate, because it makes the task of presenting currency management much more difficult. Perhaps you have to separate plain vanilla futures and options from the more exotic over-the-counter derivatives and not move forward until your prospect can recite the difference. Perhaps you should simply avoid the term *derivatives* altogether. Instead, refer to a *contract*, an *option*, a *private party agreement*, a *deferred exchange*, etc. You certainly should not promote derivatives such as embedded option strategies unless you carefully dissect them in front of your listeners, identifying each component as a long or short provision or contract. The instrument then becomes much less intimidating. Make no mistake about it—futures and options are intimidating to corporate America. One CEO remarked about how his board, without a second thought, gives blanket approval for forward contracts worth hundreds of millions of dollars in raw materials, but balks at approving twenty futures contracts for British pounds because futures are too risky.

Hedge Vehicles Come Last

Development of a currency management program does not begin with the sale of the particular financial instrument; it begins with the sale of a foreign exchange survey. Then you develop programs, policy, and models based on the results. The selection of specific hedging vehicles lies near the end of the process. By following this approach, you don't have to deal with the negative connotations of futures contracts until the principals of hedging are well understood and accepted. Your involvement implies that futures and options will play a part in the program. Leave it at that. The time to select exactly which hedge vehicles to use comes later. The credibility you've established with the company in the meantime can overcome any aversion to the use of futures. Of course, it may turn out that futures and options just don't fit the situation or the risk profile of the company. It may turn to non-leveraged techniques such as bank borrowings instead. This is another reason why the survey should stand alone as a chargeable sales product. Then you won't spend all that time with a prospect without some form of compensation.

The Individual Buyer

So far, the discussion of selling has been very general. Principles that work in almost every presentation and with almost every listener have been presented; however, there is another dimension to selling currency risk management. Rather than considering the company as a whole, take stock of the individuals who make up the organization. Each has some say in the final decision of the company, for better or worse. Robert Miller and Stephen Heiman explore these influences at length in their best seller, *Strategic Selling*. Put this book on your "must read" list. Many of the concepts below were developed from their work.[3]

Every time you contact a prospect to sell, present, educate, or inform, you essentially are asking someone (a buyer) to do something (buy). This buyer then makes a decision on whether or not to do it. The decision to buy may be in the form of final approval of the program, acceptance of the team concept, acceptance of a survey, a commitment to set time aside to listen or to bring others into the meeting, or anything else that furthers the sales process. Regardless of what it is we are selling at the moment, we assume that the person we are selling to has the authority to buy. Otherwise, why would he or she take the time to talk with us, or show interest in what we say?

There are several dynamics to be aware of in a hierarchical organization such as a corporation. First, there is one, and only one, person in the organization with the authority to make a particular buying decision at a particular moment in time. This authority oftentimes is formally bestowed on an individual—it comes with the territory. The role of the purchasing agent is a good example. Many times, however, the buying power passes from hand to hand in a much more casual fashion. Whoever has the interest, the time, the expertise, or is in the mood may be the buyer of the moment. The second time you visit, someone else may be the buyer, even when you are restating the same proposal.

There are also times that buying authority passes from one individual to another on an *unconscious* level. This is the case, for example, when no one, either in or out of the company, knows for sure who has the last word on the matter until it is expressed. This often occurs in the heat of office politics involving power plays, turf battles, defensive maneuvering, and so on. When these dynamics are in play, the person who expresses so much interest in what you say may not be the buyer, even if he implies to you that he is. He may not want to reveal that he has lost the authority to buy. He may not even be aware of the fact.

This single-buyer dynamic comes into play whether you buttonhole one individual in the hallway, or address an entire group, such as an executive committee. During a group meeting, seven or eight individuals may fire blistering questions at you, make copious notes, nod or shake their heads. It's all show. Committees do not make buying decisions. There is only one person in the group who has that authority. Even when the decision is by consensus, this is the person who sways the vote. The position or title may identify this person, but not always; therefore, it is important to know for sure who the real buyer is before walking into a meeting. When you fail to identify him correctly, he will always turn out to be the person who was nodding off in the corner; the dummy you totally ignored.

The Personal Benefit

Identifying the buyer is the first step. Your challenge is to provide him with a win. Consultative selling, remember, requires that both buyer and seller walk away winners. What does it take for a buyer to win? A common assumption is that the buyer wins when the buyer's company wins. It is essential, after all, that the company benefit from your service. Almost every manager, every employee, wants to see his or her company remain healthy. Paychecks depend on it. Knowing this, your proposal may be based solely on what benefits the company, but this benefit is too abstract to be felt on an emotional level. Fundamental to successful selling is recognition of the fact that buyers buy (and win) *emotionally.*

This is certainly no revelation. The principle of emotional buying is bedrock to the advertising industry. It is why salespeople sell benefits, not features. An owner of a hardware store, for example, does not promote the growing attributes of grass seed and vegetable seed, although they may be impressive features. Rather, he sells green lawns and bountiful gardens. These are the benefits provided by the features. The presentation of currency management works in a similar fashion. Risk reduction is a feature, and certainly core to the whole concept of hedging, but the buyer wants to know why this feature is advantageous *to him.* He needs to personally benefit before he is interested.

This is not good news. You are not selling one product to one buyer. In the process of developing a currency management program, you are selling a number of products (concepts, really) on a number of occasions to a number of buyers. They all have different needs. A potential increase in corporate earnings, for example, may drive one buyer because it means an increased bonus. It may leave a second buyer who doesn't receive bonuses completely unmoved. This person, however, may strive for increased recognition or a reduction in stress. If you do no more than correctly identify each buyer who comes along, your chances of success certainly increase. If you also correctly identify what it is that each buyer needs to have to win, and can deliver that win, you have every chance of being outstanding in this business.

Miller and Heiman categorize potential buyers by function and by the personal benefits most commonly associated with that function. Look for these "buying influences" as you make your presentation. These are the *coach*, the *user buyer*, the *technical buyer*, and the *economic buyer*. Each of these influences may impact the program as you develop it. Each may be the buyer at a particular stage, the one you must win over before proceeding to the next step.

Do you really have to sell them all? Certainly, not all of these buying influences make the final decision. Only one can financially commit the company. This is probably the chief executive officer or a director. Why not bypass a particularly obstreperous individual whom you know has no final buying authority in this process? Why not make a beeline to the final buyer? Do so at your peril. While it is true that only one person is authorized to buy any particular proposal you present along the way, this is not the case in reverse. Any number of individuals might have the authority to *not* buy; that is, they may have the power to influence the final buyer not to buy. This is why they are called "buying influences." Most often, you will have no way of knowing who can influence what. The solution, then, is to cover all the bases. Find all buying influences that can impact your program, and sell each one on how he personally benefits from currency risk management.

Eight Prospecting Considerations

The broker who prospects corporate clients for currency management business must be prepared to devote a significant amount of time to this endeavor. The objective is a long-term business relationship, so the effort put forth can be very worthwhile. Review the following considerations and plan your prospecting program accordingly.

1. Selling a currency management program requires consultative selling, a technique for providing a win-win situation for both buyer and seller.
2. The potential financial impact of a proposed currency management program requires that the broker be both credible and knowledgeable.
3. Selling the program involves a number of stages and concepts; therefore, the sale should be viewed as a process occurring over time. It includes a series of presentations or proposals.
4. All else being equal, a less technical presentation is more effective than one that is more technical. In-depth discussions of derivatives should take place only after the general concepts of currency management have been accepted.
5. Only one person will be empowered to buy or not to buy a specific proposal on a specific occasion. A subsequent proposal may involve a different buyer. In each case, the buyer may or may not be readily identifiable.
6. Although there is only one buyer at a time, there may be a number of individuals who influence the buyer's decision; therefore, everyone impacted by the program should be sold on its merits.
7. Individuals buy because of a perceived personal benefit. They do not buy features. A personal benefit creates the "win" in a selling situation. The broker must try to identify both the buyer and the buyer's personal "win."
8. Corporate functions, those who fulfill them, and their associated "wins" can be classified as buying influences. These are called the *coach*, the *user buyer*, the *technical buyer*, and the *economic buyer*. These classifications include "real" buyers as well as individuals who can influence the buyer's decision.

The Coach

The first buying influence to identify is the *coach.* This individual may or may not have actual buying authority; however, he does exert a major influence on your chances of success with the company. The coach is unique because, more than anything else, he "buys" *you.* The coach benefits personally by your success. Perhaps he wants you to succeed because he knows the importance of managing foreign exchange exposure. He sees you as the solution, and wants the recognition of presenting you to management. Perhaps you and the prospective coach hit it off right away and he simply finds satisfaction in watching you prevail.

Often, but not always, the coach is your contact person; perhaps, the one you met during the initial visit. Your *first objective* when prospecting for a new account is to *find a coach.* This person will be invaluable as he guides you through the corporate politics, opening doors. He also will help you to identify other buyers and buying influences. As this title implies, the coach will actively support you, up to a point. He will not sell for you. The reason, beside the fact that he probably is not a salesman, is because he is sold on your capabilities to sell yourself and your product.

What do you offer to acquire someone's active support? Your credibility and knowledge. Unless a prospective coach finds you credible, he will not take a chance on you. Your coach, after all, may be risking his own reputation and credibility by promoting you. Who do you look for? Someone who can relate to your knowledge base; someone who already has a basic understanding of trading and risk management. You probably will find your coach in corporate finance. Try the treasurer first, then go from there.

The Technical Buyer

The *technical buyer* rarely has any real buying authority. He is a buyer, however, because of the influence he can exert on other buyers, including those with real authority. The technical buyer is the corporate "shopper." He may be a company employee, or an outside professional with an advisory or oversight function. This buyer, more than any other, sees himself as a guardian, protecting the corporation from products and salespeople who don't measure up. He plays the devil's advocate by kicking the tires.

Technical buyers *compare.* They study the merits of a product and compare them with competing products or alternative solutions. After talking to you, they may actually solicit your competitor to come in and make a proposal, just to give the company a choice in the matter. They screen out anyone who doesn't make the grade. Nothing is approved by management without their consent, or so they believe. When selling to someone whom you mistook for an authoritative buyer, more often than not it was a technical buyer. As far as this person is concerned, until you pass muster, he *is* the buyer. Purchasing agents fulfill this role very nicely. So do the following:

- The corporate attorney
- The corporate accountant
- The bank officer
- The securities broker
- The management consultant
- The financial consultant

Technical buyers are natural cynics. Financial consultants are good examples, especially when it concerns someone else's product. When asked for an opinion of a hedging program (other than his), he immediately guards the gates. He carefully scrutinizes the program for flaws, and unhesitatingly gives a thumbs down if he finds the least discrepancy. Although he cannot give approval for the company, he may have the power to *disapprove.* In either case, the personal benefit to the technical buyer is that he gets to display his expertise and protect a client by detecting faults that others might miss. The personal benefit to most technical buyers is recognition, or sometimes the power to say no. Achieving accolades by saving the company from a bad business decision can be very satisfying. So technical buyers look for problems.

Try to avoid these people unless they truly are significant to your success. If the CEO tells you to "run it past Dan," and Dan is the corporate tax attorney, you're probably going to have a bad day. If you must sell to an important technical buyer and it's going down hill, offer to make him a member of the currency management team (assuming you can deliver on the offer). As a team player, he will be recognized and his input and scrutiny could be of value. Make the offer over lunch and pick up the tab.

The User Buyer

A particular company may have any number of *user buyers*. These are the "hands on" people. A user buyer will be involved in the actual management of foreign currency. It's up to him to make the program work for his department, and for the company as a whole. He can also make it *not* work if he feels it was foisted upon him against his will. The user buyer, therefore, is more influential than any one else once the program is up and running because he is in charge of running it. When possible, every significant user buyer should be made a part of the currency management team, and should be involved in the development of the program at an early stage.

The treasurer will usually be the primary user buyer. (If you are fortunate, he will also be your coach.) Not all user buyers are found in the area of finance, however. Sales, marketing, and production have large stakes in how currency exposures affect the company's performance. The distinction between financial and non-financial user buyers involves the personal benefit each derives from your program. Whereas treasury will gain control over the currency (a definite "win"), the user buyers in operating functions may actually *lose* control. This is the case, for example, if margins and performance figures are now to be translated at exchange rates determined by treasury, rather than by happenstance.

This loss of control can turn a neutral user buyer into an active antagonist very quickly. Any hedge program forced upon a manager without his input, especially one which affects his area of operation, will be viewed by him as a threat. Look to counter this by personal "wins" in other areas. The head of a distribution unit may not be overly impressed by the fact that hedging can reduce risk on the corporate balance sheet, but what about the program's ability to gain a competitive edge on job quotes? A reduction in accounting exposure benefits finance. Reductions in operating exposure, and the subsequent potential boost in performance, benefits the operational buyer. Remember that the performance of this person is often measured by the variances in operating income. Make the non-financial user buyer a part of the team, or at least take the time to solicit his input. Address his concerns. Keep him informed. Remember—every one has to see how they win or the program will be short-lived, if it succeeds in getting off the ground.

The Economic Buyer

This is your most challenging buying influence. The final decision to commit the company to your proposals rests with the buyer who holds the purse strings. It is common knowledge in sales that the more impact the product or service has on the company, the higher up the ladder one must look for a final commitment to buy. Currency management, of course, can have a profound impact on the corporate net worth. The final authority for this type of program will rest with one of the directors or with one of the officers, probably the CEO. If no one on this level knows you, you have not yet sold the company. Sometimes, however, you find a person at a mid-management level has been given final buying authority. Beware. That usually means that those at the executive level have not heard of your program. When they do, you may have to resell it from the beginning.

Since the directors or corporate officers are the final decision-makers, you should become very familiar with the two officers most likely to be involved, the *chief executive officer* and the *chief financial officer*. Of course, the individuals acting in these capacities may have different titles. The treasurer or the director of finance may fulfill the CFO's function. The CEO may be the president, the executive director, the general manager, or the owner. Your concern is with a particular set of responsibilities more than the title, and with the type of person who rises to the top to accept these responsibilities.

The CFO Looks for Solutions

Rarely will currency management of any kind succeed without the active and ongoing support of the CFO. After all, the program will be under his direction; therefore, you need to be well aware of what the CFO requires in the way of personal benefits before he is interested in your product.

Think of the company as a sailing ship, plying the seas of commerce. The chief executive officer is the captain. With sextant and compass, he watches the stars. The chief financial officer (CFO), on the other hand, rarely concentrates on anything that distant. Rather, he focuses on the water line. It is his duty to keep the ship afloat. The CFO does not have time to sit and project the company's position in five or ten years. He is more interested in where it is *right now*. He views things with a weather eye, and is the first to notice an approaching stormy sea. Unlike the technical buyer, the CFO doesn't look for problems. He doesn't need to. They fill his calendar daily, and each requires his urgent attention daily. He continually seeks *solutions*, on a personal as well as a corporate level. Miller and Heiman write that a solution to a problem is the most powerful of all buying motivators.[4] When wallowing in heavy seas, nothing takes precedence over keeping the ship upright. Other personal benefits, such as opportunity, growth, and recognition, can wait.

This need of the CFO is very much to your advantage. Currency management is built around problem solving. It is, after all, the method by which financial risk is transferred away from the company. When this has been effectively communicated, the CFO often becomes one of the program's stauchest promoters, and a driving force for moving it forward.

When making your presentation to the CFO, go ahead and dwell on risk reduction. On the other hand, do not carry on at all about the profit potential. If you have a "profitable" trading system that "can make you money when traded right," the CFO is the very last person you want to talk to about it. This buyer wants to *reduce* risk, not increase it with new trading adventures, nor will he exhibit a lot of enthusiasm over the novel, the experimental, or the little-known approaches to currency management. All too risky. He wants hedging techniques that have been tested, proven, and preferably carved in stone from public usage. Don't mention the word *derivative* if you can help it; the CFO's favorite financial instrument is the U.S. treasury bill.

This buyer is not a risk taker; he is a financial engineer. He will show a great deal of interest in the details of future roll overs, bull strategies in option combos, and the like, including how and when funds and securities are transferred, where accounts are located, who has custody, and so forth. He may understand these concepts at least as well as you do. Do your product homework thoroughly before meeting with the CFO. Remember that this person requires *security* and *stability*. Be prepared for questions concerning the financial strength of your firm and your length of employment. Promote this, if it is a strength. If it is not, emphasize the custodial regulations and clearing member's security of customer funds, regardless of the broker holding the account.

This buyer has a major interest in hedging *accounting* exposures, those in which the risk of exposure is most immediate and visible. If you are proposing a program that emphasizes the management of operating exposure at the *expense* of accounting exposure, give a lot forethought to how you will explain it to the CFO.

The CEO looks for Opportunities

Let's meet the captain of the ship. Whereas the CFO keeps an eye on the structure, the CEO fixes his sight on the horizon. This buyer is a futurist, and the next five years are where he lives most of the time. This buyer possesses a great deal of imagination, required of a visionary. He is charged with knowing the changes in the industry before they happen, and with making course corrections accordingly. The CEO is akin to the farmer who looks over snow-covered fields and sees wheat ready for harvest. Whether that occurs depends a great deal on his decisions and efforts. An unquenchable faith in one's self is a characteristic of both farmer and CEO. It is an essential ingredient in risk-taking and, if nothing else, the CEO is the quintessential risk taker. He tunes in to words such as *forward-looking*, *forewarned*, *strategic goals*. His personal wins include concepts such as *growth*, *opportunity*, and *success*. To achieve these, he always is seeking the high ground, the competitive advantage. The CEO has little patience with details; he can delegate those. He works almost totally with concepts.

Talk *strategically* to this buyer. There must be a competitive advantage to using your proposals. How does your program help penetrate new markets or expand existing ones? How does it help increase market share? If the chief financial officer wants a hedging system that is well-known and accepted, the CEO, on the other hand, is more interested in the system nobody knows about. Remember that this buyer, above all, is a competitor. He looks for the inside edge.

There are other distinctions between these two buyers. The CFO focuses on accounting exposures. The CEO often is more concerned with long-term operating exposures, rather than quarter-to-quarter changes in the balance sheet. In your presentation to the CEO, think about how your concept or recommendations create product differentiation, new avenues of sourcing, the ability to bid or price in local currency. The CEO strives to enhance profitability. Your presentation should illustrate how currency management does just that.

The major difference between these two buyers involves the matter of risk. Whereas the CFO is risk averse, the CEO is a gambler. If we begin to emphasize the speculative profit potential of our hedge strategy, the CFO quickly finds that he is late for another appointment. The CEO is more likely to extend the time of our meeting in order to learn the details. Knowing this, a derivative salesman might enhance the speculative aspects of a hedging program to get it past the CEO. This, of course, is unethical and quite possibly damaging to the client. The consequences may include future litigation. If there are speculative elements in your program, such as a selective hedging model, make absolutely sure that no unrealistic expectations are generated.

The CEO's decision is ultimately the one that counts, so your presentation to him is a make-or-break situation. Because you want all bases covered before approaching him, he often is the last on your list. Not always. Sometimes it is the CEO who is the most interested in currency management. He may even initiate the first contact, leaving it to you to sell others in the organization. The most important point to remember is that, no matter where you start, you must meet individuals, talk with them, and come away with everyone a winner.

The Presentation Process

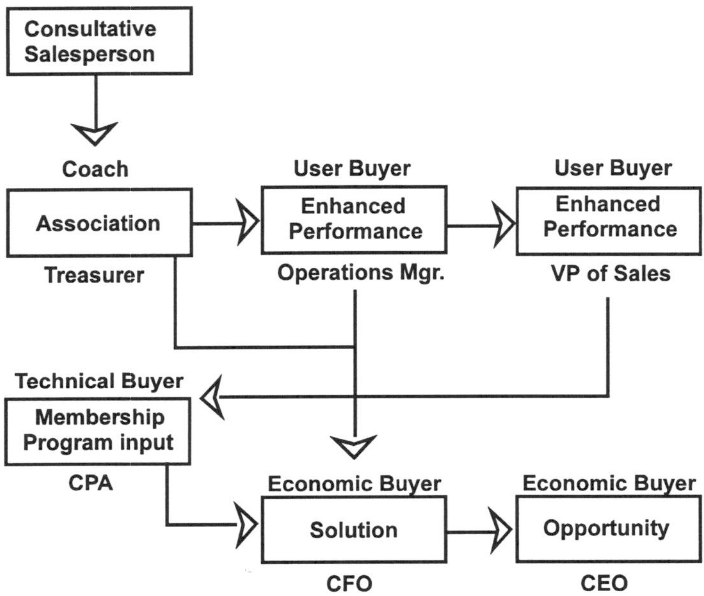

This diagram illustrates a possible presentation process for a currency management program. The consultative salesperson (futures broker) looks for the personal benefit for each buyer he encounters in order to effect a win-win situation. He or she first identifies a coach, someone who wins *because* the salesperson wins. This may be the treasurer, the financial manager, or someone acting in that capacity. The personal benefits, or "wins," are shown here within the boxes designating the various buyer positions and influences. The process culminates with a final presentation to the CEO.

The presentation is not always "uphill." The arrows often point the other way. Sometimes the CEO or CFO will start the process by finding sources to handle their exposures. The company may then be calling you.

Appendix I
Where to Go From Here

Some corporate foreign currency managers elect to turn forecasting and trading over to experts. These experts occupy such positions as Commodity Trading Advisers (CTAs), Investment Advisers (IAs), foreign exchange dealers, and futures brokers. As in any profession, some are much more knowledgeable than others. Some of these positions are regulated (exchange-related). Others are not (interbank-related). No federal or state registration is required for trading foreign exchange accounts through the interbank, off-exchange, or over-the-counter. Registration by the Commodity Futures Trading Commission (CFTC) is required for exchange-traded products such as futures or options on futures. Future exchanges are also regulated by the National Futures Association (NFA), a self-regulatory organization located in Chicago. Registration background information for all Associated Persons (brokers, also known as APs) and CTAs is on file and available to the public through the NFA.

Some APs with brokerage firms are authorized to trade futures on a discretionary basis with only the assignment of a limited power of attorney and proper account documentation. Others are not. It may be as much a matter of company policy as expertise. CTAs are authorized to trade with discretion, and are required to provide disclosure brochures relating to their past performance, yet past performance is no guarantee of future results. CTAs trade through their own brokers, or through the client's broker. Regardless of who does the trading, when a currency manager gives trading discretion, the ground rules and objectives always should be communicated very clearly before trading begins.

Market and price forecasting information is available at major banks, brokerage firms, and the exchanges. Banks and brokerage firms with foreign exchange operations solicit transaction business from corporate clients and potential clients. They often supply background educational material on request. They may provide advice, analysis, and research reports on an ongoing basis.

Market forecasting is available from numerous sources. Some compete with banks and brokers for transactional business. These include foreign exchange brokers and non-bank foreign exchange dealers. Some advertise "order-matching capability" to prospective clients, usually financial institutions and corporations. Presumably, this gives clients the same access to the latest bids and offers as enjoyed by foreign exchange dealers.

Many advisory firms supply technical information. Some supply purely fundamental information such as consensus reports, financial data from various countries, geopolitical news as it happens, and economic indicators as they are reported. When timeliness is less important, a good source for fundamental economic reports is the Federal Reserve Bank (St. Louis). Its quarterly publication, the *International Economic Conditions*, is available free of charge. It also provides economic data electronically. Referred to as "FRED" (Federal Reserve Economic Data), the data is available via computer modem. Access to the information highway may greatly increase the value of fundamental analysis as a forecasting tool. Currently, it is difficult for fundamental research to compete with technical analysis for short-term trading purposes, but instant access to fundamental information coupled with instant number crunching ability may usher in a new era of fundamental forecasting.

Many suppliers offer various kinds of technical analysis. The majority of their customers are speculators; for them, timeliness is everything. Along with the newsletters mailed out weekly or monthly, technical data and commentary arrive by fax, telephone "hot lines," computer modem, and satellite dish. Some firms also provide trading advice, alerting their clients as soon as buy and sell signals are generated by their system.

Trading systems abound. Some consist of simple pencil and paper calculations, updated at the kitchen table after each market close. The more complicated systems are often on computer diskettes available in either "black box" or "gray box" form. A black box is a trading program that, for proprietary reasons, is concealed from the public (and the user). Usually the day's open, high, low, and closing prices are entered via keyboard or downloaded at the end of the trading day, and the program is run. Instructions are given to buy or sell based on the signals generated. The signals themselves are not revealed. A gray box is similar, but there is much more disclosure of the criteria used to make the trading decisions. The problem with both, but especially with the black box, is that the user is trading in the dark. When losses occur (and they almost certainly will) the user never knows whether the system is experiencing a normal and temporary "draw down," the system bombed because of a subtle but permanent change in the market, or the system was no better than throwing darts in the first place. Computerized systems continuously evolve, fade away, and reappear in updated form. Artificial Intelligence and computer neural networks that "teach themselves" are the latest developments in the field.

For the active trader, there are quote vendors. With downloading capability and a monitor, real time quote streams can be continuously displayed. "Real time" means that you see it when it happens. There are also 5-minute delayed quotes (cheaper to obtain) and end-of-day quotes, where just the summary of the day's action is supplied (cheaper still). Some of these subscriptions come with various software packages which form charts with overlays of technical indicators and buy/sell signals.

In addition, there are risk management consultants, asset managers, and other advisory services that can supply program development, seminars, trading suggestions, and record keeping for more long-term hedging requirements. These services tend to be more client-oriented than product-oriented. When contacting any of these sources, it is important to remember that, as an industry, most participants are geared to the fast pace of speculation for profit rather than to the more time consuming development of risk management programs. The best advice is to check references with the appropriate regulatory agency or self-regulatory organization. For transaction or advisory services on futures exchanges, this is the National Futures Association.

To find these information sources, begin with the banks and brokerage firms in your area that offer foreign exchange service. Not all do, and those that do may not advertise it. For brokerage firms, find out which ones are involved in commodity or futures trading. Below are some resources for your information system.

Regulatory and Educational Sources

Federal Reserve Board
20th Street and Constitution Ave., NW
Washington, DC 20006
Office of Public Affairs: (202) 452-3204
Publications Office: (202) 452-3245
http://www.bog.frb.fed.us

Federal Reserve Bank of St. Louis
PO Box 442
St. Louis, MO 6333166-0442
Tel: (314) 444-8444 Fax: (314) 444-8731
http://www.stls.frb.org

International Monetary Fund
700 19th Street, NW
Washington, DC 20431
Tel: (202) 623-7000 Fax: (202) 623-6278
Fax for publication information: (202) 623-7201
http://www.imf.org

International Swaps and Derivatives Association, Inc.
600 5th Avenue, 27th Floor
Rockefeller Center
New York, NY 10020
Tel: (212) 332-1200 Fax: (212) 332-1212
http://www.isda.org

Global Association of Risk Professionals (GARP)
98 N. Broadway, Suite 292
Tarrytown, NY 10591
Tel: (914) 654-7803
http://www.garp.com

International Association of Financial Engineers
c/o St. John's University
Department of Finance
Jamaica, NY 11439
Tel: (516) 331-8069 Fax: (516) 331-8044

Commodity Futures Trading Commission
Three Lafayette Centre
1155 21st Street, NW
Washington, DC 20581

Tel: (202) 418-5080 Fax: (202) 418-5525
http://www.cftc.gov

National Futures Association
200 W. Madison St., Suite 1600
Chicago, IL 60606-3447
Tel: (312) 781-1300 Fax: (312) 781-1467

There are several sources on the internet for retrieving foreign exchange quotes. Two "user friendly" ones are listed below.

Federal Reserve Board
Statistics: Releases and Historical Data
http://www.bog.frb.fed.us/releases

Pacific Exchange Rate Service
(provided by Prof. Werner Antweiler,
University of British Columbia)
http://pacific.commerce.ubc.ca/xr

Risk Management Associations

International Swaps and Derivatives Association, Inc.
600 5th Avenue, 27th Floor
Rockefeller Center
New York, NY 10020
Tel: (212) 332-1200 Fax: (212) 332-1212

International Association of Financial Engineers
c/o St. John's University
Department of Finance
Jamaica, NY 11439
Tel: (516) 331-8069 Fax: (516) 331-8044

Educational and training Sources

Center for Futures Education
P.O. Box 309
Grove City, PA 16127
Tel: (412) 458-5860 Fax: (412) 458-5962

Financial Industry Institute / FII Data Center
2001 Pennsylvania Ave., NW, Suite 600
Washington, DC 20006-1807

Magazines

A few business journals specialize in the areas of risk management, trading, or both. Here are three. Some, such as *Futures Magazine*, also publish an annual source guide of professional services in the industry.

Risk
53 W. Jackson Boulevard, Suite 252
Chicago, IL 60604
Tel: (312) 554-0556 Fax: (312) 554-0558

Futures Magazine
250 South Wacker Drive, Suite 1150
Chicago, IL 60606
Tel: (312) 977-0999 Fax: (312) 977-1042

Futures and Options World (U.S. Office)
Metal Bulletin Inc. / MAR Inc.
220 Fifth Avenue
New York, NY 10001
Tel: (212) 213-6202

Appendix II Currency Exchanges Around the World

The following exchanges listed offer a variety of currency and eurorate derivatives that may be suitable for hedging purposes. No representation is made as to the accuracy of this grouping, nor has any consideration been given to trading access or factors such as credit risk, political risk and liquidity. All risk factors should be thoroughly examined before utilizing any contract in a currency management program.

U.S. dollar contracts on foreign exchanges may be used to hedge the local currency of the country in which that exchange in located. For example, the U.S. dollar contracts on the Bolsa de Mercadorias y Futuros in Sao Paulo, Brazil, could be a market in which to hedge the Brazilian Real. Currencies also may be hedged indirectly. For example, the Swedish krona can be traded on the PHLX as a cross rate, or on the Finnish Options Exchange through the Finnish Markka, assuming sufficient liquidity.

Eurorates ending in 'IBOR' or 'BOR' refer to "Interbank Offered Rate." The first letter(s) refer to the city, usually the financial center of the home country of the currency quoted. For example, 'PIBOR' is the Paris Interbank Offered Rate for the French franc, or "Eurofranc." "MIBOR" is the Madrid Interbank Offered Rate for the Spanish Peseta, or "Europeseta." The exception is the London Interbank Offered Rate (LIBOR) which refers to the U.S. dollar, or Eurodollar.

Country	Exchange	Currency	Eurorate
Belgium	Belgian Futures & Options Exchange (BELFOX)	US$/BF Exchange Rates (O)	BIBOR (F)
Brazil	Bolsa de Mercadorias & Futuros (BM&F)	US$ (commercial) (F,O) US$ (floating) (F,O) Flexible Currency (O)	one day and 30 day interbank deposits (F,O)
Chile	Santiago Stock Exchange	US$ (F)	
Denmark	FUTOP Market (Copenhagen Stock Exchange & FUTOP)		3-month CIBOR (F)
Finland	Finnish Options Exchange, Ltd.	US$/FIM (F,O) DM/FIM (F,O) SK/FIM (F,O) BP/FIM (F,O) DM/SK (F,O)	3-month HELIBOR (Forward)
	Helsinki Securities and Derivatives Exchange, Clearinghouse (HEX Ltd)	FRX Currency Derivatives (22 currencies) (F, O)	
France	March a Terme Int'l de France (MATIF)		3-month PIBOR (F, OF)
Germany	DTB Deutsche Terminbörse		1-3 month Euromark (F)
Hong Kong	Hong Kong Futures Exchange (HKFE)	Rolling Deutsche Mark (F) Rolling Japanese Yen (F) Rolling British Pound (F)	3-month HIBOR (F)
Hungary	Budapest Commodity Exchange	U.S. Dollar (F) Deutsche Mark (F) Japanese Yen (F) British Pound (F) Italian Lira (F) Swiss Franc (F) Czech Koruna (F) ECU (F)	1 & 3 month BUBOR (F)

Country	Exchange	Currency	Eurorate
(Hungary)	Budapest Stock Exchange	US$/HUF (F) Deutsche Mark (F) ECU/HUF (F)	1 & 3 month BUBOR (F)
Isreal	The Tel Aviv Stock Exchange (TASE)	U.S. Dollar Exchange rates (F,O)	
Japan	Tokyo Intn'l Financial Futures Exchange (TIFFE)	US$/JY (F)	3-month Euroyen 3-month Eurodollar (F) 1-year Euroyen (F)
Netherlands	Amsterdam Exchanges (AEX-Optiebeurs)	U.S. Dollar (F,O)	
	Financiele Termijnmarkt Amsterdam N.V. (FTA)	US$/ DG (F)	
Russia	Moscow Interbank Currency Exchange	U.S. Dollar (F)	
Singapore	Singapore International Monetary Exchange, Ltd (SIMEX)	Deferred Spot US$/JY (F) Deferred Spot US$/JY (F)	Euroyen (F,OF) Eurodollar (F,OF) Euromark (F,OF)
Spain	Meff Renta Fija (MEFF-RF)		90-day MIBOR (F,OF) 360-day MIBOR (F,OF)
Sweden	OM Stockholm AB (OMS)		STIBOR -FRA (F) HELIBOR -FRA (F)
United Kingdom	London International Financial Futures and Options Exchange (LIFFE)		1 month Euromark (F) 3 month Euromark (F, OF) 3 month Euroyen (F, OF) 3 month Euroswiss (F,OF)

Country	Exchange	Currency	Eurorate
United Kingdom			3 month Eurolira (F,OF) 3 month Sterling (F,OF) 3 month ECU (F, OF)
United States	Chicago Mercantile Exchange (CME)	Deutsche mark (F, OF) Canadian dollar (F, OF)	LIBOR (F, OF) Eurodollar Time deposit (F,OF)
	IMM (div of CME)	Swiss franc (F, OF)	3 month Eurodollar (F, OF)
		British pound (F, OF)	Euroyen (F)
(United States)		Japanese yen (F, OF) Australian dollar (F, OF) French franc (F, OF) DM/JY cross rate (F) BP/DM cross rate (F) BP rolling spot (F, OF) JY rolling spot (F) DM rolling spot (F, OF) DM currency forwards JY currency forwards	
	GEM (div of CME)	Mexican Peso (F, OF) Brazilian Dollar (F, OF) New Zealand Dollar (F, OF) South African Rand (F, OF)	
	MidAmerica Commodity Exchange (MidAm)	Australian Dollar (O) British pound (O) Canadian dollar (O) Deutsche mark (O) Japanese yen (O) Swiss franc (O)	Eurodollar (F)
	New York Cotton Exchange FINEX (div of NYCE)	U.S. Dollar Index (F, OF) Sterling/D-Mark (F, OF) Sterling/Yen cross rate (F) Sterling/Swiss Franc (F) DM/Yen (F, OF) DM/Krona (F, OF) DM/French Franc (F, OF)	

Country	Exchange	Currency	Eurorate
	New York Cotton Exchange FINEX (div of NYCE)	DM/Italian Lira (F, OF) D-Mark/Swiss Franc (F,OF) D-Mark/Spanish Peseta (F) US$/British Pound (F, OF) US$/D-Mark (F, OF) US$/Yen (F, OF) US$/Swiss Franc (F, OF) US$/Canadian Dollar (F) US$/South African Rand (F) Sterling/US$ (F, OF) Australian Dollar/US$ (F) New Zealand Dollar/US$ (F)	
(United States)	Philadelphia Stock Exchange (PHLX) Philadelphia Board of Trade (PBOT)	British Pound (O, F) Canadian Dollar (O, F) Deutsche Mark (O, F) Swiss franc (O, F) French franc (O, F) Japanese yen (O, F) Australian dollar (O, F) Spanish Peseta (O) Italian Lira (O) ECU (O,F) DM/JY cross rate (O) BP/DM cross rate (O)	

source: 1998 Source Book, *Futures*

Abbreviations

F	Futures
O	Options
OF	Options on Futures
BF	Belgian Franc
BP	British Pound
DM	Deutsche Mark
FIM	Finnish Markka
SK	Swedish Krona
HUF	Hungarian Forint
JY	Japanese Yen
DG	Dutch Guilder

Appendix III
The World of Currencies

The following table is reprinted from editions of *The Wall Street Journal*. The values represent the number of currency units equivalent to one U.S. dollar. Within a period of four years, changes in fiscal and monetary policies have produced dramatic changes in some exchange rates. Others have not budged a penny. We see, for example, that the East Caribbean dollar, the Belize dollar, the Bahrain Dinar, and the Liberian dollar, to name a few, remain firmly pegged to the U.S. dollar. Some currencies show the effects of economies wracked by inflation. Afghanistan, Algeria, Angola, Bulgaria, the Commonwealth of Independent States (Russia), Cuba, Ghana, Nigeria, Yemen and others have experienced currency devaluation of at least 50%. A few countries, Turkey, for example, appear to be stalked by real hyper-inflation.

As with a corporate balance sheet, these value columns are simply snap shots of two specific dates; they tell little about the historic events that produced them, or the current events now taking place. However, some conclusions can be drawn. We can be sure, for example, that no currency is initially valued at 100,000 to the U.S. dollar; it takes a run-away printing press to depreciate values to that level. Note that on November 7th, 1997, the entire block of Southeast Asian currencies, firmly pegged to the U.S. dollar just a few weeks earlier, were in the midst of a free fall, taking their nation's equity and debt markets with them. .

Country (Currency)	Value 11/5/93	Value 11/7/97
Afghanistan (Afghani - c)	1050.0000	4750.0000
Albania (Lek)	110.0000	145.5500
Algeria (Dinar)	19.7700	56.7992
Andorra (Peseta)	135.8900	144.5350
Andorra (Franc)	5.9113	5.7281
Angola (New Kwanza - 16, 20)	6500.3200	257128.0000
Antigua (E Caribbean $)	2.7000	2.7000
Argentina (Peso)	0.9981	0.9998
Aruba (Florin)	1.7900	1.7900
Australia (Australian Dollar)	1.4852	1.4258
Austria (Schilling)	11.9485	12.1430
Bahamas (Dollar)	1.0000	1.0000
Bahrain (Dinar)	0.3770	0.3770
Bangladesh (Taka)	39.7505	45.0000
Barbados (Dollar)	2.0113	2.0113
Belgium (Franc)	36.3100	35.2900
Belize (Dollar)	2.0000	2.0000
Benin (C.F.A. Franc)	295.5650	572.8100
Bermuda (Dollar)	1.0000	1.0000
Bhutan (Ngultrum)	31.3700	36.5320
Bolivia (Boliviano - o)	4.3950	5.3200
Bolivia (Boliviano - f)	4.4000	5.3300
Botswana (Pula)	2.5374	3.7594
Bouvet Island (Norwegian Krone)	7.3715	6.9386
Brazil (Cruzeiro - c- 4,) Real, 21	183.5900	1.1077
Brunei (Dollar)	1.5940	1.5730
Bulgaria (Lev)	30.2120	1709.0000
Burkina Faso (C.F.A. Franc)	295.5650	572.8100
Burma (Kyat)	6.1868	6.2616
Burundi (Franc)	234.5430	350.7350
Cambodia (Riel)	3500.0000	3000.0000
Cameroon (C.F.A. Franc)	295.5650	572.8100
Canada (Dollar)	1.2948	1.4047
Cape Verde Isl. (Escudo)	74.2000	92.9500
Cayman Islands (Dollar)	0.8500	0.8282
Centrl African Rp (C.F.A. Franc)	295.5650	572.8100
Chad (C.F.A. Franc)	295.5650	572.8100
Chile (Peso - o)	444.3000	466.0200
Chile (Peso - m)	412.3000	418.7300
China (Renminbi Yuan)	5.7868	8.2817

Country (Currency)	**Value 11/5/93**	**Value 11/7/97**
Colombia (Peso - o- 3)	817.0100	1290.5000
Commwlth Ind Sts (Rouble - m)	1177.0000	5907.5000
Comoros (C.F.A. Franc) (22,Franc)	295.5650	429.6075
Congo, People Rp (C.F.A. Franc)	295.5650	572.8100
Costa Rica (Colon)	148.1000	240.9650
Cuba (Peso - 23)	1.3203	23.0000
Cyprus (Pound*)	1.9470	1.9825
Czech (Koruna - 8)	29.5560	32.7270
Denmark (Danish Krone)	6.7735	6.5098
Djibouti (Djibouti Franc)	178.1650	177.7200
Dominica (E Caribbean $)	2.7000	2.7000
Dominican Rep (Peso - d)	13.0000	14.5000
Ecuador (Sucre - d)	1971.5000	4247.0000
Ecuador (Sucre -o)	1838.0000	4247.0000
Egypt (Pound)	3.3405	3.4015
El Salvador (Colon - d)	8.7100	8.7550
Equatorial Guinea (C.F.A.Franc)	295.5650	572.8100
Estonia (Kroon)	13.5300	13.6856
Ethiopia (Birr - o)	5.0000	6.6440
Faeroe Island (Danish Krone)	6.7735	6.5098
Falkland Island (Pound*)	1.4801	1.6881
Fiji (Dollar)	1.5360	1.4863
Finland (Markka)	5.7675	5.1524
France (Franc)	5.9113	5.7281
French Guiana (Franc)	5.9113	5.7281
French Pacific Isl. (C.F.P. Franc)	107.4781	104.1472
Gabon (C.F.A.Franc)	295.5650	572.8100
Gambia (Dollar) (Dalasi,24)	9.4700	10.4573
Germany (Mark)	1.7000	1.7100
Ghana (Cedi)	705.0000	2230.0000
Gibraltar (Pound*)	1.4801	1.6881
Greece (Drachma)	243.0500	269.3100
Greenland (Danish Krone)	6.7735	6.5098
Grenada (E Caribbean $)	2.7000	2.7000
Guadeloupe (Franc)	5.9113	5.7281
Guam (U.S.$)	1.0000	1.0000
Guatemala (Quetzal)	5.8240	6.1929
Guinea Bissau (Peso)(CFA Franc,25)	5000.0000	572.8100
Guinea Rep (Franc)	812.2900	1132.0000
Guyana (Dollar)	126.0000	142.8000

Country (Currency)	Value 11/5/93	Value 11/7/97
Haiti (Gourde)	12.0000	17.4131
Honduras Rep (Lempira - d)	6.9600	13.2050
Hong Kong (Dollar)	7.7275	7.7310
Hungary (Forint - 13)	99.3800	194.3400
Iceland (Krona -6)	71.3400	70.7350
India (Rupee - m)	31.3700	36.5320
Indonesia (Rupiah)	2098.5000	3300.0000
Iran (Rial -o - 17)	1661.0000	3000.0000
Iraq (Dinar-o) (m, 26)	0.3125	1200.0000
Ireland (Punt* - 7)	1.3995	1.5117
Israel (New Shekel)	2.9408	3.5407
Italy (Lira)	1642.0000	1677.3500
Ivory Coast (C.F.A. Franc)	295.5650	572.8100
Jamaica (Dollar - o)	27.5000	34.5500
Japan (Yen)	108.2500	123.7800
Jordan (Dinar)	0.6850	0.7090
Kenya (Shilling)	68.5379	63.7500
Kiribati (Australia Dollar)	1.4852	1.4279
Korea, North (Won)	2.1500	2.2000
Korea, South (Won)	807.1000	980.3000
Kuwait (Dinar)	0.2992	0.3032
Laos, People DR (Kip)	720.0000	1310.0000
Latvia (Lat - 10)	0.6100	0.5785
Lebanon (Pound)	1713.5000	1530.5000
Lesotho (Maloti)	3.3672	4.8279
Liberia (Dollar)	1.0000	1.0000
Libya (Dinar)	0.3013	0.3835
Liechtenstein (Franc)	1.5045	1.3953
Lithuania (Litas - 11)	3.9500	4.0008
Luxembourg (Lux. Franc)	36.3100	35.2900
Macao (Pataca)	7.9825	7.9861
Madagascar DR (Franc)	1850.0000	4985.0000
Malawi (Kwacha)	4.4704	17.8750
Malaysia (Ringgit)	2.5625	3.2990
Maldive (Ruflyaa)	11.9750	11.7700
Mali Rep (C.F.A.Franc)	295.5650	572.8100
Malta (Lira*)	2.5542	2.6281
Martinique (Franc)	5.9113	5.7281
Mauritania (Ougulya)	113.8100	165.8450
Mauritius (Rupee)	18.4514	21.7150

Country (Currency)	Value 11/5/93	Value 11/7/97
Mexico (New Peso - 1)	3.1470	8.2900
Monaco (Franc)	5.9113	5.7281
Mongolia (Tugrik - o - 19)	400.0000	800.3200
Montserrat (E Caribbean $)	2.7000	2.7000
Morocco (Dirham)	9.3746	9.3887
Mozambique (Metical)	5053.0729	11495.0000
Namibia (Rand - c)	3.3672	4.8279
Nauru Islands (Australia Dollar)	1.4852	1.4279
Nepal (Rupee)	46.3772	56.9500
Netherlands (Guilder)	1.9067	1.9277
Netherlands Antilles (Guilder)	1.7900	1.7900
New Zealand (N.Z. Dollar)	1.7960	1.5958
Nicaragua (Gold Cordoba)	6.2438	9.8252
Niger Rep (C.F.A.Franc)	295.5650	572.8100
Nigeria (Naira - d, m)	35.0000	80.0200
Nigeria (Naira -o)	na	21.8860
Norway (Norwegian Krone)	7.3715	6.9386
Oman, Sultanate of (Rial)	0.3850	0.3850
Pakistan (rupee - 18)	29.9000	44.0060
Panama (Balboa)	1.0000	1.0000
Papua N.G.(Kina)	0.9787	1.5279
Paraguay (Guarani - d)	1793.0000	2228.0000
Peru (New Sol -d)	2.1550	2.7125
Philippines (Peso)	27.5000	34.9750
Pitcairn Island(N.Z. Dollar)	1.7960	1.5958
Poland (Zloty - o, 27)	20619.0000	3.4730
Portugal (Escudo)	174.0500	174.6800
Puerto Rico (U.S. $)	1.0000	1.0000
Qatar (Riyal)	3.6400	3.6409
Republic of Macedonia (Denar)	na	53.4285
Republic of Yemen (Dinar)	0.4609	na
Republic of Yemen (Rial) (a, 28)	16.5000	124.0000
Republic of Yemen (Rial - o, 28)	18.0000	na
Reunion, Ile de la (Franc)	5.9113	5.7281
Romania (Leu)	1055.5000	7791.0000
Rwanda (Franc)	146.4367	293.9000
Saint Christopher (E Caribbean $)	2.7000	2.7000
Saint Helena (Pound Sterling*)	1.4801	1.6881
Saint Lucia (E Caribbean $)	2.7000	2.7000
Saint Pierre (Franc)	5.9113	5.7281

Country (Currency)	Value 11/5/93	Value 11/7/97
Saint Vincent (E Caribbean $)	2.7000	2.7000
Samoa, American (U.S. $)	1.0000	1.0000
Samoa, Western (Tala)	2.5975	2.6609
San Marino (Lira)	1642.0000	1677.3500
Sao Tome & Principe (Dobra)	240.0000	2390.0000
Saudi Arabia (Riyal)	3.7506	3.7508
Senegal (C.F.A. Franc)	295.5650	572.8100
Seychelles (Rupee)	5.2604	5.0100
Sierra Leone (Leone)	550.0000	780.0000
Singapore (Dollar)	1.5940	1.5730
Slovak (Koruna - 9)	32.8150	33.3510
Slovenia (Totar)	127.4817	161.4235
Solomon Island (Solomon Dollar)	3.1807	3.7495
Somali Rep (Shilling - d)	2620.0000	2620.0000
South Africa (Rand - f)	4.3425	na
South Africa (Rand - c)	3.3672	4.8279
Spain (Peseta)	135.8900	144.5350
Sri Lanka (Rupee)	49.0175	59.9250
Sudan Rep (Dinar)	13.0000	142.9000
Sudan Rep (Pound - c)	130.0000	1428.6000
Surinam (Guilder)	1.7850	401.0000
Swaziland (Lilangeni)	3.3672	4.8279
Sweden (Krona)	8.1600	7.4493
Switzerland (Franc)	1.5045	1.3953
Syria (Pound - d)	21.5000	41.8500
Taiwan (Dollar - o)	26.8500	30.9485
Tanzania (Shilling)	455.1372	614.5650
Thailand (Baht)	25.3500	38.5500
Togo, Rep (C.F.A. Franc)	295.5650	572.8100
Tongo Island (Pa'anga)	1.4852	1.3066
Trinidad & Tobago (Dollar - 2)	5.5200	6.1800
Tunisia (Dinar)	1.0065	1.1063
Turkey (Lira)	13499.5000	185237.0000
Turks & Caicos (U.S.$)	1.0000	1.0000
Tuvalu (Australia Dollar)	1.4852	1.4279
Uganda (Shilling - l)	1181.9231	1148.0000
Ukraine (Karbovanet - 12)	31000.0000	na
Ukraine (Hryvnia - 29)	na	1.8765
United Arab Emir (Dirham)	3.6710	3.6729
United Kingdom (Pound Sterling*)	1.4801	1.6881

Country (Currency)	Value 11/5/93	Value 11/7/97
Uruguay (Peso Uruguayo - m)	4.2400	9.9050
Vanuatu (Vatu)	122.5600	118.8800
Vatican City (Lira)	1642.0000	1677.3500
Venezuela (Bolivar - d -30)	101.0000	498.8000
Vietnam (Dong - o)	10785.0000	12206.0000
Virgin Is, Br (U.S.$)	1.0000	1.0000
Virgin Is, US (U.S.$)	1.0000	1.0000
Yugoslavia (New Dinar -14)(31)	105.0000	5.6895
Zaire Rep (Zaire - 15)	3.5100	117500.0000
Zambia (Kwacha)	350.0234	1360.0000
Zimbabwe (Dollar)	6.7913	13.4500

*U.S. dollars per National Currency unit.

+(a) Free market cental bank rate. (b) Floating rate. (c) Commercial rate. (d) Free market rate. (e) Controlled. (f) Financial rate. (g) Preferential rate. (h) Nonessential imports. (i) Floating tourist rate. (j) Public transaction rate (k) Agricultural products. (l) Priority rate. (m) Market rate. (n) Essential imports. (o) Official rate. (p) Exports. (n.a.) Not available.

Notes - Novemeber 5, 1993

+(1) Mexico, 1 January 1993: New currency called the New Peso introduced. (2) Trinidad and Tobago, 13 April 1993: floating exchange rate. (3) Colombia, 20 May 1993: Peso revised definition. (4) Brazil, 3 August 1993: New currency called the Cruzeiro Real introduced. (5) Uruguay, 1 March 1993: New currency called the Peso Uruguayo introduced. (6) Iceland, 27 June 1993: Krona devalued by approx 7.5%. (7) Irish Rep., 30 January 1993: Punt devalued by approx 10% (8) Czech, 1 January 1993: County now split into two republics Czech and Slovak (9) lovak, 10 July 1993: Koruna devalued by approx 10% (10) Latvia, 3 September 1993: Rates now being quoted for Latvia. (11) Lithuania, 21 July 1993: Exchange rates now being quoted for Lithuania (12) Ukraine, 19 August 1993: Karbovanet devalued by approx 68.66%. (13) Hungary, 30 September 1993: Forint devalued by approx 4.5%(14) Yugoslavia, 1 October 1993: Rate as of 8-20-93. Rate no longer available. (15) Zaire Rep., 3 November 1993: New currency called New Zaire introduced. (16) Angola, 13 October 1993: Kwanza devalued by approx 38.46%. (17) Iran, 14 April 1993: Rial devalued by approx 7%, currency now convertible. (18) Pakistan, 22 July 1993: Rupee devalued by approx 5.7% (19) Mongolia, 27 May 1993: Tugrik devalued by approx 62.5%.

Notes: November 7, 1997

20 - Readjusted Kwanza, 21 - new currency, 22 - new currency, 23 - specific rate for FX houses only, 24 - new name, 25 - replaces peso, 26 - official rate abolished 1/96, 27, new denomination
28 - official rate abolished 1/96, 29 - new currency, 30 - devalued approx 41% 12/95, 31 - new denomination

Source: Bank of America Global Trading, London,
Adapted from *The Wall Street Journal*, November, 8, 1993 and November 10, 1997

Appendix IV
Topic Review

Chapter One

I. Which of the following companies have a foreign currency exposure?

1. A U.S. manufacturer sells products internationally denominates its price sheets in the local currencies
2. A U.S. service provider contracting its services internationally and invoices solely in U.S. dollars
3. A distributor in the United states restricting its operations to the domestic market, but does some sourcing abroad
4. A U.S. producer only markets domestically, and only accepts invoices from foreign vendors denominated in U.S. dollars

1 only
1 & 3
1, 2 & 3
1, 2, 3 & 4

II. Laker Air was subjected to the following types of exposure:

1. Cash flow (non-contractual financial items)
2. Accounting (contractual financial items)
3. Operating (competitive position and market share)
4. Strategic (long range goals and mission)

1 & 2
2 & 3
3& 4
All of the above

III. A manufacturer can manage the foreign exchange risk of a Dutch guilder payable in several ways, including:

1. ____________________
2. ____________________
3. ____________________

IV. One of the first steps in a foreign exchange management program is to:

1. Find currency contracts to match the exposure
2. Look for a suitable foreign exchange dealer or broker
3. Identify areas of operation subject to foreign exchange exposure
4. Obtain an accurate price forecast of the currency creating the exposure

V. Foreign currency management is more important now than in the past because of:

1. An increasing number of pegged currencies
2. Increasing volatility in currency markets
3. An increasing number of foreign exchange transactions
4. Increasing stature of the U.S. dollar

1 only
1 & 2
2 & 3
2 & 4

VI. A German manufacturer previously invoiced in foreign currency, but now seeks to eliminate currency exposure by invoicing all foreign sales in Deutsche marks. This policy results in:

1. Eliminating accounting foreign currency exposure
2. Increasing total foreign currency exposure
3. Converting exposure from one form to another
4. Transferring exposure from one area to another

1 only
2 only
2 & 3
1, 3 & 4

VII. The most important criterion or criteria of a foreign currency management program is (are) that it:

1. Reduces or eliminates all exposures
2. Conforms to corporate policy and objectives
3. Reduces or eliminates operating exposure
4. Reduces or eliminates accounting exposure

1 & 2
2 only
2 & 3
2 & 4

Answers to Chapter One

I. (1, 2, 3 & 4) (1) and (3) are perhaps the most obvious examples of exposure. Any change in the rate of exchange between the dollar and the foreign currency impacts revenues or receivables (1), and liabilities (3). Not as obvious are examples of hidden exposure (2) and (4). (2) has exposure in each of its foreign markets. It is at a competitive disadvantage if the dollar strengthens. (4) can be adversely affected by foreign currency exposure, as well. If the currency of the vendor increases in value relative to the dollar, the vendor may increase the dollar price or discontinue supplying the producer.

II. (all of the above) Laker Air's revenue, or cash flow, depended on the US$ remaining at a low value in British pound terms. The relatively low value of the dollar helped induce British vacationers to travel to New York. In addition, Laker Air contracted accounting exposure in the same direction by entering into major long-term purchasing agreements denominated in U.S. dollars.

Operating exposure involves the company's competitive position. Laker Air's operation revolved around the perception that a shopping spree in New York made economic sense, a perception that changed with the exchange rate. Because the company's market niche was the New York-bound British vacationer, the exposure was strategic. Actually, Laker Air was exposed to a single risk—the variability of the dollar/pound exchange rate. This example illustrates that the differences between exposures are largely a matter of perspective.

III. The company might have an "escalator clause" written into the purchase agreement in which it is indemnified against foreign exchange loss, or it can buy guilders at the time the payable is contracted and hold them until the payment becomes due. Another way to manage exposure is to actively monitor the foreign exchange market, buying or selling guilders as the market dictates. A fourth way, is to hedge with a Dutch guilder derivative contract.

IV. (3) One of the first steps in a foreign currency management program is to identify the areas of operation subject to the exposure. In other words, first identify the risk, then find ways to manage it.

Exposure analysis may reveal that the risk is minimal, or that one exposure offsets another. Management decisions should take into account the fact that managing an exposure in one area sometimes creates an even greater exposure for the company in another area.

V. (2 & 3) There is sufficient evidence that the tremendous increase in the volume of currency trading has, in part, produced much greater volatility. Consequently, the risk of exposure has become too pronounced to leave unmanaged.

VI. (1, 3 & 4) Although accounting exposure is eliminated, the effect on total exposure is unknown because operating exposure has *increased.* The customer's ability or willingness to assume the exposure is now tested. Consequently, the risk transfers from one area (the balance sheet), to another (the market). Visible accounting exposure is converted into non-visible operating exposure.

VII. (2 only) The most important criterion is that the program fits within the overall policy of the company, and helps fulfill its short-term and long-term objectives. Unless this is accomplished, the program will almost certainly fail. Corporate objectives may well require an increase in one type of exposure to reduce another. Short of closing down operations, exposures can not be eliminated, only transferred. For this reason, (1) is an unrealistic objective.

Chapter Two

I. The three basic types of currencies are:

1 ______________
2. ______________
3. ______________

II. With regard to value, a fiat currency is:

1. Only as valuable as its redemption price
2. Intrinsically worthless, with price determined by legal tender laws
3. Intrinsically worthless, with price indeterminate
4. Only as valuable as its rate of interest.

III. A precedent in U.S. monetary policy occurred in 1862, when congress converted the "greenback" into "legal tender." As a result:

1. The U.S. dollar became a fiat currency
2. Non-acceptance of the U.S. dollar as payment of debt became illegal
3. Redemption of the U.S. dollar for gold became mandatory
4. Convertibility upon demand of the U.S. dollar into other currency became mandatory

1 & 2
2 & 3
1 & 4
1, 2 & 4

IV. So-called "hard" currencies are assumed to have certain properties, including:

1. Convertibility
2. Price Stability
3. Accessibility
4. Tradability

1, 2 & 3
2, 3 & 4
1, 2 & 4
1, 3 & 4

V. Assume that the Canadian dollar is worth approximately $0.73. Which of the following statements is correct?

1. The exchange rate of .72870 is an indirect quote.
2. The exchange rate of 1.3723 is a direct quote
3. The two quotes are ratios of each other
4. The two quotes are reciprocals of each other.

VI. The real rate of exchange varies: (select all that apply)

1. In direct proportion to the nominal rate of exchange
2. In indirect proportion to the nominal rate of exchange
3. Independently of the spot rate
4. Independently of the nominal rate

VII. Assume that the FC/HC rate is 1.00 in January. Six months later, it is 1.10. Prices in both countries remain unchanged. We know that: (select all that apply)

1. There was a change in the nominal rate of exchange
2. There was no change in the nominal rate of exchange
3. There was a change in the real rate of exchange
4. There was no change in the real rate of exchange

VIII. One U.S. dollar (HC) equals three units of FC1 and six units of FC2. Based on convention, which of the following statements is (are) expressed correctly? (Select all that apply)

1. One of the three exchange rates is 3.00
2. One of the three cross rates is .1666

3. One of the three exchange rates is 2.00
4. One of the three cross rates is .3333

IX. Explain why hyperinflation is more likely to occur in a monetary system based on a fiat currency than one based on a commodity-backed currency.

X. The government of a developing country pegs its currency to the French Franc. Recently, it increased its money supply to help finance a large government project. At the same time, it initiated a price freeze and terminated convertibility of the currency to prevent capital flight. These actions were necessary because:

1. The cross rate had changed
2. The price of the currency had changed
3. The value of the currency had changed

   1 only
   2 only
   3 only
   1, 2 and 3

Answers to Chapter Two

I. The three types of currencies are (1) *specie*, commodity currencies in the form of precious metal coins, (2) *commodity-backed*, which are redeemable upon demand for a commodity (gold or silver), and (3) *fiat*, nonredeemable paper issued as legal tender.

II. (3) Fiat currency is intrinsically worthless and considered by some scholars to be price indeterminate. This means that its value—specifically, its *external* value—is whatever the market will pay in terms of another currency (fiat or otherwise) at any given moment. Although it can be *sold* to a willing buyer, it can not be redeemed for anything of value; therefore, it has no intrinsic worth. It has *internal* value (purchasing power) only because of its legal tender status.

III. (1 & 2) To reiterate, the term *fiat* currency refers to a nonredeemable currency given legal tender status "by fiat," or government decree. *Legal tender*, as defined by the U.S. Legal Tender Act, is something that must be accepted (when tendered) in payment of "all debts, public or private." Although both commodity-backed and fiat currency may be given legal tender status, there is little need to compel acceptance of a currency that can be redeemed for precious metal. Legal tender acts provide an indeterminate amount of value to a currency; nothing in the acts stipulate *how much* legal tender must be accepted to satisfy a debt.

IV. (1, 3 and 4) "Hard" currencies are readily convertible (into other currencies), accessible (easy to acquire), and tradable (there are few exchange restrictions to limit market activity). Another characteristic is "ability to invest," implying an ample source of debt instruments denominated in the currency. Answer (2), *price stability*, is characteristic of "soft" currencies with restricted rates of exchange. Freely traded hard currencies are notoriously *unstable* with regard to price.

V. (4) .72870 and 1.3723 are reciprocals, which means 1.00 divided by either value equals the other value. (1) and (2) are incorrect because .72879 is a *direct* quote; it represents the number (or fractional amount, in this case) of U.S. dollars in one foreign currency unit. 1.3723 is an *indirect* quote, representing the number of foreign currency units in one U.S. dollar. These exchange rates can be expressed as ratios (the ratio of US$ to C$ is .72879 to 1, or US$/C$ = .72879), but they are reciprocals, not ratios, of each other.

VI. (4) Real exchange rates, which are based on the relative purchasing power between currencies, rise and fall independently of the nominal rate. The value differences between nominal and real rates change daily, resulting in price disparities between currencies that may last for years. (Note that "spot" refers to either the nominal or real rate.)

VII. (1 and 3) There is a change in both nominal and real rates of exchange. The nominal rate—price differential—increased approximately 10%. The real rate also changed; the currencies are no longer at parity because the internal value (purchasing power) remained unchanged in both currencies in spite of the change in external value or price.

VIII. (1) is correct, the others are incorrect. By convention, the term, *exchange rate* refers to two currencies, one of which is the U.S. dollar. The term, *cross rate*, refers to two currencies, *neither* of which is the U.S. dollar. We know, then, that the rate of exchange for the US$ and FC1 is either 3.00 or .3333, depending on how it is quoted. Likewise, the rate for the US$ and FC2 is either 6.00 or .1666. The cross rate refers only to FC1 and FC2; it is either 2.00 or .5000.

IX. Hyperinflation is a monetary phenomenon defining a runaway debasement (decrease in value) of the currency because of increased supply. Because a commodity-backed currency can be redeemed into the commodity that backs it (i.e., gold or silver) any major increase in supply of the currency would result in a growing demand for redemption. The finite supply of the commodity reserve, then, limits the amount of currency that can be placed in circulation. The supply of fiat currencies, however, can be increased indefinitely at little cost through use of the printing press.

X. (3 only) The *value* of the currency has changed, as demonstrated by the threat of capital flight. (1) is incorrect, because the *rate* is officially set, and remains constant compared to the French franc. In

(2), the *price* of the currency as defined refers to its external value, or what it can be bought or sold for in terms of other currencies. In this case, convertibility is precluded and the price officially established. Currency *value*, however, defines its real worth to the holder. Value can be measured in several ways, one of which is how willingly a person holds the currency rather than exchanging it for something else: another currency, goods, or services. The government actions in this scenario indicate that citizens hold the currency only because there is no other choice.

Chapter Three

I. Which of the following are examples of exchange rate regimes defined by the IMF:

1. Financial Rate
2. Composite Currency Peg
3. Export Rate
4. Managed Float

II. Currently, the exchange rate regime of the major European currencies, the Japanese yen, and the U.S. dollar is:

1. A floating system of some sort
2. A cooperative arrangement
3. A single-currency peg
4. Pegged primarily to the inflation index of the country

III. Between 1944 and 1971, the exchange rate regime of the currencies (in question 2) was:

1. A managed floating regime
2. A cooperative arrangement
3. A single-currency peg
4. A composite-currency peg

IV. A government may restrict its currency by employing various "multiple currency practices," including:

1. Fixing the exchange rate for certain types of transactions
2. Establishing parallel markets for foreign exchange purposes
3. Buying and selling the currency at a wider than normal spread
4. Taxing foreign exchange sales by commercial banks

1 & 2
1, 3 & 4
2, 3 & 4
All of the above

V. Which of the following "pegs" allows the least amount of nominal rate flexibility? Which allows the least amount of real rate stability?

1. Composite currency
2. Single currency
3. Indicator
4. Cooperative Arrangement

VI. The "Snake in the Tunnel" was replaced by the:

1. EMS
2. ERM
3. ECU
4. IMF

VII. The percentage weight of the Deutsche mark, French franc, Japanese yen, British pound, and U.S. dollar are calculated on a daily basis, based on exchange rate and relative trade importance of each. The value derived might be used to:

1. Update the value of a peg
2. Stabilize a currency
3. Settle an account
4. Produce a central bank bid or offer

1 & 2
1 & 3
2 & 4
All of the above

VIII. The monetary policy of government “A” is to prevent currency devaluation by inflationary forces. The rate of exchange is therefore re-calculated daily to ensure that it remains within policy guidelines. This is an example of an exchange rate regime known as a:

1. Adjustment to an Indicator
2. Managed float
3. Cooperative Arrangement
4. Composite-currency Peg

IX. Describe the two current trends involving currency arrangements.

X. The use of fiat currencies on a world-wide basis is a relatively new phenomenon. Many financial scholars believe there are severe shortcomings with a floating regime of fiat currencies. The primarily problem is:

1. Inflation
2. Exchange-rate controls
3. Multiple exchange rates
4. Volatility

Answers to Chapter Three

I. (2 and 4) Exchange-rate regimes defined by the IMF are:

Single-currency Peg
Composite-currency Peg
Limited flexibility *vis à vis* a Single currency
Cooperative Arrangements
Adjustment to an Indicator
Managed Float
Independent Float

(1) financial rate and (3) export rate are examples of officially established exchange rates for the purpose of restricting currency convertibility.

II. (1) Either a managed or an independently floating system. Freely traded currencies may be exchanged in any of the exchange rate regimes, from the most inflexible single-currency pegs to the most flexible floating regimes. Currently, the major currencies are all floating, with rates determined by the market. Governments often manage the "float" through intervention or interest rate changes. The rates of many key European currencies are "managed" within a range through a cooperative arrangement known as the *European Rate Mechanism.* The entire "raft" of currencies still float as a unit against currencies outside the arrangement..

III. (3) This was the era of the Bretton Woods system, based on a single-currency peg. The major world currencies were pegged to the U.S. dollar, which, in turn, was pegged to a fixed weight of gold. Although minor adjustments among the exchange rates were allowed, the system, in effect, fixed the price of every member currency through a gold standard. The collapse of Bretton Woods demonstrates the instability of a single-currency peg regime.

IV. (1, 3 &4) are common "multiple currency practices" used to restrict or control exchange rates. (2) *Parallel market*, in this context, is another name for *black market*, which, by definition, is never officially sanctioned. (3) refers to buying foreign currency at a discount and selling at a premium, sometimes practiced by a central bank to discourage capital flight from the country. (4) is an example of the practice of collecting taxes and granting subsidies. (Usually exports are subsidized, imports are taxed.) Dual or multiple market systems are also employed to restrict exchange rates.

V. (2) in both cases. The single-currency peg is the least flexible, in the sense that a currency pegged to another single currency is fixed in price, which becomes strictly a function of the other currency. (The only system more restrictive is the *unified currency system*, e.g. the euro.) Paradoxically, the single-currency peg is also the least stable in real rates. The currency peg, usually a floating major currency, is often subject to factors having nothing to do with the pegged currency. With no way of adjusting, the pegged currency is "carried along for the ride, price wise," which may create major swings in purchasing power parity, destabilizing the economy.

VI. (1) EMS. The "Snake in the Tunnel, " as it became known, was a composite-currency peg system of European currencies known as the Warner Plan. It superseded the Bretton Woods system. The objective of the Warner Plan was to peg all member currencies to a single composite, the first step toward a unified currency regime. Found to be too restrictive, it was replaced with the European Monetary System (EMS). Within this system, European central banks devised a pricing formula called the European Rate Mechanism (ERM). The end product was a composite currency called the European Currency Unit (ECU). The ECU, a currency in its own right, was used as the peg for other currencies within the EMS. This in turn, is being replaced with the euro.

The International Monetary Fund (IMF) was established in 1944, along with the World Bank, during the Bretton Woods conference.

VII. (All of the above). This is the procedure for determining the daily value of the SDR, a composite used as an exchange-rate peg. The continuously updated value is central to the stabilization of currencies that are priced based upon it. The SDR, along with the ECU, is used to settle accounts between governmental agencies, as well as between commercial interests. Both pegs are used to determine the price at which central banks buy or sell certain currencies.

VIII. (1) Adjustment to an Indicator. The currency is adjusted more or less automatically to a selected indicator—the inflation rate, in this case. When adjusted in response to a *relative* inflation rate (domestic inflation compared to the rates of inflation for major trading partners), the real rate of exchange remains stable even though the nominal rate may fluctuate widely. Brazil, for example, issued a proxy currency called the ufir a few years ago. The *ufir* was indexed to inflation (the country was in the grip of hyperinflation at the time) and used as a unit of account for collecting tax revenues.

IX. The major trend, found primarily in developing countries, is toward greater convertibility. These countries are abandoning less flexible systems, such as single-currency and composite-currency pegs, for systems with greater flexibility, such as floating systems. Mexico is a case in point. A counter-trend, however, is taking place in the industrialized countries, which seek ways to reduce volatility that goes along with a floating regime. The drive toward a unified currency by the European community is an example. The sometimes heated debate over the return to the gold standard is another.

X. (4) Volatility. Up until the demise of the Bretton Woods system (1971), fiat currency was the exception, rather than the rule. Historically, currencies were backed by something of intrinsic value, usually gold or silver. The supply/demand factors of precious metal served as constraints on the supply of currency, stabilizing exchange rates. Today, no such constraints exist; each government is free to debase its currency to whatever extent it deems necessary or expedient. In a floating regime with no price constraints, and with unlimited convertibility, turmoil in the foreign exchange markets is now commonplace.

Chapter Four

I. The PPP theory states that parity between currencies is maintained primarily by:

1. Cooperative arrangements
2. Arbitrage
3. Intervention
4. Inflation

II. A company books a one-year payable denominated in a foreign currency. The treasurer decides to manage this exposure by monitoring PPP and hedging whenever the foreign currency starts to lose purchasing power vis à vis the home currency, creating a change in rates. What is wrong with this approach?

III. Which of the following statements most accurately describes inflation?

1. A decline in the purchasing power of a currency because of decreased demand for credit
2. A decline in the purchasing power of a currency because of increased supply of currency
3. A rise in the price of goods because of increased demand for goods
4. A rise in the price of goods because of decreased supply of goods

IV. Apparently, during the 1990s, the U.S. Federal Reserve began giving more attention to a new set of indicators to predict the direction of the economy. These indicators include all of the following except:

1. The commodity price index
2. The producer price index
3. The consumer price index
4. The adjusted monetary base

V. The Current Account measures:

1. The net flow of goods and services
2. The net foreign capital inflow
3. The trade deficit
4. The capital account balance

 1 & 2
 1, 2 & 3
 3 only
 All of the above

VI. Explain how the U.S. trade deficit affects the U.S. Capital Account balance.

VII. The Federal Reserve's policy objectives concerning the management of the exchange rate of the U.S. dollar at one time or another included the following:

1. To counter disorderly markets
2. To keep exchange rates in line with underlying economic fundamentals
3. To foster stability of exchange rates around current levels
4. All of the above

VIII. The Federal Reserve "manages the float" by:

1. Dirty intervention
2. Sterilized intervention
3. Jawboning
4. Adjusting the fed funds rate

 1 & 2
 1, 3 & 4
 2, 3 & 4
 All of the above

IX. Describe the problems of managing the float.

X. The Chairman of the Federal Reserve is about to make a major announcement regarding the dollar. You are a currency trader with a substantial speculative position in Japanese yen. Your most prudent course of action is to:

1. Ignore the announcement because the Federal Reserve has only a minor influence on exchange rates;
2. Listen to the announcement, analyze the situation, then close the position if the move is warranted;
3. Instruct your foreign exchange dealer to get you out of the position immediately after the announcement if it will adversely effect your position;
4. Give up the chance for profit and get out of the position before the announcement

Answers to Chapter Four

I. (2) Arbitrage. Purchasing power parity occurs when there is free movement of goods and services across borders so competitive forces can bring prices (including currency prices) into parity with each other. Parity is achieved when profit-making opportunities based on a disparity of currency values no longer exit.

II. Changes in PPP do not necessarily correspond to changes in exchange rates, especially over the near term. PPP is more suitable as a long-term indicator (5 years or longer). Even then, predictive ability of PPP relates to changes in *real* rates, not nominal rates. (Exposure of a payable involves the risk of nominal rate change.)

III. (2) Inflation is most accurately described as a monetary (not economic) phenomenon, resulting from an increase in the supply of money; therefore, inflation is controlled by monetary policy rather than fiscal policy or foreign exchange markets.

IV. (4) The adjusted monetary base, which includes M1 and M2, measures the amount of currency in circulation. Changes in money supply have been less reliable lately as economic predictors, perhaps because of changes in public expectation regarding money supply growth rates. In the 1990s, the Fed appeared to have turned from money supply numbers to various price indices as indicators of current and future economic conditions.

V. (All of the above) The Current Account balance (the *trade deficit* when negative, the *trade surplus* when positive) is the value of exports of goods, services, and income less the value of imports of goods, services, and income (plus unilateral transfers). The trade deficit equals the net foreign capital inflow, which is the same as the Capital Account balance.

VI. The trade deficit can be identified as the U.S. dollars *exported* to pay for goods and services which exceed in value all foreign currency *imported* to pay for goods and services. These dollars must be returned, if not for goods and services, then for IOUs and assets, producing a net foreign capital inflow. Changes in this inflow reflect changes in the balance between U.S. assets abroad and foreign assets in the United States; in other words, the capital account balance. Such changes can have a pronounced, albeit indeterminate, impact on exchange rates.

VII. (4) All of the above. These are various policy positions entered into with other G-5 or G-7 member banks. They are listed in chronological order, demonstrating a tendency of the Federal Reserve to become more restrictive in its management of the floating rate regime.

VIII. (2, 3 & 4) The Federal Reserve manages the (floating) exchange rate by sterilized intervention, threats of intervention, and through open-market committee efforts (buying and selling overnight repos) to "tweak" the fed funds interest rate. It may also adjust the discount rate to make a much more emphatic statement. Changing the "earning power" of a currency usually has a direct (but not always predictable) effect on the exchange rate. Sterilized intervention has a limited short-term effect; "sterilization" refers to the practice of buying and selling dollars in the foreign exchange markets without changing the overall supply.

The Federal Reserve conducts sterilized intervention only. (A managed float is sometimes referred to as a "dirty float"; there is no "dirty intervention.")

IX. Managing an exchange rate through intervention requires international cooperation; effective intervention can only be accomplished when central banks buy or sell in concert. Such cooperation is often lacking because of conflicting national interests; for example, one country may wish to depreciate its currency to obtain a trade advantage, but to the disadvantage of its trading partners who are asked to help coordinate the move.

For the same reason, "jawboning" with threats of intervention has had less and less effect of late; the foreign exchange market can absorb all but the most rigorous buying or selling pressure exerted by a central bank, or even several central banks. Sterilizing the intervention makes it less effective because the bank adds back to the system every dollar it removes—or subtracts every dollar it adds—during the intervention process. The net supply of currency in circulation remains the same, but the geographic location of the currency has changed.

Finally, changing interest rates simply to increase or decrease the value of the currency often has an unwanted effect on the domestic economy. Central bankers who support other nations' currency policies by creating havoc at home tend not to enjoy a high degree of job security.

X. (4) Since this is a judgment call, there is no right or wrong answer. The question asks for the most *prudent* course of action. Most prudent, less adventuresome traders would get out of their positions *before* the announcement, giving up a potentially large profit to avoid a potentially large loss. (Because this is a speculative position and not a hedge, any loss would be a real loss.)

(1) is wrong because the Federal Reserve can have a momentous effect on the market *in the short term*, even though the medium- to long-term effect is much more muted. (2) and (3) would not prevent a loss. Currency markets react instantaneously; a major move could easily occur long before a close-out trade could be executed.

Chapter Five

I. Interest rate parity between the U.S. dollar and a foreign currency involves four variables. These variables do *not* include:

1. The interest rate for the foreign currency
2. The interest rate for U.S. dollars
3. The degree of arbitrage taking place
4. The (new) spot rate

II. A trader feels that the interest rate of a foreign currency is about to increase *vis à vis* the U.S. dollar. He buys the currency, assuming that its value must also increase to maintain interest rate parity. Is this a sure bet, assuming he is right about the interest rate change?

III. Which of the following statements are true? (select all that apply)

1. The difference between spot and forward exchange rates depends on the difference in Eurorate yields
2. The difference between spot and forward exchange rates depends on the difference in nominal interest rate yields
3. The difference between spot and forward exchange rates depends on the difference in real interest rate yields
4. An increase in the interest rate of a foreign currency, relative to the U.S. dollar, will result in forwards increasing in value, relative to spot

IV. Assume that a company owns a one-year receivable denominated in a foreign currency, FC. The FC eurorate equals LIBOR less 1%. The company decides to hedge the exposure with a one-year futures contract. It will (select one):

1. buy futures at a premium to spot
2. buy futures at a discount to spot
3. sell futures at a premium to spot
4. sell futures at a discount to spot

V. A foreign central bank suddenly drops its key overnight rate. LIBOR remains unchanged. In regard to the country's currency, we know that: (select all that apply)

1. The impact on the forward rate is greater than the impact on spot
2. The impact on spot is greater than the impact on the forward rate
3. The forward rate increases relative to spot
4. The forward rate may increase, decrease, or remain the same

VI. A corporate treasurer plans to purchase one-year debt instruments as a short-term investment. He can choose among instruments denominated in three currencies; Foreign Currency "A" with a 6% yield, Home Currency "B" with a 5% yield, and the U.S. dollar with a 7% yield. All foreign exchange risk is to be avoided by hedging. Which of the three currencies offers the highest earnings? (Ignore transaction costs)

1. The earnings are the same for all three
2. Foreign currency "A"
3. Home currency "B"
4. The U.S. dollar

VII. Assuming that changes in the "before" and "after" diagrams are the result of a change in interest rates, what are some of the observations that can be made about the diagram in Figure 5-11 on page 430?

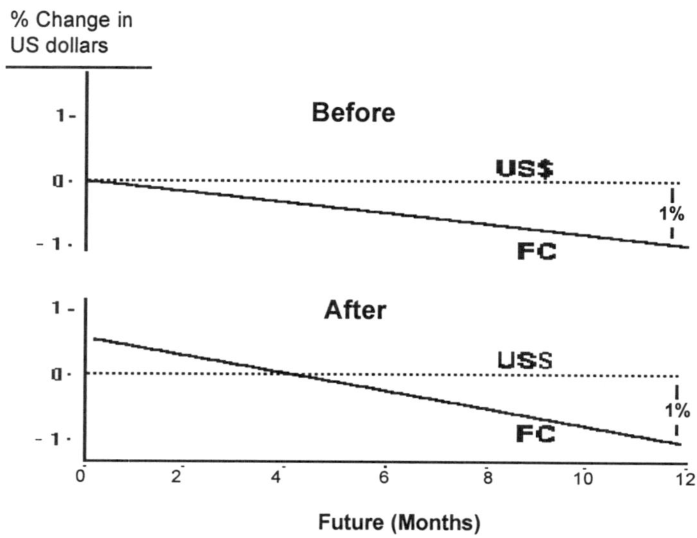

Figure 5-11: Interest Rate Result Changes

VIII. Some investors trade in and out of currencies to maximize interest rate earnings. Why is this "hot money" game a risky venture?

IX. Complete the following statement: "Differences between the spot and forward exchange rates for any two currencies are the ________________ between the same two currencies."

X. A money manager purchases a 30-day forward. Three weeks later he sells a 30-day forward. What entries are posted in his FX account after the sale?

Answers to Chapter Five

I. (3) is correct. The presence or absence of arbitrage has little to do with interest rate parity. Parity is not due to price discrepancies being "traded away." The new spot rate (4) is an indicator of the "future prospects" of the U.S. dollar (compared to the future prospects of the foreign currency). Spot is determined *in part* by variables (1) and (2); interest rate parity is expressed by the change in forward rates created by the change in spot.

II. No. The only certainty involving an increase in the interest rate is that the forward value of the foreign currency will decrease relative to spot value. This occurs because anticipated depreciation, which defines the interest rate, has increased (there now being more interest to "wring out"). The spot value, however, can move independently of changes in the interest rate. Whether it responds by going up, down, or remaining unchanged depends, in part, on whether the increase involves real as well as nominal interest rates, and how it is perceived by the market.

III. (1 & 2) The difference between spot and forward price expresses the difference between the relative eurorates. (3) is incorrect; remember that the *quoted* value is always a *nominal* value. (4) is false because a higher relative interest rate translates into a forward discount, not a premium.

IV. (3) Futures identify currency forward rates. The receivable represents an asset; therefore, the company hedges by selling—not buying—FC forward. LIBOR is the interest rate paid for eurodollars, so we know that FC has a lower interest rate yield than the U.S. dollar. A lower yielding currency is a premium currency, so the company sells the one-year futures at a premium to spot.

V. (3 & 4) All we can deduce from the drop in the interest rate relative to LIBOR is that the forwards will increase in value relative to spot. We have no idea where spot will go relative to the U.S. dollar; therefore, we cannot know beforehand whether the central bank action will cause a greater price change in spot, a greater price change in forwards, or an equal change in both, *vis à vis* the dollar. The resulting dollar value of a forward rate is completely dependent on the new dollar value of the spot rate, whatever that may be.

VI. (1) With transactions costs ignored, all options result in the same return of approximately 6%. (Note that the U.S. dollar is a foreign currency because it is not the home currency of the firm.) If the treasurer chooses the home currency instrument, he simply purchases the instrument and holds it for one year to earn 6%. There is no foreign exchange risk, and no need to hedge. If he chooses the foreign currency "A" instrument, he must purchase the instrument at spot, and sell the currency forward at a 1% premium. The end result is a 6% yield. If he purchases the U.S. dollar instrument, a treasury bill, for example, he must hedge by selling U.S. dollars forward at a 1% discount, again with the net result of a 6% investment. This "all rates equal one" phenomenon is the result of covered *interest rate parity.*

VII. Observations to be made might include the following:

1. There is a change in the nominal exchange rate, as shown in the price increase between spot and forward rates. It cannot be determined whether there is a change in the real exchange rate.
2. The FC interest rate yield was 1% over LIBOR (the U.S. rate) before, and approximately 1½% over LIBOR after the change.
3. FC strengthened relative to the U.S. dollar.
4. The one-year forward rate did not change; the impact of the change was limited almost totally to the spot rate; spot values that increase or decrease in tandem with interest rates values indicate changes in the real rate of interest, not just the nominal rate.
5. It cannot be determined whether the FC interest rate increased, LIBOR decreased, or both, nor can it be determined whether the change in interest rates (and the exchange rate) forecast stronger prospects for FC or weaker prospects for the U.S. dollar.

VIII. The only way to capture a higher yield by exchanging currencies is to leave the currency unhedged. As discussed above (question 6), the act of hedging the exchange rate results in giving back any additional interest earned. Exchange rates are usually more volatile than interest rates; therefore, assuming exchange rate risk to capture yield is a risky practice.

IX. Differences between the spot and forward exchange rates for any two currencies are the e*urorate yield differences* between the two currencies. Actually, any interest rate differential can be employed to find comparative values among currencies. Some are more accurate than others. As a rule, very short-term money market rates are most appropriate because they produce less variance in credit and country risk. Eurorates are chosen because of they are most standardized.

X. These are two positions in the account, one a purchase, the other a sale. Each has a different value date. Once a forward position is taken, it assumes a specific value date (e.g., a June 17th forward). A forward having the same value date must be used to close out the initial purchase or sale.

Chapter Six

I. The currency market consists of:

1. The cash market
2. The interbank
3. The currency pits
4. The over-the-counter market

1 & 2
2 & 3
1, 2 & 3
1, 2, 3 & 4

II. In dollar value, how much foreign exchange was transacted global-
ly in the currency markets daily in 1996?

1. $10 million
2. $50 billion
3. $1 trillion
4. $10 trillion

III. What percentage of the above transactions took place in the interbank?

1. 8%
2. 32%
3. 51%
4. 96%

IV. Which of the following quotes might be made by a foreign exchange dealer? Which by a futures broker?

1. British pound at 1.5600
2. Deutsche mark at 1.3793

3. British pound at .6410
4. Deutsche mark at .7250

V. The Deutsche mark is at 1.4119. A foreign exchange dealer quotes Deutsche marks "17 bid ask 21." This means:

1. I buy DM at 17 and sell at 21
2. I buy dollars at 17 and sell at 21
3. I buy DM at 21 and sell at 17
4. I buy dollars at 21 and sell at 17

VI. The best description of a spot/forward swap is:

1. Taking delivery of spot and selling it forward
2. Buying spot and selling forward
3. Rolling spot forward
4. Selling spot and buying forward

1 & 4
1 & 2
3
2 & 4

VII. Foreign exchange dealers are normally compensated by:

1. An undisclosed flat fee
2. A commission on the spread
3. A profit (or loss) when the trade is closed out
4. The spread between the bid and the offer

VIII. Explain why the speculator is a vital participant in the futures markets.

IX. Identify components A, B, C, D, and E in Figure 6-10 on page 436.

Figure 6-10

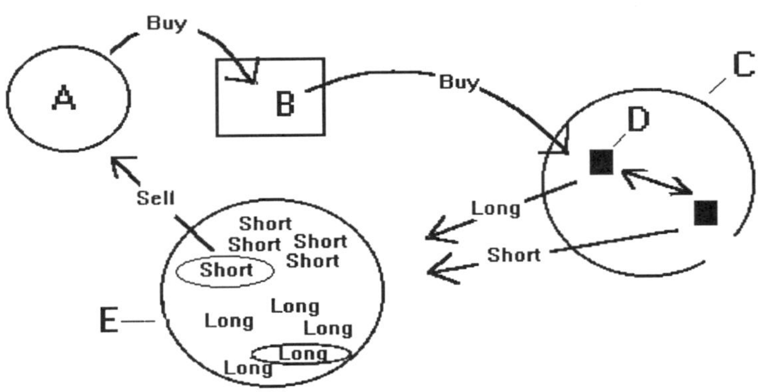

X. Which, if any, of the following statements are true?

	U.S. $ equiv.		*Currency per U.S. $*	
Country	**Tues.**	**Mon.**	**Tues.**	**Mon.**
Canada (Dollar)	.7388	.7391	1.3536	1.3530
30-day Forward	.7386	.7389	1.3539	1.3533
90-day Forward	.7382	.7386	1.3547	1.3539
180-day Forward	.7375	.7379	1.3560	1.3552

1. This is a listing of the Canadian dollar futures contract
2. The first two columns are interbank quotes
3. The last two columns are direct quotes
4. The Canadian-dollar Eurorate is less than LIBOR

Answers to Chapter Six

I. (1, 2, 3 & 4) The interbank is by far the largest, with the other markets trading derivatives of the underlying interbank spot values. "Currency pits" are the trading arenas of the futures exchanges. Currency options also trade, both over-the-counter and on various futures, securities, and options exchanges.

II. (3) Approximately one trillion dollars worth was exchanged daily. This figure pertains to the *notional* value or the size of the contract, rather than actual outlays.

III. (4) 96%. The other markets account for a thin slice of the interbank business. Still, that is approximately $40 billion worth of foreign exchange every day.

IV. Foreign exchange dealers: (1) & (2). Futures brokers: (1) & (4). The prices, 1.5600 and .7250, are *direct* quotes, referring to the amount (whole or fractional) of U.S. dollars in one unit of foreign currency. 1.3793 and .6410 are *indirect* quotes, referring to the amount (whole or fractional) of foreign currency units in one U.S. dollar. The foreign exchange dealer, in accordance with interbank tradition, quotes indirectly. The futures industry uses direct quotes. There are exceptions: the British pound is quoted directly in both markets.

V. (2) The dealer will buy dollars at 1.4117 and sell them at 1.4121. The interbank convention is to buy and sell U.S. dollars for other currencies. "17" and "21" are indirect quotes; the lower value translates into more dollars per foreign currency unit, the higher value into fewer dollars; therefore, the dealer buys more dollars at "17" and pays out fewer dollars at "21."

VI. (2 & 4) A swap is identical in configuration to a futures calendar spread, in which one month is bought and the other month is sold. "Tomorrow/next" swaps can be viewed as "one day-two day" spreads; "spot/next" swaps as "two day-three day" spreads, "spot/forward" swaps as "two day-more than two day" spreads, and forward/ forward swaps as "more than two day-more than two day" spreads. There is an exception to these comparisons. The spot CD/$ rate is a one day—not two day—forward rate.

VII. (4) Foreign exchange dealers operate as principals who buy and sell at different prices when dealing with customers and other dealers.

VIII. Speculators gives the markets the liquidity and depth required to ensure ease of entry and exit at a fair price, important considerations to the currency hedger.

IX. Customer (A) issues a buy order to his or her broker (B) who, in turn, relays the order to the exchange floor (or desk or pit) (C) where the order is filled. The "floor" broker (D) fills orders for his clients, made up largely of brokerage firms. He fills the order by transacting with an exchange member (another floor broker or floor trader, either hedger or speculator). The "fills" go to the clearinghouse, or clearinghouse "pool" (E), the custodian of member positions and funds. In the process, the clearinghouse becomes the counterparty to each purchase (long) and each sale (short). The clearinghouse records the transaction in the broker's account, and in the customer's sub-account. The broker (and by extension, the customer) and clearinghouse are now counterparties to a contract; each is responsible to the other for order fulfillment.

The open interest is the number of open contracts currently in the pool. Only one side is counted because each pair of longs and shorts makes up one contract. (Note that longs and shorts in the pool must always be equal in number.) In this case, the open interest is 3 contracts.

X. None of the statements are true. This is a listing of forwards, not futures. Futures contracts are only quoted in specific months; i.e., March, June, September, and December. The first two columns are direct quotes, used for futures pricing, the last two columns are indirect interbank quotes. The Canadian-dollar Eurorate is higher than the Eurodollar (LIBOR) rate; we know this because it is a discount currency (the forwards are lower than spot).

Chapter Seven

I. According to at least one study, the following economic indicator(s) was (were) shown to have some predictive value in forecasting currency prices:

1. Changes in productivity
2. Changes in consumer prices
3. Changes in anticipated depreciation
4. Changes in interest rates

II. Which of the following statements most accurately describe the Efficient Market Hypothesis?

1. Free markets instantly discount all available information
2. Free markets are more volatile than closed markets
3. Price forecasting in a free market is pointless
4. Future price changes result from "random walk" movements

III. According to many analysts of market sentiment, the most powerful dynamics of the market are:

1. Strong and weak hands
2. Price trends and market waves
3. Greed and fear
4. Intervention and speculation

IV. Each of the following individuals holds a sizable position in Swiss francs. In theory, which is the strongest hand? Which is the weakest?

1. The experienced floor trader with $1,000,000 in trading equity
2. The dentist with a $125,000 futures account
3. The investment manager of a $500 million dollar portfolio
4. The treasurer hedging an exposure for a small ($25 million) manufacturer

V. A technical analyst derives opinions about future price direction by:

1. Reducing currency fundamentals to a set of equations
2. Quantifying market information by analyzing the traders
3. Reviewing past market activity to the exclusion of everything else
4. Analyzing currency fundamentals with economic models

VI. Figure 7-9 illustrates what type of price chart? Describe the price movement for the three days shown.

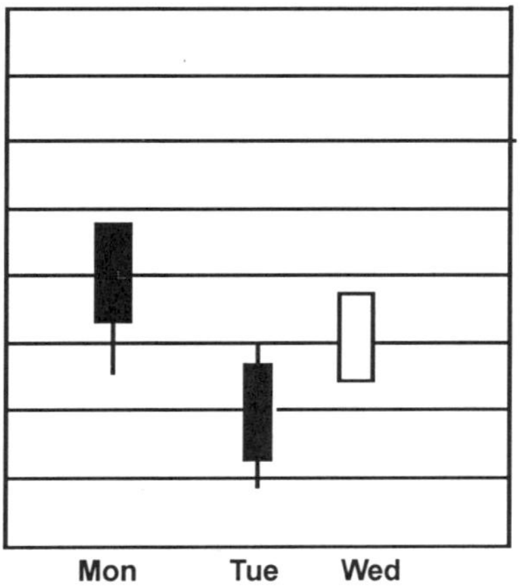

VII. As a general rule of thumb, most experienced traders will (select all that apply):

1. Sell against the trend, but near the top of the market to catch the new trend down
2. Buy on a sharp trend downward to catch the bounce
3. Place orders to buy at a point just over the chart resistance
4. Place orders to buy at a point just over the chart support

VIII. According to Elliot wave theory, the common characteristic of all natural progression is to:

1. Proceed in a series of waves that are equal in magnitude
2. Trend in four waves forward and two waves backward
3. Proceed in a "random walk" that is indicative of chaos
4. Trend in five impulse waves and three corrective waves

IX. Changes in trading volume and open interest appear to have predictive value. Based on these indicators, which of the following predictions are warranted?

indicator:
The market is trending higher. Volume and open interest are decreasing.
prediction:
1. The market is strengthening, the trend should continue
2. The market is weakening; a top is near

indicator:
The market is trending lower. Volume and open interest are increasing.
prediction:
3. The market is weakening; the trend should continue;
4. The market is strengthening, a bottom is near

X. The currency market is becoming more efficient due to the increasing trading volume and the ever-increasing speed of data dissemination and analysis. What will be the effects of this on day-to-day trading? (select all that apply)

1. Fundamental analysis will become less useful
2. Technical analysis will become less useful
3. Fundamental analysis will become more useful
4. Technical analysis will become more useful

Answers to Chapter Seven

I. (3 & 4) Changes in interest rates are probably the most important indicator for predicting (spot) exchange rates. A study by Eric Sharp also shows a correlation between anticipated depreciation and exchange rates. The same study, however, found no relationship between exchange rates, the GDP, and the CPI.

II. (1) The Efficient Market Hypothesis states that free markets instantly discount all available information. This implies that fundamental analysis is practically useless for trading purposes because the impact of new information is in the price before any orders from outside the market can be filled. In short, everything known is already in the market. In today's world of instantaneous communication, the Efficient Market Hypothesis is persuasive.

III. (3) According to market sentiment watchers, the markets are fueled primarily by greed and fear. Fear is the greater motivator of the two; losers are more prone to cut their losses than the winners are to take profits. This adds to market momentum, often resulting in major price moves beyond all apparent reason.

IV. Strong and weak hands (indicators of "staying power") do not necessarily coincide with the amount of capital available to the position holder. Theoretically, the treasurer is the strongest hand; his objective is to manage risk, not to make a trading profit. A loss—regardless of the magnitude—is simply offset by the exposure and has no influence on the trading decision. The actions of the investment manager, on the other hand, are very much determined by the profit or loss accruing in his portfolio. The weakest hand is held by the floor trader, who is very quick to take small losses before they grow into large losses. His main concern is the preservation of trading capital; he knows there will always be another time.

This answer must remain theoretical in nature because market participants do not always act in accordance with their circumstances. In the real world, hedgers are not immune to market losses, and legions of even the most experienced traders have "crashed and burned" by not following their trading rules (lack of discipline).

V. (3) Reviewing past market activity to the exclusion of all other information. A "pure" technical analyst is a staunch defender of the

Efficient Market Hypothesis, believing that any information derived from outside the market is useless for trading purposes. Technical analysis predicts future moves by studying the "internal structure" (historical price movement) of the market. Most "technicians" uses price charts as their primary tool of the trade.

(4) describes fundamental analysis; (2) describes market analysis, the measurement of sentiment, commitments of traders, etc. (1) defines econometrics, which is the technical analysis of fundamentals rather than of the market.

VI. This illustrates a candle stick chart. Originally developed by the Japanese, in recent years it has become quite popular among American chartists. It displays the same type of information as a regular bar chart (open, high, low, close), but in more graphic form. A dark "candle" represents a down move; white, an up move. The top and bottom of the cylinder portion represent the opening and closing price, the total candle height represents the daily price range.

We know, then, that on Monday the market opened at the top of the range and closed down (but not on the low of the day). Tuesday, the market opened lower and closed lower still. During the day, the market traded above the opening and below the closing price. Wednesday, the market opened higher, never traded below its opening, and closed on the high of the day.

VII. (3 & 4) Most experienced traders will not try to predict the top or bottom of the market. Rather, they wait until a trend becomes established, then go with it. "Fighting" the trend is too often a losing battle; a common characteristic of price moves is to continue beyond expectations.

Traders buy over resistance (which has given way, since the market is trading above it) and over support (which is expected to hold, based on probabilities). In like fashion, they sell under resistance, expecting it to hold, and under support, after it has broken. Trading is more of an art than a science; many successful traders use different signals and pay little heed to general rules of thumb.

VIII. (4) Elliot wave theory contends that the progression of price movement (and the movement of practically every other natural force) is a five wave sequence, designated 1 through 5, followed by three corrective waves, *a* through *c*. This predictability, according to wave theorists, is inherent in all chaotic, or non-linear, systems.

IX. (2 & 3) Increased volume shows increasing "popularity" of the move; increased open interest shows that the market is attracting new traders, who want to buy (in an up market) or sell short (in a down market). Increased volume and open interest, therefore, add momentum to the current trend, either up or down. The trend should continue or perhaps accelerate. When volume and open interest start to "dry up," it indicates that momentum is slowing. Both buyers and sellers are exiting and a market reversal may be imminent.

X. (1 & 2) There is no question that fundamental analysis gives little advantage to a trader in a market that accounts for all new information in the blink of an eye; With increasing frequency, transactions based upon the analysis of such information arrive too late to capture profits. Today more than ever, "inside information" in currency trading is a myth. Perhaps surprisingly, even technical analysis may suffer in a very crowded, fast market place. As technical analysts, all analyzing the same market, try to outwit one another, the market becomes faster and thus more difficult to get in or out before the crowd.

Chapter Eight

I. Foreign currency exposure can be most accurately defined as:

1. An asset or liability denominated in a foreign currency
2. Sourcing or selling in a currency other than the home currency
3. A currency mismatch
4. An open foreign exchange position

II. A company has a foreign currency exposure if:

1. It is at risk of an adverse move in currency value
2. Has the opportunity to gain from a currency move
3. It has taken a market position in foreign currency
4. It is involved in foreign operations

1 & 2
1 only
1, 3 & 4
3 & 4

III. One of the first steps in developing a currency management program, after identifying a foreign currency exposure, is to:

____

____

IV. The primary risk of operating exposure is its effect on:

1. Assets and liabilities
2. Cash receivables and payables
3. Operating performance and income
4. Plant and equipment

V. The primary risk of accounting exposure is its effect on:

1. Assets and liabilities
2. Cash receivables and payables
3. Operating performance and income
4. Competitive position

VI. The two major types of accounting exposure are:

1. ______________________
2. ______________________

VII. Hedge accounting practices have important implications regarding:

1. Earnings
2. Interest expense
3. Taxes
4. Currency swaps

VIII. According to FASB 52, hedge accounting provisions stipulate that hedging vehicles must have "like characteristics" such as:

1. Contractual nature
2. Same or like currency
3. Known value
4. All of the above

IX. Foreign exchange gains and losses resulting from *non-functional* currency transactions are reported:

1. On the income statement
2. In the shareholder's equity section
3. In the letter to the shareholder
4. On the consolidated balance sheet

X. Foreign exchange gains and losses resulting from *functional* currency transactions are reported:

1. On the income statement
2. In the shareholder's equity section
3. In the Letter to the Shareholder
4. On the consolidated balance sheet

XI. Cash flow exposure primarily effects the corporate:

1. Operating variance
2. Competitive position
3. Current assets and liabilities
4. Cash flow variance

XII. The primary risk of operating exposure is its effect on:

1. Assets and liabilities
2. Cash receivables and payables
3. Market share
4. Plant and equipment

XIII. Operating exposure (check all that apply):

1. Bears no necessary relationship to accounting exposure
2. Pertains to nominal rather than real rates of exchange
3. Is not necessarily associated with the currency in which prices are quoted
4. Is not necessarily associated with the country in which products are sold or inputs sourced

XIV. The management of operating exposure must take into account both the nature of the company and its:

1. Profit margin
2. Competition

3. Current financial performance
4. Financial commitments

XV. Explain the difference between strategic and value-based exposure.

Answers to Chapter Eight

I. (3) A foreign currency exposure is a currency mismatch in some area of the business. A mismatch is indicated if the business is sensitive to a change in currency values.

II. (1 & 2) Although exposure is usually associated with risk of loss, it also implies opportunity for gain. (3) & (4) may or may not indicate exposure. It depends on whether the company is sensitive to changes in currency values.

III. Quantify it in terms of risk.

IV. (3) Operating exposure refers to foreign exchange effects on the operating performance of the company, including operating income and flexibility. This involves such functions as sales, marketing, procurement and customer service, and others.

V. (1) Accounting exposure impacts the financial reports of the company, including financial performance, assets and liability changes, and contractual arrangements.

Because these measurements appear on the financial statements, accounting exposure is the most visible. (2) pertains to cash flow exposure. (3) and (4) are sensitive to operating exposure.

VI. *Transactional* and *translation* exposure. The difference between the two depends on whether the currency mismatch results from a non-functional currency (transaction) or a functional currency (translation). Transactional exposure is also referred to as "balance sheet exposure." Translation exposure is less obvious; it may show up as "consolidated after tax exposure" due to its impact on foreign operations or subsidiaries.

VII. (3) Hedge accounting, in practice, means deferred accounting. Tax reporting of hedge results is deferred until the foreign exchange gain or loss on the exposure is realized (or vice versa). The two are then netted out to determine the tax credit or debit. Currently, hedge accounting practices are limited to accounting exposures.

VIII. (4) All of these elements are "like characteristics." Accepted accounting definitions must also be taken into consideration. FASB

52 identifies a bona fide hedge for accounting purposes as one that (a) offsets an identifiable foreign currency commitment, (b) is designated as, and effective as, a hedge, and (c) must be a firm commitment in its own right.

IX. (1) Non-functional foreign currency transactions are those conducted by a company in a currency other than its own. Foreign exchange losses and gains from such transactions flow through to the income statement as an expense against operating income. This is known as "transactional exposure."

X. (2) Functional currency transactions are conducted in the home currency of the operation. They only produce an accounting exposure when they are translated on a balance sheet denominated in a different currency (the parent company functions in a different currency). The resulting gains and losses appear in the shareholder equity section of the balance sheet as "translation exposure."

XI. (1) Operating variance. Cash flow exposure is dynamic, unlike static "snap shot" values produced by accounting exposure. Gains and losses resulting from cash flow exposure can be identified by comparing the operating income from one period to another, and highlighting variances due to exchange rate fluctuations. This process is known as "variance analysis."

XII. (3) Market share. Operating exposure refers to the effects that changes in foreign currency value have on the competitive position of the company, the capacity of its customers to purchase the product or the service, and the ability of suppliers to furnish inputs.

XIII. (1, 3 and 4) Operating exposure is determined by the structure of the markets in which the company and its competitors source inputs and sell products.

Note that this exposure produces profits and losses from real-not nominal-exchange rate changes. Changes in real exchange rates impact the purchasing power of the currency. This has a direct bearing on the customer's capacity to purchase as well as the company's capacity to source.

XIV. (1 & 2) Operating exposure focuses on short- to medium-term cash flow, operating margin, sales volume and market share. (3) and (4) concern accounting exposure.

XV. Strategic and value-based exposure both impact short- to long-term operating performance, profitability, and cash flow. Both are measurements of change in real, as well as nominal, exchange rates. Both are managed with consideration given to long-term strategic options.

Unlike strategic exposure, however, value-based exposure affects all aspects of the business, including short-term financials (which are ignored when managing from a strategic exposure position). Value-based exposure management considers both monetary and non-monetary values and objectives by focusing on the overall corporate mission.

Chapter Nine

I. Examples of long and short positions might be:

1. Assets and liabilities
2. Production costs and sales receipts
3. Opposite positions of equal value
4. All of the above

II. An account is exposed to foreign currency risk if:

1. The account shows a mismatch of currency positions
2. Both long and short positions are included in the account
3. The account includes open currency positions
4. Items in the account are denominated in different currencies

III. Complete the following statement.

A hedge is the offset of a given position by an __________ position, in which the effect of the offset __________ the effects of a value change in both.

IV. Calculate the resulting gain or loss in the following hedge example. Explain why the hedge worked as intended, even though there is a net gain or loss. (Figure 9-15 on page 453)

V. "Big and Best," a U.S. office supply company, imports a line of paper products from Canada. It reduces its foreign exchange exposure of this product line by establishing a manufacturer's outlet in Vancouver and transferring the risk to the market place. Does the Vancouver outlet invoice in local or home currency?

Figure 9-15: Hedge Example

Action	Cash Market	Interbank
Book Receivable Sell Forward	Long BP 12,000,000 spot at 1.4775	Short BP 12,000,000 180 day forward at 1.4673
Six months later...		
Collect Receivable	BP spot at 1.4625	
Buy back forward		Long BP 12,000,000 at spot
Gain (loss)	?	?
Net Gain (loss)	?	

VI. When a particular price correlates significantly with the price of a related item in another market, the two markets are:

1. Converging
2. Convertible
3. Parallel
4. Establishing a basis

VII. Basis can be defined as:

1. The price difference between two markets
2. The correlation between two markets
3. The convertibility between two markets
4. The amount of gain or loss on the hedge position

VIII. Hedges should be placed in markets that correlate at a coefficiency of no less than:

1. 30%
2. 50%
3. 70%
4. 100%

IX. The "hedge triad" includes the following hedging methods *except for:*

1. Operational Strategies
2. Financial Adjustments
3. Currency Swaps
4. Transactional Hedging

X. Hedging with derivatives may entail certain risks, including:

1. Credit risk
2. Leverage risk
3. Exchange risk
4. Liquidity risk

Answers to Chapter Nine

I. (4) All of the selections are examples of long and short positions. A "long" is defined as a position that benefits the holder by an increase in value. A "short" is defined as a position that benefits the holder by a decrease in value. Conversely, a decrease in value of a long, or an increase in value of a short, adversely effects the holder.

II. (1) Foreign exchange exposure exists only when there is a *mismatch of currency positions.* This means that an existing long (or short) position is not offset by a short (or long) position equal in value and duration. Whether this condition exists in (2), (3) or (4) is indeterminable.

III. A hedge is the offset of a given position by an *equal and opposite position*, in which the effect of the offset *reduces or eliminates* the effects of a value change in both.

IV. The receivable dropped $180,000 in value from date of contract to date of collection. The corresponding decline in the short forward is $57,600, resulting in a net loss of $122,400. The hedge worked, effectively shielding the long exposure from changes in the rate of exchange. The loss is due entirely to the higher interest yield of the British pound. Actually, the hedger suffers no loss if the higher yield of the British pound is taken into account in the price of the receivable.

V. Local currency, which is Canadian dollars. We can assume that the company is invoiced for the paper products in Canadian dollars because there is a foreign exchange exposure. The Vancouver outlet acquires local currency revenue to help offset the short position. By selling in local currency, the foreign exchange risk is transferred to the market place rather than to the customer or supplier.

VI. (3) Parallel. To be considered a hedge, offsetting positions must be placed in parallel markets. The key to parallel markets is "significant correlation." (4) Basis relates to any two markets, but if prices do not correlate significantly, the basis is not predictable and, hence, not useful for hedging purposes.

VII. (1) The basis can be defined simply as the price difference between two markets. The basis may show positive price correlation, negative correlation, or no correlation.

VIII. (3) 70%—with conditions. There is no magic coefficient that serves as a cut-off point for hedge transactions. Some hedgers will not enter a market that has a correlation of less than 80% or higher. Basis risk is *usually* unacceptable under 70%. It should be noted, however, that basis risk is practically non-existent when simple currency forwards or futures are used for hedging because the forward (futures) market is a function of the spot market.

IX. (3) The currency swap is only one vehicle (of several) utilized in transactional hedging. In general, operating strategies are used for strategic and value-based exposures with very long time horizons. Financial adjustments and transactional hedging are most effective for short- to long-term accounting and cash flow exposures, with possible applications for certain operating exposures.

X. (1 & 4) The use of derivatives in a hedging program often involves *credit risk* and *liquidity risk.* Other risks associated with derivatives are *market risk*, *settlement risk*, *operations risk*, *legal risk*, and *basis risk*.

Chapter Ten

I. Complete the following statement. "For corporate management purposes, it is useful to define foreign currency exposure as the sensitivity of ___________."

II. Developing a currency management program should begin with a sensitivity analysis. This means the manager (select all that apply):

1. Measures corporate values
2. Defines the most appropriate hedging techniques
3. Identifies the exposures impacting corporate values
4. Measures the sensitivity of a particular value to a particular exposure

III. Defining corporate values as current and future cash flows helps to identify:

1. Strategic exposure
2. Cash flow exposure
3. Value-based exposure
4. Current and anticipated exposure

IV. One important factor influencing the success or failure of a start-up currency management program is the:

1. Future price action of the currency
2. The ability to perfect market timing
3. The quality of chart analysis made available
4. The corporate culture

V. According to modern Portfolio Theory:

1. No pain, no gain
2. Potential reward should compensate for the level of risk taken
3. Except for short-term government instruments (U.S. treasury bills) no return is guaranteed

4. A manager's level of tolerance for personal investment risk and business risk are much the same

VI. The most important attribute of an information system is its:

1. Sensitivity to new inputs
2. Ability to retrieve data quickly
3. Simplicity
4. Ability to process information quickly

VII. The price chart is an important tool of an information system. The manager's most important rule to follow in the use of price charts is:

1. To update the charts personally on a regular basis
2. To select the most reliable price data vendor
3. To select the type of chart (bar, point and figure, candlestick) that best fits the management style
4. To review the market activity on a regular basis with the price data vendor

VIII. An effective currency management program, regardless of the type of exposure managed, should adhere to four basic principals. Two of these are:

1.____

2.____

IX. There are at least seven reasons why currency management should be a team effort. Three of these are:

1.____

2.____

3.____

X. A written policy manual for the currency management program should address the following questions: (select all that apply)

1. Will performance be based on hedged or unhedged positions?
2. Will forwards or futures be purchased to hedge a market position?
3. Who is responsible for overseeing the program?
4. Which type of exposure is to be given management priority?

Answers to Chapter Ten

I. For management purposes, it is useful to define foreign currency exposure as the "sensitivity of some corporate objective variable to changes in foreign exchange rates."

II. (1, 3 & 4) The manager measures (or quantifies) values, identifies exposures, and determines the sensitivity of the value to the exposure. Defining hedging techniques comes later in the program.

III. (3) Value-based exposure can be best defined by equating corporate values with various cash flows of the business entity. Value-based exposure is identified in a five step process: (1) identify the relevant cash flows; (2) determine the value to the company of each cash flow; (3) identify the factors that enhance cash flow value; (4) determine sensitivity of these factors to currency exposure; (5) focus on exposures having the most impact on the selected factors.

IV. (4) The corporate culture is a key factor in whether the currency program ever gets off the ground. Corporate culture is the amalgamation of senior management's opinions, perceptions, and misconceptions, including those regarding risk and exposure.

V. (2) According to modern Portfolio Theory, the amount of reward must compensate for the level of risk undertaken to capture that reward. In other words, the greater the risk, the greater the (anticipated) reward. This relationship is used to construct questionnaires that measure risk tolerance levels. Statement (4) is the presumption that validates such measurements.

VI. (3) Simplicity is paramount in developing an information system. The chances of receiving reliable information in a predictable manner depends almost completely on how easily—and how routinely—the data can be gathered, analyzed, and transmitted.

VII. (1) The manager should update the charts personally on a regular basis. This is, by far, the best way to maintain a "feel" for the market, and to stay on top of events as they unfold.

VIII. The four basic principals that should underlie all currency management programs are: (1) to effectively protect profits; (2) to promote continuity of business; (3) to enhance competitiveness both at home and abroad; (4) to promote good citizenship both at home and abroad.

IX. The following statements are seven arguments for team formation (the concept is key; the wording is optional):

1. Value-based exposure involves the impact of foreign exchange in all areas of the business. No one individual can monitor all of them.
2. Currency management draws on knowledge and expertise from many disciplines, including sales, marketing, engineering, and finance
3. Currency management may involve board resolutions, information systems and forms, foreign exchange accounts, and other items and activities that cross functional lines of authority.
4. Teams facilitate the communication of updated information across functional lines, necessary for monitoring the markets and updating the management plan.
5. Senior management involvement is crucial for the acceptance of the program's objectives, and should be present during goal setting.
6. Team members offer needed support and encouragement during the "down" times.
7. Currency management decisions and results must be completely and consistently disclosed. The team acts as a check and balance system.

X. (1, 3 & 4) A policy manual should address strategic, not tactical, decisions. Specifics such as the selection of contracts or the timing of a hedge can be covered by the hedge model or trading rules, but should not be considered general policy matters. When policy becomes too cumbersome, the program is prone to indecisiveness and second guessing.

Chapter Eleven

I. The management of a toy manufacturer has made certain currency management decisions regarding a popular line of toys that it produces in Italy and markets throughout Europe and the Middle East. Match each decision with the type of currency exposure it addresses.

A. Accounting exposure
B. Cash flow exposure
C. Operating exposure
D. Strategic exposure

1. Fourth quarter inventory located in Milan will be hedged
2. The company will continue to manufacture in Italy
3. European distributors will receive a price increase. Middle Eastern distributors will continue with current price sheets
4. Distributor price sheets will be denominated in local currency for European markets, and in Italian lira for Middle Eastern markets

II. The Fordoche Company has determined that its U.S. manufacturing operations produce long positions in certain foreign currencies. Explain how this might occur.

____

____

III. Developing an operating strategy to hedge currency is suitable for: (select all that apply)

1. Operating exposure
2. Cash flow exposure
3. Strategic exposure
4. Value-based exposure

IV. Strong currency invoicing is an example of:

1. A financial adjustment
2. Cash flow exposure
3. Hedge accounting
4. Long-term transactional hedging

V. The results produced by financial adjustments must be monitored on a daily basis and the hedge "readjusted" to conform with the current price trend of the currency being managed.

1. True
2. False

VI. A manager closes out a long forward Spanish peseta position and simultaneously buys peseta forwards for a value date farther in the future. This is an example of a:

1. Foreign exchange swap
2. Currency spread
3. Forward roll-over
4. Transactional hedge

VII. Which two factors determine the periodic payment between the counterparties of a currency swap?

1. ______________________
2. ______________________

VIII. Since payments are exchanged periodically throughout the duration of a currency swap, why must one party make a compensation payment when the swap is closed out?

____

____

IX. One method of consolidating exposure is to permit a manufacturing or marketing unit to invoice in foreign currency and then sell the receivable to a unit created by the parent corporation specifically for that purpose. This is known as:

1. Netting
2. Reinvoicing
3. Factoring
4. Centralized settlements

X. The following factors should be considered in the siting of a currency netting or consolidation unit:

1. Tax implications
2. Foreign exchange regulations
3. Political considerations
4. Communications

Answers to Chapter Eleven

I. (1-A) The consideration whether or not to hedge inventory is a current financial decision involving an accounting exposure. (2-D) The major, long- range decision to manufacture in Italy is an example of strategic exposure management planning. (3-C) Marketing and engineering decisions that affect short- to medium-term operating performance are operating exposure considerations. (4-C) or (4-B) Decisions regarding currency denomination of future revenue and expenses can be based on either operating or cash flow exposure management considerations, depending on circumstances.

II. Fordoche competes domestically against Canadian dollar cost-based products. An increase in the Canadian-dollar value therefore translates into a competitive advantage for Fordoche, giving the company a long Canadian dollar position. Also, from the standpoint of competitive pricing, exports to foreign countries create long foreign currency (short U.S. dollar) positions relating to those countries.

III. (1, 3 & 4) Operating strategies are usually long-range, major decisions involving a restructuring of the operation, with all the expense and time that entails. This type of currency hedging, therefore, is suitable only to long-term exposures intrinsic to the business. Cash flow exposure effects usually are temporary and measured over a much shorter duration of time.

IV. (1) Strong currency invoicing is an example of a financial adjustment for hedging purposes. Other financial adjustments are home currency invoicing, home currency sourcing, same currency sourcing, long-term, fixed-rate borrowing, and leading and lagging. All of these might be appropriate responses to cash flow exposure, as well as short- to medium-term operating exposures.

V. (2) Hedges in the form of financial adjustments might or might not be subject to changes based on a market view or forecast. Medium-term (six months to a year) or long-term (one year or more) market views might call for readjustments to the hedge, but changes based on daily, or even weekly, price moves are almost always inappropriate for this type of hedging method.

VI. (3) Closing one forward position and simultaneously reinstating the same position at a later value date is called a forward roll-over. Roll-overs can be effected on a routine basis to replicate long-term borrowing of the currency. (4) assumes that the roll-over is implemented for hedging purposes, which may or may not be the case.

VII. The two factors that determine who pays and how much are (1) the difference in interest rate yields of the two currencies, and (2) the difference in credit ratings of the two parties. These factors together determine the amount of debt service each pays to borrow the currency exchanged in the swap.

VIII. The swap is initiated at a specific spot rate of exchange for the two currencies. During the life of the swap, changes in interest rates (reflected by changes in the forward rate) are offset by periodic payments equal to the interest rate differential. Changes in the spot rate are not a function of interest rates and are not offset until the swap is closed out. At that time, the final payment compensates the party which incurs the foreign exchange loss from the change in spot.

IX. (3) The distinctive feature of factoring is that the receivables are actually *sold* to the factoring unit (at a discount), which then assumes profit and loss responsibility for its collection and for any change in the exchange rate. A reinvoicing unit (2) underwrites the exchange rate between the time the invoice is issued and the time it is collected. It does not actually purchase the invoice.

X. (1, 2, 3 & 4) These are all considerations that should be taken into account when setting up a consolidation unit. The tax structure, the political situation, and foreign exchange restrictions of the host country are important factors in the success of the operation. Of course, the factors involved in moving funds rapidly, securely, and efficiently between countries also must be carefully weighed.

Chapter Twelve

I. Items or activities that can produce transactional exposure include:

1. A payable denominated in a foreign currency
2. The sale of a fleet of airliners to a foreign corporation
3. A job bid on a project in another country
4. The labor costs incurred by a foreign subsidiary

II. The CEO and the CFO of a corporation often view currency exposure in different ways. The CEO may place a higher priority on the management of operating exposure. The CFO often considers accounting exposure the most troublesome. What accounts for the difference is perspective?

____

III. One important objective of a hedge model is to:

1. Plan a course of action ahead of time
2. Insure that the hedge complies with corporate objectives
3. Provide assurances that no unwarranted risk is being taken
4. All of the above

IV. A company sells abroad on very thin margin and invoices in local currency. Management has little tolerance for foreign exchange loss. An appropriate currency management program could incorporate a:

1. Range hedge model
2. Classic 100% hedge model
3. Trend following model
4. Option strategy

V. A company feels that its currency management efforts should produce a profit. It is willing to tolerate a high degree of market risk. The least appropriate hedge model for this objective is a:

1. Range model
2. Classic 100% hedge model
3. Trend following model
4. Option strategy

VI. The most popular trading system for hedging purposes is:

1. Black box
2. Top- and bottom-picker
3. Trend follower
4. Elliot wave

VII. The frequency of false signals generated by any trading system is ____________ to its level of sensitivity.

1. Directly proportional
2. Indirectly proportional
3. Unrelated
4. Finely tuned

VIII. An effective trading unit for managing accounting exposure consists of: (select all that apply)

1. The company's hedge policy
2. An accounting system
3. An information system
4. A check and balance system

IX. A trading unit analyzing currency to develop a hedge strategy should pay close attention to: (select all that apply)

1. The exchange rate regime
2. The historical volatility of the currency
3. The medium- and long-term price range
4. The broker's near-term trading advice

X. A successful currency management program will be developed around:

1. A specific currency price
2. Corporate objectives
3. The currency price trend
4. The transactional hedge instruments

Answers to Chapter Twelve

I. (1, 2 & 3) Items (1) and (2) may produce assets and liabilities on the balance sheet denominated in a foreign currency. (3), although a contingent liability, produces a transactional exposure. Item (4) is a translation—not transactional—exposure since costs are incurred in the functional currency.

II. Whereas operating exposure is perhaps more pervasive than accounting exposure, it is often hidden from view. Accounting exposure is very visible, and appears in the financial reports for which the CFO is directly responsible.

III. (4) An effective hedge model is a pre-determined plan of action within acceptable risk parameters which furthers the goals and objectives of the company.

IV. (2) An appropriate hedge in this case would be a classic 100% hedge. 100% of the exposure is hedged 100% of the time. This model keeps the chance of both opportunity gain and market loss to an absolute minimum. The margin is therefore secured.

V. (2) In this case, the classic 100% hedge would be the least appropriate because it precludes any chance of gain from exchange rate moves. Possibility of gain must be a part in any program that is expected to increase—and not just protect—profitability. Of course, the program may not be profitable, but loss-producing instead. The tolerance for market risk must be high enough to allow for this.

VI. (3) Trading with the trend is favored by most traders; therefore, the most popular type of trading system for hedging, as well as for speculating, is the trend following system. Attempts to pick tops and bottoms is always a riskier venture because it requires trading *against* the trend. Elliot waves are difficult to discern and often perplexing to all but the most ardent student. "Black boxes," or systems generating buys and sells based on unseen, proprietary signals require a great deal of faith—usually more than corporate managers are willing to muster.

VII. (1) Directly proportional. The more sensitive the trading system, the more readily it will generate false signals (for example, a buy signal just before the market drops). On the other hand, the more insensitive the system, the less chance that it will generate any timely signal, false or otherwise. A profitable trading system depends on fine tuning of signal sensitivity.

VIII. (1, 2, 3 & 4) These items should all be incorporated in a trading unit. Also included should be the hedge model, specific trading rules, outside information resources, and service providers.

IX. (1, 2 &3) The analysis should include the currency characteristics, such as its record of volatility and its correlation with other currencies, that might provide natural hedges. Short-term trading advice has little relevance when developing a hedging strategy.

X. (2) All currency management programs should begin with corporate objectives foremost in mind. The program is best constructed from the "bottom up," (determining the results desired and building from that point.) Current price and direction are not useful information for program development because they are subject to constant change. The choice of markets and hedging vehicles, such as forwards or options, are tactical decisions that should be made on a case-by-case basis within the framework of the program's objectives and policies.

Chapter Thirteen

I. Which of the following client advantages are offered by the foreign exchange dealer? By the futures broker?

1. Ready access to a 24-hour market
2. No margin deposit requirement
3. Personalized service
4. Full disclosure of client costs

II. What conflict of interest might a client encounter with the foreign exchange dealer?

____

III. Ralph, the currency manager, has developed a close business relationship with Nick, the futures broker. Ralph holds a market position to hedge a six-month payable. Nick calls Ralph to inform him that CPI figures are to be released after the close. The "talk on the street" is that the dollar will react negatively. He advises Ralph to cover the hedge and reinstate it the next morning at a better price. Nick has advised Ralph on several occasions to get out of the market in front of major economic reports. Is this good advice?

1. Yes
2. No

IV. There are two basic types of orders. These are:

1. Verbal and written
2. Open and closed
3. Immediate and deferred
4. Day and GTC

V. Three basic types of order designations are (select all that apply) :

1. Market orders
2. Ex-pit orders
3. OB orders
4. Stop orders

VI. A client is informed that the current market price is 7650. He instructs his broker to buy at 7690. This constitutes a:

1. Price limit order
2. Loss limit order
3. Stop order
4. Stop limit order

VII. A limit order is *not* appropriate for the following conditions or objectives (select all that apply):

1. A volatile market
2. A thin market
3. Liquidating a hedge
4. Capping a loss

VIII. What are the two leading types of losses as caused by trading derivatives?

IX. A hedger suffers two back-to-back losses on his derivative trades. First, his company took a $100,000 dollar market loss. Secondly, a miscommunicated order resulted in a $20,000 loss. Which of these losses should be of greater concern to the company? Why?

____

____

X. One major trading rule is to "know your position." This is especially important when:

1. Trading futures under volatile market conditions
2. Selling forwards in a thin market
3. Entering into a currency swap agreement with a solid AAA counter-party that affords you a number of options
4. Purchasing options on futures contracts

Answers to Chapter Thirteen

I. (1) and (2) are advantages offered by the dealer. The interbank market trades 24 hours a day, so trades can be initiated at any time—assuming the dealer provides 24-hour access. Trading in currency futures is limited to regular trading hours (7:20 AM to 2:00 PM, CT, for the Chicago Mercantile Exchange). Note, however, that some brokers and exchanges provide access to foreign exchanges for round-the-clock trading capability. In regard to (2), trading through a bank dealer is based on a line of credit. No margin is required.

(3) and (4) are advantages offered by many futures brokers. The relationship is more personal, especially if the broker is located nearby. Brokerage transaction costs are fully disclosed, whereas dealer transaction costs are included in the spread.

II. The dealer buys *from* and sells *to* the client, rather than *for* the client. This may constitute a major conflict of interest because a favorable price to one is unfavorable to the other. The conflict exists because normally the dealer does not disclose his profit on the trade. One way to ensure a fair price is to obtain quotes from more than one dealer (and let each know you are shopping around). This involves a bit of "fancy footwork" on the phone because quotes change every few seconds..

III. (2) Lifting positions in front of news may be prudent for speculation; it is almost never appropriate for hedges.

The major conflict of interest involving the client-broker relationship is the fact that the broker is compensated only when a trade occurs, regardless of the resulting profit or loss to the client. The conflict is significant because the personal relationship between the client and the broker often promotes client dependence on the broker for advice.

IV. (4) The two basic types of orders are Day and GTC. Day orders expire at the end of the day in which they are issued. GTC, or good till canceled, orders remain in effect until they are filled or canceled by the client. Many foreign dealers do not accept GTC orders. Some brokers and exchanges now cancel GTC orders after a certain period of time, such as 30 days, which must then be reinstated by the client. This reduces the chance of a forgotten order that fills unexpectedly.

V. (1, 3 & 4) The three basic order designations are market, OB (or limit) and stop orders. *Market* orders fill immediately at whatever price is available. *Limit* and *stop* orders specify a certain price, and do not fill unless, or until, that price occurs.

VI. (3) This is an example of a stop order. The buy price is higher, or the sell price is lower, than the current price. It is often used to close out a position in order to stop a loss from accruing, or to limit the size of the loss. It may also be used to enter the market on a price break-out above resistance or below support.

VII. (3 & 4) The liquidation of a hedge assumes that the purpose of the hedge no longer exists. At that point, any market position becomes speculative, a risky position for any risk manager to undertake. The same holds true when attempting to limit a loss by "playing the market" to improve the position. The rule is to just get out—immediately—or enter a stop order.

(1 & 2) When there is no compelling reason to get in or out of the market immediately, volatile, thin, and choppy markets are best traded with limit orders to improve the chance of receiving the desired price.

VIII. The leading type of loss is *market loss*, in which the market simply goes the wrong way. The second leading type is loss due to error, usually in the form of miscommunication between the client and the dealer or broker. There are numerous ways for errors to occur. Buying instructions are relayed as sells or vice versa; a limit order becomes a market order; "GTC" is marked instead of "DAY," etc.

IX. The first loss of $100,000 should be no cause for concern. Market losses are intrinsic to hedging. No matter how costly, they should be tolerated as the opportunity cost of hedging.

The second loss of $20,000 should create a great deal of concern. Errors should not be tolerated, no matter how minor. First, they represent *real* losses, with little or no chance of recovery. Secondly, they are preventable. The vast majority of errors can be avoided by (1) taping the phone conversations relating to order entry, and (2) requiring that the dealer or broker to read back the order *verbatim.*

X. (3) All hedge strategies require due diligence and careful monitoring. The swap, however, with its customized provisions (embedded options) is the most complex. It is the complexity—not the risk—that results in a break-down of understanding regarding the direction of the hedge. Not knowing whether the company is net long or short is an obvious road to disaster. This demonstrates the importance of another trading rule, which is stress testing the model. The more complex the hedge, the more important is becomes to devise "what if" scenarios to make sure the corporate position under any condition is well understood.

Chapter Fourteen

I. The dollar value of a C$1,000,000 contract quoted at 1.3329 can be calculated in the following manner:

1. Multiply the quote by the number of units
2. Divide the quote by the number of units
3. Divide the number of Canadian dollars by the quote
4. Divide 1.00 by the quote, then divide by the number of units

II. Hedging a foreign currency exposure valued at $5,000,000 with forward contracts requires a foreign exchange credit line of $5,000,000.

1. True
2. False

III. A currency manager wishes to hedge a 1.5 million British pound liability for one year with forward contracts. He finds, however, that value dates farther out than 6 months are too thinly traded for desirable pricing. He therefore:

1. Sells 3 million British pounds six months forward, then buys 1.5 million pounds spot six months later
2. Sells 1.5 million British pounds for six months, allowing the remaining six months to go unprotected
3. Initiates a swap by selling 3 million pounds spot and simultaneously buying 1.5 million pounds six months forward
4. Sells 1.5 million pounds six months forward, then rolls the position over for another six months on or before the value date

IV. The above-mentioned manager sells British pound forwards at 1.55. Two days later, the price drops to 1.54, resulting in a credit in the foreign exchange account. The manager can:

1. Withdraw the credit since it is payable upon demand

2. Withdraw the amount of the credit that exceeds the margin required
3. Not withdraw the credit because it must remain in the account
4. Transfer the credit to an interest-bearing account, as long as it remains with the bank

V. The 1.5 million British pound liability is unexpectedly paid one month before the forward contract matures. The manager therefore takes the following action:

(1)____

The payment is unexpectedly delayed for an uncertain period of time after the exposure matures. The manager therefore takes the following action:

(2)____

VI. A "perfect hedge" is one in which the gain or loss from the exposed position precisely offsets the loss or gain from the hedge position, leaving a zero balance. The perfect hedge almost never occurs, because of: (select all that apply)

1. Interest rate differentials
2. Differences in time and duration
3. Slippage
4. Transaction costs

VII. Match the following characteristics with the market with which it is best associated, interbank or futures exchange:

1. Disclosure
2. Liquidity
3. Credit risk
4. Flexibility

VIII. With a proxy hedge, such as the sale of the U.S. dollar index against long positions in European currencies, a greater amount of consideration should be given to:

1. Market risk
2. Basis risk
3. Basket risk
4. Transaction risk

IX. A currency manager hedges a Mexican peso receivable by buying futures contracts. The receivable is due May 15th. The futures prices for Mexican pesos are:

June .11940

Sept. .11070

Dec. .10320

The manager decides to buy Dec. because it is the lowest priced. Why is this a mistake?

____

X. Explain why futures hedges should be placed in the *same* or the *next nearest* contract month to the exposure whenever liquidity permits.

____

____

Answers to Chapter Fourteen

I. (3) The value of a contract that is quoted indirectly, such as this one, is calculated by dividing the number of currency units by the price. (1,000,000 divided by 1.3329 equals $750,244). Multiplying the quote by the number of currency units (1) determines the dollar value of contracts quoted directly.

II. False. The credit line is used to credit or debit only the difference between the current price and the initial price of the forward contract. A forward valued at $5,000,000 would have to drop to zero value before the entire amount is debited. (Or, if sold short, the price would have to double.) The size of the credit line required can be estimated by analyzing the historical volatility of the currency over the span of time that the forward position remains open.

III. (4) The manager hedges the amount of the exposure with the most distant forwards that are hedgeable, in this case, six months. When the forward value date arrives, he closes out the contract by buying it back and simultaneously selling another forward for the same amount six months forward. This is called a *roll-over*, or *rolling the hedge forward.*

IV. (3) and (4?) The position is marked to the market each trading day, with credits and debits entered in the account after the close. In general, credits accruing in a foreign exchange account are not available, but remain in the account until the position is closed out; however, some banks offer flexibility in this regard, based on their relationship with the client.

V. (1) The manager simply buys the contract by buying a forward that has the same value date as the original forward. On the value date, both contracts become spot and cancel each other out, leaving a net credit or debit in the account.

(2) The manager buys the contract back. If he buys on the value date of the forward, he actually buys spot currency, not a forward. Since the forward is now also a spot position, both positions are netted out, the same as above. Upon entering the buy order, the manager simultaneously enters a sell order for a new forward with a new value date one or two days out. When that forward also becomes spot, the process is repeated. These roll-overs take place

automatically upon request, and are known as a *spot-forward* or *tomorrow-next swaps*.

VI. (1, 2, 3 & 4)—All of these factors influence the amount of gain or loss on the hedge position. (1) The greatest price disparity between the two markets derives from interest rate yield differences. The exposure is valued at spot, whereas the hedge is valued at the forward or futures price. (2) The hedge position and the exposed position may be closed out at different times, resulting in different prices. (3) Derivative prices may vary from their implied spot price because of market conditions at the time the trade was made. (4) The transaction cost, whether a part of the spread or a separate commission, must be factored into the gain or loss on the hedge.

VII. (1) *Futures exchange*. The cost of transaction, comprised of commission and fees, are separate items not included in the price of the currency. (2) *Interbank*. This is the most liquid market in the world, with over $1 trillion dollars worth of currency traded daily. It trades 24 hours a day, unlike the exchanges that are active only during regular trading hours. (3) *Futures Exchange*. The exchange, through its clearing operations, guarantee every side of every contract. There has never been a loss to the client due to default. (4) *Interbank*. Every tradable currency can be bought or sold for any future value date, as long as banks for both currencies are open for business on that date.

VIII. (2) Basic risk. Even parallel markets that correlate highly, such as spot and its derivatives often display price variances due to timing and other market characteristics. Proxy hedges involve markets interrelated to a much less degree. Without the ability to convert, without the assurance of convergence, price correlation may break down altogether. This results in an especially high basis risk for most proxy hedging strategies.

IX. The receivable is due May 15th, at which time the manager must sell the futures contract. Assuming that interest rate differentials remain somewhat stable, he ends up buying low and selling low, for no additional gain. He does pick up a greater basis risk because of the length of time between the futures last trading date and the day he must liquidate it for whatever its price at the time.

X. If the exposed position outlasts the hedge position, an additional transaction must be undertaken to reinstate the hedge. Besides the extra transaction cost, unnecessary risks relating to basis and interest rate fluctuations are introduced. If the hedge position outlasts the exposed position, it is a simple matter to liquidate the hedge early with little additional risk. This is why either the same or *next* month beyond the exposure liquidation should be chosen.

As implied in answers 8 and 9, the risk does increase when the contract being liquidated still has a significant amount of time remaining before it can be converted to spot. For this reason, the next *nearest* month should be chosen when selecting futures contracts.

Chapter Fifteen

I. Without knowing either the trade or the market price, which of the following is certain to have a positive value:

1. A long futures contract
2. A long futures option
3. A long forward contract
4. A long currency spread

II. A trader exercises an option. We know, therefore, that:

1. The trader is long and takes a profit
2. The trader is short and takes a profit
3. The trader is long and takes a loss
4. The trader is short and takes a loss

III. A buyer exercises a PHLX cash option by exchanging his Deutsche marks for U.S. dollars. We know, therefore, that the buyer exercised:

1. A U.S. dollar call option
2. A Deutsche mark call option
3. A U.S. dollar put option
4. A Deutsche mark put option

IV. A buyer who wishes to exercise a PHLX call option for French Francs must first establish:

1. A foreign exchange account in the United States
2. A futures account in the United States
3. A cash account in France
4. A futures account in France

V. The options below refer to Mexican peso futures options. Which of the following traders are long pesos? Which are short?

1. A buyer of a call option
2. A buyer of a put option
3. A writer of a call option
4. A writer of a put option

VI. The option premium is composed of one or both of two components. These are:

1. Delta
2. Strike price
3. Time value
4. Intrinsic value

VII. How does the accounting of a short option position differ from that of a long option position? Assume the positions pertain to call options on futures.

____

VIII. Under what circumstances would a company hedge an accounting exposure with options rather than forwards or futures contracts? (Select all that apply)

1. The exposure is conditional, and not contractual
2. There is a high tolerance of market risk
3. There is low tolerance of market risk
4. The company wants the opportunity to profit in foreign exchange

IX. A company hedges a liability by buying 5200 calls and selling 5400 calls. This is an example of a:

1. Classic hedge
2. Timing hedge
3. Range hedge
4. Selective hedge

X. A currency manager intends to hedge a 10,000,000 French franc position with cash options. After analyzing recent volatility, he purchases options for 30,000,000 francs. This is an example of:

1. Over hedging
2. Texas hedging
3. Speculating
4. Delta hedging

Answers to Chapter Fifteen

I. (2) An option, by definition, is an asset with positive value. The buyer of an option has acquired certain (valuable) rights that afford him the opportunity to profit without the risk of loss. (Rights that are unavailable with the other choices.) It is interesting to note, therefore, that the phrase, "buying" or "selling" a futures or forward contract is a misnomer. Rather, traders take long or short positions in the market. Value, either positive or negative, occurs only after the market moves away from the transaction price.

II. (1) The trader is long (he is the buyer) and takes a profit. The seller's option might be exercised, but sellers do not exercise. Only the buyer to whom he sold the option has that right. And because exercise is a right—not an obligation—the buyer will exercise only to take a profit.

III. (4) A Deutsche mark put option. The Philadelphia Stock Exchange only trades foreign currency options, so it can not be (1) or (3); therefore, it is a Deutsche mark call or put. The Deutsche mark call conveys the right to "buy" Deutsche marks, the put conveys the right to "sell" them. We know it is a put because the option buyer is, in effect, selling Deutsche marks for dollars.

IV. (3) A cash account in France. PHLX options are cash options. (Options on futures trade on the CME.) Whereas options on futures are exercised into futures contracts (a deferred exchange of currency), cash options exercise into spot (an immediate exchange of currency). Because the option is a call, the buyer is exchanging dollars for francs and must have a cash account in France into which the francs can be deposited.

V. (1) and (4) are long pesos. (2) and (3) are short. Note that the question refers to long and short peso positions, not *option* positions. Option writers (sellers) are, by definition, short options. An easy way to avoid confusing the two is to remember that holders of long currency positions profit when the currency goes up; holders of short currency positions profit when the currency goes down. In this example, the call options increase in value when the peso rises in value; the puts increase in value when the peso price declines.

VI. (3 & 4) Premiums are made up of time value plus intrinsic value, if any. Time value depends on the amount of time remaining in which the option has the potential to increase its intrinsic value—the amount by which the option is "in-the-money."

VII. A short option on futures position is accounted for in the same manner as a short futures position. The premium collected by the writer is deposited in the account, where it serves as margin. Additional funds may be required to maintain a minimum margin amount. Margin is required because the writer must buy back the option at whatever it costs at the time, in order to close out the position or finance the resulting short futures position if the option is exercised. The position, therefore, is marked to the market on a daily basis. Because increases in premium value represent a loss in the account, it is subject to calls for additional margin.

Unlike a short futures position, decreases in premium value are not credited to the account. The best the writer can hope for is to keep the entire premium already collected, which happens if the option expires worthless (out of the money).

A long option position is accounted for quite differently. The account is charged the premium, which must be paid up front by cash in the account. There is no other liability. Like the writer's account, the premium is marked-to-the-market on a daily basis. Unlike the writer's account, however, it is not subject to margin calls. The premium amount can be withdrawn by the holder when the option is sold. If the holder exercises rather than sells, the option is replaced by a long futures position in the account. This position, like all futures positions, requires margin to be deposited in the account.

This difference in accounting procedures demonstrates the much higher risk involved in option writing than in option buying.

VIII. (1, 3 & 4) The option hedge *precludes* loss while retaining the opportunity for profit. This is especially important if the exposure is conditional. A hedge loss could not be offset if the exposure does not occur. Of course, the option advantages come at a cost which, if not recouped, can be considered a loss. Nevertheless, it is often more palatable (politically speaking) to suffer a premium loss as the "cost of doing business" than a market loss from "guessing wrong."

IX. (3) The range hedge model predicts a price range. The hedge is placed when the market is within that range. The hedge is lifted when the market moves out of the range in a profitable direction. It is reinstated when the market moves back into the range. The option strategy in this example has the same effect. The predicted range is 5200 to 5400. If the market rises above 5400, the hedge is, in effect, "lifted." There is no additional hedge gain because further profitable increases in premium value of the 5200 calls are now offset by the (loss-producing) increases in premium value of the 5400 calls. When the market falls back below 5400, the 5400 calls, now out of the money, have no further effect—the hedge is "reinstated."

X. (4) Delta hedging is the practice of matching the price move of the option with the price move of the underlying currency. Because of variations in volatility, measured as delta, the prices usually move at different rates. We assume that the volatility indicates a 0.33 delta, which means that the option premium moves one tick for every three tick move in the underlying currency value; therefore, three times the currency amount in options is required for the change in premium value to offset the value change in the French franc.

Chapter Sixteen

I. Consultative selling strives to achieve a situation in which:

1. The buyer wins and the seller loses
2. The seller wins and the buyer loses
3. The seller and buyer both win
4. Neither party wins, but the company benefits

II. Prospect for currency management business only when:

1. There is a chance for immediate compensation
2. The prospect will pay for a foreign exchange survey
3. You are assured that futures will be part of the program
4. There is an opportunity for a long-term client/consultant relationship

III. In consultative selling, your most important sale is:

1. Your credibility
2. The financial strength of your firm
3. A competitive commission structure
4. Your firm's research capability

IV. Before your first appointment, you should know all you can about:

1. Your product or service
2. The prospect's exposure
3. The prospect's operation
4. All of the above

V. The best way to build credibility with a prospect is by:

1. Achieving a highly developed product knowledge base
2. Fully disclosing all material facts

3. Proposing personal benefits to the company
4. Correctly identifying all buying influences

VI. During a presentation, technical jargon should be kept to a minimum because:

1. Technical analysis is not very predictive
2. Chart patterns can rapidly change
3. It is difficult to understand
4. All of the above

VII. The *single buyer* theory implies that:

1. Only one person has the authority to buy any given thing at any one time
2. Buying decisions can be influenced only by one person
3. Only a single buyer is authorized to commit the company financially
4. The buyers must always benefit on an individual basis

VIII. In any given sales situation, the buyer wins when:

1. The company wins
2. The features have been fully recognized
3. A personal benefit has been obtained
4. He or she foresees higher bonus payments

IX. Usually the most important buying influence during your initial contact is the:

1. Coach
2. Treasurer
3. CEO
4. Economic buyer

X. Before the company is committed to your program, it must be approved by the:

1. CFO
2. Economic buyer
3. Technical buyer
4. CEO

XI. Match the buying influence with its most probable "win":

1. Coach	New opportunity
2. CFO	Financial solutions
3. Chief Operating Officer	Increased performance
4. CEO	Your success

Answers to Chapter Sixteen

I. (3) Consultative selling strives for a win-win situation between buyer and seller. Anything less is economically indefensible or unethical. The only way to prospect for currency management business is with a consultative selling approach.

II. (4) The only way to justify the time, effort, and often the delayed compensation involved in prospecting for currency hedging business is when the objective is a long-term business relationship.

III. (1) Unless credibility is first established, nothing else offered will be of interest to the prospect.

IV. (4) You should be prepared to answer fully all questions regarding your product or service, and to ask *relevant* questions regarding the company's operation and exposures. The more you know in advance about the company, the more relevant your questions, and the more credible you are.

V. (2) Anything *less* than full disclosure of all material facts is construed as unethical business practice or fraudulent. This includes omissions of facts as well as misleading statements. A sales presentation that is less than forthright quickly undermines any credibility of the presenter.

VI. (3) The probability of a presentation's being too technical is much greater than of its being too basic. Brokers and analysts in the financial industry all too often fail to recognize this fact. A presenter who talks over the heads of the audience is often considered arrogant and the speech intimidating. A speaker rarely gets a second chance to redeem himself.

VII. (1) At any given time, only one person within a corporation is authorized to make a specific buying decision concerning a specific product on any specific occasion. This "authority" may be (a) formally recognized; as with the role of purchasing agent; (b) informally recognized; i.e., the decision is of no great import and is made by whoever is available; (c) unrecognized, such as when power shifts occur because of office politics.

VIII. (3) The "win" in a win-win situation always involves a personal benefit for the buyer. This may or may not be the same benefit enjoyed by the company as a whole. A personal benefit satisfies someone on an emotional level, something a "feature" does not do.

IX. (1) The most important buying influence at the initial stage of prospecting is the coach. This buyer helps smooth the way by opening doors, identifying other buyers, and identifying what might personally benefit them.

X. (2) Only the economic buyer has the authority to commit the company financially. This is the buyer entrusted with the purse strings. It may be the CEO, a director, the major stockholder, or someone else.

XI. (1) The coach attaches his star to yours and wins when you succeed; (2) The CFO seeks financial solutions more than anything else; (3) The COO is a user buyer who benefits personally by enhanced operating performance; (4) The CEO looks for new opportunities for the company.

Appendix V
Currency Price Charts

Prices can be charted in a variety of ways. The most suitable format depends on its particular purpose. If the object is to measure volatility over a certain time span, a bar chart or candlestick chart might be the most appropriate. If the long range trend is of primary concern, a simple line chart can adequately display the trend direction.

Australian dollar	(chart 1)
British pound	(chart 2)
Canadian dollar	(chart 3)
Deutsche mark	(chart 4)
Japanese yen	(chart 5)

Long term candlestick charts show the trend of major currencies against the dollar over a ten year period. Each line represents a monthly range; the "candlestick" defines the opening and closing prices of that range. In these examples, which price is the open and which is the close is not determinable nor significant. The candlestick effect helps keep focus on the trend by "filtering out" temporary volatility. Prices are spot, quoted directly. (note: Japanese yen x 100)

Brazilian real	(chart 6)

The monthly range bar chart showing open, high, low, and close over a 29 month period plots the nearest CME futures price of the real. This clearly depicts the effect of the "crawling peg," by which the currency is officially devaluated at a steady, pre-determined rate over time.

Mexican peso (chart 7)

A weekly candlestick chart of nearest CME futures prices illustrates the high near-term interest rates, reflected in discounted forwards, as a consequence of devaluation after the lifting of the peg in late 1995.

Indian rupee (chart 8)
Indonesian rupiah (chart 9)
Korean won (chart 10)

Simple line charts (rupee, rupiah) and candlestick chart (won) of daily prices from January, 1997, clearly illustrate the rippling effect on regional exchange rates from the collapse of the pegged currency regime in Southeast Asia. Note that exchange rate (indirect quote) moves higher as the currency devalues.

*Charts courtesy of INO GLOBAL Markets, http://www.ino.com

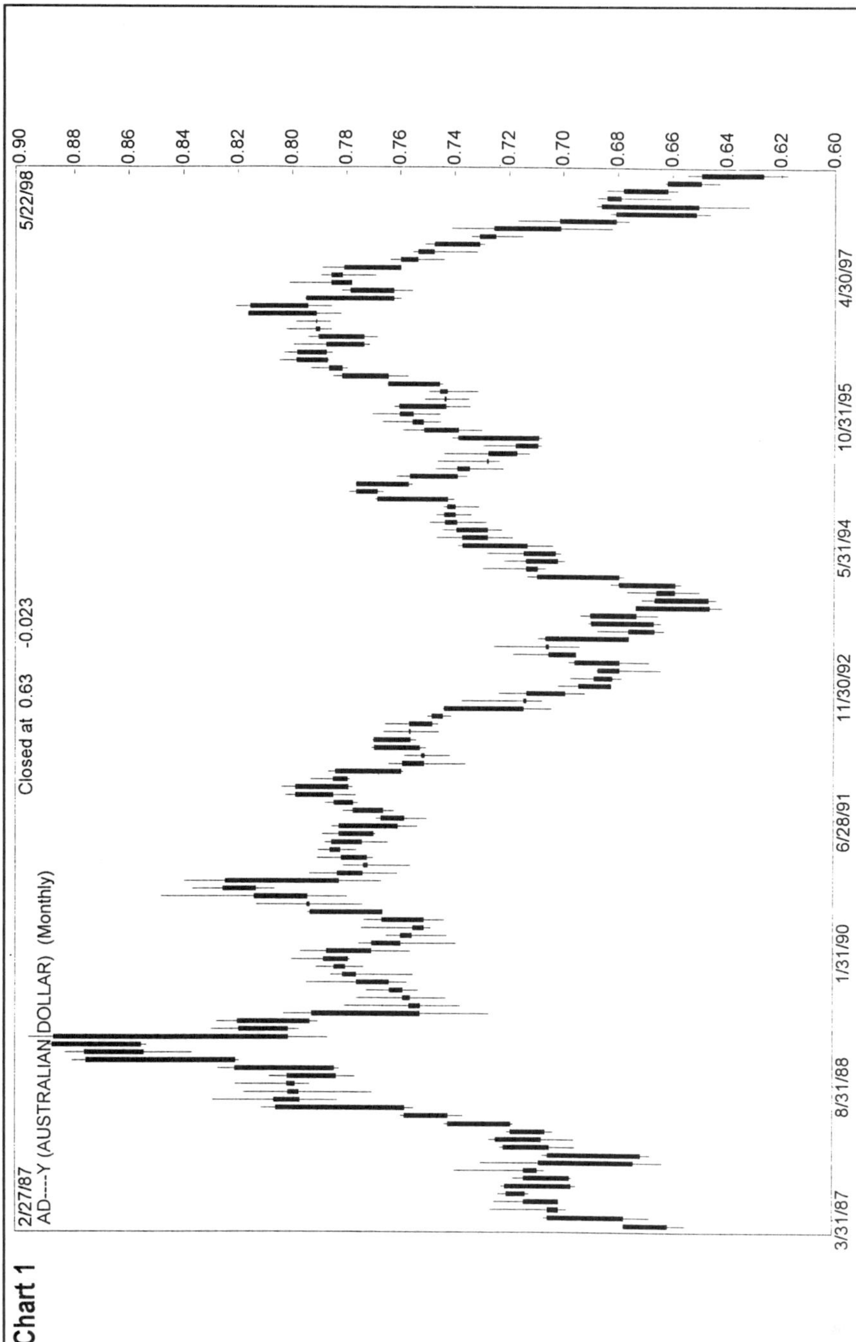
Chart 1
2/27/87
AD----Y (AUSTRALIAN DOLLAR) (Monthly)
Closed at 0.63 -0.023
5/22/98
0.90
0.88
0.86
0.84
0.82
0.80
0.78
0.76
0.74
0.72
0.70
0.68
0.66
0.64
0.62
0.60
3/31/87
8/31/88
1/31/90
6/28/91
11/30/92
5/31/94
10/31/95
4/30/97

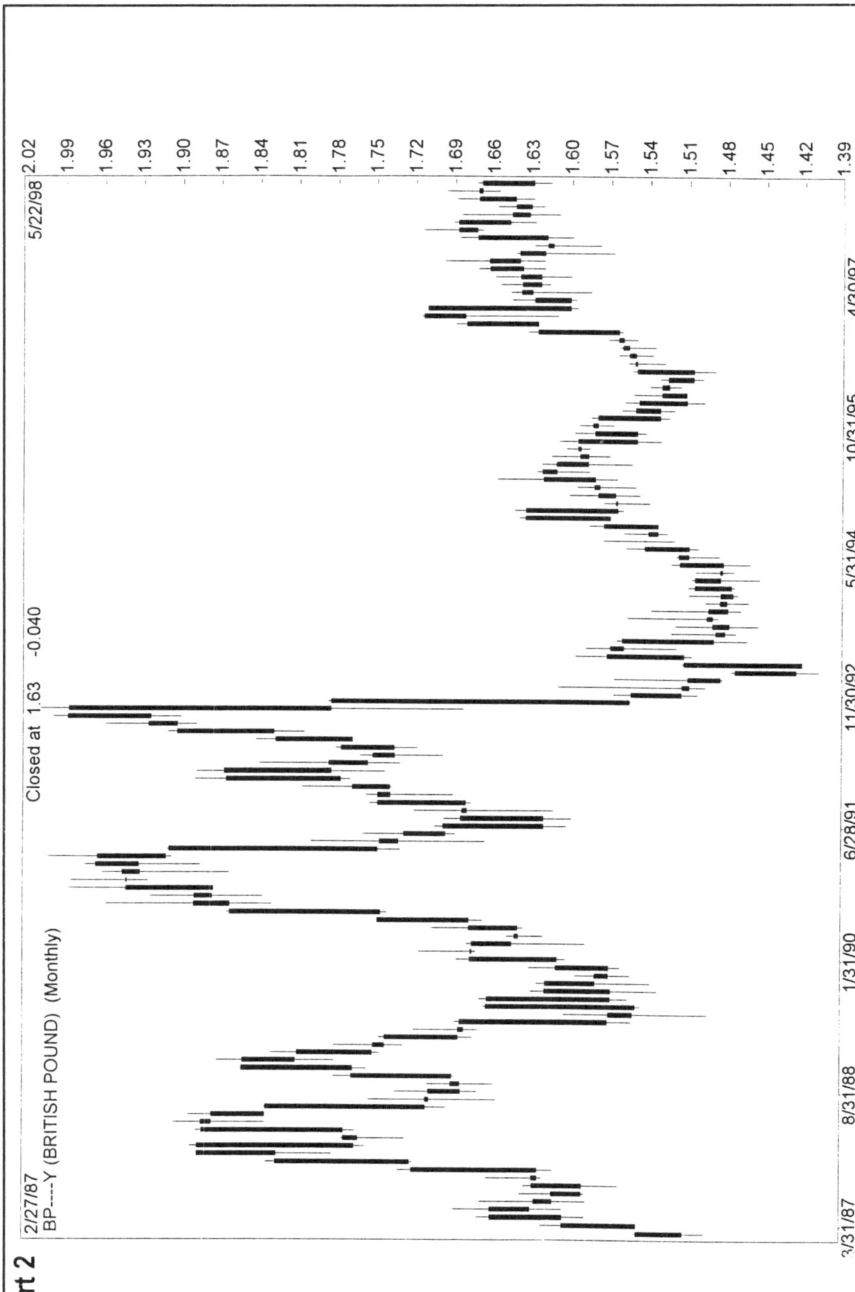
2/27/87
BP----Y (BRITISH POUND) (Monthly)
Closed at 1.63 -0.040
5/22/98
2.02
1.99
1.96
1.93
1.90
1.87
1.84
1.81
1.78
1.75
1.72
1.69
1.66
1.63
1.60
1.57
1.54
1.51
1.48
1.45
1.42
1.39
3/31/87
8/31/88
1/31/90
6/28/91
11/30/92
5/31/94
10/31/95
4/30/97

Chart 2

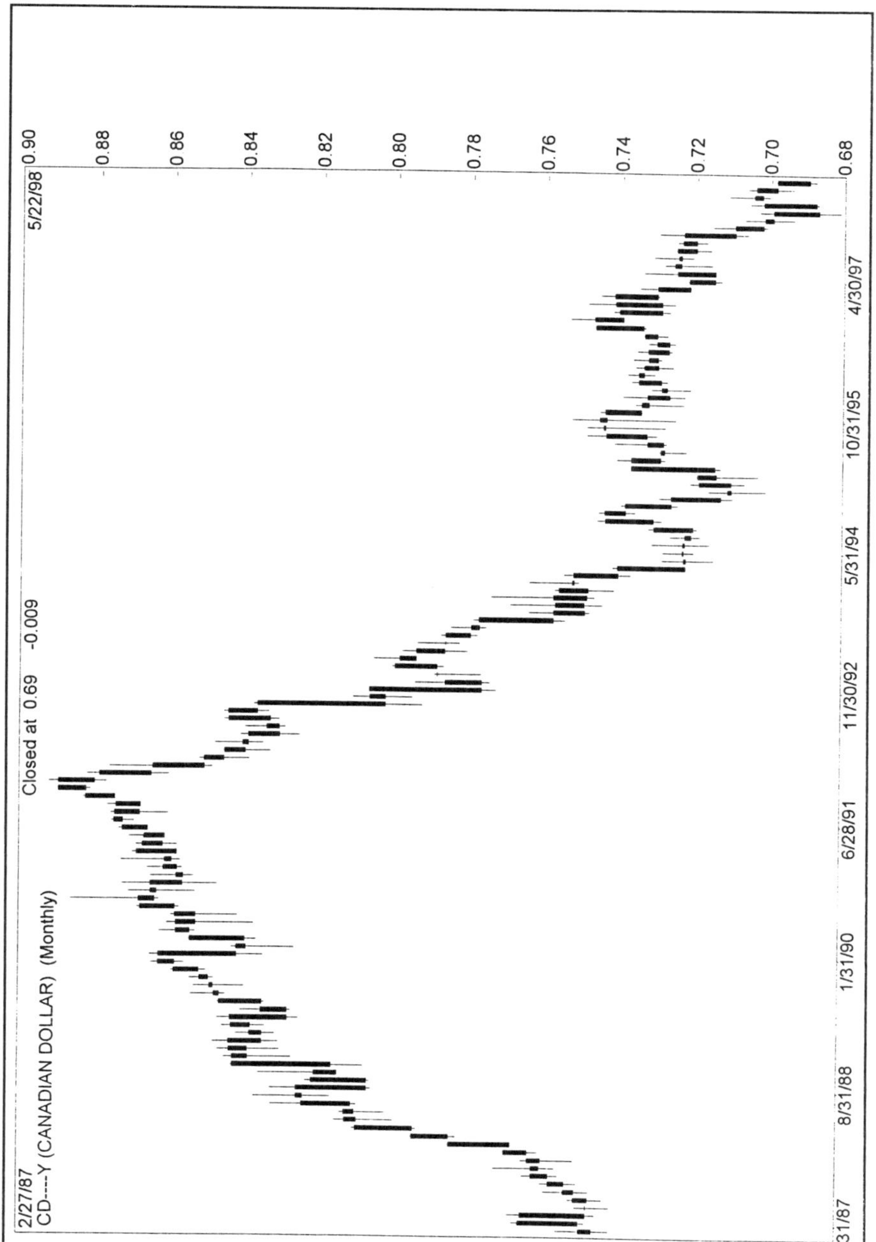
2/27/87
CD----Y (CANADIAN DOLLAR) (Monthly)
Closed at 0.69 -0.009
5/22/98
0.90
0.88
0.86
0.84
0.82
0.80
0.78
0.76
0.74
0.72
0.70
0.68
3/31/87
8/31/88
1/31/90
6/28/91
11/30/92
5/31/94
10/31/95
4/30/97

Chart 3

Chart 4

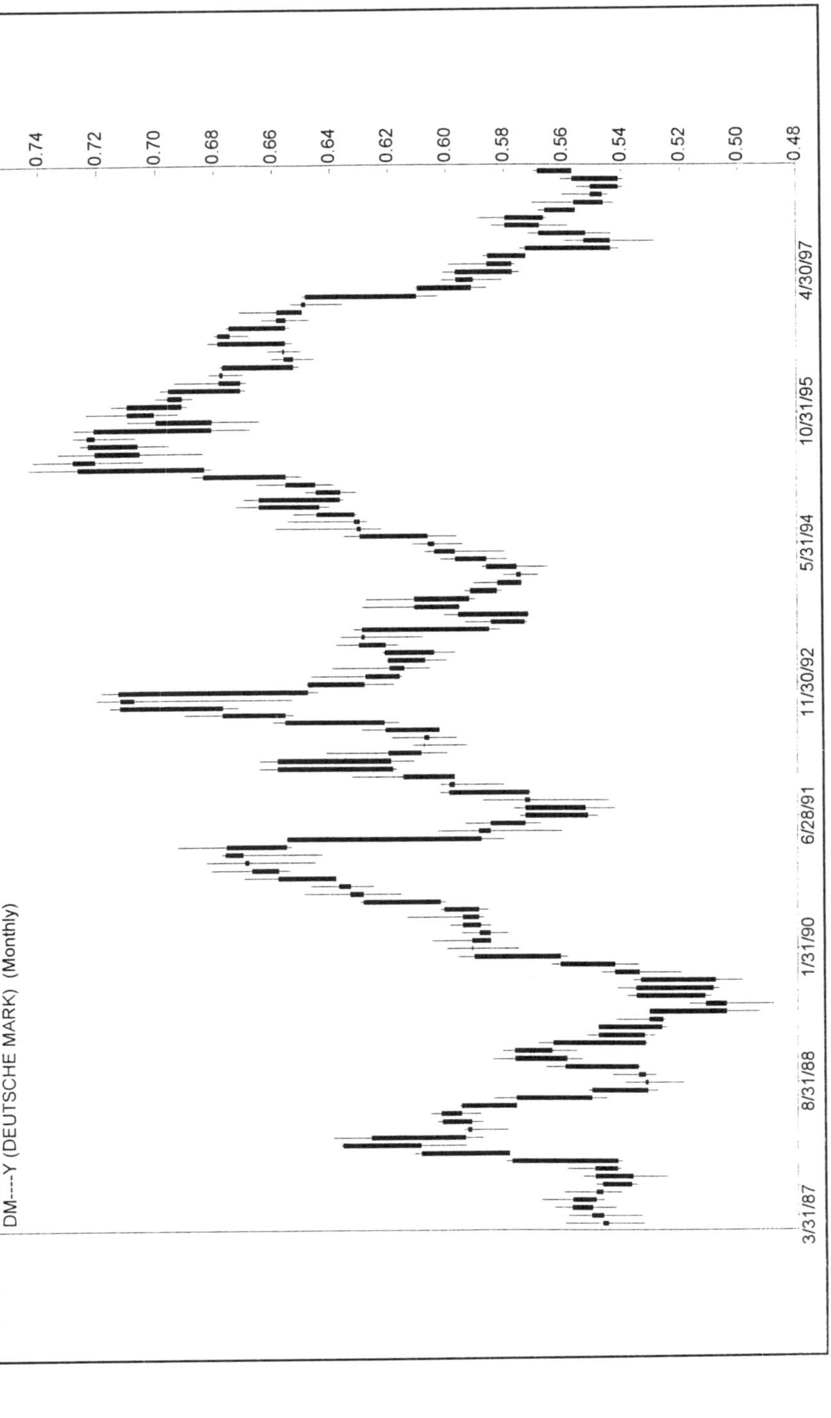
2/27/87
DM---Y (DEUTSCHE MARK) (Monthly)
Closed at 0.57 + 0.012
5/22/98
0.76
0.74
0.72
0.70
0.68
0.66
0.64
0.62
0.60
0.58
0.56
0.54
0.52
0.50
0.48
3/31/87
8/31/88
1/31/90
6/28/91
11/30/92
5/31/94
10/31/95
4/30/97

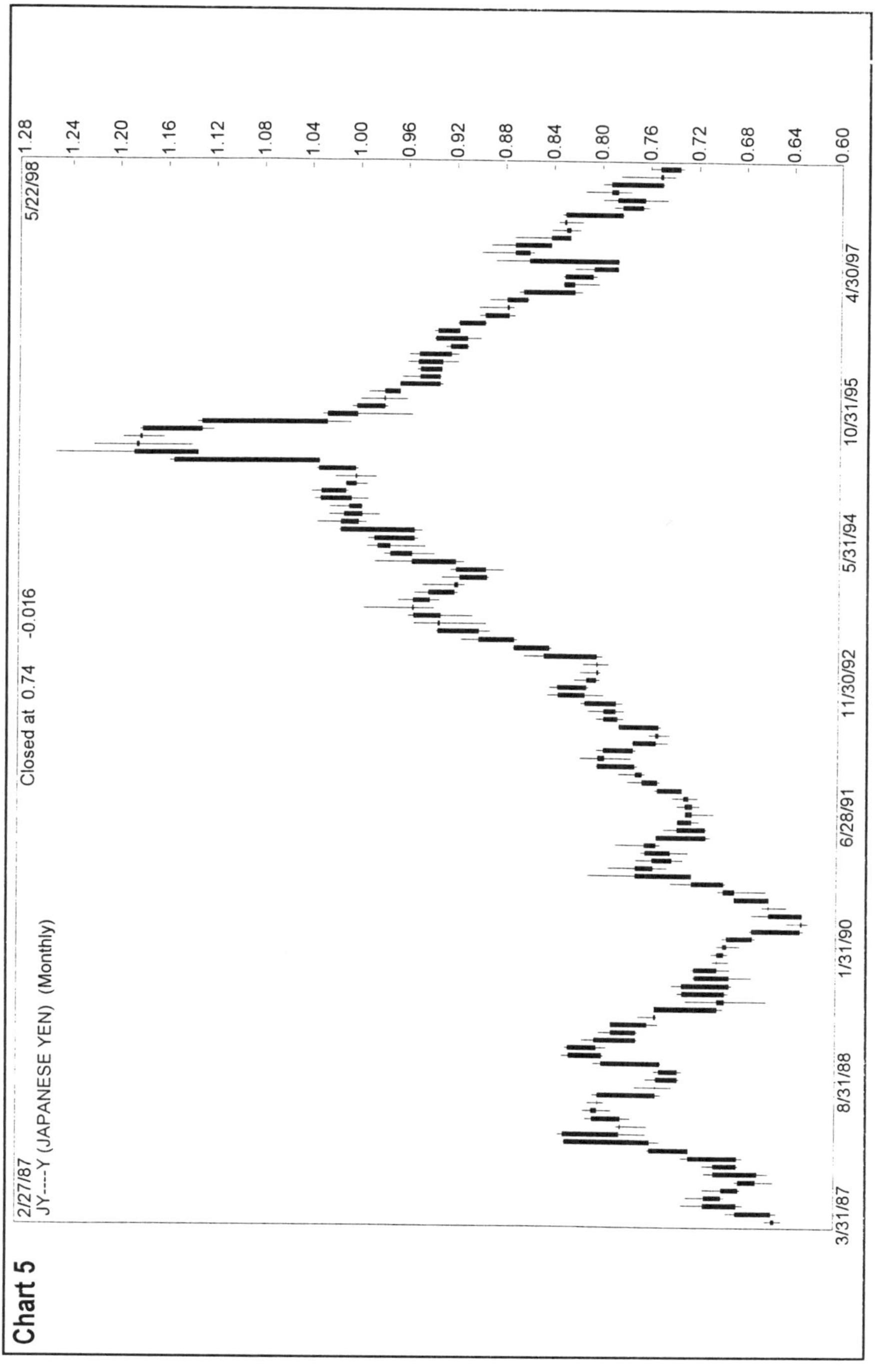
2/27/87
JY----Y (JAPANESE YEN) (Monthly)
Closed at 0.74 -0.016
5/22/98
1.28
1.24
1.20
1.16
1.12
1.08
1.04
1.00
0.96
0.92
0.88
0.84
0.80
0.76
0.72
0.68
0.64
0.60
3/31/87
8/31/88
1/31/90
6/28/91
11/30/92
5/31/94
10/31/95
4/30/97

Chart 5

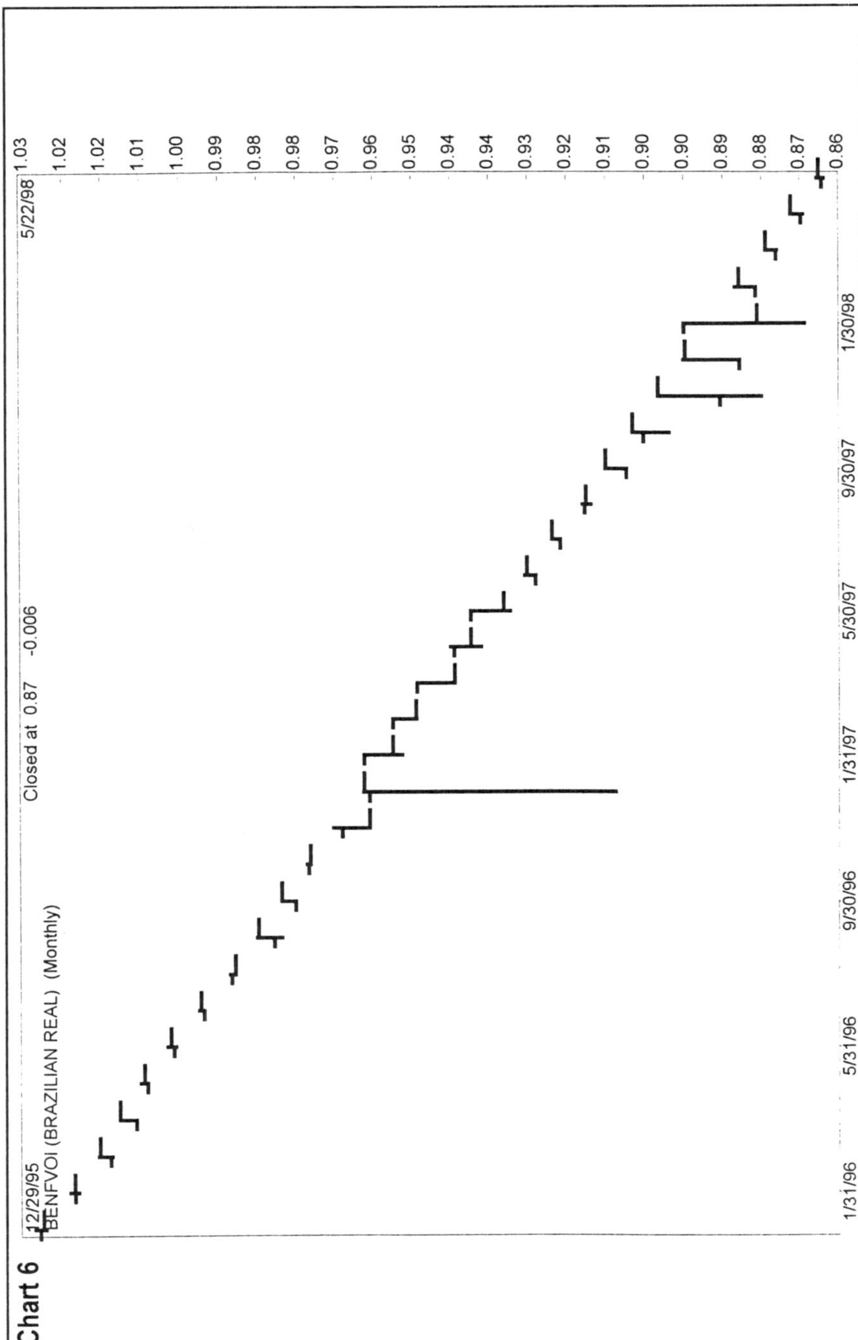
BENFVOI (BRAZILIAN REAL) (Monthly)
Closed at 0.87 -0.006
12/29/95
5/22/98
1/31/96
5/31/96
9/30/96
1/31/97
5/30/97
9/30/97
1/30/98
1.03
1.02
1.02
1.01
1.00
0.99
0.98
0.98
0.97
0.96
0.95
0.94
0.94
0.93
0.92
0.91
0.90
0.90
0.89
0.88
0.87
0.86

Chart 6

Chart 7

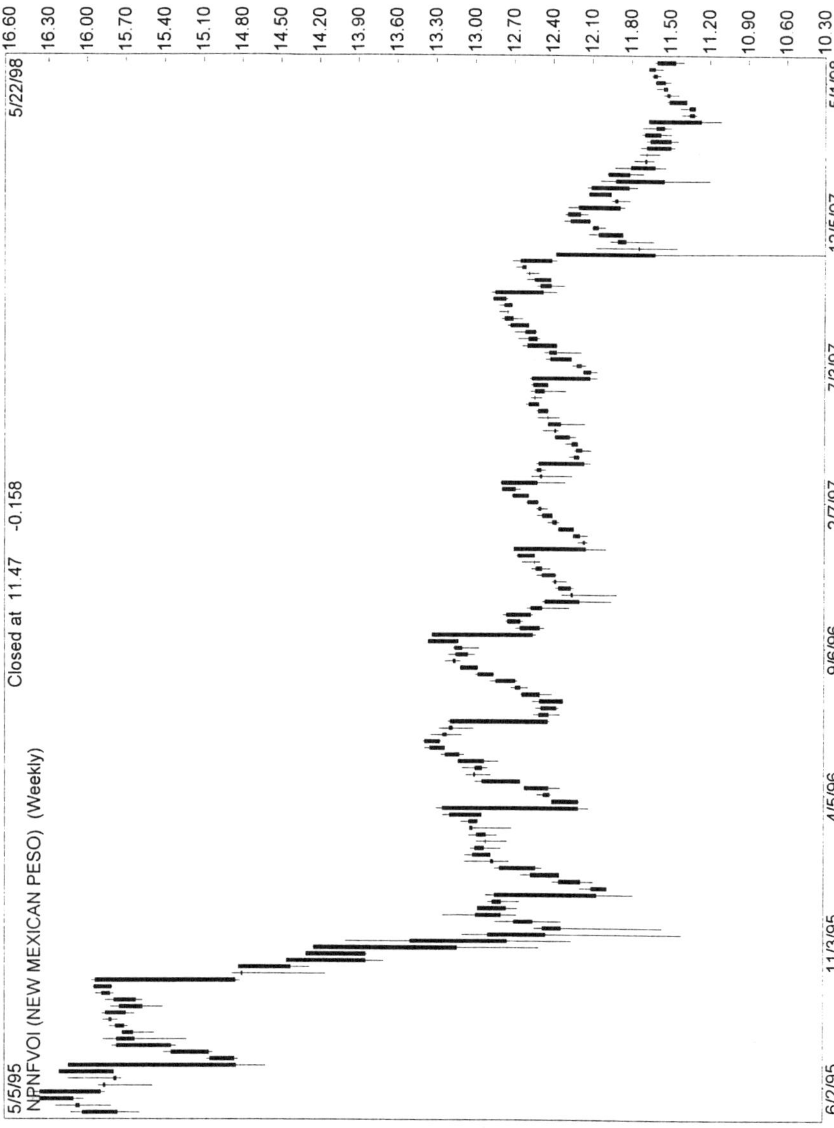
NPNFVOI (NEW MEXICAN PESO) (Weekly)
Closed at 11.47 -0.158
5/5/95
5/22/98
6/2/95
11/3/95
4/5/96
9/6/96
2/7/97
7/3/97
12/5/97
5/1/98
16.60
16.30
16.00
15.70
15.40
15.10
14.80
14.50
14.20
13.90
13.60
13.30
13.00
12.70
12.40
12.10
11.80
11.50
11.20
10.90
10.60
10.30

Chart 8

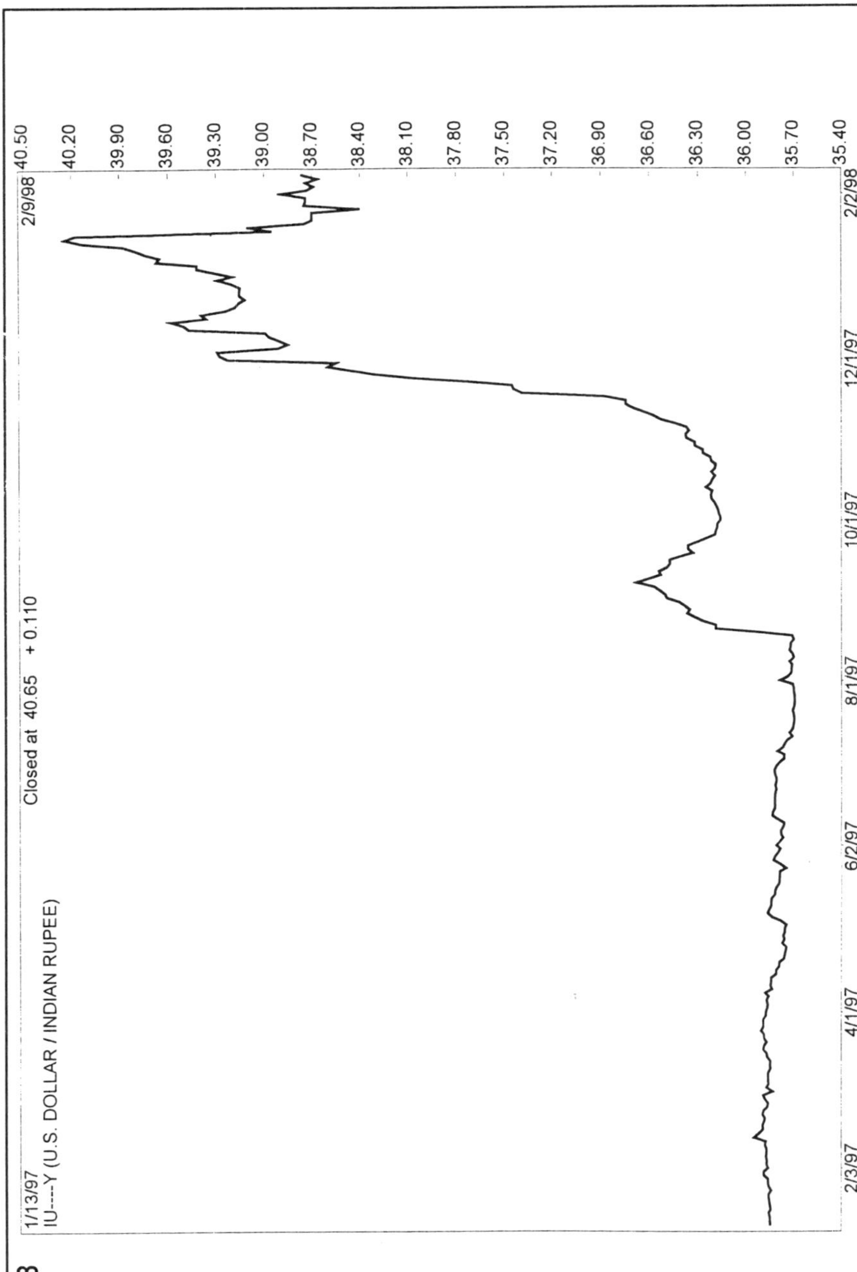
1/13/97
IU---Y (U.S. DOLLAR / INDIAN RUPEE)
Closed at 40.65 + 0.110
2/9/98
40.50
40.20
39.90
39.60
39.30
39.00
38.70
38.40
38.10
37.80
37.50
37.20
36.90
36.60
36.30
36.00
35.70
35.40
2/3/97
4/1/97
6/2/97
8/1/97
10/1/97
12/1/97
2/2/98

Chart 9

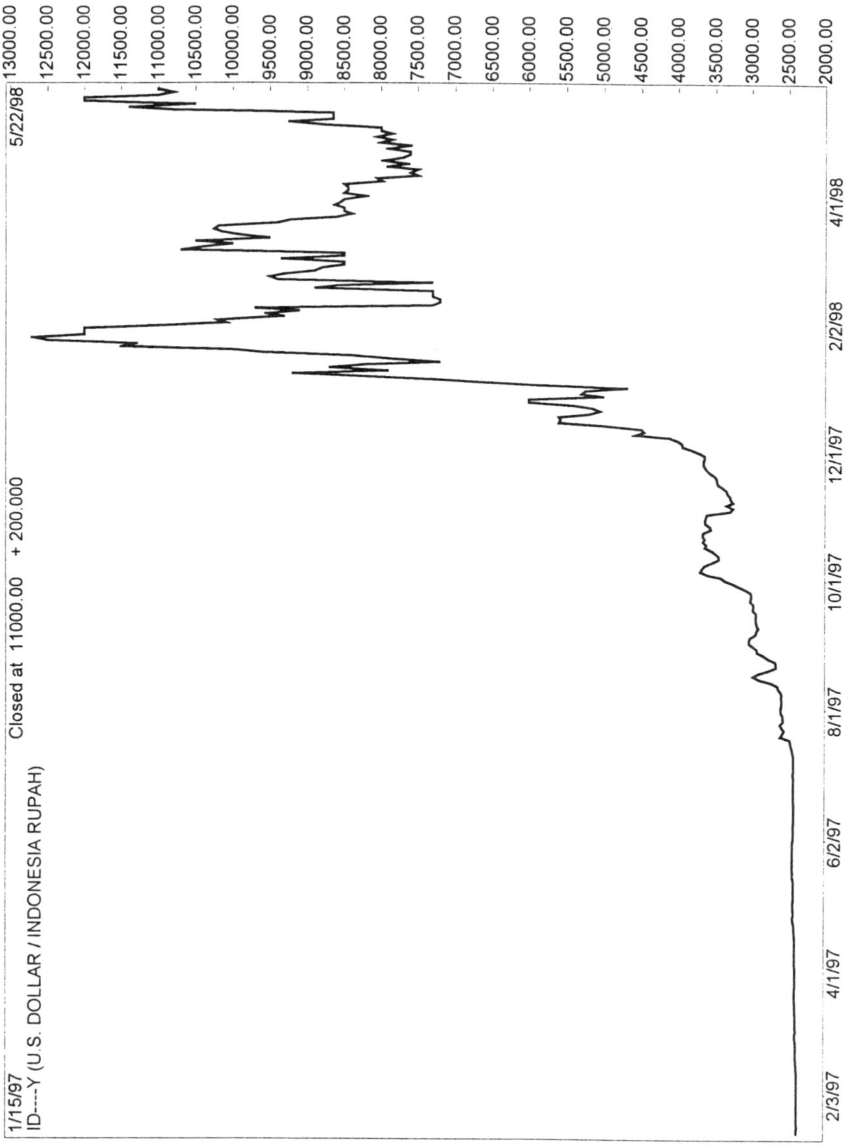
1/15/97
ID----Y (U.S. DOLLAR / INDONESIA RUPAH)
Closed at 11000.00 + 200.000
13000.00
12500.00
12000.00
11500.00
11000.00
10500.00
10000.00
9500.00
9000.00
8500.00
8000.00
7500.00
7000.00
6500.00
6000.00
5500.00
5000.00
4500.00
4000.00
3500.00
3000.00
2500.00
2000.00
2/3/97
4/1/97
6/2/97
8/1/97
10/1/97
12/1/97
2/2/98
4/1/98
5/22/98

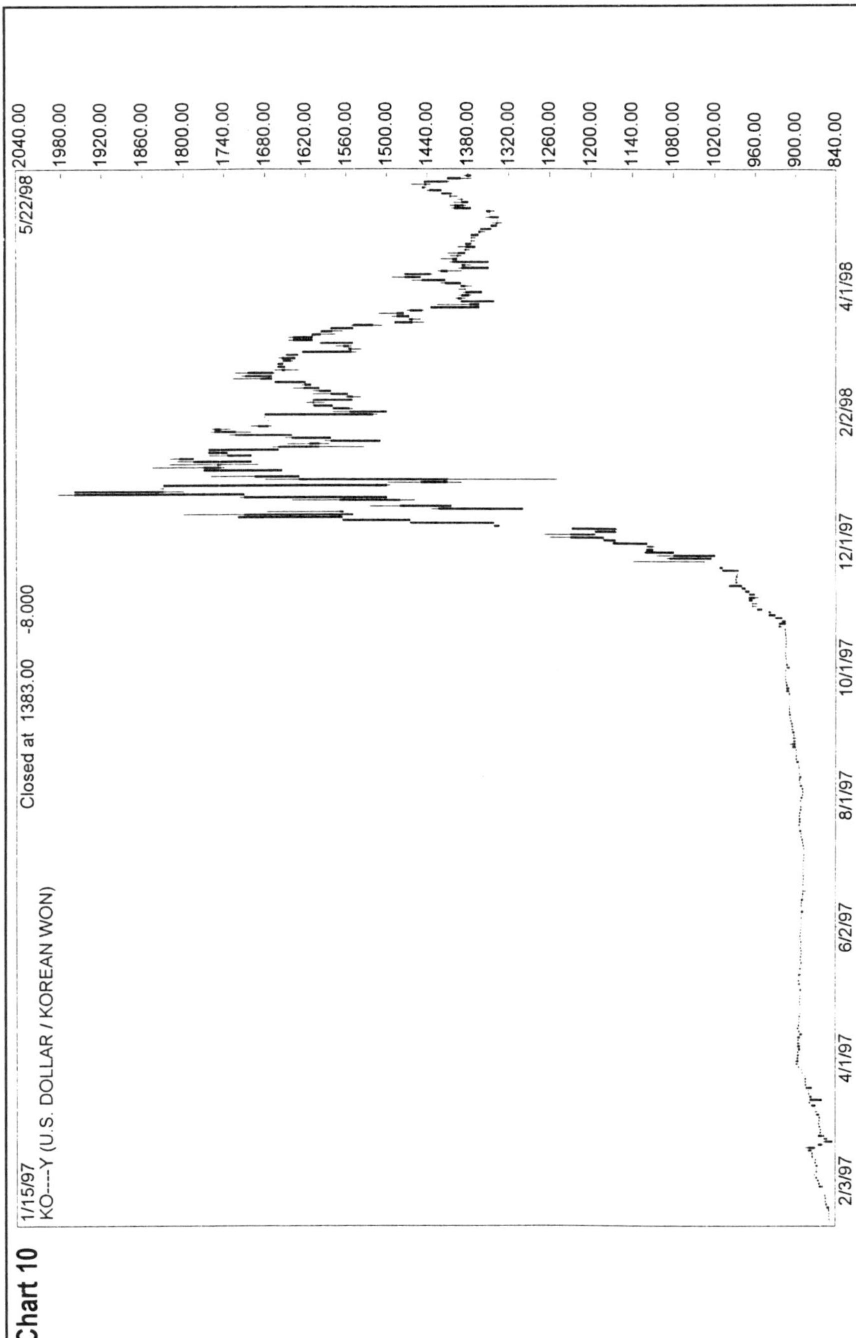
1/15/97
KO---Y (U.S. DOLLAR / KOREAN WON)
Closed at 1383.00 -8.000
5/22/98
2040.00
1980.00
1920.00
1860.00
1800.00
1740.00
1680.00
1620.00
1560.00
1500.00
1440.00
1380.00
1320.00
1260.00
1200.00
1140.00
1080.00
1020.00
960.00
900.00
840.00
2/3/97
4/1/97
6/2/97
8/1/97
10/1/97
12/1/97
2/2/98
4/1/98

Chart 10

End Notes

Introduction

1. Taming the Derivatives Beast, *The Economist*, May 23, 1992.
2. Mary Ann Burns ed., "Interview: Chicago Exchange Leaders Confront Challenges," *Futures Industry*, vol. 3, no. 2, March/April 1993.

Chapter One

1. Gregory J. Millman, *The Floating Battlefield: Corporate Strategy in the Currency Wars* (New York, NY: AMACOM, 1990).
2. Editorial, "Getting Around the 'S' Word," *Futures*, no. 14, December 1992, 8.
3. Millman, *The Floating Battlefield.*
4. Editiorial Staff, "Selling Risk Management Concepts," from "Politics of Risk," *Corporate Risk Management*, vol. I, no. 1, September/October 1989, 8.

Chapter Two

1. John Stuart Mill, *Principles of Political Economy*, Vol. II (New York, NY: D. Appleton and Co.), 23.
2. Neil Wallace, "Why Markets in Foreign Exchange are Different from Other Markets," *Quarterly Review* (Federal Reserve Bank of Minneapolis), Winter, 1990, 12-18.
3. Rep. Ron Paul and Lewis Lehrman, *The Case for Gold* (Washington, DC: Cato Institute, 1982) 75, 83.
4. Paul, 85, 88, 91.
5. Paul, 37-57

6. Gary O'Callaghan, "The Structure and Operation of the World Gold Market", IMF *Occasional Paper* No. 105, (Washington, DC: International Monetary Fund), based on a review of the paper by IMF Survey, November 8, 1993, 345.
7. Gary O'Callaghan, "The Structure and Operation of the World Gold Market."
8. "Iraq Arrests Currency Traders," *The Wall Street Journal*, August 25, 1994, A8.
9. William Baumol and Alan Blinder, *Economics, Principles and Policy*, 4th ed. (USA: Harcourt Brace Jovanovich, 1988).

Chapter Three

1. These countries are Australia, Canada, Japan, New Zealand, and the United States, as reported in the *Annual Report on Exchange Arrangements and Exchange Restrictions*, 1991. This report is published annually by the International Monetary Fund, Washington, DC.
2. Hans M. Flickenschild and Martin G. Gilman, "Developments in International Exchange and Payments Systems," *World Economic and Financial Surveys* (Washington, DC: International Monetary Fund, 1992). Flickenschild and Gilman directed a staff team from the Exchange and Trade Relations Department of IMF to research and present this survey.
3. *Annual Report on Exchange Arrangements and Exchange Restrictions*, (Washington, DC: International Monetary Fund, 1991).
4. These bonds were named after Robert Roosa, Undersecretary for Monetary Affairs, U.S. Treasury, 1961-1964.
5. *Annual Report on Exchange Arrangements and Exchange Restrictions*, 1991.
6. Member nations of the CFA are Benin, Burkina Faso, Cameroon, Central African Republic, Chad, Comores, Congo, the Ivory Coast, Equatorial Guinea, Gabon, Mali, Niger, Senegal, and Togo.
7. David G. Pearson, *The Wall Street Journal*, January 21, 1994.
8. Malcomb Forbes made this comparison during a panel discussion at a Washington, DC seminar on September 14, 1994, marking the 50th anniversary of the Bretton Woods affair. The seminar, produced by *Empower America*, was chaired by Senator Jack Kemp. The panel was moderated by Robert Bartley, Editor, *The Wall Street Journal*.

Chapter Four

1. Michael T. Belongia, "The Signals in Money," *International Economic Conditions* (The Federal Reserve Bank of St. Louis, August 1993), 1.
2. GDP (Gross Domestic Product) is the same as GNP (Gross National Product) except that it excludes revenue produced abroad by American companies. The Federal Reserve is currently phasing out GNP in favor of the more precise GDP designation.
3. Horace W. Brock, "Determinants of Exchange Rates," *Management of Currency Risk*, vol. 1, ed. Boris Antil, (London, England: Euromoney Publications PLC, 1989), 63-86. *Editor's note*: "This framework was originally developed in a 1985 project undertaken for the Global Capital Markets Program of the Morgan Bank. The intent of the porject was to develop a framework that permitted traders and sales people to intepret better the news as it breaks around the world."
4. The G-5 countries are the United States, Japan, former West Germany, France, and the United Kingdom. The G-7 countries include Canada and Italy in addition to those above (with the change to Germany).
5. Kristina Jacobson, "US Foreign Exchange Operations," *Economic Review*, Federal Reserve Bank of Kansas City, September/October, 1990.
6. Jacobson, "US Foreign Exchange Operations," 7031.
7. Milton Friedman, "Dejà Vu in Currency Markets," *The Wall Street Journal*, Sept 22, 1992, A18.

Chapter Five

No notes for Chapter Five.

Chapter Six

1. Horace W. Brock, "Determinants of Exchange Rates."

Chapter Seven

1. Eric Sharp, "Tracking Currency Rates via Fundamental Factors," *Futures*, vol. 20, no. 3, February, 1991.

2. Dr. William Schmidt is president of *Golden Harvest*, a futures research facility in Jackson, MI.
3. James Gleick, “A Geometry of Nature,” *Chaos; Making a New Science* (New York, NY: Viking Penguin, Inc., 1987), 83-102.

Chapter Eight

1. Christine R. Hekman, “Measuring the Impact of Exposure,” *Management of Currency Risk*, vol. 1, 51-54.
2. *Accounting Standards: Original pronouncements as of June 1, 1982*, Vol. 1,”Statement No. 52, Foreign Currency Translation” (Stamford, CT: Financial Accounting Standards Board dist. by McGraw Hill, 1982), 1410.
3. *Accounting Standards*, 1409.
4. Boris Antl, “Accounting Exposure,” *Management of Currency Risk*, vol. 1, 25.
5. Antl, 23.
6. Antl, 26.
7. Donald R. Lessard and John B. Lightstone,”Operating Exposure,” *Management of Currency Risk*, vol. 1, 29-40.
8. Millman.
9. Gregory J. Millman, “Trading can be Safe—If Controlled,” from “Politics of Risk,” *Corporate Risk Management*, vol. 1, no. 2, November/December, 1989, 41.
10. Portia Richardson, “Currency Shifts Can Take Byte Out of U.S. Computer Companies,” *Corporate Risk Management*, vol. 1, no. 2, November/December 1989, 18.
11. Millman, *The Floating Battlefield.*
12. Helmut Hagemann, “Strategic Exposure,” *Management of Currency Risk*, vol. 1, 41-42. Editor’s note: “This chapter was reproduced by permission of *Harvard Business Review*. Adapted from “Anticipate your long-term foreign exchange risks,” by Helmut Hagemann (March–April 1977), copyright 1877, by the President and Fellows of Harvard College (all rights reserved).

Chapter Nine

1. Other derivatives are used, including interest rate futures and swaps, and certain commodities such as gold, that can be used as currency pegs.

2. Nicholas Bray, "Two Agencies Issue Guidelines on Derivatives," *The Wall Street Journal*, July 27, 1994, A10.

Chapter Ten

1. Editorial Staff, "Selling Risk Management Concepts" from "Politics of Risk," *Corporate Risk Management*, vol. 1, no. 1, September/October 1989, 8.
2. The definition according to FASB 52 is 3 years of inflation at a rate of 100% or more.

Chapter Eleven

1. Bruce Babcock Jr., "How Well do Popular Methods Perform—A Frame of Reference," *The Dow Jones-Irwin Guide to Trading Systems* (Homewood, IL: Dow Jones-Irwin, 1989).
2. Satyajit Das, "Currency Swaps," *Management of Currency Risk*, vol. 1, 263-279.
3. Sam Borenstein, "Multi-currency Management Centres," *Management of Currency Risk*, vol. 1, 215-229.

Chapter Twelve

1. Bruce Babcock, Jr., *The Dow Jones-Irwin Guide to Trading Systems*, (Homewood, IL: Dow Jones-Irwin, 1989).

Chapter Thirteen

1. Spot for Canadian dollars in North America is one business day after the transaction takes place.
2. One business day for Canadian dollars beginning with the December 1994 contract.

Chapter Fourteen

No notes for Chapter Fourteen.

Chapter Fifteen

No notes for Chapter Fifteen.

Chapter Sixteen

1. Gary Shoup, *Currency Risk Management: A Broker's Handbook*, (Grove City, PA: Center for Futures Education, Inc., 1995) 163-186.
2. John Walsh, *How to Sell Futures*, (Grove City, PA: Center for Futures Education, Inc., 1992).
3. Robert B. Miller & Stephen E. Heiman, *Strategic Selling* (New York, NY: Warner Books, Inc., March 1986): 69-99.
4. Miller & Heiman, 122-123.

Index